VOCATIONAL EDUCATION AND THE NATION'S ECONOMY

VOCATIONAL EDUCATION AND THE NATION'S ECONOMY

Edited by
Warren G. Meyer

Seventh
Yearbook

American Vocational
Association
Washington, D.C.

ISBN: 0-89514-000-4

Published 1977 by
THE AMERICAN VOCATIONAL ASSOCIATION, INC.
1510 H Street, N.W., Washington, D.C. 20005

Printed in the United States of America

PREFACE

The seventh yearbook of the American Vocational Association is a volume dealing with vocational education's role in maintaining national economic health. Among the many charges of the Vocational Education Act of 1963, the mandates to improve the quality of existing programs and respond to the needs of youth and adults posed challenges that vocational education still pursues vigorously.

The Education Amendments of 1976 stress comprehensive planning as a means to more effective utilization of all resources available to vocational education. We are living in a period of disenchantment with education—on the part of students, parents, and taxpayers. People are looking to vocational education as a means not only of improving the nation's productivity but as a cure for many of society's ills. Vocational education is seen as a way to instill a more realistic purpose in our educational system. This public attitude has generated national recognition for vocational education, but it has brought a host of special interest groups calling for special attention. How will vocational education survive, let alone grow, in a technological, "no-growth" society?

Vocational educators with a sound knowledge of economics can contribute much in searching for solutions to this problem. Three fundamental issues to be resolved with the help of economic analysis are: What types and how much output is to be produced? How should the production of the various forms of education be organized? And how should educational output be distributed? The authors of this book lend insight into the means of arriving at the answers to these questions, which transcend the educational system.

The Board of Directors of the American Vocational Association selected the theme of the 1977 yearbook and appointed the editor, Warren G. Meyer. The content was planned by the editor and his advisory committee, consisting of: Dr. Darrell R. Lewis, associate dean of the College of Education and professor of economic education at the University of Minnesota; Dr. Merle E. Strong, professor in the Department of Educational Administration and director of the Wisconsin Vocational Studies Center at the University of Wisconsin; and Dr. Gordon Swanson, professor and director of graduate studies for the Department of Vocational Education at the University of Minnesota. All advisory committee members and chapter authors were approved by the AVA Board.

Warren G. Meyer, editor of the 1977 yearbook, was a secondary school teacher, an adult education field instructor, and a state supervisor of distributive education before joining the faculty of the University of Minnesota in 1946. His occupational experience before becoming an educator consisted of merchandising and managerial positions in Wisconsin, New York, Illinois and Michigan. Professor Meyer initiated the distributive teacher education program at the University and was its chairman until his retirement in June 1976.

Professor Meyer has written and edited many works, including two professional books, and he is senior author of a high school textbook. As a member of the graduate faculty, he has been advisor to numerous masters and doctoral candidates. In recognition of his teaching ability, he received the Horace T. Morse Award conferred by Standard Oil, and the Academy of Distributive Teacher Education Award.

An active member of AVA since becoming an educator, Professor Meyer has served on the first AVA research committee, the public relations committee, and numerous divisional committees. He is a past president of the Council for Distributive Teacher Education, an affiliate of the Distributive Education Division of AVA.

Professor Meyer's degrees in economics and business and his occupational experience in retailing and service industries, together with his education assignments and published materials on economics education provide the balance between practice and theory necessary to edit a yearbook on vocational education and the nation's economy. He is eminently qualified for this task.

LOWELL A. BURKETT
Executive Director
American Vocational Association

INTRODUCTION

Vocational Education and the Nation's Economy is a book by leaders in vocational education and pacesetters in economics education. Its purpose is to help readers improve their understanding of the economics of vocational education, encourage them to develop further their competencies in this realm, and to stimulate interest in broadening the scope of vocational education curricula to include content that will upgrade the economic literacy of vocational education recipients. The authors share their expertise with a variety of readers ranging from local instructors to high-level decision makers in vocational education.

It was the recommendation of the 1977 Yearbook Advisory Committee that the scope of this volume be limited to vocational education in the schools because it did not seem feasible to treat this all-embracing topic in its entirety without sacrificing the depth needed to meet the objectives of the project. The economics of education is a very complex branch of economics; yet it seems to be the most appropriate starting point when launching a discourse on vocational education and our national economy.

The chapters of this book provide excellent opportunities for exploring basic problems and issues in the economics of vocational education because the authors differ sufficiently in their views to produce a lively discussion. In some areas they approach a topic from different perspectives and philosophical orientations. The editor made no attempt to change the intent of the authors, their only constraint being to remain within the parameters of the topic to which they were assigned.

Section I is a mini course in the economics of education which lays the foundation for the chapters that follow. It describes this relatively new field of economics and explains the concept of human capital, which forms the basis of a procedure for economic analysis and comparison of educational programs.

Section II accompanies the reader through a set of sequential steps in the economics of vocational education, beginning with goals and objectives and ending with a discussion of programmatic investments. Knowing how a program is evaluated and improving one's competencies in this task are valuable possessions.

Section III takes a different tack, dealing with economic literacy and identifying what teachers and workers should know about economics. It describes candidly the current status of economic literacy in the United States and directs the reader's attention to fruitful sources of information. A new approach to the assessment of economic literacy is proposed.

Section IV is addressed primarily to teachers and curriculum specialists in six areas of vocational education. Each author addresses the economic roles and contributions of the occupational field served and offers suggestions on teaching applied economic understandings and skills.

This volume contains knowledge of concern to all vocational educators and their allies and supporters. It is intended as a practical resource to which they can turn when planning their work as teachers, curriculum planners, administrators and other decision makers. It should be found in places where planning takes place rather than on a library shelf.

Many individuals contributed to the organization and preparation of this book, but special recognition must be given to the 1977 Yearbook Committee: Dr. Gordon Swanson for sharing his deep insight into vocational education throughout the project; Dr. Darrell Lewis for his guidance in the realm of the economics of education; and Dr. Merle Strong for his helpful advice as a former yearbook editor. Last but not least, Ms. Toni Lydecker, AVA publications editor, provided expert assistance in preparing the manuscripts for publication. Many thanks to all.

W.G.M.

Minneapolis, Minnesota
April 1977

CONTENTS

Vocational Education and the Nation's Economy

Warren G. Meyer

When vocational educators invest time and effort to improve their understanding of the economics of education, the returns promise a variety of benefits. That a working knowledge of this type of economic inquiry is essential to being in tune with the times needs no documentation; economic factors have always influenced many kinds of educational decisions. This is especially true today, when there is high concern for economy in nearly all types of public institutions. But specifically, how can vocational educators improve their lot through a working knowledge of the economics of education? What can they gain from better insight into the role of vocational education in the nation's economic welfare? What can be done to improve the productivity of vocational education? And how can vocational educators help raise the level of economic literacy among their clients?

KNOWING THE ECONOMICS OF EDUCATION

Education is an integral part of a competitive, market-centered economic system, and as our socioeconomic needs grow, our educational program is subjected to increasing economic analysis. Until recently, education has been supported largely on faith in the concept that the door of democracy is unlocked by education. Heretofore, we have achieved economic health and commercial success largely because of the advantages derived from our natural resources, American ingenuity, and expertise in technology; but this leadership is being challenged by other nations. We have reached a time when the national economic shoe begins to pinch, and economists are allocating more time to examining the effectiveness and efficiency of all types of education. The international commercial posture of other highly developed nations may have been epitomized by Khrushchev's challenge a number of years ago:

> We declare war upon you—in the peaceful field of trade. We declare a war we will win over the United States. The threat to the United States is not the intercontinental ballistic missile, but in the field of peaceful production. We are relentless in this, and it will prove the superiority of our system (*Congressional Record,* 1960).

The cold war may have abated, but international competition in trade has intensified. Japan and West Germany, as well as the USSR, have made phenomenal commercial progress during the past two decades and threaten our economic supremacy; our balance of trade causes alarm. Thus a new nationwide wave of general economic concern faces decision makers who control the destiny of education, an important factor in economic welfare. The implications for vocational education are clear—we must upgrade the economic literacy of vocational education personnel and that of the clientele served in order to fulfill our mission and achieve our goals.

Economics and Moral Values

Economics is an important factor in the formulation of moral values—a concept that was not fully appreciated by this writer for many years. The incident that brought about an awakening merits sharing. While passing over Belgium with a highly educated young newspaper editor from Innsbruck, Austria, as my seatmate, I looked at the ground below. Amazed at the density of the population, I remarked to my new friend, who had just finished a three-month educational exchange program in the U.S., "I can't believe my eyes; the villages down there are closer together than the farm dwellings in most of the state in which I live." His response was, "What you see reveals the basic problem in Europe. Tell me what you think is the primary concern of the people who live there." I couldn't answer immediately. "Simply this," he said, rescuing me from my predicament, " 'Do I survive or do I perish?' You Americans are always concerned about whether something is right or wrong. Those people have this concern too, but their primary interest is survival." As A. H. Maslow found, physical and safety needs take precedence over social or love needs; and unless there are sufficient resources to satisfy physical and safety needs, they impinge on our social behavior. Thus I began to realize the importance of economics and its effect on our way of life. I also gained a new perspective on the role of competition, and with the years took a much greater interest in the contributions of vocational education to our national economic welfare. Indeed, economic vitality impacts on our entire way of life.

Economic Roles during Critical Periods

Two earlier experiences illustrate other facets of the economic role of vocational education during critical times. Having experienced the Great Depression and having participated in the Vocational Education National Defense program (VEND) during the early years of World War II, I often have pondered the pivotal role of vocational education during national emergencies such as war, economic depression, and periods of severe social stress.

War emergencies. Khrushchev was right on one count: namely, that wars are won or lost on the home front. Had it not been for the service of vocational education during World War II, the outcome might have been much different.

In that period, all vocational education services were involved in the battles of productivity and maintenance of morale, each contributing in its own way. Men and women in industry and agriculture who were exempt from military service in order to produce war materials and food were given excellent skill training; home economics and distributive educators combatted a deterioration of health and morale through educating those who remained at home about the conservation of food and essential materials and how to cope with distribution problems such as rationing, ersatz product uses, and the black market.

One very effective medium during the war emergency was the Training Within Industry (TWI) program that helped prepare new and experienced supervisors in business and industry to teach new workers and to supervise them. Some of this instructional material is still used in business and industry and in education. Thus the economic impact of vocational education during war emergencies is an important economic phenomenon—one that is difficult to measure, but critical to national welfare as reflected in federal legislation. It should be considered when evaluating the benefits of vocational education.

When reading in the *Congressional Record* about the debates that preceded the Smith-Hughes Act, one soon learns that economic welfare and national defense were dominant reasons for its passage in 1917 (*Smith-Hughes Act in the Making*, 1952). War recovery problems of an economic character were a basic reason for the George-Barden Act of 1946 —training war veterans for entry and reentry into the labor force.

Economic depressions. The intervening George-Deen Act, however, is undergirded with another kind of economic consideration. The target of this 1936 legislation was to stimulate the economy, which was still battling the Great Depression. Funds to step up vocational training in the three established fields (agriculture, trade and industrial, and home economics education) were greatly increased, and money was earmarked for training employed workers in the distributive occupations in order to help small businesses in their recovery efforts and to encourage entrepreneurship.

Periods of severe social stress. The Vocational Education Act of 1963 was aimed at reducing unemployment among youth groups, an economic problem, but it also had a socioeconomic purpose—the elimination of inequalities in educational opportunity in vocational education. One of the basic economic questions in education focuses on this problem (see Chapter 2). The 1963 Act and those that followed also contained provisions for productivity effectiveness and efficiency, directives that were not present in earlier laws. Program evaluation was made mandatory, and accountability became the order of the day.

Current economic concerns. Current national problems of concern to vocational educators center on energy use—an economic problem of supply and demand. Indeed, education in general, and vocational education in particular, are highly involved in our economic welfare; and personnel in these occupations must be sophisticated in societal economics in order to meet their responsibilities in the maintenance of our economic system. Much more could be said about the bond between vocational education and economic welfare and about the need for vocational educators to understand the societal aspects of the economics of education, a subject that will be approached from different perspectives in later chapters.

Returns to Investment of Program Components

Nearly all vocational educators want to do their best in their particular jobs. They are deeply concerned about their commitments to society, and they think that the best way to contribute is through their work in the educational unit to which they belong. A moderate degree of sophistication in the economics of vocational education reveals individual benefits that are often overlooked. Therefore, it seems appropriate at this juncture to outline, for staff members of component parts of a vocational education program, some of the more important returns to investment of a working knowledge of this branch of economics.

Most conscientious vocational educators hold their own specialty in high esteem—this is as it should be. Unfortunately, in their enthusiasm for their own fields, there is a strong tendency to lose sight of the goals of the total vocational education program, of which they are a part, and of its role in the entire educational system. Some of them become overly competitive and step on a few toes, thereby defeating their own purposes; such behavior may also complicate the maintenance of good human relations, thereby interfering with productivity.

Another condition, one that may arouse indignation among some staff members, is a seemingly inequitable allocation of resources among component parts of a vocational program. (Readers may have witnessed vocational education programs in which one or two fields appear to dominate the others excessively.) What can be done to provide staff members with total program perspective and to maintain proper allocation of offerings among program components? Development of an understanding of the economics of education on the part of program personnel *can* help to realize these goals.

First, an economic perspective usually helps a program proponent to arrive at realistic program goals—goals that take into account population and manpower needs, available resources, and economic factors pertaining to operation in consonance with other instructional units.

Second, since resources are limited, there will always be competition for those resources. Therefore, the ability of vocational educators to analyze the underlying economic reasoning of concerned parties and to use economic information and skills in persuasion can be critical factors in a program's welfare or even survival.

Third, an appreciation of the economics of education can be useful in deriving satisfaction from an environment in which program economies are realized through cooperation with other fields of vocational and general education. It's much more enjoyable to work in a cooperative setting with a common goal than one where each worker is distrustful of the motives of others.

Fourth, economic understandings can be instrumental in precluding the divide-and-conquer strategies of those who attempt to inhibit the achievement of given ends. For example, one way for higher level decision makers to defeat a proposal for funding is to encourage disagreement among groups or individuals requesting the money and to delay allotments until there is agreement among those wanting the funds. Understanding the economics of educational decisions and the need for unity may aid the parties making the request to maintain a coherent and consistent stand.

Fifth, understanding the economics of education can be useful in identifying latent assets and hidden or ignored liabilities. The more one knows about the inherent strengths, weaknesses, and economic or other motives of competitors, the better are the probabilities of achieving an end.

This list of benefits to staff members could be extended; however, it seems that the case for an understanding of the economics of vocational education has been made. Yes, there usually *are* reasons why one program unit gets red carpet treatment from higher level decision makers while another gets the "brush-off." The ability of the program's proponents to apply the principles of the economics of education in presenting their case often may account for the difference.

Appraisal of the Use of Economics of Education

One may envision the economics of education as a tool, a problem solving facilitator, a logical procedure, or a way of thinking—one that is used in approaching problems in vocational education and arriving at facts for decision making. Its stance is one of objectivity in the investigation of relative effectiveness and efficiency of production. What can one expect in this regard?

Utility of the economics of education. Economics, per se, usually does not provide the complete answer to an inquiry, and sometimes the economic information provided is not even the most important factor in decision making; but frequently it tips the scales in one direction. Economic principles aid decision makers in devising ways of doing the best with what we have. They serve as guides in measuring the inputs and outputs of production so that alternative methods and procedures can be compared on the basis of some accepted set of criteria.

Although economic analysis of data lends an aura of objectivity to educational decision making, and its procedures are designed to reduce if not eliminate bias, the information gleaned from a study is no better than the quality of the data and information used in the investigation. An economic analysis can be manipulated or an investigator may be misled; therefore, it generally is advisable to check the procedure and data before accepting the results of a study.

Attributes of the economics of education. Quantifying educational data for economic analysis poses some difficult problems. For example, decision makers vary widely in their beliefs about the "human wants" to be satisfied through educational services. One cause of this problem is that the economics of education relates to a wide variety of expected benefits—those of educators, employers, law makers, learners, and others (Ellis, 1975, 15-20); and sometimes these expectations conflict. Thus, to answer the first question in the economics of education (what should be produced?) is particularly difficult, especially from the standpoint of society. The question of anticipated benefits calls for reasonable agreement among decision makers on mission, goals, and objectives of the educational unit being analyzed. (See Chapter 4, "Toward Economic Goals and Objectives for Vocational Education.")

A second obstacle occurs in differentiating among the learning outcomes. Isolation and measurement of a large number of the anticipated outcomes is a very difficult task. Even in vocational education, where some of the outcomes (e.g., earnings of graduates) are more tangible than in general education, the measurement of program outcomes is in an embryonic stage. This problem is treated in several later chapters.

One complicating factor in the measurement of learning outcomes is the perishability (or durability) of learnings—some are more durable than others. For example, the possession of some manual skills may persist longer than a person's retention of factual information. Another difficult task is the isolation of learning outcomes that may be attributed to schooling from those caused by improved technology.

Although the difficulties inherent in educational economic analysis may seem almost insurmountable, much progress has been made during the past few decades. (See Chapter 3, which deals with the development of human capital.) Measurement of program outputs in vocational education is advancing rapidly beyond the stage where the sole criterion of measurement is placement of graduates in jobs related to their training.

IMPROVING VOCATIONAL EDUCATION'S PRODUCTIVITY

Vocational education is constantly shooting at a moving target—a condition that challenges educational economists. If its sole responsibility were to fulfill manpower needs for training, the mission would be *relatively* simple, but vocational education now has an explicit mandate to serve population needs as well. Even looking at the manpower needs assessment alone, the task is not easy because manpower demands change rapidly due to economic conditions (prosperity and recessions or depressions), continuous technological advancement, and numerous shifts in the social and political obligations of those who purchase manpower services.

The Vocational Education Act of 1963 focused on the education of people (development of individuals), in contrast to earlier manpower-oriented mandates. The concept of providing occupational education as a part of career education for *all* people, wherever they might be, was added to the original commission, introducing new variables into economic analyses. This legislation also stressed vocational education for individuals with special needs (another complex problem for educational economists) and called for rigorous accountability. Thus, the quest for more effective and efficient production had to be applied to new educational outcomes as well as to those already in force.

Economic Assessment

During the last two decades educational economists have developed a system for evaluating educational productivity that is parallel to the one used for evaluating the productivity for physical goods. This system, based on the concept of *human capital,* is explained in Chapter 3. Benefits derived from education are balanced out against costs. The relationship between these two elements (costs and benefits) is used in deciding whether an investment is equal or superior to alternative uses of funds. The system can be used to evaluate an expenditure of public funds, *societal* returns to investment, or to appraise an individual's investment in schooling, *private* returns to investment.

As suggested earlier, many educational costs and benefits are difficult to calculate. Also, there are conceptual weaknesses in estimating the size and direction of economic influences on educational investment decisions. According to Perlman (1973, xi), imperfect as the system may be as a guide to decision makers, it is the best we have, and should be used—with caution—in policy decisions and in the allocation of resources. This value judgment warrants further discussion.

Human capital. Capitalization—as it refers to human capital—allows money values to be placed on an individual as an economic entity. It facilitates the measurement of returns to investment in a person and aids in making decisions about the merits of investing in an individual or particular group of people. A person in whom no investment has been made can be compared to unused land; future earning power and current asset value is limited until the land (or the mind) is cultivated. To raise personal economic productivity, an individual must be developed as a human resource; investments such as education and training must be made in the person to increase future earning power.

The human capital approach compares added return from investments (benefits) to their costs in dollars. Here the economist and humanist often disagree. The humanist objects to dollar measurement of benefits. The human capital proponent argues that the economic component is just one of many factors to be weighed in long-run decisions pertaining to expenditures of time and money. Some people confuse one's "human capital value" with value as a human being. The difference may be illustrated by contrasting an individual's net worth with value as a person; e.g., a gangster may be wealthy but rate low in our social hierarchy.

Opposing viewpoint. Although the cost-benefit approach to economic analysis that is favored by human capital advocates may seem to be the best we have, it is appropriate to highlight opposing points of view. The expression "man is not a machine" can be used against the human capitalists on their own grounds. The following quotation by Perlman (1973, 8) capsulizes the argument of opponents of the system. It partially explains why some educators favor the use of cost-effectiveness analysis, another approach to program appraisal that is discussed in Chapter 7.

> Workers do not necessarily supply their services to the highest bidder because they value working conditions, chances of promotion, job location, etc., as well as wages. Similarly, the individual worker, unlike the firm, cannot have income maximization as his goal; a 168-hour work week can be very tiring. He does maximize his satisfactions, or utility, from the allocation of his time, which he divides between income-generating work and leisure . . . In short, labor analysis is complicated by the fact that work is done by people who cannot separate themselves from the services they render and who therefore must expend time and effort in providing these services . . . These same immeasurable elements prevent pat conclusions regarding the merit of investment projects in man. Individuals do not decide whether schooling "pays" solely on monetary considerations . . . Similarly, public decisions on educational investment are influenced by indirect results from the projects —the effect on economic growth and social changes, for example.

Elements of cost-benefit analysis. Although the costs of education and the benefits derived therefrom are explained in Chapters 3 and 7, which discuss cost-benefit analysis as it

Table 1

COSTS OF EDUCATION

To Society	To Individuals
Direct Costs	**Direct Costs**
Teachers' salaries	Tuition & fees
Nonteaching salaries & wages	Supplies purchased by student
Supplies & equipment	Transportation
Supplies purchased by student	
Transportation	
Indirect (Opportunity) Costs	**Indirect (Opportunity) Costs**
Opportunity cost of capital outlay	Earnings foregone by student
Foregone interest	
Depreciation	
Earnings foregone by students	
Costs of tax exemption	
Exemption from property tax	
Exemption from income tax	
Foregone earnings of mothers	
(those who must forego jobs to stay at home and provide early childhood education)	

Table 2

BENEFITS FROM EDUCATION

To Society (External Effects)	To Individuals (Private Benefits)
Residence Related Benefits	**Employment Related Benefits**
1. Intergenerational benefits (future benefits to family)	1. Increased earnings (subject to adjustments for intelligence, ambition, informal education at home, family wealth, social mobility)
2. Neighborhood benefits	2. Broadened employment opportunities
3. Taxpayer benefits (less unemployment, law enforcement costs, taxes)	3. On-the-job training options (flexibility, can learn job faster)
Employment Related Benefits	4. Hedging against technological change (increased ability to adjust to changing job opportunities, additional benefit from on-the-job training)
1. Effect on quality of production	**Education Associated Benefits**
2. Effect on productivity of other workers	Eligibility for additional education
Society Related Benefits	**Nonmarket Benefits**
1. Maintenance of competition & market-centered economy	1. Ability to prepare own income tax returns & other forms & reports
2. Effect on political democracy	2. Do-it-yourself options for home & personal use
3. Effect on equality of opportunity	**Personal Living Benefits**
4. Spillover effect on research & services	1. Income-leisure options
5. Effect of training workers for specialized skills when bottleneck to economic development exists	2. Way of life options
6. Effect on cultural levels	
7. Effect as hedging against war emergencies	

applies to vocational education, it seems appropriate to present in outline form the potential items for consideration in such studies as a precursor and handy reference for the discussions that follow (see Tables 1 and 2).

Measuring Instruments

Accurate economic analysis depends on the existence of valid and reliable instruments with which to measure program outcomes. Several yearbook authors have voiced the need for good instruments to measure the outcomes of vocational training. It is generally agreed that shortcomings in this realm have retarded progress in program evaluation. Therefore, it seems appropriate to describe briefly a set of evaluative devices which the writer believes have particular potential for use in vocational education program evaluation. These instruments may add a dimension to those currently being used (Lofquist & Dawis, 1969).

A set of inventories based on the theory of work adjustment (Dawis, Lofquist & Weiss, 1968) has been developed by the federally funded Minnesota Studies in Vocational Rehabilitation over a 20-year period. These instruments may be used nationwide by teachers and researchers to augment guidance and placement, classroom and on-the-job instruction and improvement of job performance, and program evaluation. Three of the instruments of particular worth in evaluation are the: Minnesota Importance Questionnaire (MIQ), Minnesota Satisfaction Questionnaire (MSQ), and Minnesota Satisfactoriness Scales (MSS). These instruments, together with occupational reinforcer patterns (ORPS) or vocational needs profiles for 148 published occupations to date (32 more are still to be published), enable users to assist students from the time they embark on occupational training through their occupational adjustment. Twenty dimensions of work needs form the basis of the four instruments:

ability utilization
achievement
activity
advancement
authority
company policies
compensation
co-workers
creativity
independence
moral values
recognition
responsibility
security
social service
social status
supervision—human relations
supervision—technical
variety
working conditions

Briefly, the instruments and the factors measured are as follows:

MIQ—satisfactions sought in an ideal job

MSQ—satisfactions derived from present job
MSS—satisfactoriness to supervisors and employers
ORPS—norms of work satisfiers in 148 occupations

Computer printouts compare an individual's needs pattern with each of the ORPS in descending order of similarity and likewise with occupational clusters. Thus, practitioners can (1) help applicants select an occupational cluster or occupation that is compatible with their needs patterns; (2) place students in part- or full-time positions that correspond to their needs patterns—comparing ORPS with MIQ patterns; (3) follow up on placements to see that the students receive the satisfactions sought (MSQ); (4) acquire information on the satisfactoriness of their students' work performance (MSS); (5) provide classroom instruction and encourage supervision in concert with students' needs (MIQ, MSQ & MSS). Likewise, researchers may evaluate program effectiveness in performing these functions.

When used in conjunction with vocational education programs or program components, these instruments can shed light on program productivity. The theory of work adjustment and its measurement instruments seem to be compatible with the new emphasis on individual (people) needs as well as being in tune with the improvement of worker productivity.[1]

Micro-Economic Studies in Vocational Education

Macro-economic studies, as the name implies, treat global concerns—how the entire economy behaves—whereas micro-economic studies deal with much smaller components (e.g., the vocational education system or fields of vocational education or even parts of those fields). Educational economists are interested in all of these.

In some situations, micro-economic studies dealing with part of the total vocational education program may be more helpful in achieving program improvement than broader studies that deal with the program as a whole. Such studies of smaller program components can provide valuable information for grass-roots practitioners who are in a position to take positive action, whereas the broader-based studies seem to them more global, less meaningful and designed for their superiors. Moreover, the people on the firing line may feel that their fields or particular specialties are quite different from the other components and that the larger studies are suspect, mixing apples and oranges. Opinions concerning uniqueness vs. commonality among vocational fields and parts of fields range widely, and there are philosophical, pedagogical and organizational reasons for the larger measures; but the economist's concern for the examination of reasonable alternative methods of production, using appropriate measures in the process, dictates analysis of the smaller units as well as the larger ones.

Altman (1966) directed a study of general vocational capabilities (skills and knowledges) that portends opportunity for improvement of micro-studies in vocational education which involve the individual occupational fields. While attempting to identify capabilities that can be generalized across a reasonable variety of job requirements, vocational content was ordered along a continuum from hardware to people (mechanical-electrical, spatial, chemical-biological, symbolic and people). Content categories along this continuum were found to be compatible with a cross-cutting set of psychological processes arranged in a hierarchy of complexity (sensing, detecting, rote sequencing or chaining, discriminating or identifying, coding, classifying, discrete estimating, continuous tracking, logical manipulation, rule using, decision making, and problem solving). Altman contended:

> The most important implication of the study was that there is a definable and well-structured domain of vocational capabilities which has not previously been well defined and which is not being systematically taught by our educational institutions. This domain is compatible with and intimately related to existing academic disciplines and specialized vocational training. It can be a focal point for the development of vocational awareness, vocational choice and career planning. If properly exploited, it also promises to enhance the flexibility with which students can apply the results of their educational experience (Altman, 1966, xiii).

Categories of the hardware-to-people continuum—and the hierarchy of psychological processes—appear to be associated with occupations in the several vocational education fields in approximately the following way trade and industrial education (mechanical-electrical-spatial); agricultural, home economics, and health (chemical-biological); office (symbolic) and distributive (people). Of course, each vocational area transcends categories and likely includes some competencies in each, but a field may be characterized generally by one or more of the categories.

The AIR study could be a harbinger of a new direction in vocational education research which investigates differences as well as commonalities in methodology and delivery systems among vocational education fields and elements of those fields. Such evidence would provide insight into administrative problems involving combination of fields into viable units and preclude the assumption by some that common methods of instruction are effective and efficient in all vocational areas.

Thus, if the hardware-to-people continuum or psychological process hierarchy has merit, economic analysis designers should recognize the unique characteristics of the various specialized programs in order to improve the productivity of the total vocational education program. The AIR study is not conclusive, but it does suggest an area of inquiry that may contribute to the improvement of vocational economic analysis.

Employer Inputs

How should production of the various forms of education be organized? This is one of three questions in the economics of education discussed in Chapter 2. Vocational education is noted for its variety of delivery systems and the involvement of outside sources, particularly management and labor, in the production process. Employers have participated in occupational training since colonial times, when through an apprenticeship arrangement they were responsible for an apprentice's general education as well as for teaching a trade. Employer involvement in vocational education has had its ups and downs; however, during the past few decades cooperative vocational education has become relatively popular, largely because of the low unemployment rate of its graduates compared to high school graduates in general. Attractive as any type of delivery system involving input from outside agencies may be, shifting a production function to an employer or other instrumentality does not alter the cost of production unless that educational process results in economies not realized in the traditional delivery system. Thus, economic analysis must include all costs, regardless of who performs the function—there is no such thing as a free lunch.

Regardless of the sector of society, the most important natural resource is the human resource. If even a small percentage of it is wasted, the cost to society is heavy. Wasted time, costly mistakes, theft, training costs, extra supervision, and low morale all have a devastating effect on a corporation's income statement and the costs are passed along to consumers in most cases. Business and industry and education are frequently thought of as independent operations, but the need for cooperation becomes more apparent as education seeks assistance from employers and as their personnel participate in educational planning, guidance counseling, and instruction.

As cooperative effort of employers increase, costs of education are added to the cooperating agency's expenses, and analyses become more complex. In addition to the regular schooling costs, supporting agencies bear such expenses (or investments) as: costs of training (including apprenticeship), on-the-job training of cooperative education student trainees, company tours for students (field trips), resource visitors to schools, donations of instructional equipment and materials, remedial instruction in fundamentals, and specialty training of employees. Additional costs include expenses associated with participation in school management such as those listed by the Conference Board (Finley, 1973) in a survey of school related activities: serving on school boards, advisory committees and panels of consultants, sharing methods of accountability control with schools, helping schools update technology, offering budget and financial advice, doing survey and evaluation projects for schools, advising on plant management, helping school administrators with labor relations problems, offering advice on organizational design, helping schools introduce new record systems, and offering supplementary personnel for management training. Of course, the cooperating agencies reap some benefits such as good will and tax deductions from their investments, but this does not alter the cost of education.

Some benefits that accrue to education from employer involvement in production may not be available in a delivery system operated by the school alone—for example, development of competencies in the operation of office or industrial machines that are not feasible in school, and co-worker relations competencies. In distributive education, it would be virtually impossible for a school to finance a laboratory with equipment equivalent to that of the modern shopping center, supervisory services, customers and co-workers of all ages. Additional outcomes resulting from employer contributions must be considered, even in programs where students do not enter employment.

IMPROVING ECONOMIC LITERACY

Economic understanding and personal development can help individuals achieve success and satisfaction in the world of work, no mean outcome in itself. But equally important, these investments in human capital can qualify young men and women to become agents of change to help bring about not just a healthier economy but a better society (see the concluding statement of Chapter 12). If this statement by W. Lee Hansen is true, what can be done to improve economic literacy in the United States? What is the role of vocational education in such an endeavor? What can be done to improve the effectiveness and efficiency of production in the present delivery system in teaching economic competencies? These nationwide issues are treated in an excellent manner in Chapters 11 and 12. This discussion will be confined to the role and delivery system of the development of economic understandings and skills for vocational education in general, since Section IV is devoted to the economic contributions and organization for teaching economic competencies in the six major vocational education fields.

Vocational Education's Economic Role

Everyone seems to realize that vocational education has an important economic role; but during the first half century of federal financial participation, instruction in technical competencies heavily overshadowed other types of content, including economics instruction. At the high school level, social studies was assumed to have filled the gap in most vocational education services. Among the vocational fields, agricultural education included applied economic understandings and skills in its curricula and home economics dealt with consumer economics and other selected economics topics in a limited perspective, but very little economics instruction existed in the other occupational fields until the early 1960s. Management and labor did not show great concern for the low level of economic literacy that prevailed among workers and the general public. Apparently the Vocational Education Act of 1963, with its emphasis on serving people and its mandates for accountability, generated interest in economics, which led to a concern for including economics in vocational instruction.

Since economic competencies are useful to everyone and all students take social studies courses, outside agencies and organizations such as the Joint Council on Economic Education supported and gave leadership to the social studies cause. Also, general business education (the general education component of business and office education) included selected economic content in its curriculum and some schools offered courses in economics in their business education departments; thus, business education became active in the movement which was resisted by many skill-subject teachers. In 1961 the National Task Force on Economic Education prepared a report, *Economic Education in the Schools,* which became a springboard for economics education curriculum development.

Early lack of concern for economic education. Current interest in teaching economic understandings and skills in vocational education is evident, but one may wonder why economics was not stressed at the outset—such knowledge might provide clues to solutions of current curriculum enrichment problems. Of course, there were many reasons for the delay, a few of which will be called to mind here. The delegation of economics to social studies teachers has been mentioned. Lack of mandated accountability for instructional outcomes has been implied. But probably the most compelling reason is that a large percentage of vocational education personnel have not been sufficiently sophisticated in economics to teach the required understandings and skills. This does not suggest lack of academic ability on the part of vocational educators, but rather that the educational and experience backgrounds of many vocational teachers have not included the study of economics or an environment conducive to its learning. Many vocational educators, especially trade and industrial teachers, entered professional education directly from business and industry, having been selected on the basis of their expertise in their fields rather than for their academic achievement.

Another reason for the delay in teaching economic competencies to vocational education students may be attributed to the lack of concern on the part of vocational education leaders and decision makers. Computer printouts of research and publications identify few studies or articles about teaching economic understandings and skills to the participants of vocational education programs. The reasons for this are not clear. Vocational education decision makers in general conform to federal laws and the rules and regulations relating to those laws; they are usually sensitive to the expressed needs of those who support vocational education. Perhaps the lack of leadership in teaching economics competencies to vocational education students in the past reflects the general posture of the nation, and new leaders will take the initiative in improving the economic literacy of workers. Apparently employers and employees are beginning to sense the need for better economic understanding. Recent surveys have indicated that high school graduates often regret not having developed a better background in the area of economics (Shirey, 1977).

The final reason to be mentioned here for vocational education's tardiness in teaching economics relates to the impression of economics in the minds of those who have taken college courses in economics, especially teachers. Needless to say, their perceptions of economics can be improved. On the positive side, however, hope lies in current efforts to improve the teaching of economics, both at the college and high school levels. There has always been controversy between the content fields (discipline areas) and education departments concerning the administration of teacher education, each group claiming superiority in the preparation of teachers. In fact, each of the two approaches has strong appeals, but the interdependence between them has not been recognized until recently. Lack of appreciation of learner needs and insufficient sophistication in student motivation on the part of college economics instructors may be, at least in part, the reason for poor teacher attitudes toward economics. Fortunately, the Joint Council on Economic Education and many state councils on economic education are helping to bridge the gap, and perhaps there will be more cooperation among administrative units of colleges and universities in teaching economics in the future.

Economic education inhibitors. Other than dissatisfaction with the way economics is taught, why do many individuals have a negative feeling about economics? Disagreement among economists may cause lack of confidence for some of them; stress on dollar measurement turns off some humanists; and the complexity of economics discourages many. In addition, it appears that some private sector interest groups and unsophisticated educators probably reinforce these negative attitudes about economics by focusing primarily on certain isolated facts and figures about profit, thereby mystifying students and the lay public. The following case illustrates this point.

As Hansen states in Chapter 12, "Interestingly, pollsters ask about profit per dollar of sales rather than profit per dollar of capital invested: this reveals their own lack of sophistication in economics." Though he uses this situation to demonstrate ignorance of economic understanding, it also serves to illustrate the mystery that is generated about our market-centered economy.

Many business personnel seem to lament the fact that the general public is grossly misinformed about the monetary rewards of business owners and managers and that they highly overestimate the profit per dollar of sales. Profits of 1 to 7 percent seem ridiculously low to most laypeople, and they wonder why companies assume large risks on such small margins and how they can afford to pay executives and board members such high salaries—a logical cause for skepticism. Unfortunately (from the lay viewpoint), very few business firms publicize their return on capital invested—which, after all, is the reason for being in business. Profit per dollar of capital invested is more in line with consumer estimates of profit and a more reasonable figure in their minds. Whatever the purpose of highlighting the lower profit margin on sales may be, the situation illustrates how selected economic facts and figures in isolation cause skepticism. This phenomenon is not limited to the field of business and economics.

Assume for the moment that workers (or students) understood an income statement and how turnover of inventory enables a firm to reinvest the capital and earnings derived therefrom each time the stock is sold, adding to the profit of previous stock turnovers. Suppose further that they understood the role of expense control in earning a profit. Wouldn't it be much easier to teach the impact of various daily work activities on the firm's profit—facilitating stock turnover, conservation of materials, avoiding wasted time, and so on? An example concerning motivation illustrates the importance to learners of meaningful company practices. The writer, when teaching adult retail selling classes, was unable to achieve anticipated motivation for learning suggestion selling until he related it in figures to its effect on the firm's profit in the income statement.

Improving Productivity of Instruction

Although the authors of Section IV relate many excellent ways of motivating and instructing individuals to study economics, I shall make a few generalizations and add a suggestion or two.

The real answer to improving economic literacy rests with educators who share the truths about our economic system with their clients. The "secret" of motivation is to teach economics from the learner's point of view. Shirey (1977), a businessman, describes the rationale for a student to be concerned about understanding our business system as follows.

> First, students eventually will have to know how to live and work in a world where businesses operate within the principles of free enterprise, and they have a stake in the preservation of the system so that they'll not be deprived of its benefits during their lifetime. Secondly, they must not only under-

> stand the tasks assigned but also the goals to be reached. This involves understanding the system under which enterprises operate and the necessity of profit and productivity in business so that recommendations in these areas can be seen as progressive steps on the part of business enterprises.
>
> Having this larger frame of reference—becoming goal-oriented rather than task-oriented—will completely change the students' perspective as they view jobs in which they function. They'll see [beyond] the piece of paper, the order, the invoice or the letter [to] . . . the customer behind it—and it is really King Customer who continues to call the shots. . . .
>
> Thirdly, if students are to prosper in the system, they must understand how it works—how wealth is created and where it comes from. There is an increasing tendency today to think that wealthy [people] become so because of what they earn rather than understanding the basic precept that what we ultimately own is dependent not upon what we make, but what we save.

These recommendations relate to the business and industrial sector; however, their underlying motivational vein applies to all vocational education. The basic concept in the quotation above is that an understanding of the system in which learners work generates attitudes that are personally and economically helpful and enhance their satisfaction from work. Unfortunately, many teachers do not capitalize on opportunities to teach these broader understandings and attitudes. There is a strong urge for them to terminate instruction after a skill has been mastered and hurry on to the next content area, when it would be much more conducive to permanent learning and attitude formation to continue teaching content that relates the skills to economic goals and the system under which the learner works.

Vocational education has a definite bearing on work attitude formation and consequent worker productivity. Some individuals see their work as only a *job*—a means of earning money. Others are sufficiently interested in what they do to perceive their work as a *task,* and they take pride in performing a task well. Still others think of work as an *occupation* and identify themselves with that occupation. Finally there are those who believe that their work is part of a *career*; they are dedicated to it and receive personal satisfaction from their contributions to society through it. Economic understanding and skills can help workers move from one of these work attitude levels to another—job orientation, task orientation, occupation orientation and career orientation. Understanding the economic implications of daily work activities can be a strong factor in motivating individuals to do so.

Effective Delivery Systems

Returning to Shirey's concept of relevant content and appropriate teaching methods, several delivery systems offer attractive opportunities for learning how our business system works, together with the improvement of economic understandings in general. Junior Achievement, Inc., a national educational organization sponsored by private businesses, teaches the American private enterprise system through firsthand experiences. High school youths, regardless of career objectives, select a business (usually one that manufactures a product), organize it, operate it and finally dissolve it. JA's methods and techniques warrant examination by vocational educators.

Another type of delivery system that has received legislative support and offers excellent potential for improving economic literacy is cooperative vocational education. This plan of public school instruction combines classroom learning with employment, thereby affording an actual life laboratory of economic activity and excellent opportunities for guided activities pertaining to our economic system. This delivery system was appraised in a bulletin of the National Association of Secondary School Principals (1973) as follows:

> Specific occupational training programs appear to be generating the most enthusiasm among students, employers, and school officials, inasmuch as students feel these programs are providing them valuable training, employers feel they are getting their money's worth, and school people are satisfied with the learnings and with job placements after the training period . . . cooperative education programs are more likely than any other type to provide students with job related instruction in school . . .

Commercial textbook publishers are beginning to supply instructional materials on economics that are specificially designed for vocational education students (Klaurens, 1971). Agricultural education offers comparable opportunities for the acquisition of economic understandings and skills through its program for young farmers.

Last to be mentioned here, simulation programs in the various vocational fields provide good opportunities for teaching economics. Students organize and operate simulated businesses or industries. Such programs, when offered during the junior year of high school, enable cooperative vocational education students to obtain a perspective of the economic environment before entering employment with a cooperating employer.

A final observation about teaching economics pertains to

the use of analyses of private returns to investment in schooling—returns on an individual's investment in education as compared to those of society. If relevance is a key to motivation in the study of economics, what could be more appropriate than studying the economic feasibility of one's own schooling? The subject seems especially timely for vocational education students when making various career decisions. The concept of human capital provides latitude for an interesting study of one's own return to investment in schooling, as well as that of society.

Enrichment of Instruction in Economics

What can be done to promote the development of instruction in economic understandings and skills of those who matriculate in vocational education programs? What are the resources, both within and outside of the field?

There comes a time in one's professional development when the return to investment of one's time in investigating the expertise of other disciplines exceeds that of studying the disciplines underlying his or her own field. For example, within vocational education each occupational field has its own areas of strength and weakness. Members of a particular field may seek to correct the weaknesses of their field by studying fields that are stronger in those areas. Also, going beyond the vocational family, vocational educators can help the cause of economic literacy by eliciting help from educational economists and the organizations whose purpose is to update and improve the teaching of economics.

One such organization is the Joint Council on Economic Education, mentioned earlier, which publishes numerous materials at various educational levels—curriculum guides, teachers' manuals, tests of economic understandings, and teacher education materials, including its latest release, *Master Curriculum Guide in Economics for the Nation's Schools* (Hansen et al, 1977). Part I contains a framework for teaching economics: a concise statement of basic concepts and generalizations for teaching economics. Part II, available in the fall of 1977, treats strategies for teaching economics.

CONCLUDING STATEMENT

Vocational education and the nation's economy is a broad topic that can only be introduced in one volume. For discussion purposes in this limited treatment, it may be divided into three broad areas: the economics of education, the economics of vocational education, and improving the economic literacy of vocational education recipients.

In order to approach the subject of vocational education and the nation's economy, one needs to have at least an acquaintance with the economics of education—a complex field of economics, a relatively new one, and one that still has a long way to go before it is perfected. Some educational economists have developed a system of human capital evaluation which parallels that of physical capital, but the inputs and particularly the outputs are difficult to isolate and measure. A system of cost-benefit analysis restricts all measures to dollar values, which stirs the disapproval of many educators. Another analytical procedure that does not require dollar measurement of outcomes, i.e., cost-effectiveness analysis, meets with more favor among educators (see Chapter 7).

Understanding the economics of education alone is insufficient competence to appraise the outcomes of vocational education and compare the effectiveness and efficiency of alternative productive processes. When designing studies concerning the productivity of vocational programs, vocational educators should give careful consideration to the uniqueness of program components; and when delivery systems involve inputs by outside agencies such as employers, the costs accruing to those agencies should be included in the analysis. Even though the cost-benefit or rate-of-return analysis provides a faulty economic guide to investors in vocational education, it serves a useful purpose and should be used (with caution) in policy formation pertaining to investments.

Although vocational education has served economic and national security purposes of society for years, little attention has been given to the instruction of vocational students in economic understandings and skills. Since economic literacy is a strong factor in career development and work satisfaction, balanced vocational education requires the inclusion of this type of instruction. Assistance in the identification of relevant economic concepts and instructional materials and methods is available both within and outside vocational education, and it should be sought.

NOTE

1. Information about these tests may be obtained from Vocational Psychology Research, Department of Psychology, N660 Elliott Hall, 75 East River Road, University of Minnesota, Minneapolis, Minnesota 55455.

REFERENCES CITED

Altman, James W., project director. *Research on General Vocational Capabilities (Skills and Knowledges) Final Report.* Pittsburgh, Pennsylvania: American Institute of Research, March 1966.

Dawis, Rene V.; Lofquist, Lloyd H.; and Weiss, David J. *A Theory of Work Adjustment (A Revision).* Minnesota Studies in Vocational Rehabilitation, xxiii. Minneapolis: 1968.

Economic Education in the Schools . . . A Report of the National Task Force on Economic Education. George Leland Bach, Chairman. New York: Committee for Economic Development, 1961.

Ellis, Mary. "A Report to the Nation on Vocational Education." Prepared for Project Baseline, Northern Arizona University, and Ellis Associates, Inc., College Park, Maryland, November 1975.

Finley, G. J. *Business and Education: A Fragile Partnership.* New York: The Conference Board, Inc., 1973.

Hansen, W. Lee; Bach, G. L.; Calderwood, James D.; and Saunders, Philip. *Master Curriculum Guide in Economics for the Nation's Schools—Part I, A Framework for Teaching Economics: Basic Concepts.* New York: Joint Council on Economic Education, 1977.

Klaurens, Mary K. *The Economics of Marketing.* Occupational Manuals and Projects in Marketing. New York: Gregg Division of McGraw-Hill Book Company, 1971.

Lofquist, Lloyd H., and Dawis, Rene V. *Adjustment to Work.* New York: Appleton, Century, Crofts Division of Meredith Publishing Company, 1969.

Perlman, Richard. *The Economics of Education: Conceptual Problems and Policy Issues.* New York: McGraw-Hill Book Company, 1973.

"School-Supervised Work Education Programs." *Curriculum Report* 3. Washington, D.C.: National Association of Secondary School Principals, Curriculum Service Center, 1973.

Shirey, David. "Free Enterprise and the Business Student." *Business Education Forum* 31 (April 1977): 3-5.

The Smith-Hughes Act in the Making—The Growth of the Concept of Federal Aid to Vocational Education. Revised October 1952. Los Angeles: California State Department of Education, Bureau of Industrial Education in Cooperation with the University of California, Los Angeles, October 1952.

Section I:
The Economics of Education

An Introduction to the Economics of Education

Darrell R. Lewis

Why are economists concerned with education? What are some of the conceptual issues within education to which economists might offer some insight? What is the economic magnitude of education as an industry? Answers to these queries should provide readers of this yearbook with the background needed to pursue and relate to one another many of the specific problems and issues dealt with in ensuing chapters.

WHAT IS ECONOMICS ALL ABOUT?

The first step in our introduction to the economics of education is to obtain a clear conception of what economics is and what economists do. In this regard, there are more than five hundred different definitions of the term *economics*, ranging from lengthy statements to Jacob Viner's tautology, "Economics is what economists do." For our purposes in this introductory chapter, *economics* is defined as the social science that describes human efforts to satisfy human wants by utilizing scarce resources. As a social science, economics involves dealing with human actions which cannot be controlled as can, for example, the physical elements used by the chemist. An economist has society as his laboratory and thus cannot engage in the kind of experimentation favored by the physical scientist. As is true of the social sciences in general, economics is not an exact science and forecasts of economic developments are thus subject to considerable inaccuracies. Economics is, however, the social science with the most sophisticated body of theory—that is, the one with the greatest predictability accuracy of all the social sciences.

Our definition of economics underscores human wants and the scarcity of resources as essential elements in the study of any human activity. Economics is concerned with "doing the best with what we have." If our wants are virtually unlimited and our resources are scarce, we cannot conceivably satisfy all of society's material and service wants. The next best thing is to achieve the greatest possible satisfaction of these wants. Economics is, without a doubt, a science of efficiency—efficiency in the use of scarce resources.

Such economic efficiency is concerned with the allocation of resources among competing uses. It is also concerned with "inputs" and "outputs." Specifically, it is concerned with the relationship between the units of scarce resources which are put into the process of production and the resulting output of some wanted service or product. Thus, economic efficiency has to do with inputs of scarce resources and outputs of useful services and products.

The Production of Knowledge

Our economic interest in the area of education is not confined to education per se, but encompasses the much larger category of knowledge. One prominent economist, Fritz Machlup (1962), has written a monumental study in which knowledge as a whole, with education as one of its components, is investigated. Machlup states that there are two broad types of knowledge, the type that is designed to yield a large payoff in the future (investment) and the type that gives its recipient immediate pleasure (consumption). Knowledge of either type can be acquired in numerous ways—at formal institutions like schools; through the written word, as in books, magazines, and newspapers; or through audio and visual media such as radio, television, and the cinema. Machlup justifies the entrance of an economist into an analysis of knowledge by noting:

> The production of knowledge is an economic activity, an industry, if you like. Economists have analyzed agriculture, mining, iron and steel production, the paper industry, transportation, retailing, the production of all sorts of goods and services, but they have neglected to analyze the production of knowledge. This is surprising because there are a good many reasons why an economic analysis of the production of knowledge seems to be particularly interesting and promising of new insights (1962, 9).

He acknowledges that, among the major subdivisions of the knowledge industry, education is by far the most important. Education is not, however, a homogeneous category since there are multiple means of acquiring education. Education can be acquired in the home, in school, in church, in the armed forces, through the communications media, by training on the job, through self-education, and by learning from experience. Although most economists have focused primarily on education in the school, the concepts which they developed are equally applicable to other educational categories.

CONCEPTUAL ISSUES IN THE ECONOMICS OF EDUCATION

The economics of education embraces many different questions and draws on a wide variety of skills, conceptual models, and analytical techniques—ranging from human capital theory to program budgeting. However, economists focus on one unifying theme, the "economizing of educational resources." Thus, in this pursuit of efficiency within the educational industry, three fundamental questions are addressed by economists: What types and how much educational output is to be produced? How should the production of the various forms of education be organized? And how should the educational output be distributed?

What and How Much Is to Be Produced

With such a large amount of society's resources invested in producing educational goods and services within the context of Machlup's "knowledge industry," an analytical framework must be found which will promote rational decision making in this area. Since economic resources available for human investment are limited, investments should be made in the areas where they have the greatest positive impact on the production of educational goods and services. But what are those areas? How much of individual and public investment resources should go into physical resources? How much into human resources? What goods and services are to be produced and in what quantities does society want these goods and services produced? These are fundamental questions which must be answered by both the individual and society, regardless of the economic or social order. There is no way to avoid them. Efficiency becomes important because neither the individual nor society has unlimited resources. Hence, achieving efficiency in the production of educational goods and services is a relevant problem, whatever the individual's or society's political persuasion.

Although there are a number of different methods of inquiry in the economics of education, the concepts of *human investment* and *human capital* have provided a central focus for much of this work. These concepts have provided a method of analysis whereby it has been possible to apply existing economic theories of investment in physical capital to human investment decisions. The concept of *human investment* is meant to include those activities involving the diversion of resources from current consumption to those designed to augment the stock of human knowledge, skills, and capabilities. It is this stock of *human capital* which actually produces the stream of future output during its expected lifetime.

Through this human investment/human capital conceptual framework, it becomes possible to relate the future outputs of activities to the inputs required to perform these activities; it becomes possible to address the questions of "what and how much is to be produced" within the educational industry. This is most commonly done by comparing the value of the inputs with the value of the outputs—i.e., comparing costs and benefits. These comparisons require an allowance for the fact that at least some of the outputs or benefits are expected to materialize far in the future. Thus, as in any capital market, the time stream of the benefits or returns must be "discounted" to yield the true amount and present value of the payoff. Ordinarily, the resulting figure is expressed as the *internal rate of return* on investment; or as that rate of discount which equates the present value of returns earned throughout the expected future life of the worker with the present value of costs, most of which are incurred early and during the training period.[1] If the expected return is large relative to that available from other sectors of the economy (or large relative to alternative types of activities within the educational sector), that fact is taken to suggest that additional resources might profitably be devoted to that activity.

With such an analytical framework, both *private* and *social rates of return* can be determined. The private rate refers to individual investment decisions and the social rate to public ones. The basic computational differences between the two rates result from those costs of education which individuals do not directly finance (e.g., governmental expenditures) and those benefits (e.g., taxes) which individuals generate for society but do not directly receive. These additional social costs and benefits are added to the private determinations when social rates of return are computed. The whole treatment is directly analogous to that accorded to investment in physical capital, such as plant, machinery, and the like.

Recognizing and employing the conceptual framework of human capital opens the way for explaining past economic growth, planning the alteration of such growth in the future, and altering the distribution of productive abilities. Consequently, human capital opens up new dimensions in economic analysis, manpower planning and educational policy. Labor's productivity is not to be treated as an unknown or as a constant. It may be modified by individual decisions and public policy. Rational (i.e., efficient) decision making is not only desirable but possible within the educational sector.

Organizing Production

In the economics of education, one of the advantages of thinking in terms of human investment is that it immediately focuses attention on the production problem. What factors create human capital? What is the most efficient method of combining these factors? What is the best technology to use in production at various levels and for various outputs? In economics, similar questions could be raised concerning any other commodity; many of the same types of answers and problems arise. In the economics of education, we attempt to answer these questions by finding the production function for human capital; the technical or physical relationship between inputs and outputs is referred to as a *production function relationship.* Economists may search for national human capital production functions, production functions for particular skills, and production functions for particular educational sectors, institutions, classrooms or even individuals. In each case economists wish to know the precise inputs (resources) which enter the production process, the precise relationships between factors within the production process, and the outputs (benefits) which result from these production processes in education.

The inputs to education can be specified and quantified without great difficulty. As evidenced by our discussion of cost data later in this chapter, most of the various resources used to produce education are fairly obvious and can be evaluated in dollar terms; e.g., teachers, buildings, books, and the time and effort of the students themselves. On the other hand, the outputs of education present greater difficulties, both in concept and measurement, than the inputs. The nature of the outputs of the educational process are not fully understood, since some are intangible; this has made it difficult to assign a value to all of education's outputs. For lack of a better measure, economists have been forced to rely heavily on earnings as a measure of educational output. Accordingly, many of their analyses deal primarily with the financial returns as a single result of education.

It is, nonetheless, recognized that there are other important, if less tangible, educational benefits—both to the individuals who receive education and to the societies which participate. Obviously, there are both consumption and investment types of returns to individuals from most types of educational investment. Beyond this is a variety of additional benefits which "spill over" to other people, whether educated or not. These *neighborhood effects* or *external benefits* accrue to others through, for example, raising the general level of literacy or causing people to be more responsible citizens.

In addition to the development of national (aggregated) production functions, a number of efforts have been made to determine the nature of the production function for the various sectors and units within education as a part of the application of systems analysis to educational decision making. Possibilities for increased efficiency in education have been examined through the use of program budgeting, linear programming, and a number of studies dealing with teacher salary evaluations. Possibilities for various *economies of scale* (size) have also been explored (see Chapter 9). More recently, major efforts have been directed to learning more about specific school and teacher effects.

How society steers resources into the production of desired goods and services is very much a part of the economics of education. Consequently, issues of educational finance are a natural outgrowth of the work dealing with the organization of production in the economics of education. Who should pay for education? Should the government support public and private education? If so, which level of government should take what share of the burden? In financing the various educational activities, should the government support individuals or institutions? What share of total costs should be borne by the taxpayer, as opposed to the direct beneficiaries of the educational process? These and similar questions are all related to the organization of production in education today.

Distributing Output

How society divides or rations its output among its various units is also a fundamental question which every society must somehow answer. It is also a set of questions which economists are directing at education. Which members of our society should have access to what educational activity? Who are the individuals most likely to benefit from education? What is the effect of education on the distribution of income? Obviously, these types of questions involve not only economics but politics and ethics as well. Nevertheless, they are of growing concern in the economics of education.

With much of the disciplined inquiry in the economics of education focused on the economic value of education and the efficiency of resource allocation, both within education and among other sectors of the economy, there is an increasing awareness of the role which public policy can play in improving the economic status of low-income and minority young people. For example, inequalities in the distribution of both natural abilities and of human capital are being recognized and the factors which produce human capital are being isolated as first steps toward reducing such inequalities. Consequently, the economics of education and the analysis of human capital are becoming key ingredients in studies of poverty and racial inequality and in government programs to alter both. Most manpower training programs are based on the explicit assumption that productivity determines earnings.

On the other hand, there is also increasing awareness of a possible conflict in the goals of efficiency and equality of educational opportunity in the economics of education. For example, it is generally observed that individuals who obtain more education are also the ones who come from wealthier and otherwise advantaged families. It is thus concluded that the educational system may maintain and perpetuate such an unequal distribution of income. Some types of educational reform (e.g., school desegregation and the provision of additional resources for select types of children) may not necessarily lead to greater economic efficiency in the educational process; nevertheless, they may be desirable in a just society.

EDUCATION AS AN INDUSTRY

In the United States, education is a large-scale endeavor in both social and economic terms. In fact, it is the largest single industry in the United States today. Consequently, the purpose of this section is to explore the magnitude and trends of some of the resource imputs, costs, and relationships among sectors within education.

Education is the primary activity of approximately 62.3 million Americans. Included are 58.9 million students enrolled in schools and colleges, 3.1 million teachers, about 300,000 instructional staff members—superintendents, principals, supervisors and others (Simon, 1976, 8-11). This means that in a nation with over 214 million people nearly three out of ten persons are directly involved in education and nearly 8 percent of our Gross National Product (GNP) can be attributed to the educational process.

Student Enrollments

With approximately 28 percent of our total population involved as students in some type of formal education and with the largest proportion of these people abstaining from full-time employment, it is indeed appropriate to take note of the magnitude of the student population when reviewing the size and form of education as an economic industry.[2] Moreover, changes in school-age populations and educational participation rates are the major determinants of changes in demand for educational employment services (teachers) and other educational expenditures. (See Table 1.)

General trends in enrollments. Total enrollments in regular educational programs from kindergarten through graduate school increased for 27 consecutive years before reaching an all-time high of 59.7 million in the fall of 1971 (Simon & Frankel, 1976). During the decade from 1964 to 1974 enrollments in formal education programs increased by seven million—from 53 million to over 60 million. However, such enrollment is expected to decrease to 56 million by 1984.[3] The small decreases that occurred at the elementary level in recent years reflect the fact that there are now fewer children 5 to 13 years of age.

Trends in education beyond high school. The largest relative increases in enrollment during the past decade were registered in public higher education, with non-degree-credit vocational and technical education leading all areas of expansion. Projections to 1984 continue this expansion, but at a more moderate pace of 9 percent—again with vocational and technical education leading the way with a 50 percent increase projected. Enrollments in education beyond high school nearly doubled during the decade from 1964 to 1974, increasing from 5.3 million to 10.2 million, and they are expected to rise to 11.6 million by 1984. In 1984, 15.5 percent of this enrollment is expected to be in vocational and technical education, as compared to 11.7 percent in 1974 and only 6.2 percent in 1964 (Simon & Frankel, 1976).

Enrollment trends in adult education. The adult population, with its recent increase in educational participation, constitutes an expanding pool of potential students. The combination of an expanding adult population and the growing perception of education as a consumer commodity should

Table 1

SUMMARY OF UNITED STATES TRENDS IN FORMAL EDUCATION: 1964-65 TO 1984-85

Characteristic	Fall 1964	Fall 1974	Percent Change, 1964 to 1974	Fall 1984[1] (projected)	Percent Change, 1974 to 1984
	Thousands			*Thousands*	
I. School-age population					
5-13	35,373	33,903	-4	30,213	-11
14-17	14,229	16,880	19	14,279	-15
18-21	11,542	16,194	40	15,839	-2
18 (nearest birthday)	3,350	4,166	24	3,610	-13
II. Enrollment					
K-grade 12	47,716	49,756	4	44,900	-10
K-8	35,025	34,419	-2	31,500	-8
9-12	12,691	15,337	21	13,300	-13
Public	41,416	45,056	9	40,600	-10
K-8	30,025	30,919	3	28,500	-8
9-12	11,391	14,137	24	12,100	-14
Nonpublic	6,300	4,700	-25	4,200	-11
Higher education (post-secondary)					
Degree-credit	4,950	9,023	82	9,811	9
Public	3,180	6,838	115	7,780	14
Private	1,771	2,185	23	2,031	-7
4-year	4,239	6,825	61	6,939	2
2-year	711	2,198	209	2,872	31
Undergraduate	4,342	7,833	80	8,475	8
Graduate	608	1,190	96	1,336	12
Full-time	3,418	5,817	70	5,845	0
Part-time	1,532	3,206	109	3,966	24
Full-time equivalent	3,924	7,015	79	7,325	4
Non-degree credit	330	1,200	26	1,799	50
Public	288	1,150	29	1,723	50
Private	42	50	1	76	52
III. Instructional staff					
Elementary and secondary classroom teachers	1,865	2,387	28	2,360	-1
Elementary	1,086	1,311	21	1,379	5
Secondary	779	1,076	38	981	-9
Public	1,648	2,159	31	2,134	-1
Elementary	940	1,161	24	1,229	6
Secondary	708	998	41	905	-9
Nonpublic	217	228	5	226	-1

Table 1

SUMMARY OF UNITED STATES TRENDS IN FORMAL EDUCATION: 1964-65 TO 1984-85 (CONTINUED)

Characteristic	Fall 1964	Fall 1974	Percent Change, 1964 to 1974	Fall 1984[1] (projected)	Percent Change, 1974 to 1984
	Thousands			*Thousands*	
Other instructional staff (public)	165	257	56	254	-1
Higher education					
Resident courses	367	633	73	695	10
Full-time equivalent . .	274	493	80	541	10

	Constant 1974-75 dollars 1964-65	1974-75	Constant 1974-75 dollars 1984-85[1]
IV. Total expenditures by regular educational institutions:		*Billions of dollars*	
All levels	$68.6	$108.4	$122.3
Public	53.2	88.4	99.9
Nonpublic	15.4	20.0	22.4
Elementary and secondary schools	46.0	68.2	70.1
Public	40.6	61.6	63.4
Nonpublic	5.4	6.6	6.7
Institutions of higher education	22.6	40.2	52.2
Public	12.6	26.8	36.5
Nonpublic	10.0	13.4	15.7
		Dollars	
Current expenditure per pupil in average daily attendance in public elementary-secondary schools	$802	$1,255	$1,464

[1]Projections are based on assumptions given in Appendix A of *Projections of Education Statistics to 1984-85.* Users should check the acceptability of these assumptions for their purposes.

SOURCE: Data are adapted from tables in Simon and Frankel (1976, 8-10) and in National Center for Education Statistics (1976, 72-86).

contribute to further growth for the educational participation of adults. There has been a steady increase in adult education enrollments since 1957. During that year, 7.8 percent of the population 17 years and older were engaged in some form of adult education; the percentage rose to an estimated 13.3 percent by 1975. The actual number of participants more than doubled during that period, increasing from 8.2 million to 18 million (National Center for Education Statistics, 1976a, 11).

Enrollment trends, K-12. Elementary school enrollments (K-8) during the decade 1964-74 increased and then decreased—35.0 million in 1964, 36.8 million in 1969, and 34.4 million in 1974. The recent decrease is expected to continue until 1981, when estimated enrollments will be 30.8 million and then begin to increase again, reaching 31.5 million by 1984.[4]

Senior high school enrollment (grades 9-12), which increased 2.6 million during the 1964-74 decade—from 12.7 million to 15.3 million—is expected to decrease rapidly to 13.3 million in 1984 as the children born in the low birthrate years of the late 1960s progress through high school.

Enrollment-size factors. The two basic factors affecting changes in enrollments are population changes and the percentage of the population enrolled in educational programs. Not only has population growth historically contributed to the substantial growth in student enrollments, but a far greater proportion of young people is now enrolled and spending much more of their time in school.

Increases in the percentage of our population 5-17 years

Table 2

SUMMARY OF UNITED STATES TRENDS IN SCHOOL PARTICIPATION RATES FOR ALL INDIVIDUALS 5-17 YEARS OLD

Years	Percent Enrolled	Percent Attending Daily
1869-70	57.0	59.3
1939-40	84.0	86.7
1971-72	88.1	90.2

SOURCE: National Center for Education Statistics, 1976, 2-6.

old who are enrolled in school and the percentage attending daily persisted for a century, as shown by Table 2. A hundred years ago, 57 percent of the individuals in the school-age population were enrolled in the public elementary and secondary schools, while nearly 60 percent of them were attending daily; thus, fewer than 35 percent of the appropriate age group were actually attending school on a regular basis. Increases in both the percentage of population enrolled and attendance were steady through 1939-40. Despite a drop in participation in the 1950s, by 1971-72 both enrollment and attendance were within one percent of all-time highs for the public schools, with 88.1 percent enrolled and 90.2 percent of the enrollees attending daily. The figures are especially noteworthy because the school term itself has been getting longer. Average term length has grown from 132.2 days in 1869-70 to 179.3 days in 1971-72 (National Center for Education Statistics, 1976a, 2-6).

Because current participation rates for elementary and secondary schools are high, the enrollment changes between the early 1960s and the middle 1970s can be attributed primarily to population trends. In contrast, the dramatic increase in enrollment in education beyond high school has been due largely to increasing rates of involvement—i.e., more of the relevant age group participates in higher education. Significantly, the proportion of the college-age group attending some formal postsecondary institution is over twice as great in the United States as in any other country of the world. Most of this growth has been in public institutions, with the most rapid growth in public two-year institutions.

Future enrollment-based problems. The uneven pattern of expected enrollments definitely poses problems to be considered in planning for the future. Making provisions for adequate educational services over time and yet avoiding the costly wastes of partially filled buildings and underutilized teaching staffs when enrollments decline is a serious economic problem. Elementary school enrollment (K-8) peaked in 1969-70, and secondary schools followed in 1975-76; for colleges the phenomenon will occur in 1981-82. Elementary enrollments will decline, at least until 1981-82, when the elementary school-age population is expected to increase again, with secondary and college-age populations increasing in later years.

Employment in Education

The figures on participation in public school programs just given attest to the importance society attaches to education. Regardless of whether credit for the growth in enrollments in education goes to a generalized belief in the economic, consumptive or social values of education or to interests in the credentialing, social conditioning or custodial role of schooling, a moment's reflection suggests that such expansion implies a major commitment both in time and in resources devoted to educational activities. Education provides a major source of employment.

Approximately 7.7 percent of the total civilian labor force (over seven million people) is employed by the formal educational sector of the American economy. This figure includes both instructional and maintenance support personnel. This industry employee group is two and one-half times larger than the total federal civilian employment. It is about equal in number of employees to the construction, mining, and transportation industries combined (Council of Economic Advisers, 1976). It is also larger than the combined labor forces of Norway, Sweden and Denmark—certainly a potent economic and political group in our society.

Growth in the number of personnel employed in education has been dramatic. The number of public elementary and secondary school teachers has increased more than tenfold during the last century; in 1870 there were 201,000, and in 1974 there were 2,387,000. In 1974 there were more than 2.6 million professional personnel employed in the public and private elementary and secondary day schools—teachers, principals, supervisors, psychological service personnel, and librarians (90 percent being classroom teachers).

The explosive increase in higher education instructional staff is even more dramatic—from 6,000 in 1869-70 to 633,000 in 1974-75. Much of this growth has taken place during the last ten years. As recently as 1964 there were only 367,000 higher education instructional staff members. The rate of increase in educational employment, however, has declined in recent years and is actually projected for some absolute declines at the secondary level during the next ten years. This is in line with the reduced growth experienced and projected in enrollments.[5]

Educational Expenditures

As a percent of GNP, formal education has expanded to the point where it is a major consumer of goods and services.

In 1929 education accounted for 3 percent of GNP; by 1969-70, the $70 billion spent on education accounted for 7.5 percent of GNP. Since 1969, education's share of GNP has not exceeded 8.0 percent, though the dollar sums have increased steadily (National Center for Education Statistics, 1976b).

Comparative investments in education. Only a few countries allocate such a substantial portion of their GNP to education. This high proportion, together with the high GNP for this country, means that our expenditures per student, even given the large numbers of students receiving education, greatly exceed those of other countries. For example, during 1974 government expenditures (excluding nonpublic expenditures) on education as a percent of the GNP amounted to 6.5 percent for the United States and 8.6 percent for Canada. Yet current expenditures per student in public elementary and secondary schools were $860 for this country and $748 for Canada (National Center for Education Statistics, 1975). Similarly, public expenditures of $3,150 per student enrolled in higher education are higher for the United States than for all countries in the world except for the Netherlands (National Center for Education Statistics, 1976a, 175). Clearly, the ability to provide educational services is a function of size of GNP as well as of willingness to pay.

The educational expenditures of the state and local governments also reflect upon the economic impact of education. During the decade 1962-72, education was consistently the largest item in the budgets of state and local governments. Expenditures for education accounted for 37 cents per dollar spent in 1962-63 and for 39 cents per dollar spent in 1971-72. The total spending by state and local governments for education rose from $23.7 billion in 1962-63 to $64.9 billion in 1971-72 (National Center for Education Statistics, 1976b, 29).

Trends in expenditures. Total annual education expenditures—including current expense, capital outlay and interest—have risen spectacularly in the United States, climbing from $3 billion in 1929-30 to over $108 billion in 1974-75. In 1974-75 dollars, they increased from $68.6 billion in 1964-65 to $108.4 billion in 1974-75 and are expected to be $122.3 billion in 1984-85. It is noteworthy that expenditures have increased faster than both enrollment and instructional staff.

Annual current expenditures for public elementary and secondary schools in 1974-75 dollars increased 71 percent—from $31.8 billion in 1964-65 to $54.3 billion in 1974-75. They are expected to increase another 5 percent to $56.9 billion by 1984-85. Increased enrollment, together with increased expenditures per pupil, have accounted for the increase in current expenditures. Expenditures have been increasing and are expected to continue to increase, but at a much slower rate in constant dollars for practically all of the major items included in current expenditures, such as administration, instruction, operation and maintenance of plant, fixed charges, and other school services and programs. Annual current expenditures per pupil in 1974-75 dollars increased from $802 in 1964-65 to $1,255 in 1974-75 and are expected to increase to $1,464 by 1984-85.

True cost of education. It has been estimated by many economists that the true cost of education in our society today is close to 15 percent of our GNP rather than the normally assumed 8 percent of GNP. The total expenditures described in the preceding paragraphs do not provide a complete view of the magnitude of investment in education. It is now generally recognized that one important part of the educational cost to society is represented by the earnings foregone by students attending school. Such foregone earnings for students in regular secondary and postsecondary educational institutions has been estimated as over 50 percent of the direct total expenditures above (Cohn, 1975, 96). In addition, the costs of educational effort by the military and other nonregular federal and private schools should also enter any such calculation of total resource costs. These have been estimated as another 7 percent of resource costs to be added to the total costs of education (Simon & Frankel, 1976, 71). Finally, an approximation for the private purchase of books and supplies and for the "imputed rent" of educational buildings and equipment must also be made and is estimated as approximating another 20 percent of current direct expenditures (Cohn, 1975, 109).

Such costs of formal education, of course, are still only a part of the total costs of education. Not included in our discussion are costs of on-the-job training, the costs of education of children provided by parents, the costs of church-related education provided outside the parochial schools, and the like. These various sums might raise outlays on education by another 30 percent.

Certainly, education in our economy is "big business" and an industry of significant size and importance.

NOTES

1. Similarly, the methodology for *cost-benefit ratios* can also be applied to the questions of how much education an individual should acquire or society should provide. In general, each person can profit-

ably acquire more education so long as the present discounted value of the benefits is equal to or exceeds that of the costs.

2. It is common practice to include in the total economic costs of education an estimate of the "income foregone" of persons enrolled in formal educational institutions.

3. As indicated by Table 1, these totals include daytime enrollment in all regular public and nonpublic elementary and secondary schools; degree-credit enrollment in publicly and privately controlled institutions of higher education in programs leading to a bachelor's or higher degree; and non-degree-credit enrollment in programs that extend not more than three years beyond high school and are designed to prepare for a technical, semiprofessional, or craftsman-clerical position.

4. The projected decrease of six million elementary students between 1969 and 1981 is based on the assumption that the school-age population on which the projections are based will remain through 1984 substantially as now projected by the Census Bureau (1975). The population projection is based on a fertility rate of 2.1 births per woman, which represents replacement level. Replacement-level fertility is that required for a population to replace itself indefinitely, given mortality rates and in the absence of migration. The 2.1 births per woman is also compatible with the most recent birth expectation data.

5. These historical data are derived from Table 1 (Simon & Frankel, 1976; National Center for Education Statistics, 1976a).

REFERENCES CITED

Cohn, Elchanan. *The Economics of Education.* Cambridge, Mass.: Ballinger Publishing Company, 1975.

Council of Economic Advisers. *Economic Report of the President with the Annual Report of the Council of Economic Advisers.* Washington, D.C.: U.S. Government Printing Office, 1976.

Foster, Betty J., and Carpenter, Judi M. *Statistics of Public Elementary and Secondary Day Schools, Fall 1975.* Washington, D.C.: National Center for Education Statistics, U.S. Government Printing Office, 1976.

Machlup, Fritz. *The Production and Distribution of Knowledge in the United States.* Princeton: Princeton University Press, 1962.

National Center for Education Statistics. *The Condition of Education, 1975.* Washington, D.C.: U.S. Government Printing Office, 1975.

National Center for Education Statistics. *The Condition of Education, 1976.* Washington, D.C.: U.S. Government Printing Office, 1976a.

National Center for Education Statistics. *Digest of Education Statistics, 1975.* Washington, D.C.: U.S. Government Printing Office, 1976b.

Simon, Kenneth A., and Frankel, Martin M. *Projections of Education Statistics to 1984-85.* Washington, D.C.: National Center for Education Statistics, U.S. Government Printing Office, 1976.

U.S. Department of Commerce, Bureau of the Census. "Population Characteristics, Fertility Expectations of American Women: June 1974." *Current Population Reports,* Series P-20, no. 227. Washington, D.C.: U.S. Government Printing Office, 1975.

Investment in Human Capital

William E. Becker, Jr.

At the turn of the century, about 70 percent of those who graduated from high school pursued additional formal schooling; those who continued their postsecondary education, however, represented only about 7 percent of the people born around 1881. After World War I there was a sharp decline in the percentage of high school graduates who continued their formal education. This reduction was the result of a large increase in the number of students graduating from high school, with little corresponding change in the number of students entering two- and four-year institutions of postsecondary learning.

During the 1950s the percentage of high school graduates continuing their formal education increased; and by 1970, 60 percent of all high school graduates attended postsecondary institutions. Those who continued their education at such institutions represented about 50 percent of the population born around 1950. This growth in education and in human capital represents in part a shift in policy toward providing more education to all of the people in the United States (Finch, 1946; Folger & Nam, 1967; Taubman & Wales, 1975a). Also, the educational supply process changed.

During the last 80 years, the educational processes and the institutions providing instruction beyond the high school level have undergone great change. Emphasis has shifted back and

Constructive criticism of an earlier draft of this chapter was provided by John Hause, Darrell Lewis, Jack Rodgers and N. J. Simler. Warren Meyer's editorial comments were also useful. Any errors which may still remain, however, can only be assigned to me.

forth between a liberal education and technical or specialized training. New disciplines were founded with a proliferation of courses being introduced into the curricula (Wolfle, 1954). Many four-year colleges changed their status to universities; numerous two-year colleges and technical schools were founded; normal schools became four-year colleges, while statewide higher education coordination boards expanded their authority (Jencks and Riesman, 1968). Such technological changes in educational delivery systems may have brought about a better-educated population or higher-quality stock than existed earlier.

To an economist, these population distribution changes in the amount of education received and the quality changes resulting from new processes and institutions through which people gain their education reflect an investment decision of those being educated and of society as a whole. Since formal schooling requires a commitment of student time, in addition to direct monetary outlays on the part of the student and society, it is an investment decision. Furthermore, the effect of these schooling decisions—number of years and type of training—is not consumed during one period of time but persists over the student's entire lifetime, which affects the individual's income and life-style. For society, the distribution and quality of education embodied in the working population influence total current productivity of the economy and influence economic growth itself.

These private and social outcomes of an investment in education are referred to as *returns to education.* The return to education resulting from an increase in the amount of education received and the quality of education given is the central focus of this chapter.

First, the theoretical relationship between changes in years of schooling and income returns to additional education is discussed. It is demonstrated that an increase in the educational levels of the working age population results in a reduction in the rate of return to additional years of schooling—assuming that the quality of schooling is constant. The income effects of technological change in the educational process itself are addressed in the second section. It is shown that an improvement of the quality of education that individuals are receiving may cause the rate of return to education to rise for any given level of education considered. The idea that formal education is nothing more than a "screening device" is discussed in the third section. It is shown that screening may raise the schooled individual's income, but need not benefit society in general.

Current empirical estimates of the returns to education and implications for the future of education are provided in the last two sections of this chapter. In these two sections it is suggested that the technological change which has occurred in education has tended to offset the effects of increases in the amount of education people receive. However, evidence is provided which suggests that the rate of return to additional years of schooling is currently declining.

HUMAN CAPITAL DEEPENING

The effect of increased investment in education on general economic growth and on private returns to education (benefits to the learner) can take numerous forms. As a starting point, the effect on economic growth is most easily addressed by considering the impact of education investment on society's ability to produce. The effect on private returns to education is considered as an implicit or internal rate of return on *human capital*—measured as accumulated years of schooling and as the real investment cost of education to our working population. Another measure of the return to be considered is the proportion of a nation's total production going to human capital.

Vocational educators, and educators in general, believe that additional education will raise people's ability to perform the task for which they receive training. For example, an individual's ability to take dictation is raised by a semester of shorthand training; and a student's ability to process data is enhanced by learning Fortran. One might argue, therefore, that an increase in educational attainment of the entire working age population, referred to as *human capital deepening*, should also result in an increase in society's productivity as a whole. In fact, Denison (1962) argues and attempts to show that education has been a major source of economic growth in the United States.

The above argument may be interpreted to imply that as educational levels—years of schooling—rise for the working population, Gross National Product (GNP) should follow.[1] The law of diminishing returns, however, suggests that GNP will not grow proportionately to a growth in educational levels. This is true because in the production process, added investment in schooling may be combined with relatively fixed factors of production. For example, with fixed and full computer facility utilization, a doubling of computer programmers will not lead to a doubling of data processing and, in turn, a doubling of final output. It simply may imply longer lines at the card reader or portable terminals.

Less than proportional growth in the GNP resulting from more education is represented in Figure 1 by the production curve labeled aa in Diagram A.[2] As average educational levels rise from six to twelve years, GNP rises from 2 million to 3.2 million dollars. (Human capital deepening raises the GNP.) Each additional year of schooling, however, adds a smaller increment to output. This is referred to by economists as *diminishing marginal product.* Classical economic theory suggests that human capital deepening will not only result in reductions in education's marginal product, but in a reduction in returns to education as well; an input receives the value of its marginal product. This is represented in Figure 1 by the marginal value product curve bb in Diagram B; as educational levels rise from six to twelve years, returns to a year of education fall from $833.33 per year to $666.66 per year.[3]

Just as physical capital has a rate of return, so too does human capital. For instance, if six years of school for a population of 100 costs $1 million (cost includes both direct costs such as tuition and indirect costs such as lost earnings), and twelve years for the same size population costs $2 million, then the *gross rates of return* for this human capital would be, respectively, 5 percent ($833.33 per year, times 6 years, times 100 students, divided by $10 million) and 4 percent ($666.66 times 12 years, times 100 students, divided by $20 million).[4]

Although the return per year of schooling and the rate of return per year of schooling may decrease with additional years of schooling, individual total earnings may rise with additional schooling. In our example, individual earnings for an elementary education are $5,000 ($833.33 per year times 6 years) and $8,000 ($666.66 times 12 years) for an individual with a high school education. The contribution to total earnings (value added) by six additional years of schooling is $3,000 per person; the *value added rate of return* for six additional years investment in schooling is calculated to be 3 percent ($3,000 additional return divided by $100,000 additional cost). For the entire working population of 100 persons, human capital's share of the GNP rises from $500,000 to $800,000 with the value added being $3,000,000. The social value added rate of return is by assumption equal to the private value added rate of return, 3 percent.[5]

As educational levels rise, however, the fixed factors become scarce relative to the variable education factor. That is,

Figure 1

EDUCATION, GROSS NATIONAL PRODUCT AND RETURNS TO SCHOOLING AND OTHER FIXED FACTORS

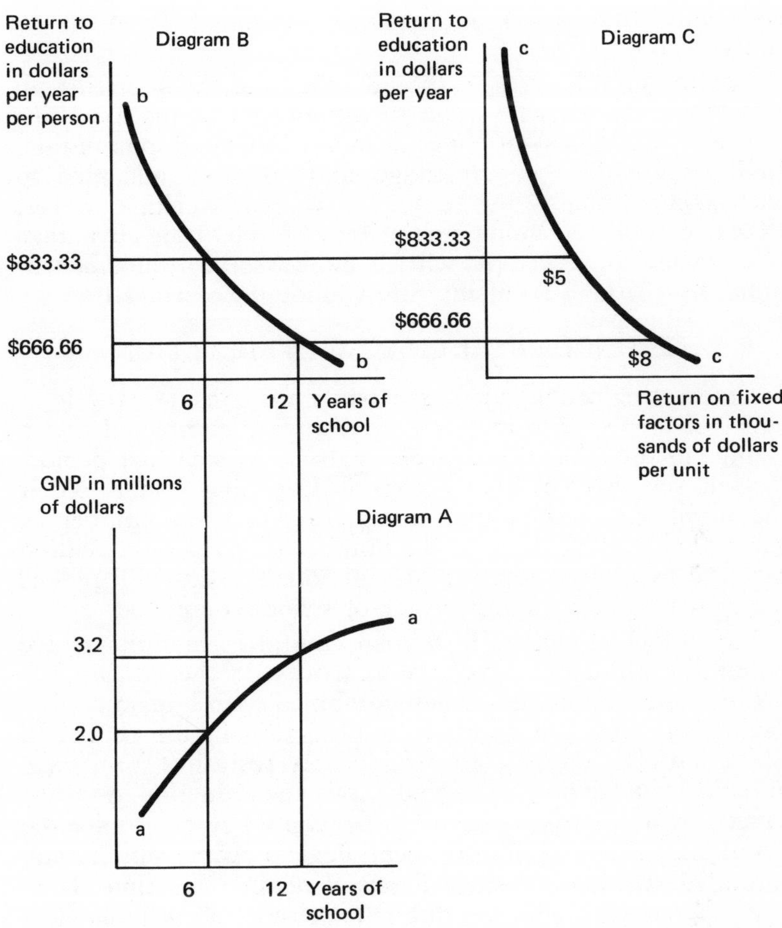

in the production process individuals with more education are combined with the same amount of fixed factors. The economic return to these fixed factors, therefore, rises relative to the return to education. Such a factor-price curve is represented in Figure 1, Diagram C. As the return to a year of schooling falls from $833.33 per year of schooling, the fixed factors' return rises from $5,000 to $8,000 per unit of the fixed factors. Assuming 300 units of the fixed factors, the fixed factors' total share of GNP rises from $1.5 million ($5,000 per unit times 300 units) to $2.4 million ($8,000 per unit times 300 units) as education levels go from six to twelve years.

In our example, it is to the advantage of those getting an education, the workers—and to the owners of the fixed factor, the capitalists—to have a more educated population. GNP rises while the percentage share of GNP allocated to each group remains the same. In the real world, however, human capital deepening may or may not be to the advantage of everyone concerned. As will be shown, some groups benefit more than others from increased amounts of education.

TECHNOLOGICAL CHANGE IN EDUCATION

An interesting problem is posed when one considers the joint effect of an increase in years of schooling completed and a change in the educational process itself. As was just demonstrated, the effect of human capital deepening—where either the number of individuals completing a given number of years of schooling rises, or the number of years of education received by a given number of individuals rises—will reduce the return to education per year of school completed.

Technological change in human capital formation—where either the ability of students improves or the educational process itself improves—when combined with human capital deepening, need not result in a reduction in the return to education. The increase in productivity resulting from technological change may more than offset the reduction in return caused by an increase in the human capital stock. To see the simultaneous effects of both technological change and human capital deepening, consider Figure 1 again. This time, however, start with the productivity effect of technological change in education. An increase in the ability of students entering and finishing a given training program, or an improvement in the educational process itself, implies an increase in the GNP at each level of education being considered.

For example, if the "new math" raised students' problem solving aptitude, then they should be more productive as workers. Or, if teaching typing by a "straight copy method" is replaced by a "production method," then the students' productivity in the work force should be higher when they terminate their training.

The GNP effect of such an educational improvement is represented in Figure 2, Diagram A by a movement from the production function aa to a′a′. For each year of schooling of the working population, more output than was given by production function aa will be forthcoming—a labor force with six years of schooling is now associated with a GNP of $3.2 million, for example. This increase in productivity also implies an increase in the marginal value product curve at each level of schooling. In Diagram B this is a movement from marginal value curve bb to b^1b^1. The resultant shift in the factor price curve is represented in Diagram C as a movement from cc to c^1c^1.

A simultaneous increase in years of schooling from six years to twelve years and an increase in the quality of schooling received—either because of "brighter" or more "motivated" students or better educational process—can now be seen to result in an increase in the return to human capital. To see this, first consider just the effect of a movement from six to twelve years of schooling. Such capital deepening, as described in the previous section, caused the return to years of schooling to fall from $833.33 per year to $666.66 per year —a negative difference of $166.67. The offsetting effect of technological change in the schooling process causes an increase in return to years of schooling, at the twelfth grade level, of $300 per year ($966.66 per year minus $666.66 per year). Therefore, a net increase of $133.33 ($300.00 per year minus $166.67 per year) results, with the return to education becoming $966.66 per year of schooling for a twelfth-grade education.

In the real world, effects of an increase in the years of school completed and technological changes occurring over time are extremely difficult to differentiate. Most recently, however, sets of data have become available from which it is possible to adjust for the earnings impact of many important factors that both influence earnings and tend to be directly associated with education; e.g., mental ability, family background, tuition costs. The later sections deal with some of the more precise return to education estimates which have evolved from these broad characteristic samples.

Figure 2

EDUCATION, GROSS NATIONAL PRODUCT AND RETURNS TO SCHOOLING AND OTHER FIXED FACTORS

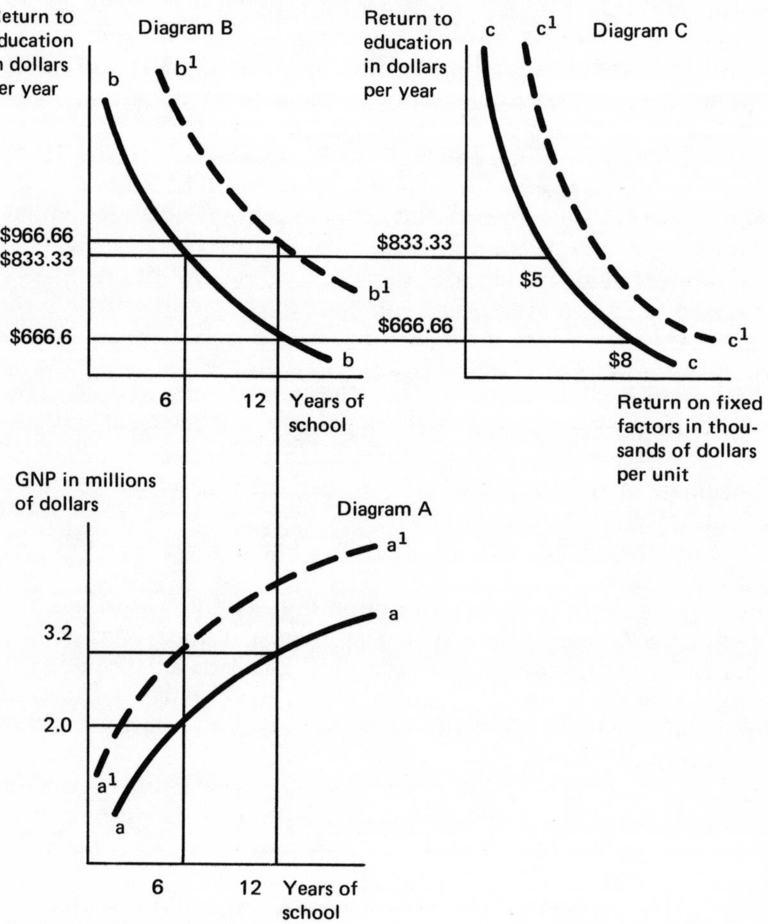

EDUCATIONAL SCREENING

Within the economics profession there is a faction who assert that the primary result of formal education is the screening of individuals; that is, ranking students in terms of their ability and aptitude or matching individuals with jobs for which they are best suited. Such screening functions are also given by some educators as key functions of schooling. The idea of grading and designating one curriculum to be a vocational program and another to be a liberal arts program is in part based on a screening philosophy.

Stiglitz (1975), as well as others, has shown that the consequence of viewing education as simply a screening device in which individuals are ranked can lead to quite different results from those derived in classical human capital theory. Private returns to education (or screening) will be positive, but with no change in productivity being brought about by schooling, social returns will be negative.

To see the results of a screening process in which individuals are simply ranked, consider a population in which individuals can be described by a single characteristic A. Let this characteristic be proportional to an individual's productivity. However, individuals of higher ability A_H can receive a higher income W_H only if they can be identified as being more productive than the lower ability A_L individuals.

While individuals may know their own abilities, in the absence of any information the market does not. The market treats all individuals the same. That is, in the absence of identification, individuals receive an income equal to the man value of the population. (Such would be the case, for instance, on an assembly line.) The mean income is given by

$$\overline{W} = p\,(A_H\,H + A_L\,L)\;/\;(H + L)$$

where H equals the number of high-ability individuals in the population, L equals the number of low-ability individuals and p is the coefficient of proportional income-ability conversion. If the difference between W_H and $\overline{W}$ is greater than the cost of schooling (screening), then those knowing that they have higher ability would be willing to pay for schooling. Those schooled would receive the higher income W_H. Those not schooled get an income W_L which is less than $\overline{W}$. (This would be the equivalent of forming two assembly lines—one for the more able and one for the less able.) The gain to those schooled may exceed the loss to the nonschooled. Society as a whole, however, is made worse off by schooling.

For example, if H = 25 people, L = 75 people, A_H = 200 I.Q. points, A_L = 100 I.Q. points, W_H = \$200 and W_L = \$100, then

$$\overline{W} = (\$1)\,\frac{(200\text{ I.Q.})\,(25) + (100\text{ I.Q.})\,(75)}{100} = \$125$$

If education costs \$60, then the individuals who know that they are of higher ability will pay for schooling. As a result of the school's screening function, the market identifies those who are more able. Each more able individual gains \$15 (\$200 − \$60 − \$125), a total gain of \$375 (25 × \$15). The private return to education for these individuals is clearly positive. However, each lower-ability individual has a loss of \$25 (\$125 − \$100) for a total group loss of \$1,875 (75 × \$25). The social return to education is thus negative, as the population as a whole lost \$1,500 (\$1,875 − \$375).

On the other hand, if education is inexpensively screening individuals by assigning them to jobs for which they are best suited, then it is possible to show that education is still providing a productive function to society. It is providing a positive kind of "externality" in the form of information. For example, assume that there are two types of output produced by society, each valued at \$100 per unit, and two kinds of individuals. Individuals of characteristic A_X can produce 100 units of output X and zero units of output Y. Individuals of characteristic A_Y can produce 100 units of output Y and zero units of output X. If the size of the population is 100, with 50 of each type of individual, then random assignments of jobs would imply an output for society (GNP) of \$5,000. On the average, half of society would be in the wrong occupation. With equal income distribution, however, all individuals share in the output, with each individual receiving \$50.

If education can screen individuals by assigning them to their most productive jobs at a cost of less than \$5,000, then society and individuals can gain from screening. At an educational cost of \$1,000, for instance, society's net GNP would be \$9,000. All individuals would be in their most productive occupation. With the cost of education paid equally and with equal income distribution, each individual would receive \$90. The private and social return to education is clearly positive for this type of screening.

As will be shown in the next sections, the critical empirical question in assessing the screening argument is whether or not education results in an increase in productivity. If it does this, it is adding something to human capital. If it does not, then it may benefit a few at the expense of others.

RETURNS TO EDUCATION

A widely documented and universally accepted fact is that additional years of schooling tend to be associated with additional earnings. However, the actual size of the earnings differential for additional years of schooling and the rate of return to private and social investment in education are not universally agreed upon.

Using the observed earnings differential between those with different amounts of schooling as the "return" and the cost of extra schooling as the "investment," most studies show the private rate of return—that accruing to the individual being educated—for primary and secondary schooling to be quite high, ranging from 20 to 30 percent. Because almost all elementary and secondary training is subsidized, social rates of return to those levels of education are much smaller. Estimates of the private rate of return to postsecondary education tend to be on the order of 10 to 15 percent in most studies. Social rates of return for postsecondary training typically are several percentage points below these limits.

On balance, work by Taubman and Wales (1975b), Hause (1971, 1975) and Wachtel (1975) suggest that rates of return to private investment in postsecondary education are only slightly less than returns to physical capital—generally thought to be 13 to 15 percent. Although these studies attempt to filter out the influence of mental ability (I.Q.), family background and other nonschool variables which affect earnings, none of these calculations includes either private nonmonetary returns to investment in schooling or nonmonetary returns to society as a whole. Unfortunately, results from recent studies dealing with nonmonetary private and social returns to education are still quite ambiguous. (For a discussion of possible nonmonetary returns to education, see Part 2 of Juster [1975]).

The possibility that quality changes have occurred in United States education is high. Taubman and Wales (1975b), as well as others, have demonstrated that there has been a systematic tendency for the relative average ability of entering college freshmen to increase over time. Juster (1975) notes that much of the increase has resulted from an extremely rapid rise—from 50 percent to about 90 percent between the 1920s and the 1960s—in the proportion of the most able high school seniors attending college. In addition, there was nearly as rapid an increase in the proportion of students in the upper quarter of their high school graduating class attending college. Also, the Taubman and Wales evidence indicates that the relative average ability of those not going to college has declined steadily over time. Supporting the findings of Taubman and Wales are the findings of Rosen (1975) that there is no evidence that high school graduates of several decades ago acquired less knowledge in high school than current high school graduates do. When taken together, Rosen's findings of no such "vintage effects," and the Taubman-Wales findings that the average ability of non-college-bound high school graduates has declined, suggest that the value added by high school instruction has increased over time. The effectiveness of schools seems to have increased sufficiently to offset any decline in terminal student abilities, with lower-ability current high school graduates becoming just as efficient learners as high school graduates in the past.

Economists such as Freeman (1976) and Machlup (1973), however, question whether or not the value added by postsecondary education will continue to be as high during the next couple of decades; their evidence suggests that it will not. Between 1969 and 1974, for instance, Freeman's United States Bureau of Census data show that the ratio of college to high school graduates' mean income for all full-time male workers fell from 1.53 to 1.35. Freeman argues that 1969 was the peak for returns to postsecondary education. We are now supposedly entering a period in which the effects of further human capital deepening will not be offset by income effects induced by quality changes in education. It must be noted, however, that this prediction is based on evidence from a relatively short time period. This time period can also be characterized as one of general economic depression.

Although schools may have become more effective over time, especially before 1969, there are differences in the quality of training offered by schools at a point in time. There are marked differences among schools in the amount of resources used; and there are corresponding differences in the private costs such as tuition fees paid by those attending schools. Wachtel (1975) hypothesized that higher-cost and supposedly higher-quality institutions considerably enhance the income generating ability of their graduates over lesser-cost and lesser-quality institutions.[6] This is especially true for postsecondary institutions where the variance of resource cost is extremely high.

After separating the direct and indirect costs of education, Wachtel found that the rate of return on the direct investment component (cost actually paid) tends to run from 10 to 15 percent, while that on the indirect component (foregone earnings) is quite small, as low as 1 or 2 percent. Wachtel's findings support his hypothesis and suggest that a movement away from full-time high school attendance will raise GNP and personal earnings if accompanied by an increase in the quality of schooling provided: "That is, part-time attendance can be compensated for by an increase in direct investment of less than two standard deviations." The current move in education toward greater evening and extension class offerings may yield greater fruit in the future if instructional standards for these classes are also raised.

THE BEST EDUCATION FOR INCREASING PRODUCTIVITY

Taubman and Wales (1975b) argue that in part education is productive because it is used by employers as a relatively inexpensive screening device. That is, employers require a community college degree for certain kinds of jobs on the grounds that this approach is more likely to be successful in identifying potentially more productive employees or that it involves lower cost—at least for the employer, if not for society in general—than the use of alternative devices. According to this argument, at most only a fraction of the increase in earnings resulting from education can be attributed to skills learned. Individuals receiving a degree get higher incomes because the institution granting the degree has produced a screening function which is valued by employers.

This screening argument suggests that the best education is the one which screens students in terms of their future productivity. However, the Taubman-Wales' interpretation of supporting evidence is highly controversial. As Juster (1975) notes, their interpretation rests on evidence concerning the returns to educational differences within given occupational categories; yet very little of the within-occupation variance in earnings can be explained in their data. A very large part of the total variance is due to causes which could not be identified. This unidentified source of variance might or might not be systematically associated with particular characteristics of the individuals involved. Therefore, the observed effect of education on earnings could well be a biased estimate of the true effect, the degree of bias being dependent on the extent to which the unidentified source of earnings variance within occupations is correlated rather than random.

Berg (1971) has also done a series of tests that he argues confirm the screening argument. Berg observes that although the change in skill requirements between 1940 and 1965 for a large number of jobs was rather small, the education requirements for these jobs rose greatly. Furthermore, since there seems to be little relationship between increased educational requirements and changes in output per worker, employers must simply be using educational levels for screening potential employees.

Berg's screening argument says that employers are willing to pay more for more highly educated rather than less educated employees, even though their productivity differences do not warrant extra pay. But if this is to be believed, why doesn't some employer move in and hire the less educated but equally skilled workers at lower salaries? Is one to believe that employers are not sufficiently intelligent to figure out how they can turn a larger profit, or is output per worker the wrong productivity measure to use? [7]

If we put aside Berg's and Taubman-Wales' emphasis on the screening function of education, and concentrate on the human capital or training aspect of education, insight into what may be the best education can be gained from the study by Beaton (1975). Beaton's study is based on the National Bureau of Economic Research-Thorndike sample. The NBER-TH sample is a relatively high income, heavily entrepreneurial and almost entirely white male group. It is therefore a very select and successful group of the United States population.

Contrary to screening theory, respondents in the Beaton study unanimously regarded "one's own performance" and "hard work" as their major factors associated with success; being "lucky" or "unlucky" was considered unimportant. Activities and social awareness were regarded by respondents as relatively unimportant functions of school.

In regard to the educational process itself, respondents in the Beaton study overwhelmingly considered the acquisition of basic skills to be the single most important function of the educational process, with career preparation next, followed by general knowledge. Interestingly, Taubman and Wales (1975b) and Hause (1975) also found basic skills such as "arithmetic computation" to have a strong effect on earnings in the early stages of many occupations.

On the other hand, the data revealed that the more successful respondents, at the peak of their earning potential, tend to rank general knowledge as more important and career preparation as less important. The same is true for the respondents with a higher level of education. This may indicate that the members of the highly educated and relatively successful group regard the acquisition of general knowledge as contributing more to their success than the preparation for specific careers. As Juster (1975, 41) notes, "These results are consistent with the well-documented fact that the majority of people settle in careers that have little direct relevance to their specific training in schools."

Recent trends in education rates of return, however, may be causing students and schools to design programs which are not general and basic. Freeman (1976) reports that while average returns to post-high school training may have fallen since 1969, the returns for business sector specialists such as accountants, engineers, and secretaries, and for independent practitioners have remained strong. Not surprisingly, therefore, many students and school administrators cognizant of this fact may have shifted their emphasis to specific skill training and screening for initial job entry. They have downplayed the possible importance of a "liberal education" for future success as given by the NBER-TH sample.

In the community colleges, vocational programs—including secretarial, practical nursing, and commercial courses—have become more attractive than liberal arts, causing some schools which previously had stressed transfer to four-year colleges to shift their emphasis in the direction of the job market. Similarly, in the case of four-year colleges the 1970s have been a period of reallocation of training from academic to business and government career fields. This may have potentially significant implications for the composition of our labor force, leadership and economic growth. As more and better students select specific technical training and career screening, at the expense of general academic training, Galbraith's "scientific-educational estate" will lose influence and power. Economic growth as well may or may not suffer.

NOTES

1. GNP reflects a society's total productivity. It measures the dollar value of all goods and services produced and rendered within the society in a given year. After adjusting for inflation, GNP figures can be used to compare a society's productivity over time and among nations.

2. The variable educational input, fixed factor input, and GNP output data are assumed to be as follows:

Years of school	Fixed population	Other fixed factors	Man years of schooling	GNP	Return for 100 man years of schooling
5	100	300	500	$1,916,664	—
6	100	300	600	$2,000,000	$83,333
11	100	300	1,100	$3,133,334	—
12	100	300	1,200	$3,200,000	$66,666

3. For simplicity, only one working year is considered. To obtain the total present value of the return to education over a lifetime, or any other period of time, economists consider the income received year after year which results from a given number of years of schooling and then use discounting formulas to establish the present value of such an income stream. Mincer (1975) provides examples of income streams for alternative terminal years of schooling. Fleisher (1970, 93-101) provides an easy-to-follow description of present value calculations for discounting a stream of income.

4. For simplicity, all cost figures are assumed to be borne by the individual being schooled and are discrete, one-time costs. In the real world, costs are incurred over time, which necessitates the use of present value procedures in calculating rates of return. Furthermore, individuals seldom bear all costs of education themselves. To the extent that students do not bear the cost of education generally, society must; and the private rate of return will exceed the social rate of return. For an interesting debate on who pays and who gains from education, see Hansen and Weisbrod (1969) and Pechman (1970).

5. If individuals receiving the additional years of schooling only paid $30,000 of the $100,000 additional cost, then the private value added rate of return would be 10 percent ($3,000 additional return divided by $30,000 added cost), while the social value added rate of return would still be 3 percent.

6. Astin (1968) questions the use of financial measures as indexes of institutional excellence; however, Rock, Centra and Linn (1970) report that the cost of instruction per student is highly correlated with high performance on the Graduate Record Examination. For a review of other studies dealing with institution quality and student performance, see Solmon (1973).

7. Dore (1976) discusses the human capital theory versus the screening theory debate and identifies "casual strands" which might help to explain the correlation between earnings and education.

REFERENCES CITED

Astin, Alexander W. "Undergraduate Achievement and Institutional 'Excellence'." *Science* 161 (August 1968): 661-68.

Beaton, Albert E. "The Influence of Education and Ability on Salary and Attitudes." *Education, Income, and Human Behavior*. Edited by F. Thomas Juster. Berkeley, California: Carnegie Commission on Higher Education and New York: National Bureau of Economic Research, 1975, 365-96.

Berg, Ivar. *Education and Jobs: The Great Training Robbery*. Boston: Beacon Press, 1971.

Denison, Edward F. *The Source of Economic Growth in the United States and the Alternatives before Us.* New York: Committee for Economic Development, 1962.

Dore, R.P. "Human Capital Theory, the Diversity of Societies and the Problem of Quality in Education." *Higher Education* 5 (February 1976): 79-102.

Finch, Frank H. *Enrollment Increases and Changes in the Mental Level of the High School Population.* Applied Psychology Monograph, no. 10, American Psychological Association. Oxford University Press: 1946.

Fleisher, Belton M. *Labor Economics: Theory and Evidence.* Englewood Cliffs, New Jersey: Prentice Hall, Inc., 1970.

Folger, John K., and Nam, Charles B. *Education of the American Population.* A 1960 Census Monograph. Washington, D.C.: Government Printing Office, 1967.

Freeman, Richard B. *The Over-Educated American.* New York: American Press, 1976.

Hansen, W. Lee, and Weisbrod, Burton A. *Benefits, Costs and Finance of Public Higher Education.* Chicago: Markham Pub. Co., 1969.

Hause, John C. "Ability and Schooling as Determinants of Lifetime Earnings, or If You're So Smart, Why Aren't You Rich?" *American Economic Review* 61, no. 2 (May 1971): 289-304.

———. "Ability and Schooling as Determinants of Lifetime Earnings, or If You're So Smart, Why Aren't You Rich?" *Education, Income, and Human Behavior.* Edited by F. Thomas Juster. Berkeley, California: Carnegie Commission on Higher Education and New York: National Bureau of Economic Research, 1975, 123-49.

Jencks, Christopher, and Riesman, David. *The Academic Revolution.* Garden City, New York: Doubleday and Company, Inc., 1968.

Juster, F. Thomas, ed. "Education, Income, and Human Behavior: Introduction and Summary." *Education, Income, and Human Behavior.* Berkeley, California: Carnegie Commission on Higher Education and New York: National Bureau of Economic Research, 1975, 1-43.

Machlup, Fritz. "Perspectives on the Benefits of Postsecondary Education." *Does College Matter?* Edited by Lewis C. Solmon and Paul J. Taubman. New York: Academic Press, Inc., 1973, 353-63.

Mincer, Jacob. "Education, Experience, and the Distribution of Earnings and Employment: An Overview." *Education, Income and Human Behavior.* Edited by F. Thomas Juster. Berkeley, California: Carnegie Commission on Higher Education and New York: National Bureau of Economic Research, 1975, 71-93.

Pechman, Joseph A. "The Distributional Effect of Public Higher Education in California." *Journal of Human Resources* 5 (Summer 1970): 361-70.

Rock, Donald A.; Centra, John A.; and Linn, Robert L. "Relationship Between College Characteristics and Student Achievement." *American Educational Research Journal* 7 (January 1970): 109-21.

Rosen, Sherwin. "Measuring the Obsolescence of Knowledge." *Education, Income, and Human Behavior.* Edited by F. Thomas Juster. Berkeley, California: Commission on Higher Education and New York: National Bureau of Economic Research, 1975, 199-231.

Solmon, Lewis C. "Schooling and Subsequent Success." *Does College Matter?* Edited by Lewis C. Solmon and Paul J. Taubman. New York: Academic Press, Inc., 1973, 13-32.

Stiglitz, Joseph E. "The Theory of 'Screening' Education, and the Distribution of Income." *The American Economic Review* 3 (June 1975): 283-300.

Taubman, Paul, and Wales, Terrence. "Education as an Investment and a Screening Device." *Education, Income, and Human Behavior.* Edited by F. Thomas Juster. Berkeley, California: Carnegie Commission on Higher Education and New York: National Bureau of Economic Research, 1975a, 95-119.

———. "Mental Ability and Higher Educational Attainment in the Twentieth Century." *Education, Income, and Human Behavior.* Edited by F. Thomas Juster. Berkeley, California: Carnegie Commission on Higher Education and New York: National Bureau of Economic Research, 1975b, 47-67.

Wachtel, Paul. "The Returns to Investment in Higher Education: Another View." *Education, Income, and Human Behavior.* Edited by F. Thomas Juster. Berkeley, California: Carnegie Commission on Higher Education and New York: National Bureau of Economic Research, 1975, 151-70.

Wolfle, Dael. *America's Resources of Specialized Talent.* The Report of the Commission on Human Resources and Advanced Training. New York: Harper and Brothers, 1954.

Section II: The Economics of Vocational Education

Toward Economic Goals and Objectives for Vocational Education

Charles J. Law and Katy Greenwood

The purposes of this chapter are: (1) to document the belief that educating for employment is one of the functions of the American public school system, (2) to support the contention that vocational education is the component of public education which can most effectively address that economic function, and (3) to encourage a broad interpretation of the economic function of vocational education.

The goals and objectives of vocational education and general education are interrelated; therefore, they must be analyzed from that perspective. Likewise, all educational goals must be studied as they relate to societal goals. Bruner (1973, 100) declares, "The psychologist or educator who formulates pedagogical theory without regard to the political, economic, and social setting of the educational process courts triviality and merits being ignored in the community and the classroom."

Vocational education operates within a political, economic, and social environment. Educational decision makers have given much attention to the political and social environment; but the economic function of vocational education either has been so obvious as to merit little discussion, or it has been regarded as having little, if any, value. Either of these suppositions has created an unfortunate situation because it is the economic force that has given primary direction to vocational education programs.

Many of our conceptual and operational problems can be traced to a misunderstanding of the economics of vocational education. If an economic function is assigned by society to a subsystem—in this case vocational education—and at the same time responsibility for that function is not assumed by the entire system, the subsystem and the total system will be incompatible. In our present system this incompatibility occurs continually. Before we analyze present realities and are able to understand this incompatibility, we need a historical base.

A HISTORICAL PERSPECTIVE: 1890-1917

The early advocates of vocational education did not hesitate to state their views of its economic function. The support which these parties gave vocational legislation was based primarily upon economic benefits. American industry was attempting to compete profitably in world markets. The industrial spokesmen made known unequivocally their wish that the main instrument for achieving national wealth and power should be the American public school system. Likewise, organized labor spoke to the economic function of vocational education. It stated its concerns about the proposed modification of the school system. Naturally, such interest groups as industry and labor were not always mutually supportive. It was easier to propose that American schools be adapted to the needs of American industry that it was to make this an accomplished fact. Even in this era of economic expansion, many people were unwilling to accept as an article of faith the idea that "what was good for business" was, in fact, "good for America."

Prominent educators could be found on both sides of the issue. Underlying all the rhetoric was the philosophy of John Dewey, whose beliefs must be analyzed separately. Even though he is quoted often, his ideas concerning vocational education have not been implemented to any noticeable degree. Also, it is to Dewey that this cycle of debate about vocational education will return when we recognize that not only can vocational education revitalize all education, but that a revitalized educational system can drastically change American society.

National Association of Manufacturers

The National Association of Manufacturers (NAM) made an early decision to promote vocational education as a major component in its effort to put America into a competitive position in the world market. The association's support for vocational education was logical: (1) Germany was the world's leading economic power; (2) German national policy supported trade schools; (3) America had all of the ingredients necessary for competition except a vocational education program; therefore, (4) the addition of vocational education would enable America to compete in the world market.

The NAM took its mandate on education from its founders. One such person was Thomas B. Egan, chairman of the first organizational meeting, who said that ". . . the prosperity of any locality [is] dependent upon the prosperity of business in it; and therefore, the proper test for any proposed policy is whether it [will] be good or bad for business" (Wirth, 1970, 32).

The manufacturers wanted a generous supply of labor of all types. They were willing to let the laws of the marketplace determine wages. Anthony Ittner, an early leader in the movement, was particularly zealous in proposing short-term training courses to create a situation which had no restrictions on supply.

The NAM began to maximize its efforts to demand that American schools follow the German pattern. In German schools, the members saw a process which would provide not only skills but loyal economic and political attitudes within students. Yet there was not complete accord among American industrialists who held typical American values. Their belief in the "rags to riches" saga was real. Despite different positions taken by individuals within the NAM, the association did support vocational education as a factor of economic control.

The Labor Movement

Organized labor addressed the changing economic role of the public schools. Early activities of the labor movement showed a distrust of vocational education motives. This was particularly true when industrial advocates praised vocational education as one way to eliminate the "abuse" of the apprenticeship system and to keep wages at a low level by creating an oversupply of trained laborers. Organized labor opposed such proposals; however, labor did become an ardent supporter of vocational education for different economic reasons.

Before automation restructured the economy of this country, it was in the best interest of the working family to seek employment for their children as early as possible to add to family income. As work conditions improved, so did wages. Yet an oversupply of trained labor tended to keep wages low. The labor movement saw a possible solution through vocational education. By delaying the entry of children into the labor force, adult workers would receive increased wages;

also the capabilities of their children would be improved by added schooling. Such schooling was assumed to be more beneficial if it were of a vocational nature; likewise, retention of the children of workers in vocational programs seemed to be greater than that of the traditional curriculum. Therefore, labor sought to influence the direction of the economy vis-a-vis vocational education. Thompson (1973, 43) observed that "Interest in child labor [by organized labor] grew out of the attempt to reduce the labor force, not from a moral conviction that the growth and development of children was stifled by early work."

Educators

Educators were drawn into the affray.[1] Their concern dealt with a different set of problems—or so it was thought. According to Lazerson and Grubb, "Foremost among these [problems] was the emergence of the high school . . . The influx of working class and immigrant children threatened to destroy the high school's traditional function" (Lazerson and Grubb, 1974, 21-22).

Education was criticized harshly. The training of students for specific jobs would answer the charges of industrial critics of education. However, such a philosophy contradicted a basic belief about American public education, i.e., a common education for all students. The fundamental issue for educators was the degree to which vocational education contributed to, or impeded, commonality and democracy in education. Lazerson and Grubb (1974, 21-22) perceived, "What emerged was a redefinition of the idea of educational opportunity and a rejection of the common school idea."

The greatest criticism was that the content of the instructional program was not usable in daily life, nor was it deemed useful for future occupations. Indeed, it seemed that the common school system deprived many children of the instruction they needed most. The new definition of democracy in education gave every student the right to schooling and placed upon the state the responsibility of providing education commensurate with his/her abilities and potential. If education for democracy was to be a reality, instruction had to be modified and made applicable to the socioeconomic background, needs, interests, abilities, and aspirations of all children.

From this concept of democracy in education developed the division of the curriculum into multiple occupational categories. It then became necessary to place students in the "proper" categories. Therefore, as Lazerson and Grubb report, ". . . vocational education was first justified, then glorified, as the only basis upon which a mass educational system could be made democratic" (1974, 25).

Vocational education was legitimized as a function of the public schools *only* after the redefinition of equality of educational opportunity. This redefinition—juxtaposed with the already potent arguments that vocational education would maximize economic efficiency and growth, increase upward social mobility, retain pupils in school longer and, at the same time, teach moral values inherent in the Protestant work ethic—made the force for vocational education almost irresistible.

John Dewey

Educators accepted the new role of vocational education with varying degrees of excitement. However, as mentioned earlier, few attempted to implement the concept as it was developed by John Dewey. It may be that Dewey's concepts are so complex that anyone who attempts to follow his logic will stop short of making any real adaptation out of sheer perplexity. On the other hand, Dewey's ideas may connote so much common sense that they invite repudiation.

Dewey (1915, 283-84) saw a dramatic role for vocational education. Most educators accepted the nature of technology as a "given" and they tried to adapt their students to industrialism as directly as possible. Not so with Dewey. He declared, "The kind of vocational education in which I am interested is not one which will 'adapt' workers to the existing industrial regime . . . [We should] strive for a kind of vocational education which will first alter the existing industrial system, and ultimately transform it" (Dewey, 1915, 42).

The issue for Dewey was the contrasting philosophies of (1) adding vocational-technological studies to the curriculum in order that students might gain insights into the complexities and issues of the industrial society or (2) permitting vocational programs simply to train students to serve industry. He preferred the former. Others also spoke out for such a revolutionary concept. Leavitt (1914, 79-81) asked, "Why should we hesitate to lay hands on industry in the name of education, when we have already laid hands on the school in the name of industry?"

The pedagogical question which arose, with all its social, political, and economic ramifications, was the degree to which the educational system would be *active* or *reactive*. If the system were only to react to the needs of society, then schools should be tied to the needs of the business-industrial complex. If, however, the system were to act to influence change, it then became obligated to take advantage of the multisensory and practical experience dimensions of the business and industrial complex and to demand use of that educational potential.

The difference in these two concepts should be noted. The reactive role is relatively safe and secure. The active role is highly insecure and unsafe, for it can change the world—and changing the world always has been dangerous. John Dewey fought for the latter option. He did not think that his task was easy. He felt that if there were a chance for reform, it would be accomplished only when the humane aspects of science were combined with the ideals of democracy. This condition called for the restructuring of habits and attitudes of the entire culture. Every institution would have to make its particular contribution. However, one had to begin somewhere; therefore, Dewey supported the type of school reform which vocational education offered. It seemed to be a logical starting point. The minds of the young are pliable, and their habits are not so structured as to defy transformation. Dewey acknowledged that this was a long-term approach. However, even if change did occur in the schools, still more than half of the job would remain when one attempted to change the adult culture.

Dewey felt that mechanization had exerted dangerous influences on American life. Techniques were beginning to be viewed as an end rather than as a means to some worthwhile goal. Also, there appeared to be standardization and homogeneity of thought coming from the school system instead of the uniquely inherent human ability to think critically. He objected, "If the schools do nothing more than fashion people to meet the needs of the system, if education fails to give people the insights to challenge the distortions of the system, then men are more enfeebled" (1930, 81-82).

He outlined his approach to the problem in five propositions:

> (a) The only hope for civilizing the technological society is to cultivate "new habits of mind and sentiment." (b) These cannot be formed by approaches which reject the machine culture—but somehow the industrial society itself, including man's work in it, must be converted into an agent for human liberation. (c) Both man's mind and machine age culture must be seen as emergents with nature. The habits of intelligence which may become the instruments for salutary change must be identified

> and consciously cultivated, both in schooling and through the workings of all institutions. (d) A "dualistic humanism" which separates mind from matter and turns to intellectualist elitism must be rejected as futile. (e) The changes effected by technology have such a radical effect on human life that the new habits of intelligence required to cope with change must be cultivated throughout the entire population (Wirth, 1970).

Dewey projected what should happen, and he felt that vocational education could provide part of the answer. He was afraid, however, that "vocational education will be interpreted in theory and practice as trade education, as a means of securing technical efficiency in specialized future pursuits" (Dewey, 1916, 369-70).

Dewey supported vocational education as an economic function of the public schools in the broadest possible sense. He rejected the concept which he saw emerging under David Snedden and Charles Prosser (circa 1914) as too narrow. He felt that these programs, intended to provide training only for useful employment, failed to deal with the all-important value issues. To Dewey, it was a matter of practicality, not philosophical inclination, to encourage the raising of value questions about the consequences of industrial development. The effects of industrialization had to be analyzed by both workers and managers on a continuing basis. Wirth (1972, 203) notes, "Technology was too powerful a force to be set loose without careful social monitoring."

Summary

During the early days of vocational education, its economic function was identified clearly, though consensus seldom prevailed. The business-industrial block recognized vocational education's economic function. It sought a surplus of well-trained labor in order to compete successfully with Germany. Labor movement leaders recognized that vocational education performed an economic function by both keeping young people in school and out of the labor market, thus holding wage levels high. The educators saw the economic function partially, but they quickly centered their attention on the selection process necessary in order to carry out this function. (This reaction of educators is not to be denigrated, since it caused the differentiation of curricula and of staffing, stimulated the advent of the guidance movement, and instigated both the junior high school and the concept of a comprehensive senior high school.)

Nevertheless, it was John Dewey who saw the full economic potential of the vocational education movement in public education. His concept was so pervasive that it had either (1) eluded the practitioners of the art until today, or (2) intimidated any would-be practitioner by the simple audacity of its intention. He, above all people, appears to have been the prime revolutionary.

THE INTERLUDE: 1917-1976

Actual Interpretation

Vocational education paid little, if any, heed to Dewey's admonitions. Instead, it set itself upon a narrow path designed by the industrialists and the apostles of industrialism. Bagley's concept of social efficiency affected the movement. He claimed, "Social efficiency is the standard by which the forces of education must select the experiences that are impressed upon the individual" (Bagley, 1905, 60).

Ultimately, Charles A. Prosser and David Snedden became spokesmen for the new movement. They defined vocational education in a very narrow context. Its only purpose was to train for useful employment. Prosser insisted that all vocational content be specifically for an occupation and "have little or nothing in common with corresponding content in any other occupation. [There] must be as many specific courses or groups of courses as there are occupations for which it proposes to train" (Prosser, 1950, 233).

Prosser was certain that if vocational education were to succeed, its administration could not be left to the general educators. There were several reasons for this viewpoint, not the least of which was that general educators were "impractical" and "cut off from this world of work." Besides, their educational psychology, he felt, had proved to be ineffective.

Since he wished to exclude general educators from managing vocational education, Prosser fought as long as possible for a separate school system. He had to compromise, but basically he created a framework which permitted vocational programs to remain separate. He was the main architect of the Smith-Hughes Bill and, as Barlow observed (1967), "The Smith-Hughes Act did establish a Federal Board for Vocational Education, separate from the U.S. Office of Education and responsible to Congress" (114-15). As executive director of the Federal Board for Vocational Education, Prosser established the initial tone of administration. Wirth reports (1970), "States were given the option of setting up separate boards, or of administering vocational education under . . . their general boards of education" (232-35). Essentially, he devised a separate system which only gave the appearance of operating as an integral part of the total educational system.

The Vocational Education Literature

Despite this narrow interpretation and implementation of vocational education—or perhaps because of it—vocational education writers who have supported the program since 1917 seemingly have chosen to concern themselves more with the social and political realities surrounding vocational education than with its concomitant economic function. Why? Is it because the economic function truly is so obvious as to cause it to be disregarded, or is it because vocational education writers are acutely uncomfortable with what Prosser stated so vehemently and seek to overcompensate?

Regardless of the cause, much can be found in the literature concerning such social and political topics as (1) the development of vocational education policy, (2) equality of opportunity, (3) distribution of income, (4) social compensation, (5) work satisfaction, (6) national defense, and (7) productivity and commercial leadership.

The nearest things to critical analysis to be found in the literature are statements of "principles of vocational education." Our problem with these writings is two-fold: (1) They deal with the principles which operate from some elusive philosophical base but never describe that base. They simply assume that such a base is there and that it should remain inviolate. (2) We believe that the principles discussed have evolved over the years and should not be attributed solely to the original leaders of the movement. A thorough reading of the original manuscripts will divulge some of the early leaders contradicting these supposedly inviolate principles.

Some of these "principles" to which we allude are enumerated by Barlow (1974) in the fourth yearbook of the American Vocational Association (19-22). The principles listed relate very broadly to the following: (1) citizenship, (2) general education, (3) clientele, (4) theory and practice, (5) cooperation, (6) the national nature of the problem, and (7) individual instruction. With all due respect to Dr. Barlow, when we analyze these principles in light of our stated problems with such writings,[2] we disagree with his statement that ". . . the vocational education movement rests upon a solid foundation of basic principles that do not change with time" (1967, 23).

Instead, we believe that not only has our interpretation of these principles changed, but that our entire philosophy has changed. Vocational education's problem is that these philosophical changes have not been noted. Otherwise, it is difficult to understand how Barlow can give the credit that he does to Prosser and his dictums and, at the same time, state his own belief that:

> If the position is taken that a person's vocation is what he does to earn a living, then "vocational subjects" is a variable and not a constant. Whether or not a subject is vocational is determined by the will of a person and is not a characteristic of the subject (1967, 28).

Summary

While leading vocational education writers of the period 1917-1976 seem to have spoken of everything but the economic function of vocational education, manpower experts frequently have addressed this issue. In addition, the Educational Amendments of 1976 make the administration and implementation of such programs more narrowly definitive than ever.

CHANGE AND VOCATIONAL EDUCATION: 1976 AND BEYOND

It is time to examine all aspects of vocational education. In addition to social and economic analyses, this examination must include a determination of the following factors:

1. The degree to which society assigns an economic function to vocational education.
2. The degree to which vocational education is a part of the total educational establishment.
3. The degree to which the total educational establishment is willing to assume its economic function.
4. The changes in the economic picture of America.
5. The careful determination of the breadth and depth of the economic impact which vocational education is to have on American society.

We shall consider these five concepts, state the available facts, draw some inferences, and raise some questions. Few answers are given, since the purpose is to start dialogue and not bring closure to the discussion of the economic role of vocational education.

The Economic Function Presently Assigned to Vocational Education

Though the vocational literature does not speak often of the economic function of vocational education, the Congress of the United States speaks definitively on this point. In the

Education Amendments of 1976, vocational education is defined as follows:

> Section 195. (1) The term "vocational education" means organized educational programs which are directly related to the preparation of individuals for paid or unpaid employment, or for additional preparation for a career requiring other than a baccalaureate or advanced degree.

The legislation further specifies that upon receipt of applications for these monies from a local educational agency,

> (5)(a) that the State shall, in considering the approval of such applications give priority to those applicants which (i) are located in economically depressed areas and areas with high rates of unemployment, and are unable to provide the resources necessary to meet the vocational education needs of those areas without federal assistance, and (ii) propose programs which are new to the area to be served and which are designed to meet new and emerging manpower needs and job opportunities in the area and, where relevant, in the State and the Nation (U.S. Congress, 1976, 96-145).

The legislative intent of the Congress does specify the economic responsibility of vocational education, at least in that part of vocational education in which the federal government is a partner. Of this, there can be no misunderstanding.

Vocational Education as a Part of the Educational Establishment

Though such stalwarts as Snedden and Prosser attempted to establish two separate types of high schools, technically this concept was rejected by the decision makers of the early twentieth century. A major step was taken when the Cardinal Principles of Secondary Education were reported by the Commission on the Reorganization of Secondary Education. This report recommended the establishment of comprehensive secondary schools. The commission felt that class distinctions could be negated by mingling all classes of youth in one high school. The commission was ". . . against any and all plans . . . which [were] in danger of divorcing vocational and social-civic education . . . [and it was] for the infusion of vocation with the spirit of service and for the vitalization of culture by genuine contact with the world of work" (National Education Association, 1918, 16).

Has this concept worked? One has only to observe the factions, the infighting, the divisiveness, and the misunderstanding that exist between vocational education and general education to form one's own opinion. To quote one critic, however, "the comprehensive high school idea became a disappointment [to everyone]" (Ellul, 1967, 126-29).

The early vocationalists and the advocates of the comprehensive high school approached the problem with such opposing concepts that any type of success has been hard to achieve. In addition, educators alone cannot create nor should they alone be held accountable for creating truly workable comprehensive high schools. When one observes the impact of social class distinctions upon the school, racial and sexual divisiveness, and the status differentiations based upon hierarchies of skill as evolved within the corporate bureaucracies, one marvels that the high school has survived, much less that it has been successful. In addition, the kinds of communities which Americans have established make it very difficult to achieve the ideal of democracy in education to which most people subscribe.

Perhaps the biggest problem is that while schools have assumed a career-sorting function, this fact has not been acknowledged by professional educators. The comprehensive school is still being touted as a great equalizing force, though much evidence could be mustered to disprove such a belief. Ellul comments:

> Only as American society has threatened to disintegrate under the stresses of population explosion, pollution, racism, and overseas adventurism, has it become apparent how much we have lost of the substance of democratic, humanistic values. We are now in the testing time to find out if they can be recovered at all under the circumstances of the twentieth-century life. The debate over the creation of the comprehensive school reveals the tension between the drives for democratic processes and the career-sorting, efficiency demands of technocracy (Ellul, 1967, 126-29).

If this criticism is accurate, two questions face vocational education: (1) Can the dream be recaptured by redirecting vocational education, perhaps in the way John Dewey envisioned it? or (2) Will vocational education simply become training and be moved out of public school education? These may be our alternatives.

The Economic Function of the Total Educational Establishment

If vocational education accepts its economic function—either narrowly or broadly conceived—but such function is not accepted by the entire educational system, then a state of dysfunction must occur. Does the entire public educational system accept such a function?

It is difficult to answer this question. On the one hand are the statements of thinkers as Jerome Bruner and Leon

Lessinger. In a paper titled "Educational Stability in an Unstable Technical Society," Lessinger points out that there are two camps of informed opinion regarding the role of vocational education in the high school. One group believes that the rapid development of technology makes it futile for the schools to offer any training except that of a general education. The other group sees the value of teaching skills which are immediately applicable, and thus saleable, as youth enters the labor market, with subsequent retraining as needed. He believes that

> . . . [both] have merit, but neither position is adequate. Analysis of the occupational world indicates that both positions must be utilized in varying proportions according to the nature of the job family for which the pupil is preparing. More importantly, underlying all the professional, skilled, and technical occupations, lies a substantial set of behaviors which can be taught, described, and are remarkably stable. It is this stable structure which should be carefully considered by educators (Lessinger, 1965, 208).

On the other hand, there are the sentiments of those who appear to question this role, but who seem to have nothing better to offer. We can infer only that consensus does not exist yet, though we may be moving in that direction. Until consensus is reached, the incompatibility of vocational education with the total educational system either will continue or vocational education will be forced out of the public schools.

We have been critical of vocational education leadership, but all the responsibility for the failure of vocational education to be compatible with total education does not rest with vocational education. If vocational education, in order to perform its economic function, is forced out of the comprehensive public school system into a separate school system —public or private—or to a training agency, then general educators must bear part of that responsibility. The economic function of education to train for jobs *will* be performed. The only question is "where?"

The handwriting is on the wall. Unless the comprehensive high school does assume its proper economic function, then vocational education will be forced out. This would be detrimental because all persons then will lose something. Such losses were envisioned by Alfred North Whitehead when he said, "There is something between the gross specialized values of the mere practical man, and the thin specialized values of the mere scholar. Both types have missed something; and if you add together the two sets of values, you do not obtain the missing element" (Wirth, 1970, 209). To him, the function of education enabled a person to comprehend

> . . . a technology in its completeness: this is the essence of technological humanism, and that is what we should expect education . . . to achieve . . . it could be achieved by making specialist studies . . . the core around which are grouped liberal studies which are relevant to these specialist studies [or vice versa]. *But they must be relevant; the path to culture should be through man's specialism not by by-passing it* (Wirth, 1970, 232-33, emphasis ours).

Though Whitehead spoke to the problem at the university level, his concept applies equally to the comprehensive high school. The question is, "Will educational leadership respond, or will this critical function pass from its grasp?" Again, we wonder.

Economic Change in America

Even if one could assume that vocational education has a clearly defined economic function, that vocational education is a full partner in a truly comprehensive high school, and that the total education establishment fully assumes its economic function, there still would remain at least two critical factors. The first deals with the changes in our economy. Some of the questions about those changes for vocational education include these:

1. What is the employment situation today? Tomorrow? Four years from now? For young people? For minorities?
2. Should the school be held responsible for the employment of its graduates or the *employability* of its graduates?
3. Does the Protestant work ethic have the same meaning today as it did in 1917?
4. What about vocational education for avocational purposes?
5. Must young people be held in school and thus kept out of the labor market for longer periods of time? If so, what effect does this have on the secondary school curriculum? On the postsecondary curriculum?
6. Where will skills be taught?

A few concrete answers are available. The only specific area we shall mention is that of youth unemployment. As reported by Guzzardi, there are more teenagers now than ever before, and a smaller proportion is going to college and into the armed forces. Therefore, they are coming into the work force in great numbers "and the high rates of unemployment among them last summer—about 20 percent for all Americans between ages 16 and 19, and about 35 percent for blacks in that age group—have become notorious" (Guzzardi, 1975, 124).

Willard Wirtz, former Secretary of Labor, called attention constantly to these high rates of unemployment. He also raised serious questions concerning whether specific training at the high school level is the answer. He believes that most 18-22 year-olds, no matter how skilled, may be forced to accept low-paying, unskilled jobs until they are mature enough to compete with older workers. One alternative which he suggests is to keep youth in school for at least two additional years.

The most dramatic statements concerning economic change are found in the writings of George C. Lodge. In his book, *The New American Ideology,* he identifies the following changes which, if he is correct, will affect profoundly our entire culture.

> First, communitarianism is augmenting and replacing individualism. For most people today, fulfillment occurs through their participation in an organic social process . . . Second, *rights of membership* are communitarian rights that public opinion holds to be consistent with a good community. They represent a revolutionary departure from the old Lockean conception, under which only the fit survived . . . Third, our method for controlling the use of property is changing radically. Where once we entrusted this function to open competition in the market place, we are now applying the criterion of community need to the utilization of resources . . . Fourth, the role of government is inevitably expanding to embrace the concept of the state as a planner . . . Finally, and perhaps most fundamentally, comes the growing acceptance of *holism* . . . The perception of reality now demands that we perceive entire systems, not only the parts thereof. The old idea of scientific specialization has given way to a new consciousness of the interrelatedness of all things (1975, 17-20).

If these are correct assessments—and we suspect they are—then great changes are forecast for vocational education. Even if vocational education performs its economic function and if total education fully assumes its economic role, this new ideology still will require an entirely different approach from that of today—a different approach, but not an unexplored approach. We are led to believe that vocational education, if it were implemented according to Dewey's vision, would answer the educational questions raised by this new American ideology as stated by Lodge.

Impact of Vocational Education on the Economy

Even if the first three factors in Lodge's analysis could be assumed to be compatible, two factors remain—one relating to the changing economy and one pertaining to the determination of how broadly and deeply one is willing to interpret the economic role of vocational education. There are at least two alternatives:

Alternative One. The economic function of vocational education can be narrowly defined with the same result that Lazerson and Grubb saw in past vocational education when they said (1974):

> The impact of vocationalism also revealed the extent to which American education had accepted the ethics of the emerging corporate order. Vocational education was part of a broader rationalization of the schools, which included specialization of function, cost accounting, research and testing departments, and development of a science of administration. The ideal school system had come to be modeled after a modern corporation, both in its hierarchical and bureaucratic organization and in its purpose; students were raw materials to be processed in an efficiently run plant, and the criterion of success was the price the finished product could bring in the market place. Hence the enthusiastic acceptance of vocational education into the public schools, despite its contradiction of earlier ideals, paralleled the enthusiastic acceptance by educators of the industrial order. With the vocational education movement, educators saw their role as *serving* the industrial order and adapting students to its requirements. Economic criteria had become a primary force in educational decision making (49-50).

Alternative Two. The economic function can be identified broadly. Goodman and Goodman stated this approach as follows:

> The *sine qua non* for a man who desires to be cultured is deep and enduring enthusiasm to do one thing excellently. So there must first of all be an assurance that the student genuinely wants to make beer. From this it is a natural step to the study of biology, microbiology, and chemistry; all subjects which can be studied not [only] as techniques to be practiced but as ideas to be understood. As his studies gain momentum the student could, by skillful teaching, be made interested in the economics of marketing beer in public-houses, in their design, in architecture; or in the history of beer drinking from the time of the early Egyptian inscriptions, and so in social history; or, in the unhappy moral effects of drinking too much beer, and so in religion and ethics. *A student who can weave his technology into the fabric of society can claim to have a liberal education; a student who cannot weave his technology into the fabric of society cannot claim even to be a good technologist* (1960, 19-20).

CONCLUSION

Early in this chapter, we stated our purposes. We believe that we have documented the American public school's economic responsibility for the economic function of educating for employment. It should be discussed just as openly as we discuss the social and political functions of that system. We believe that we have shown vocational education to be that facet of public education which most effectively can address that economic function. We now suggest that the economic function of education, as exemplified in vocational education, be subjected to further critical analysis with a possible interpretation that is more comprehensive than has been true in the past.

Universally, we assume that "form follows function." We are familiar with the form(s) of vocational education. Its edifices surround us (though some are in a sad state of disrepair). In this chapter, we began a critical analysis of the economic function of vocational education. We have raised (or implied) the following very sensitive questions regarding that function. Is the function a legitimate one? Is the function one worth performing for individuals and society? Should schools and education perform such a function? Could others perform the function better? Is the function compatible with other basic human functions? With other educational functions? Is there a better function which education might address with its limited resources? What are the consequences of performing such a function? Of not performing such a function? Does the function make any real sense?

If our belief in vocational education has been reaffirmed by asking these sensitive questions and obtaining at least a reasonable semblance of an answer—and it has—the most important question still remains, *"Cannot vocational education perform a larger, more important, inherently better function than it presently does and at the same time lose none of its present effectiveness?"*

We don't often ask such questions of our technology, our schools, our churches, our towns, our modes of transportation, our programs of vocational education, nor our programs of education; but the only way to achieve more effective learning is through asking difficult questions about the most appropriate proportion of means and ends. Answers to such questions will not do away with the economic function of education. Instead, it will revitalize that function and align it properly with other generally accepted functions.

Vocational education is difficult to analyze because education is not a rigid structure; its chief component is people. The problem of vocational education planning is not like arranging people for a play, nor even sending players into a game. None of us is purely passive. We are all involved in the action. Nor do we proceed according to a predetermined script; instead, we are agents of our free wills. So we often forget our corporate purpose. Occasionally, therefore, it is good to view ourselves as integral parts of an elaborate scheme and to recognize that our actions do contribute to the "wholeness" of society. When this is done, even in a cursory manner as we have done here, we gain an insight into the true goals of vocational education. Potentially, they are much more comprehensive than we had dared ever to dream.

NOTES

1. Much of the information included in this section is based upon *American Education and Vocationalism* (Lazerson and Grubb, 1974).

2. For a more definitive analysis see "A Search for a Philosophy of Vocational Education," an unpublished paper by Charles J. Law (1976).

REFERENCES CITED

Bagley, William C. *The Educative Process.* New York: The Macmillan Company, 1905. Quoted in Arthur G. Wirth, *Vocational-Liberal Studies Controversy between John Dewey and Others (1900-1917).* St. Louis: Washington University, September 1970, 184.

Barlow, Melvin L. *History of Industrial Education in the United States.* Peoria: Charles A. Bennett Company, 1967.

———., ed. *The Philosophy for Quality Vocational Education.* Washington, D.C.: American Vocational Association, 1974.

Bruner, Jerome S. *The Relevance of Education.* New York: W. S. Norton and Company, Inc., 1973.

Dewey, John. "Splitting Up the School System." *The New Republic* (April 17, 1915).

———. *Democracy and Education.* New York: The Macmillan Company, 1916.

———. *Individualism, Old and New.* Milton Balch and Company, 1930.

Ellul, Jacques. *The Technological Society.* New York: Random House, 1967. Cited by Arthur G. Wirth, 1970, 126-129.

Goodman, Percival, and Goodman, Paul. *Communitas.* New York: Vintage Books, 1960. Quoted in Arthur G. Wirth, 1970, 233.

Guzzardi, Walter. "Education for the World of Work." *Fortune* (October 1975).

Law, Charles J. "A Search for a Philosophy of Vocational Education." Paper presented at a meeting of the National Association of State Directors of Vocational Education, Washington, D.C., May 12-16, 1976.

Lazerson, Marvin, and Grubb, W. Norton. *American Education and Vocationalism.* New York: Columbia University, Teachers College Press, 1974.

Leavitt, Frank M. *How Shall We Study the Industries for the Purposes of Vocational Guidance?* U.S. Bureau of Education, *Bulletin* no. 14. Washington, D.C.: Government Printing Office, 1914.

Lessinger, Leon. "Educational Stability in an Unstable Technical Society." *California Journal of Secondary Education* (March 1965).

Lodge, George C. *The New American Ideology.* New York: Alfred A. Knopf, Inc., 1975.

National Education Association. *Cardinal Principles of Secondary Education: A Report of the Commission on the Reorganization of Secondary Education.* U.S. Bureau of Education, *Bulletin* no. 35. Washington, D.C.: Government Printing Office, 1918, 16.

Prosser, Charles A., and Quigley, Thomas H. *Vocational Education in a Democracy.* Revised ed. Chicago: American Technical Society, 1950. Quoted in Arthur G. Wirth, 1970, 233.

Thompson, John F. *Foundations of Vocational Education—Social and Philosophical Concepts.* New York: Prentice-Hall, Inc., 1973.

U.S. Congress. House. *Report.* H.R. 94-1701, 94th Cong., 2d sess. (Sept. 27, 1976), 96-145.

Wirth, Arthur G. *The Vocational-Liberal Studies Controversy between John Dewey and Others (1900-1917).* Final Report, USOE Project no. 70305, Grant no. OEG 08 070305 3662 90850. St. Louis: Washington University, September 1970.

———. *Education in the Technological Society.* San Francisco: Intext Educational Publishers, 1972.

The Vocational Education Industry

Garth A. Hanson and E. Charles Parker

The word *industry* sparks a myriad of thoughts in people's minds. It might connote *bigness, production, assembly line, workers, factories, payrolls, sales, planning,* or *profits*; but seldom does it suggest *education.* Webster defines *industry* as "any branch of trade, production, or manufacture or all of these collectively."

Vocational education is an industry in every sense of the word. True, there are no assembly lines, factories, or profits as one usually pictures them. However, there is a product. The product of the vocational education industry is a trained person: one who has mastered entry-level skills, upgraded existing skills or retrained for a new occupation. Vocational education is a large, significant industry affecting millions of people as students and thousands of people as teachers, counselors, and administrators. Billions of dollars are spent in the process and the product is used in virtually every other industry in America.

Vocational education is taught by many institutions and agencies and in many different settings. Although many people think of vocational education in terms of the public secondary school, the impact of the vocational education industry is much greater than that. The purpose of this chapter is to discuss not only the public school sector, but other aspects of the vocational education industry as well: private vocational schools, apprenticeship programs, employer training opportunities, armed forces training, the GI Bill for veterans and dependents, federal employment and training programs, and home study programs, just to name a few.

Any significant industry produces an economic impact, not

just within itself but within every other industry it touches. There are normally a number of support industries that depend heavily upon the major industry for sustenance. The automobile industry, for example, provides the lifeblood for the steel, rubber, paint, plastics, and many other support industries. Without the major industry, many support industries simply would not survive.

Vocational education has its support industries, too. These industries include those which produce textbooks, instructional materials, capital equipment, buildings, facilities, safety devices, and other physical necessities. These are identified to call attention to the ripple effect of the industry.

One previously unmentioned industry is seldom thought of as a support industry. It is the teacher education industry—the prime supplier of teachers, counselors, and administrators for most educational programs.

There are other business, industry, government and education support industries too, perhaps some that are more important to the economy than those mentioned above. Suffice it to say that these industries exist, contributing to the economy of the United States and collectively providing jobs and income for millions of people.

THE VOCATIONAL EDUCATION INDUSTRY

The vocational education industry differs from most industries that manufacture assembly-line products, for people are its product—people with the skills needed to produce, distribute and consume goods and deliver services needed in America today. Vocational education processes or services its product from a very tender age to the grave. But the product is never really finished. There is no other industry quite like it.

Here is an illustration of how an individual might be involved with the education industry. A high school junior named Pat enrolls in a basic electricity course, a part of the vocational curriculum in a comprehensive high school. Pat likes electricity and would like to pursue it as a career, but can't work it into the curriculum until after graduation. She has a part-time job while in high school that includes working in a small appliance repair shop. Upon graduation she decides to enroll in a postsecondary private vocational school. When the course is completed, Pat joins the armed forces and finds that the electricity experience provides opportunities for greater training through the military programs. Deciding not to make a career of the military, Pat takes a job in the private sector, fully trained by the vocational education industry.

Many things will change in the technology of electricity throughout Pat's lifetime, so periodic enrollment in vocational courses of various kinds sponsored by different institutions and agencies provide her with the necessary skills to maintain an adequate living with up-to-date skills. The education industry has "manufactured" its product; the product has been sold; both the buyer and the seller are pleased with the results. The entire economy has benefitted in the meantime.

THE PUBLIC SECTOR

Public Agencies for Vocational Education

Public vocational education includes secondary training in grades 7-12, postsecondary training in grades 13-15 (usually excluding the baccalaureate degree), and adult vocational and technical programs for persons of any age (usually above high school age) which are funded by federal, state, and local dollars.

Vocational education is defined in Public Law 94-482, the Education Amendments of 1976, as "organized educational programs which are directly related to the preparation of individuals for paid or unpaid employment, or for additional preparation for a career requiring other than a baccalaureate or advanced degree." The agencies of the public sector engaged in vocational education are also defined in the Education Amendments of 1976 and consist of the following:

Specialized high school. Used exclusively or principally for providing vocational education to persons who are available for study in preparation for entering the labor market.

The department of a high school. Used exclusively or principally for providing vocational education in no less than five different occupational fields to persons who are available for study in preparation for entering the labor market.

Technical or vocational school. Used exclusively or principally for providing vocational education to persons who have completed or left high school and who are available for study in preparation for entering the labor market.

The department or division of a junior college, community college or university. Operates under the policies of the state board and provides vocational education in no less than five different occupational fields, leading to immediate employment, but not necessarily leading to a baccalaureate degree.

All of these agencies include at least five areas of vocational education instruction. The most popular programs emphasize agriculture, distributive occupations, health occupations, home economics related occupations, office occupations, technical education, and trade and industrial instruction. There are also programs in consumer and homemaking skills but the relationship between training and industry is not as direct as with the above-mentioned areas. Special programs for the disadvantaged and handicapped are given high priority. Complete curricula are designed to prepare workers within these specific occupational areas.

An example of how each of these seven vocational areas relates directly through instructional programs to the jobs listed in the *Dictionary of Occupational Titles* is shown in Table 1. These are examples of how specific occupations are served.

The first significant federal legislation for vocational education was the Smith-Hughes Act (PL 64-347) passed in 1917, which provided funds for programs in agriculture, trades and industry, and home economics. There has been much legislation affecting vocational education since that time. The Vocational Education Act of 1963 was one of the great landmarks. The Amendments of 1968 changed the 1963 Act somewhat, adding dollars and students to programs at all levels. When the Education Amendments of 1976 were passed, more dollars and programs again were added.

Through 1975, more than 110 million persons have received vocational training under these acts. Enrollments in 1964, 1970, and 1975 are shown in Table 2 to indicate the growth pattern by adult, secondary, and postsecondary classifications.

An indication of the distribution of federal, state, and local funds can be seen in Table 3. This report for fiscal year 1975 shows a total expenditure of over $4 billion in the public school sector of the vocational education industry.

Directly Funded Programs

Many public agencies engaged in vocational education are not connected with the school system in any way. These programs usually are for persons who have left the secondary school. They include vocational rehabilitation, veteran's assistance, the military, and various manpower programs (Comprehensive Employment and Training Act, Job Corps, Work Incentive Program and others) mostly administered through the Department of Labor. Although a few programs have been retained under direct federal control, most manpower programs are now planned and managed by state and local gov-

Table 1

EXAMPLES OF CURRICULA OFFERING TRAINING FOR SPECIFIC OCCUPATIONS

Major vocational area	Instructional program	Occupational title
Agriculture	Agricultural mechanics	Farm equipment mechanic
	Soil	Soil conservationist
	Forestry	Forest aide
Distribution	Floristry	Floral designer
	Distributive services	Purchasing agent
	Recreation & tourism	Recreation director
Health	Dental assistant	Dental assistant
	Medical lab assisting	Medical lab assistant
	Occupational therapy	Occupational therapy aide
Home economics	Care & guidance of children	Child care attendant
	Food management, production, & services	Cook
Office	Peripheral equipment operator	High-speed printer operator
	Secretaries	Legal secretary
	Quality control clerk	Claim examiner
Technical	Commercial pilot training	Commercial airplane pilot
	Electronic technology	Electrical technician
	Scientific data processing	Programmer, engineering & scientific
Trade & industry	Body & fender repair	Automobile body repairer
	Aircraft operation	Flight engineer
	Product design	Industrial designer

SOURCE: U.S. Department of Labor, Bureau of Labor Statistics, 1976.

ernment units. These programs are supervised to various degrees by the federal government, however.

Comprehensive Employment and Training Act of 1973. In 1975, its first year of operation, the Comprehensive Employment and Training Act (CETA) served over 1,500,000 individuals. Approximately 650,000 received work experience training; 377,000 persons received public service training; 317,000 received classroom training; 75,000 received on-the-job training; and approximately 90,000 received many services designed to improve their employability.

During the same year, 431 eligible units of government, called prime sponsors, received CETA funds. These programs served the following purposes (U.S. Department of Labor, Bureau of Labor Statistics, 1976):

1. Outreach to make needy persons aware of available employment and training services
2. Assessment of individual needs, interests, and potential; referral to appropriate jobs or training; and follow-up to help new workers stay on the job
3. Orientation, counseling, education, and classroom skill training to help people prepare for jobs or qualify for better jobs
4. Subsidized on-the-job training
5. Allowances to support trainees and their families and needed services, such as child care and medical aid
6. Labor market information and job redesign to open up positions for employment and training program graduates

Table 2

ENROLLMENTS IN VOCATIONAL EDUCATION BY LEVEL OF INSTRUCTION

Fiscal Year	Adult	Secondary	Postsecondary	Total
1964	2,254,799	2,140,756	170,835	4,566,390
1970	2,666,083	5,114,451	1,013,426	8,793,960
1975	4,024,104	9,426,376	1,889,946	15,340,426

SOURCE: U.S. Department of Health, Education, and Welfare, 1964, 1970, and 1975.

7. Transitional public service jobs
8. Special programs for groups such as Indians, migrants, nonnative speakers of English, ex-offenders, and youth

Job Corps. During fiscal year 1974, training was provided for over 63,000 Job Corps members in 61 centers in 31 states and Puerto Rico. Persons were trained in clerical occupations, sales, service skills, forestry and farming, food service, automobile and machine repair, construction trades, electrical appliance repair, industrial production, transportation, and health occupations.

Those entering the Job Corps in fiscal year 1974 were youth between 16 and 21 years of age, mostly school dropouts who had poor academic records and who were economically disadvantaged. The purpose of the program is to help persons with this type of background become employable and productive. The program provides basic educational and vocational skills, as well as social skills, counseling, medical and

Table 3

TOTAL EXPENDITURES FOR VOCATIONAL EDUCATION IN FY 75 (IN THOUSANDS)

Level	Federal	State/Local	Total
Secondary	$319,546	$2,273,869	$2,593,415
Postsecondary	148,488	993,930	1,142,418
Adult	40,326	233,997	274,323
Disadvantaged	109,127	209,914	319,041
Handicapped	48,588	56,745	105,333
Total	$508,360	$3,501,796	$4,010,156

NOTE: Figures for disadvantaged and handicapped are included in secondary, postsecondary and adult classifications.

SOURCE: U.S. Department of Health, Education, and Welfare, 1977.

dental treatment, and other support. The program provides for full-time residential living.

Work Incentive Program. The Work Incentive Program (WIN) helps recipients of Aid to Families with Dependent Children (AFDC) secure and keep jobs. It was created as a program by the 1967 Amendments to the Social Security Act. Since 1972 and the new Amendments, the program has been known as WIN II.

The program is administered jointly by the Department of Labor and the Department of Health, Education, and Welfare through state employment and training agencies and welfare agencies throughout the U.S. WIN II may provide participants with job development services and referrals, preparation for finding employment, subsidized employment, limited training, and supportive services such as child care. During fiscal year 1975, there were over 975,000 participants, of whom approximately 170,000 moved to unsubsidized jobs.

Other government training programs. Certain government agencies administer training programs for many of their employees. Such agencies include the Federal Bureau of Investigation (FBI), police academies, and fire departments. Much of the training obtained through these agencies can be considered vocational in nature. It represents a significant contribution to the economy of the United States.

Armed Forces

The armed forces represent one of the nation's largest sources of trained manpower. Military training programs include recruit training, specialized skill training, officer acquisition training, professional development training, and flight training. Specialized training provides military personnel with skills for technical jobs such as radio communication and aircraft engine repair, and for administrative and service-related specialties such as clerical work and military police duty. Specialized skill training is the most significant classification of training as far as numbers trained and the influence felt within the service.

The following is a list of enlisted personnel in each of the nine major occupational training groups on June 30, 1975 (U.S. Department of Labor, Bureau of Labor Statistics, 1976):

Infantry, gun crews, and seamanship specialists	223,558
Electronic equipment repairers	179,077
Communications and intelligence specialists	122,538
Medical and dental specialists	83,803

Other technical and allied specialists	33,872
Administrative specialists and clerks	323,253
Electrical and mechanical equipment repairers	360,006
Craftworkers	86,574
Service and supply handlers	192,611
Total	1,605,292

Note the concentration of persons trained in the mechanical and technical areas. The military programs provide a great source for trained civilian workers.

In addition to this specialized training, the military offers a variety of on-base and off-base educational opportunities, including home study. These opportunities include tuition assistance programs which pay up to 75 percent of tuition fees for off-duty study at accredited schools. Not all of this training is vocational, but much of it is.

The GI Bill. The current GI Bill (PL 89-358) became effective June 1, 1966. It was enacted by the Congress primarily to provide educational opportunities to veterans whose career goals may have been impeded by service in the armed forces after January 31, 1955. Opportunities are available to military service personnel on active duty who have completed two or more years of service.

A second purpose of the GI Bill is to provide vocational rehabilitation to help veterans to overcome handicaps resulting from service-connected or service-aggravated disability. A third educational program aids survivors or dependents of veterans who died from service-connected causes or whose service-connected disability is rated permanent and total.

Over the past 10 years, through fiscal year 1976, over 6.5 million veterans or active-duty personnel have trained with the help of the GI Bill. During fiscal year 1976, 2.8 million persons trained under PL 89-358. An additional 100,000 dependents received educational benefits and 29,000 persons received training under the vocational rehabilitation program (Veterans Administration, 1977).

Of the 2.8 million persons trained in fiscal year 1976, 422,000 were trained in vocational-technical programs, including flight training, apprenticeship, on-the-job training, and cooperative farms programs. This number does *not* include any of the 205,000 persons enrolled in correspondence courses, of which a large percentage were undoubtedly enrolled in vocational courses. These vocational programs were made available at a total cost of $671,607,388. (Note: The total federal dollars spent in fiscal year 1976 in public vocational education as a result of PL 90-576 [1968 Amendments] was less than $600 million.)

THE PRIVATE SECTOR

Vocational Schools

In 1974 nearly 8,000 private vocational schools were operating and certified in the United States. Students of these schools were primarily secondary school leavers and came from all types of economic backgrounds. One hundred twenty-nine of these schools were listed as correspondence schools.

Table 4 shows the number of private schools and classifies them as proprietary and nonprofit schools. Enrollments shown include full-time and part-time students.

Proprietary schools are owned and managed by an industry or an individual to meet a specific need. There are many high-

Table 4

ENROLLMENTS IN PRIVATE NONCOLLEGIATE POSTSECONDARY SCHOOLS WITH OCCUPATIONAL PROGRAMS (1973-74)

Type of School	Number of schools	Enrollments		
		Full-time	Part-time	Total
Cosmetology/barber	2,401	91,841	21,802	113,643
Flight	1,477	23,806	51,157	74,963
Business/office	1,241	180,156	139,544	319,700
Hospital	1,077	62,298	395	62,693
Trade	678	94,200	32,142	126,342
Vocational/technical	588	83,794	28,811	112,605
Technical institute	163	38,947	10,313	49,260
Other	199	8,824	19,335	28,159
Total	7,824	583,866	303,499	887,365

SOURCE: U.S. Department of Labor, Bureau of Labor Statistics, 1976.

quality private schools in existence. Most of them focus on placing the student on the job immediately upon graduation from the program. Most private school curricula provide for job-related courses almost exclusively, requiring a minimum of nonvocational courses. Each curriculum is tailored to the needs of a specific occupation.

Proprietary schools traditionally offer specialized subject matter courses which lead to jobs in relatively few industries. A majority of these courses can be classified easily into the following industries: cosmetology/barber, flight, hospital, and business/office. Accumulatively, these represent over 78 percent of the total private school market (see Table 5).

Table 5

NUMBER OF PRIVATE NONCOLLEGIATE POSTSECONDARY SCHOOLS WITH OCCUPATIONAL PROGRAMS

Type of school	Number of Schools in U.S.		
	Proprietary	Nonprofit*	Total
Vocational/technical	515	73	588
Technical institute	150	13	163
Business/office	1,208	33	1,241
Cosmetology/barber	2,397	4	2,401
Flight	1,472	5	1,477
Trade	571	107	678
Hospital	24	1,053	1,077
Other	175	24	199
Correspondence	126	3	129
Total	6,638	1,315	7,953

*Includes schools supported by a religious group.

SOURCE: U.S. Department of Labor, Bureau of Labor Statistics, 1976.

Those in the private sector of vocational training are in business to make a profit. When they do, they stay in business; when they don't, they cease to exist. They are a part of the private enterprise system.

Business and Industry Training

Apprenticeships. There seems to be no substitute in quality for the apprenticeship program. It provides a thorough knowledge of the craft on a hands-on basis. The instructor is one skilled in that craft. The classroom is the factory. Simulation, obsolete equipment, and unskilled teachers do not exist. The student either succeeds or fails.

The following list shows the numbers officially registered in apprenticeship programs for 1975 (U.S. Department of Labor, Employment and Training Administration, 1976a):

Beginning-of-year totals	284,562
Added during the year	83,018
Cancelled	55,338
Completed	45,765
End-of-year totals	266,477

These numbers represent only those registered with the Department of Labor. There is no way of estimating the number who were actually training in apprenticeship programs, but were not officially registered.

The following is a list of the top 10 occupational groupings in apprenticeship programs (U.S. Department of Labor, Employment and Training Administration, 1976c):

Carpenters	36,594
Electricians	32,640
Plumbers	18,405
Machinists	14,861
Pipefitters	12,717
Sheetmetal workers	11,647
Tool and die makers	10,984
Structural steel workers	8,982
Auto and related mechanics	8,254
Bricklayers, stone, and tile sets	7,832
Others	103,561
Total	266,477

Most apprenticeship programs have committees of employers and local trade unions which interview applicants, review the trainee's progress, and determine when an apprenticeship has been completed satisfactorily. The Department of Labor's Bureau of Apprenticeship and Training

(BAT) registers but does not finance apprenticeship programs.

Training craftworkers to meet future manpower requirements has become a common goal for employers, unions, and government manpower officials. Many apprentices work for a while only to "drop out" to become journeymen. Since this happens so frequently in all programs, the high number of cancellations is not necessarily a negative indication. There is no question that apprenticeship programs contribute significantly to the manpower delivery system.

Training by Employers

The nature and quality of training by employers varies greatly, ranging from highly effective to inadequate. At one extreme is a very formal, sophisticated training which surpasses most formal school instruction in its scope and achievements. Airline pilot training, technical machine operation, and significantly complex equipment training are examples. Perhaps the most common type of training by employers consists of a simple procedure where the employee is trained until proficiency is acquired. The employee "just picks up the skills" by observation, working during lunch, asking questions, and seeking promotion. Some efforts are currently being made to collect these data, but the results will be guesstimates at best. Suffice it to say that this category probably represents the largest classification of vocational training; it is the easiest to get in and out of; and the quality of instruction varies greatly.

THE IMPACT OF ENVIRONMENTAL FACTORS ON THE VOCATIONAL EDUCATION INDUSTRY

In addition to being a manpower delivery system, the vocational education industry must serve the individual needs of its students. The product is delivered with adequate skills for a specific service to an employer; in return, the employer compensates the person for services performed. Generally speaking, as long as the compensation for the services rendered is adequate, employees stay, improve their skills, get promoted, and increase their productivity. As soon as the compensation falls short of expectations for services rendered, they consider changing their work environment.

An employee's compensation comes in dollars, prestige, satisfaction, a sense of accomplishment, pride, and personal growth. It is a major function of the vocational education industry to provide education where abilities can be developed to meet job specifications. The vocational education industry does not deliver its product until such time as the vocational student finds employment which adequately meets personal needs. Personal needs usually change as one's environment changes. Any industry dedicated to delivering saleable skills must therefore be able to meet changing personal needs. The following must be considered in meeting these needs.

The Home

Vocational education can only be delivered to persons who want to learn. An attitude of wanting to learn begins in the home or wherever young children spend their early childhood. Parents and guardians, whose environment is often created by their own career choices, serve as a component of the child's environment. A child learns a life-style, an attitude about work, a desire to plan (or not to plan), intellectual curiosity, a desire to excel, a plan for a career. In this setting, ability development is begun.

As persons grow and develop, the home continues to affect vocational education, although a person's ability to control the home environment changes with age. Children are highly impressionable. If the family is habitually on welfare and the parents do not have the ability or interest to obtain skills or earn a living, the child may be conditioned to expect a life on welfare. If the family, on the other hand, is work-oriented, that child may be highly motivated to obtain skills, improve them, and constantly strive for more training.

As a teenager, the home can be a place where one learns how to work, a place to eat and sleep, or a place of negative influence. As an adult, the home may become a domicile to support, an integral part of a career plan, or a stimulating career influence. If an attitude for learning has not been developed, the vocational education industry cannot produce a product. An industry cannot produce any product without the raw material with which to work.

The Schools

For the purpose of this chapter, let's assume that school systems develop student abilities. A child enters the school system with a background from the home and the neighborhood. The school ascertains what abilities currently exist. An educational program is outlined and the procedure begins. Many assume that all school experiences develop personal abilities. This may or may not be true. What is true is that schools have a great impact upon the development of persons for the world of work.

The Job Market

In an industrial society, jobs must be available where persons can exchange their talents and abilities for pay (in whatever form). Jobs must be generated; the economy must be developed; housing must be furnished; taxes must be paid; transportation must be provided. All of this depends upon the availability of jobs, which must be filled by qualified workers.

GUIDANCE AND PLACEMENT

Matching People and Jobs

As experts in the labor and education forces argue over the number of unemployed, there are in the United States at any given time many persons who are not well-matched to the jobs they hold. Probably now, more than at any other time since the Great Depression, more Ph.D.s are driving taxicabs and waiting on tables than ever before. Often second and third generations of families are on welfare; most have never held a job for any length of time. In a time when it may be easier and pay more to be on welfare than to be employed, matching people to jobs is especially important.

Among the individuals who need job-finding assistance are those who are chronically dependent, socially hostile, mentally retarded, physically handicapped, emotionally disturbed, or economically or culturally disadvantaged. Some find themselves displaced because of technological change or other reasons and others are underemployed. Still others are overemployed, a condition where it will be only a matter of time before the requirements of the job and personal inabilities to handle the work will catch up with them; inevitably, unemployment will follow.

The vocational education industry has finally become aware of the need to shore up this part of the delivery system. Congress recognized the problem in the Education Amendments of 1976. Under Part D of Title II of that act, entitled "Guidance and Counseling," Congress said that:

> (1) Guidance and counseling activities are an essential component to assure success in achieving the goals of many education programs; (2) lack of coordination among guidance and counseling activities supported jointly or separately by Federal programs and by state and local programs has resulted in an underutilization of resources available for such activities; and (3) increased and improved preparation of education professionals is needed in guidance and counseling, including administration of guidance and counseling programs at the state and local levels, with special emphasis on inservice training which takes educational professionals into the work-

> places of business and industry, the professions, and other occupational pursuits, and that increased and improved use of individuals employed in such pursuits are needed for effective guidance and counseling programs, including (a) bringing persons employed in such pursuits into schools, and (b) bringing students into such workplaces for observation of, and participation in, such pursuits, in order to acquaint the students with the nature of the work.

Congress then authorized the appropriation of $20 million for fiscal years 1978 and 1979 for guidance and counseling.

Suffice it to say, then, that Congress has recognized the need to be specific in identifying the problems relating to guidance and counseling needs. The vocational education industry has long trained individuals for a job, turned them out of the classroom, and forgotten them. It has been like an automobile manufacturer's producing automobiles and letting them sit in their storage lots without any effort to market them. In order for an industry to succeed, the product has to be matched with a buyer.

Counseling needs to take place before students enter programs, while they are in programs, and as they leave those programs. It is also very important that workers have the opportunity for additional career counseling periodically after they get on the job.

The economic drain on a large industry which does not match the product to the buyer is devastating. The return on the investment that it takes to develop this vast resource makes the effort to properly place the product very worthwhile.

Improving Health and Security

Many tragic tales of employee bondage to the employer have been told over the centuries. It wasn't until the turn of this century that real strides were made to provide appropriate working conditions and advancement opportunities for workers. The atrocities of child labor abuse, manual laborers working until they literally dropped dead on the job, and the dead-end jobs where there was no opportunity for the workers to better themselves are being greatly reduced. Some say the pendulum is swinging so far away from those times that the worker is endangered psychologically by the lack of work on the job rather than by the overabundance of it.

Several issues have been raised to emphasize the change. Minimum wage and hour laws have been passed. Unions have performed a needed service in providing maximum worker benefits through bargaining with management. Safety has been emphasized to the extent that places of business have been closed rather than to jeopardize the lives or well-being of their employees, a drastic change from past practices. Other changes include the addition of old-age survivor's benefits and anti-discrimination laws.

One major contribution that the vocational education industry has to offer is a reprieve to the underemployed. Where else can a person obtain the assistance needed to upgrade skills, learn of opportunities for advancement, receive counseling for self-improvement, and in more and more cases, actually receive placement assistance in finding that new position? The vocational education industry plays a significant role in helping people improve their health and security.

SUMMARY

The vocational education industry has contributed much to the manpower supply in the United States. There is currently some question as to whether or not it is the primary delivery system it should be. At the time of this writing, Congress is deliberating major changes in the Comprehensive Employment and Training Act of 1973, with appropriations proposed at approximately 12 times the amount appropriated for vocational education. Since Congress usually places a dollar value on the importance attached to each bill, vocational educators should be concerned about this proposal.

The vocational delivery system varies greatly in its effectiveness. The one thing that seems sure about the delivery system as it now exists is that it must change to more adequately meet the needs of its public. The following are some of the considerations which need to be made:

1. Vocational education will need to do a better job of selling what it is producing to all publics—business, industry, parents, administrators, and students.
2. The vocational education concept will need to include training which more closely meets the needs of a larger part of the education industry.
3. Vocational educators must think of programs in terms other than secondary education.
4. Vocational education will need to expand beyond the classroom walls where appropriate.
5. Manpower delivery systems outside of vocational education will need to recognize the delivery capabilities of vocational education.
6. Leaders of education and industry must recognize the accomplishments of vocational education to date as they move into the future. The best of the existing

structure should be incorporated into the manpower delivery system as it develops.

There is no question that manpower will continue to be trained for jobs throughout the economy. It is difficult to comprehend that vocational education might ever be eliminated from the school (even though the form may change somewhat). The questions currently being asked throughout the vocational education industry are: Who will do the training? Who will draw the programs together? Who will do the best and most effective job of training persons for the jobs they need? In seeking answers to these questions, vocational educators can and should make the proud traditions of the past the beginning of an even more proud future.

REFERENCES CITED

U.S. Congress. "Education Amendments of 1976." *Public Law 94-482.* 94th Congress (October 12, 1976).

U.S. Department of Health, Education, and Welfare, Office of Education, Bureau of Occupational and Adult Education. "Annual Reports, Vocational and Technical Education." Washington, D.C.: 1964, 1970, 1975.

————. "Summary Data, Vocational Education FY 75." *Vocational Education Information,* no. 1. Washington, D.C.: 1977.

U.S. Department of Labor, Bureau of Labor Statistics. "Occupational Projections and Training Data." *Bulletin,* 1918. Washington, D.C.: U.S. Government Printing Office, 1976.

U.S. Department of Labor, Employment and Training Administration. "Apprentice Action Data." *Report,* no. 9. Washington, D.C.: 1976a.

————. "Apprentice Registration Actions, by Personal Characteristics—State Summary." *Report,* no. 7. Washington, D.C.: 1976b.

————. "State and National Apprenticeship System: Report by Selected Occupational Grouping." *Bulletin,* 77-6. Washington, D.C.: 1976c.

Veterans Administration. "Veterans Benefits under Current Educational Programs." *Information Bulletin,* no. IB 04-77-1. Washington, D.C.: 1977.

The Economics of Planning Vocational Education

George H. Copa

Limited resources, the appearance of viable alternatives to expenditures on education, decentralization in decision making, and the stress on accountability have resulted in a recent reemphasis on planning in education. This trend is made explicit for vocational education by the expanded requirements for planning in new federal legislation (U.S. Congress, 1976). In order to develop the planning capacity being requested, the planning process itself must be made explicit for critical examination of its ability to result in plans which meet the needs of the people in our changing society. Absence of an explicit description of the planning process and its subsequent examination can result in plans which bear little relationship to the wishes of the constituency for which the plans are made or to the administrative context within which plans must be implemented. This chapter focuses on the economics of planning vocational education, which requires an examination of the planning process for vocational education from an economic perspective—a perspective which is concerned with the use of scarce resources to produce a selected output.

PLANS AND PLANNING

A plan can be conceived as a definition of how one is going to get somewhere or obtain something in the future; it is usually characterized in terms of time, cost, and performance expectations. A plan is the result of the process of planning. Planning requires decision making about future actions.

Friedman (1973, 19) has referred to planning as "the application of a scientific and technical intelligence to organized action." This definition identifies the planning characteristic of using the best current knowledge and experience in an organized way to make decisions; the implication is that information and thought are essential to planning. In a later treatise, "Emerging Methodology of Planning," Ozbekhan (1974, 65) says:

> Planning is to act on some object.
> Planning is to act on some object for some purpose.
> Planning is to act on some object for the purpose of effecting change(s) in the object.
> Planning is the definition of the purpose of the change(s) one wishes to effect in the object.
> Planning is the design of the actions which will change the object in the manner that has been previously defined.

As aptly stated, planning takes on the additional characteristics of being purposeful, focused on change, and concerned with defining the reason for change and the design of action. Planning as a process requires knowledge of where one is (i.e., the present situation), where one wants to be (i.e., goals), alternative courses of action available, and means/ends relationships.

WHY PLANNING?

From an economic perspective, planning is done to improve efficiency and to avoid surpluses or shortages in production. Improvement of efficiency refers to reducing the cost per unit of production. Reduction in cost per unit of production may come through selection of inputs used in the process or changes in the production function used to combine resources to produce a product. In the case of vocational education, one of the foremost products is better-educated or prepared workers. Inputs used include teachers, classrooms, instructional materials, time, and students. The production function for vocational education refers to how these inputs are combined to produce better-prepared workers. A typical production function at the micro level is to use one teacher in one classroom with one set of textbooks for one hour per school year with 20 students in grades 11 and 12. Another production function commonly used with adults is one teacher in one classroom for three evening hours per week for ten weeks with 15 students ages 25 to 65. The focus of planning in improving the efficiency of vocational education has to do with decisions such as: (1) which teacher, (2) how many teachers, (3) how many classrooms, (4) which instructional materials, (5) length of program, (6) scheduling of program, and (7) which students. The goal is to use resources to minimize cost per unit of production (in this case, a better-prepared worker). Planning can improve efficiency by forcing thinking and communication about future expectations, by keeping discussions and production focused on selected goals, and by facilitating control of the production process by comparing it to a plan.

The second reason for planning involves the avoidance of surpluses or shortages in production. Economically, surpluses are caused by supply exceeding demand at a given price per unit of production. Shortages are the opposite situation, where demand exceeds supply at the going price per unit of production. We have said that one product of vocational education is a better-prepared worker. Surpluses in production of this product would exist when there are more better-prepared workers than society is willing to use at a given wage rate. Shortages would exist when society is willing to use more better-prepared workers than are presently available at the prevailing wage rate. Note that in defining *shortage* and *surplus,* they are referenced to a given price per unit; in the case of workers, this is the wage rate. The economic assumption is that if the price per unit changes, a new balance would be struck between supply and demand. As an example, it is assumed that if a surplus of workers exists, a reduction in wage rate would be followed by an increase in demand, all other factors remaining the same.

Shortages and surpluses are undesirable from the standpoint that resources are not being used to their maximum benefit. This is particularly critical for resources such as workers because if they are not used, their production is lost for all time—it is not a resource which can be stored for use at a future time.

Planning is useful in avoiding shortages and surpluses by focusing on the selection of production goals for future time periods and the use of a plan as a comparative tool in monitoring progress toward the goals. For vocational education, planning has typically meant deciding how many workers with various types and amounts of preparation will be needed at some future time—e.g., next month, next year, five years from now. In this context, planning involves deciding "what should be," whereas in the context of improving efficiency, concern was with deciding how to produce "what should be" for the least cost in terms of using scarce resources.

MISSION AND PERFORMANCE REQUIREMENTS OF VOCATIONAL EDUCATION

In order to continue a discussion of the economics of planning an entity such as vocational education, it is necessary to define at least a partial context for the entity. In defining this context, stress will be placed on describing a general mission and set of performance requirements similar to the prospectus for a business sector in our economy. These specifications, in turn, provide a context in which the planning process is applied for vocational education. Note that specification is in terms of a general mission, not specific goals, and performance requirements within which vocational education must function. The purpose of planning is to identify the specific goals and production function within this broader context.

In specifying the mission and performance requirements for vocational education, heavy reliance will be placed on the contents of current federal legislation as a benchmark. There are other ways of approaching a definition of the parameters of vocational education; however, the federal legislation is perhaps the most accepted and commonly used.

Given the benchmark of current federal legislation, vocational education is one of society's planned and organized processes for providing education for work. By definition in a document describing society's intent, vocational education means "organized educational programs which are directly related to the preparation of individuals for paid or unpaid employment, or for additional preparation for a career requiring other than a baccalaureate or advanced degree" (U.S. Congress, 1976, 2211).

It should be recognized that this federal act is an amendment to a previous act and that it is reasonable to expect more amendments or whole new acts defining vocational education. Thus, the definition is not permanent and can be changed to meet the felt needs of society.

As a planned and organized process in actual operation, vocational education operates within a context. This context evolves from the documents already mentioned, from interpretations of those documents by persons operating the process, from knowledge of how persons develop their preparedness for work, and from existing cultural values, resource availability and technology. The context can be thought of, more specifically, as a set of performance requirements which society perceives that vocational education should meet. These performance requirements include both objectives (desired ends) and operating constraints (limitations within which the desired ends are to be achieved); it is expected that these performance requirements will change over time.

Desired End

The desired end for vocational education is the mutual satisfaction of the individual and society through the individual's participation in the work role (Moss, Smith and Copa, 1972). The individual receives satisfaction from what he does in the work role (content) and the environment in which he performs the role (context, e.g., working conditions, rate of pay, co-workers). Society receives satisfaction from the quantity and quality of the worker's performance, and from the relevance of the job to society's needs.

Limited Work Roles

The definition of vocational education referred to earlier stipulates that programs are designed to prepare individuals for employment other than that requiring a baccalaureate or advanced degree. This stipulation delineates the types of work roles, or more specifically, occupations, for which vocational education provides preparation. The occupations generally excluded by this stipulation are those labeled "professional" by the U.S. Department of Labor. This legal delimitation of the work roles of concern to vocational education indicates that vocational education is not responsible for all education for work.

Realistic in Terms of Employment Opportunities

Although the managers of vocational education do not have direct control of the occupations which are relevant to society, they are required to be aware of society's needs and operate accordingly. The 1976 Amendments state that individuals participating in vocational education will have access to programs which are: ". . . realistic in the light of actual or anticipated opportunities for gainful employment . . ." (U.S. Congress, 1976, 2170). If vocational education is to result in maximum mutual satisfaction to the individual and society, and one way in which society and the individual get satisfaction is from having an individual in a relevant work role, then vocational education managers must be aware of the work roles society wants filled, i.e., employment opportunities.

Concern for Individual

Vocational education is an educational process directed at the individual. It is a planned, organized learning experience intended to make individuals aware of their response potential in a role or to alter the role behavior of an individual in a manner which will facilitate interaction and result in fuller self-actualization of the individual and society. Vocational education is directed at changing the individual's interactions in a work role, although sometimes it may not affect cultural values and work role requirements.

Equal Educational Opportunity

One of the values in our culture which is relevant to any educational program supported by our society is the concept of equal educational opportunity. As a performance requirement, it means that individuals have an equal opportunity to pursue the education of their choice. This requirement can be operationalized in several dimensions to more closely define the context of vocational education. These dimensions are: "ready access" and "suited to needs, interests, and ability to benefit."

Ready access. In clarifying the purpose of vocational education, the Vocational Amendments of 1976 state that vocational education should provide programs so that

> Persons of all ages in all communities of the State, those in high school, those who have completed or discontinued their formal education and are preparing to enter the labor market, those who have already entered the labor market, but need to upgrade their skills or learn new ones, those with special educational handicaps, and those in postsecondary schools will have ready access to vocational training or retraining . . . (U.S. Congress, 1976, 2169-70).

The interpretation of this statement is that vocational education should provide equal educational opportunity by being accessible in geographic proximity, cost, and time scheduling to all persons regardless of age, race, and sex. The requirement for ready access is often at odds with efficiency in achieving the desired ends for vocational education. Accessibility as a dimension of the equal educational opportunity performance requirements has direct implications for the quantity or number of programs to be offered and the geographic location of those programs in a state.

Suited to needs, interests, and ability to benefit. In its concern with the individual's preparation for a work role and with providing equal educational opportunity, vocational education must be attuned to the individual's needs, interests, and ability to benefit from participation (U.S. Congress, 1976, 2170). The interpretation of this dimension is that vocational education must be suited to an individual's development with respect to preparation for work and level of satisfaction with a work role—or adjustment for the role if not yet working—in the sense that if more development can take place, the satisfaction of the individual will improve.

The status of an individual's development in terms of preparation for work can be assessed by using the following categories: awareness, orientation, exploration, career specialization (initial and continued) (Moss, Smith and Copa, 1972). Awareness is characterized by an individual's ability to recognize and discriminate among occupations and to think about himself in occupationally relevant dimensions of motives and abilities. Orientation involves the ability to do reality testing of the individual's abilities and motives and their relationship to his concept of occupations. It results in a clarification of his perception of himself in relation to occupational motivational satisfiers and ability requirements. The final stage of career specialization is characterized by a refinement of abilities and motivational patterns for a selected occupation(s). This stage covers the span of time from an initial decision to specialize in a particular occupation through continued preparation to maintain ability and motivational pattern for that occupation or to change ability or motivational pattern to fit a new occupation. Individuals are in a career specialization state during most of their work life. The word "most" is used to indicate that at various times the individual may wish to move to the exploratory state—particularly to retrain for a different occupation.

This dimension does *not* imply that vocational education must provide preparation for all or any select group of these stages. Rather, it is authorized to do any or all. The requirement is that if vocational education provides training to an individual, it must be compatible with the stage of development with respect to work of that person if equal educational opportunity is to result. Adherence to this requirement means that vocational education must be able to provide preparation for a wide variety of occupations and ability levels with respect to capability to perform a work role.

Society has identified two particular groups of people with special needs whom vocational education is to serve: the handicapped and the disadvantaged. At present, society's performance requirement is that 25 percent of federal funds given to vocational education at the state level be used for programs serving handicapped or disadvantaged individuals (U.S. Congress, 1976, 2185).

"Ability to benefit" implies that the participant in a vocational education program, as well as society, should be more satisfied with the participant's performance in a work role following participation in a vocational education program. As such, it necessitates that some opportunity to benefit does in fact exist for the individual and society before an individual participates in vocational education.

Enforcement of these dimensions of equal educational opportunity will require an assessment of the needs, interests and present level of satisfaction of the population to be served by vocational education. In the absence of this information, planners of vocational education, although cognizant of the concern for the individual, may fail to get maximum effect in changing individual and societal satisfaction. An assessment of this nature provides the baseline from which to measure the achievements of vocational education in this dimension of providing equal educational opportunity.

Time

The performance requirements which follow from this point give particular emphasis to the economic context for planning vocational education. First, vocational education works within a given time horizon. Time can be thought of in the very short run as a time schedule, i.e., high school programs of vocational education normally operate between 8:30 a.m. and 3:45 p.m. in 50-minute blocks of time, all the way to the very long run, i.e., 50 years or more from now. Generally, the shorter the time horizon being considered, the more fixed are the factors affecting the production of vocational education. (Land, labor, capital, and management are the factors of production.) Some factors may be more fixed than others. For example, even in a short time, it may be possible to secure more labor, i.e., another teacher; however, it may be very difficult to acquire more capital, i.e., a new classroom. The long run as a time requirement refers to a time period which is long enough that most factors of production are variable, i.e., new land can be purchased and a building constructed.

If actions taken to maximize the "desired ends" for vocational education in the long run do not result in maximizing their attainment in the short run, it may be necessary to subordinate short-run objectives to long-run objectives in order to maximize effectiveness over time.

Available Resources

Resources available to conduct vocational education also act as a performance requirement on what vocational education can accomplish. Resources can include land, labor, capital and management. Although resources can be combined in many different ways and substituted for one another, vocational education cannot use more resources than it has.

Technology

Technology as a performance requirement refers to how land, labor, capital, and management are combined to accomplish a given end. More efficient and effective processes of vocational education are continually being explored, but the level of development is always a given at a particular point in time.

The technology of vocational education can be described in terms of content, purpose, institution, and function. Content refers to the subject matter of a program and usually is categorized according to occupational groupings. The more traditional content areas are agriculture, distributive, health, home economics, business and office, technical, and trade and industrial.

Another means of describing the technology of vocational education is to focus on its purpose relative to the needs of individuals to be served. Traditional categories based on "purpose" are: awareness, orientation, exploration, specialization (i.e., preparation for the first job), continuing specialization (i.e., updating, upgrading, retraining).

Institution refers to the types of institution in which the program is operated; the more traditional levels are secondary (e.g., high school, secondary vocational centers) and postsecondary (e.g., postsecondary area vocational-technical institutes, community colleges). More recently, with the inception of "career education," elementary and junior high schools are also being used in describing the process of vocational education. Note that the purposes and institutions categories are not necessarily parallel; that is, several programs with different purposes may be offered at the same institution. In general, however, elementary programs at elementary schools focus on awareness, orientation, and exploration, secondary school programs on exploration and specialization, postsecondary school programs on initial and continuing specialization.

Function as a technological description of vocational education refers to how resources are used, given a program with a particular content, purpose, and institution. Function describes the ways vocational education influences individuals —through recruitment, guidance, instruction, and placement.

The technology of vocational education can also be characterized in other ways such as mode (i.e., individualized, small or large group, computer assisted) and place of instruction (i.e., classroom, shop, laboratory, on-the-job, home).

Planning

The most recent federal legislation states that one of its purposes is to "assist states in improving planning in the use of all resources available to them for vocational education and manpower training by involving a wide range of agencies and individuals concerned with education and training within the State in the development of the vocational education plans" (U.S. Congress, 1976, 2169). To enforce their intent, the Congress mandated a five-year state plan and annual program plan and accountability reports involving the active participation of a specified group of agencies and individuals in a detailed process. These requirements imply a concern for increased planning activities of higher quality, more comprehensive planning of total occupational preparation services, and involvement of those who will be affected by the plan.

Efficiency

Efficiency is also a value that our society endorses. It can be interpreted to mean that once a decision is reached on *what* must be accomplished, and on the *parameters,* i.e., performance requirements, within which one must operate, the task should be done in the most efficient manner, i.e., least costly in terms of resources used. For vocational education, efficiency is interpreted as a performance requirement stating that vocational education should provide training for only those work roles for which it can train more efficiently than other agencies (e.g., private schools, firms, family) for individuals with special needs not served by other agencies, and where other agencies cannot provide enough training. This performance requirement should be the last to be applied to the operation of vocational education after the other performance requirements have been enforced.

MAJOR PLANNING DECISIONS

Given the above context, the economics of planning vocational education can be viewed in terms of the major decisions needed. From an economic perspective, these decisions concern scale, product mix, production function, schedule, and location of vocational education services.

Scale

The decision about scale is one of deciding how much vocational education should be provided. Questions of scale relate specifically to the capacity of institutions providing vocational education services. Focus is on projections of the number of people who want preparation for work, labor market demand for prepared workers, and resources available. Also, concern is with the substitutes for vocational education services such as on-the-job training, other educational programs, and self-instruction. Decisions about scale should be based on benefits vocational education can produce more efficiently than competitors providing the same kind of services and on the "value" of the benefits of vocational education relative to the benefits of other services which could be provided with public funds, e.g., health, transportation and housing. Comprehensive planning of occupational education services should avoid gaps and duplication and, more broadly, take into account all human services related to the question of scale. Viewed at the micro level, scale decisions concern class size and institution size to maintain efficiency and quality service.

Product Mix

The proportion of vocational education programs offered in terms of content (e.g., agriculture, home economics, business), level (e.g., secondary, postsecondary, adult), and purpose (e.g., exploratory, specialization, continuing) is the focus of planning decisions concerning product mix for vocational education. Given that scale has been determined, product mix decisions concern the internal allocation of resources within vocational education itself. Here the needs of individuals to be served and labor market demand must be made much more specific to be useful. In addition, the information about alternative sources of supply for prepared workers must be considered in greater detail. Questions about the capacity, effectiveness, accessibility, and cost of alternatives to vocational education become relevant as decisions are made on a program by program basis. Discussions also center on the specialization versus flexibility of preparation of individuals.

Production Function

Production function concerns relate to how the product mix will be produced. What are the best formulas to prepare workers for various occupations? How long should the program be and how much should be in the classroom, laboratory, shop, or on-the-job? Should instruction be group-centered or individualized? How many resources should be spent on guidance, instruction, administration, evaluation? Decisions are being made on how to allocate scarce resources to meet a particular program mix goal. Many factors come into play at this micro level of planning, e.g., facilities available, curriculum materials, on-the-job training stations, length of time student can spend.

Schedule

Decisions about schedule refer to the timing of vocational education services, ranging from whether to add and delete programs to when a given program should be operated. Long-range versus short-range planning is at issue. Scheduling decisions are particularly important in avoiding surpluses and shortages, since these occurrences are often a function of time. For example, at the micro level, contrast the scheduling implications of constant-length programs with those allowing continuous entry and exit.

Location

Geographic location of programs requires decisions about numbers of institutions and their spatial distribution in a given geographic area. The issue of vocational programs in area centers versus home high schools is tied to the location question. Location of programs is highly correlated to accessibility and thereby the requirement of equal educational opportunity.

STRATEGIES FOR PLANNING

Several approaches to planning vocational education through making the major decisions cited above are available. The strategies vary in their complexity, dynamics, information requirements, and factor stress. Each has its advantages and disadvantages.

Manpower Requirements Approach

Using the manpower requirements approach, the one critical factor in planning is the labor market demand (Lecht, Teeple, & Paredes, 1970; McNamara & Franchak, 1970; Braden, Harris & Paul, 1970; Young, 1973; Copa & Irvin, 1974; U.S. Department of Labor, 1974a). In this approach the manpower requirements to produce a desired set of goods and services in the economy are estimated. Vocational education programs are then matched to occupations and estimates made of the number of completions needed for each program. At the macro level, manpower requirements are usually specified in terms of the number of new positions to be filled in a selected set of occupations for a given time period and geographic area; at the micro level it may include a detailed listing of the knowledge and skills needed by workers in the various occupations (Braden & Paul, 1975). Information needs include projection of labor market demand for detailed occupations, a cross classification system between occupations and vocational education programs, estimates of supply of prepared workers coming from sources other than vocational education and from vocational education. Alternative sources of supply may include the unemployed, programs sponsored under the Comprehensive Employment and Training Act, on-the-job training, private vocational schools, and other education programs not particularly directed at vocational education.

Many states are now approaching this planning strategy in preparing tables describing enrollment and labor force projections for their state plans for vocational education. Advantages of this approach include its logical simplicity and pragmatic focus on a primary purpose of vocational education —preparation of workers. Its limitations lie in the limited ability to make accurate labor market projections (Kidder, 1972), the almost universal lack of information documenting labor market supply from all sources (including vocational education), the lack of a valid and comprehensive means of cross classifying occupations and vocational education programs (U.S. Department of Labor, 1975; The California Manpower Management Information System, 1976), the limited concern for other factors such as wages as a means of altering either or both supply and demand (perhaps more effectively than changing the scale or mix of products of vocational education) (U.S. Department of Labor, 1974b) and lack of consideration that vocational education has purposes in addition to preparing workers to meet manpower requirements (i.e., general education components) (Evans, 1971).

Social Demand Approach

The social demand approach assumes that potential students of vocational education are wise consumers and that it does not pay to try to second-guess the labor market. Here, the one major factor used in deciding planning questions is the demand for vocational education services by individuals (Copa, Persons & Thomas, 1973; Copa & Maurice, 1976). Vocational education programs under this approach are sensitive to the wish of potential and current clients. Programs are provided on the basis of interest, applications, enrollments and completions. If the program attracts students and holds them until completion, it is satisfactory.

Primary information requirements are indicators of individual demand (e.g., interest assessments, application counts, enrollments, completion percentages). An obvious advantage of this aproach is the limited information requirements and the complete disregard for manpower projections information. Disadvantages lie in the ability of potential students to be able to recognize, first, their needs and second, the needs of society, i.e., jobs for which they wish to prepare, the high cost of following through with programs to meet all of social demand, and the difficulties in projecting social demand. The concern about potential students not being able to recognize the needs of society is particularly true at the postsecondary level, where the investment of dollars and opportunity costs are substantial and preparation is relatively specialized (non-transferrable). Adult-level vocational education may be particularly appropriate for the social demands approach to planning programs; in fact, this approach is most commonly used in current practice for adult programs. As adults, potential students are assumed to be wiser consumers, partly because they are usually already in the labor force. Also, program feasibility is usually based on the number of students enrolled, since a major part of program costs must be recovered from program participants.

Rate of Return Approach

The rate of return approach is particularly suited for taking advantage of planning as a means to improve efficiency, in contrast to the two previous approaches, which take advantage of planning as a means to avoid shortages and surpluses. In the rate of return approach, focus is on estimating the discounted costs and benefits to individual and society of participating in vocational education (National Planning Association, 1972). Participation in vocational education is viewed as an investment and concern is with the costs and benefits which can be measured in dollars. Discounting of costs and benefits allows a long-range perspective in making planning decisions. Costs to the individual include direct costs for items such as fees, tuition, books, as well as opportunity costs of income foregone while the individual is in school. This approach makes the decision more critical as costs rise, such as in the case for postsecondary programs, where both instructional and opportunity costs may be high for both individual and society.

Information requirements for this approach include detailed estimates of costs and benefits of programs to individual and society. Benefits usually come through follow-up studies of individuals who have participated in the program, focusing on increase in wages. Using this approach, priority is given to programs with the highest net difference between benefits and costs.

Disadvantages involve heavy reliance on past or present data on costs and projections into the future, difficulty of separating consumption versus investment aspect of education, lack of data systems to allow accurate and consistent estimation of costs (let alone benefits), limitation of measuring only those benefits which can be translated into dollars, and the short-run unresponsiveness of wages (a primary benefits indicator) to more education. Advantages are the philosophical perspective of viewing vocational education as an investment and the ability to treat the decision to participate in vocational education as a separate decision for each individual.

Possibilities and Factors

A decision matrix characterizes the possibilities and factors approach, with possible decision alternatives on one dimension and factors or criteria to be used to choose among alternatives on the other dimension (Young, Clive, & Miles, 1972; Iowa Department of Public Instruction, 1974). Several factors can be used in choosing among alternatives; therefore, this approach often encompasses the three previously described approaches in that factors relating to manpower requirements, social demand, and cost and benefits are often included. In addition, factors such as availability of other sources of training, accessibility to handicapped and disadvantaged, and availability of teacher and facilities can be taken into account (Zymelman, Horowitz, Herrnstadt, & Woodruff, 1973; Copa, Geigle, & Imade, 1976). The number of factors is limited only by convenience, availability of information, and the planner's ability to interpret results.

Factors can be considered sequentially with "go/no go" decision rules or considered all at once. Decision alternatives such as the funding of various programs can be contrasted with each other or some standard norm, the latter allowing the consideration of one program at a time. The advantage of this approach is its ability to capture the context of the planning decision at hand; as such it provides the basis for modeling the planning process. Thought and discussion are focused on defining alternatives, defining and weighing factors, and considering trade-offs—these are the very essence of the planning process. The approach often yields as much benefit in going through the planning process as from the resulting plan itself. Disadvantages are the large information requirements as more factors are added, which also lead to increased complexity in interpretation of exactly why a particular alternative was selected and another rejected.

Dynamic Analysis Approach

Dynamic analysis involves consideration of the total system or environment in which planning decisions are made from a perspective that the environment is dynamic, i.e., always susceptible to change. The approach requires the modeling of the planning process with its important variables (Arnold, 1969; Center for Occupational Education, 1973). Both the variables and relationships are considered to be dynamic in that they are expected to change. The result is more emphasis on the planning process and its fit to the environment and less on any one particular plan. The perspective is that the plan is old the moment it is constructed. The techniques used in dynamic analysis include linear programming (McNamara, 1970; Smith, Collins, Hopkins, Isaac & Jain, 1974) and system simulation models; the latter being more dynamic and flexible in depicting the results of a changing environment.

The advantages with dynamic analysis are a closer fit to the real world and the possibility of testing planning decisions with alternative future environments—perhaps even the development of alternate futures not even contemplated with the more static planning strategies. The disadvantages are the requirement for large volumes of information, the development and validation of accurate models, and the increased difficulty of explaining and interpreting why particular decision alternatives are selected; in fact, a very real problem is to sort through the myriad of alternatives to identify those most appropriate to consider.

ISSUES IN PLANNING

With the renewed emphasis on planning called for in new federal legislation and the present state of the art, several issues become important in improving planning for vocational education (Lawrence & Dane, 1974; Morgan, Lawrence & Champion, 1974). First, what skills and knowledge are most important in planning vocational education? A recent assessment of skills required for state planning of vocational education identified seven areas of competence as being important: political, economic, cultural, organizational, personal, and inquiry and communications (Copa & Geigle, 1976). The three most important competencies as judged by state directors for vocational education and executive directors of state advisory councils for vocational education were:

1. Identify, collect, interpret demographic and manpower data for projecting annual and long-range employment needs by occupational category and skill level.
2. Develop measurable vocational education program goals and objectives.
3. Interpret policies and procedures established by State Boards of Education and Vocational Education (p. 58).

If the planning process is to improve, an important aspect is the further education of planners; the questions are where to start and how to deliver.

Second, the state plan for vocational education was originally viewed as a compliance document rather than a plan (O'Reilly, 1975). The challenge is to continue the trend toward developing a "working" plan for vocational education at all levels. The standards for the planning document must be updated as new planning techniques are developed and experienced. For example, most state plans for vocational education contain projected data about vocational education programs and employment, which represent a manpower requirements approach to planning vocational education. This is one of the "first generation" approaches to planning—and many geographic areas may not even be doing an effective job of implementing this relatively simple approach. How is the drastic change in planning practice to be made? Which of the planning strategies or combinations should be selected as a next step in purposefully organizing the complexity which exists to make better decisions about future actions for vocational education?

Third, the planning process uses large volumes of information about past, present, and future (Copa & Geigle, 1976; Morgan, Ballenger & Lawrence, 1974; Drewes, Nerden, Lawrence & Oglesby, 1975). In many cases, the information exists as numbers but validity and reliability are very questionable. An important issue is accurate and comprehensive information as a limitation in the planning process (Porter, 1976; Drewes & Katz, 1975).

Fourth, how can *use* of accurate information be stimulated? Given that the information is available and that it is accurate, the challenge is to get it used in decision making. For this reason, as much thought should be given to the planning process (e.g., identifying the important factors, relationship between factors and goals) as to the gathering of supporting information; they are like "horse and carriage." It may well be that they cannot be developed separately if utilization is an important final criterion.

Fifth, who needs to be involved in planning to assure that plans will be implemented and will represent the needs of the people (Rieder, 1976)? What are the roles of student, parent, labor union, employer, taxpayer in planning vocational education? How are they to be involved? Where in the process is each most effective? New federal legislation on vocational education is unusually prescriptive as to the involvement of others in planning vocational education. Related to this problem is the amount of autonomy to be given to state and local educational agencies in their planning: Which level is best able to make which planning decisions, and how are planning decisions to be articulated?

Sixth, research and development is an essential ingredient in improving the state of the art in planning vocational education. For some of the important needs in improving planning capacity, no new knowledge or product is available. In some aspects of planning vocational education, there is little about which to counsel inservice educational planners. A programmatic research and development program should be developed that focuses particularly on those aspects of planning which are critical and for which knowledge is particularly limited.

Seventh, planning can be overdone. The challenge is to capture the benefits of planning in the planning process without including its negative aspects. Powerful anti-planning arguments can be made when planning limits flexibility, creativity, innovation; limits responsiveness to specialized needs and changing circumstances; and represents plans for the people rather than by the people (Hayek, 1944). Efforts must be made to ensure that the negative characteristics do not describe the planning process used for vocational education. If the production process is relatively efficient, shortages and surplus do not exist (or if they do there are many alternatives and more effective ways of eliminating them), and the environment is relatively stable, then the benefits of intensive and costly planning efforts are indeed likely to be small.

REFERENCES CITED

Arnold, Walter M. *Vocational Technical and Continuing Education in Pennsylvania: A Systems Approach to State-Local Program Planning.* Harrisburg, Pennsylvania: Pennsylvania Department of Public Instruction, 1969.

Braden, Paul V.; Harris, James L.; and Paul, Krisham K. *Occupational Training Information System Final Report.* Stillwater, Oklahoma: Research Foundation, Oklahoma State University, 1970.

Braden, Paul V., and Paul, Krishan K. *Occupational Analysis of Educational Planning.* Columbus, Ohio: Charles E. Merrill Publishing Company, 1975.

California Manpower Management Information System. *Cross-Code Index.* Vols. I-IV. Ventura, California: California Manpower Management Information System, Ventura County Superintendent of Schools Office, 1976.

Center for Occupational Education. *Dynamic Analysis and Strategic Planning: Revised Basic Program Plan.* Raleigh, North Carolina: Center for Occupational Education, North Carolina State University at Raleigh, July 1973.

Copa, George H., and Geigle, Erwin K. *National Conference for State Vocational Education Planning Staffs.* Minneapolis, Minnesota: Minnesota Research Coordinating Unit for Vocational Education, University of Minnesota, November 1976.

———; Geigle, Erwin K.; and Imade, U. O. *Factors, Priorities, and Information Needs in Planning Vocational Education: Views of Selected Educational Planners in Minnesota.* Minneapolis, Minnesota: Minnesota Research Coordinating Unit for Vocational Education, University of Minnesota, March 1976.

———, and Irvin, Donald E., Jr. *Occupational Supply and Demand Information: A Format with Implications for Planning Education for Work.* Minneapolis, Minnesota: Minnesota Research Coordinating Unit for Vocational Education, University of Minnesota, September 1974.

———, and Maurice, Clyde. *People's Need for Additional Job Training: Development and Evaluation of a Procedure for Assessment.* Minneapolis, Minnesota: Minnesota Research Coordinating Unit for Vocational Education, University of Minnesota, November 1976.

———; Persons, Edgar; and Thomas, Paul. "Individual Demand for Vocational Education: Structure and Determination." Minneapolis, Minnesota: Minnesota Research Coordinating Unit for Vocational Education, University of Minnesota, February 1973.

Drewes, D. W., and Katz, D. S. *Manpower Data and Vocational Education, A National Study of Availability and Use.* Raleigh, North Carolina: Center for Occupational Education, North Carolina State University at Raleigh, 1975.

———; Nerden, Joseph T.; Lawrence, John E. S.; and Oglesby, Elizabeth H. *Questions in Vocational Education.* Raleigh, North Carolina: Center for Occupational Education, North Carolina State University at Raleigh, 1975.

Evans, Rupert N. *Foundations of Vocational Education.* Columbus, Ohio: Charles E. Merrill Publishing Company, 1971.

Friedman, John. *Retracking America: A Theory of Transactive Planning.* Garden City, New York: Anchor Press/Doubleday, 1973.

Hayek, Friedrich A. *The Road to Serfdom.* Chicago: University of Chicago Press, 1944.

Iowa Department of Public Instruction. *Iowa Priority Program Areas Requiring Specialized Training of Less than Baccalaureate Degree.* Des Moines, Iowa: Iowa Department of Public Instruction, 1974.

Kidder, David E. *Review and Synthesis of Research on Manpower Forecasting for Vocational-Technical Education.* Columbus, Ohio: The Center for Vocational Education, The Ohio State University, February 1972.

Lawrence, John E. S., and Dane, J. K., eds. *State Vocational Education Planning: An Assessment of Issues and Problems.* Raleigh, North Carolina: Center for Occupational Education, North Carolina State University at Raleigh, 1974.

Lecht, Leonard A.; Teeple, John B., and Paredes, Maria-Aurora. *Relating Manpower and Demographic Information to Planning Vocational-Technical Education.* Washington, D.C.: Center for Priority Analysis, National Planning Association, September 1970.

McNamara, James F. *A Mathematical Programming Model for the Efficient Allocation of Vocational Technical Education Funds.* Harrisburg, Pennsylvania: Bureau of Educational Research, Pennsylvania Department of Education, 1970.

———, and Franchak, Stephen J. *Planning Vocational Education Programs in Pennsylvania: Guidelines for the Use of Labor Market Information.* Harrisburg, Pennsylvania: Research Coordinating Unit, Pennsylvania Department of Instruction, 1970.

Morgan, Robert L.; Ballenger, William L.; and Lawrence, John E. S. *Management Information Systems for Vocational Education: A National Overview.* Raleigh, North Carolina: Center for Occupational Education, North Carolina State University at Raleigh, 1974.

———; Lawrence, John E.; and Champion, Douglas W. *A National Survey of Problems in State Planning for Vocational Education.* Raleigh, North Carolina: Center for Occupational Education, North Carolina State University at Raleigh, 1974.

Moss, Jerome Jr.; Smith, Brandon B.; and Copa, George H. "Some Major Concepts in a Rationale for Education for Work (Career Education)." Unpublished manuscript. Minneapolis, Minnesota: Minnesota Research Coordinating Unit for Vocational Education, University of Minnesota, 1972.

National Planning Association. *Policy Issues and Analytical Problems in Evaluating Vocational Education.* Final Report, Parts I and II. Washington, D.C.: Center for Priority Analysis, National Planning Association, 1972.

O'Reilly, Patrick A. *The State Planning Process in Vocational Education.* Project Baseline Supplemental Report. Flagstaff, Arizona: Project Baseline, Northern Arizona University, December 1975.

Ozbekhan, Hasan. "The Emerging Methodology of Planning." *Fields Within Fields,* no. 10 (Winter 1973-74), 63-80.

Porter, G. William. *Data Needs in Vocational Education.* Vol. I, Summary of Procedures and Results, Project EDNEED I. Raleigh, North Carolina: Center for Occupational Education, North Carolina State University at Raleigh, March 1976.

Rieder, Corine H. "Planning for Vocational and Technical Education in the United States: Context, Process, Issues." Paper presented at the International Conference on Vocational Education, Denver, Colorado, June 1976.

Smith, Gene H.; Collins, Bill D.; Hopkins, Charles O.; Isaac, Margaret P.; and Jain, Rakesh. *The Development and Testing of a Linear Programming Technique for Optimizing Occupational Training Program Combinations.* Stillwater, Oklahoma: Oklahoma State Department of Vocational and Technical Education, 1974.

U.S. Congress. *Title II—Vocational Education.* P.L. 94-482. Washington, D.C.: Government Printing Office, October 12, 1976.

U.S. Department of Labor. "Matching Occupational Classifications to Vocational Education Program Codes." *Tomorrow's Manpower Needs,* Supplement 3 (revised). Washington, D.C.: Government Printing Office, 1975.

———. "Occupational Manpower and Training Needs: Information for Vocational Counseling and Planning for Occupational Training." *Bulletin* 1824. Washington, D.C.: Government Printing Office, 1974a.

———. "Occupational Supply: Concepts and Sources of Data for Manpower Analysis." *Bulletin* 1816. Washington, D.C.: Government Printing Office, 1974b.

Young, Robert C. *Manpower Demand: Information Guidelines for Educational, Vocational Education, and Manpower Planning.* Columbus, Ohio: The Center for Vocational and Technical Education, The Ohio State University, June 1973.

———; Clive, William V.; and Miles, Benton E. *Vocational Education Planning: Manpower, Priorities and Dollars.* Research and Development Series no. 6B. Columbus, Ohio: The Center for Vocational Education Research, The Ohio State University, 1972.

———; Zoints, Stanley; and Bishop, Albert B. *Linear Programming for Vocational Education Planning.* Columbus, Ohio: The Center for Vocational and Technical Education, The Ohio State University, December 1973.

Zymelman, Manuel; Horowitz, Morris; Herrnstadt, Ernie; and Woodruff, Alan. *Cost Effectiveness of Alternative Learning Technologies in Industrial Training—A Study of In-Plant Training and Vocational Schools.* Bank Staff Working Paper no. 169. Washington, D.C.: International Bank for Reconstruction and Development and International Development Association, December 1973.

Cost-Benefit Analysis and Cost-Effectiveness Analysis in Education and Vocational Education

J. Robert Warmbrod

During the past several years writers and researchers have given special attention to the economics of education in general and to the economics of vocational education in particular. Since a primary purpose of vocational education is preparation for employment, vocational education programs are, in some respects, more amenable to an economic assessment of benefits and costs than is education in general or some of the other special-purpose programs within the public educational system.

As with many public social programs, vocational education is being subjected to rigorous economic analysis, which necessitates that costs and benefits, both monetary and nonmonetary, be quantified. Onc assertion is that vocational education programs should be required to meet the test of economic efficiency and that alternative methods for achieving the objectives of vocational education should be identified and compared in terms of costs and benefits to each other and to present programs. The concern includes not only the efficient use of resources allocated to vocational education, but also a consideration of alternative programs to which present or additional funds can be allocated for accomplishing the purposes of vocational education. Actually, the argument is that the costs of vocational education must be justified on the basis of outcomes. An important part of this argument is that the more common measures of the

---

Portions of the chapter are drawn from the author's *Review and Synthesis of Research on the Economics of Vocational-Technical Education* (1968).

economic utility of vocational education, such as percentage of graduates employed and percentage of graduates working in occupations for which they were prepared, are inadequate and incomplete measures of the economic benefits of vocational education.

The purpose of this chapter is to provide an orientation to some general concepts of the economics of education and to the application of cost-benefit and cost-effectiveness techniques to the assessment of vocational education programs. The writing and research cited are primarily the efforts of economists whose special interests and expertise include the study of the economics of education and the application of these concepts and techniques to the study and analysis of vocational education at the secondary and postsecondary levels.

ECONOMICS OF EDUCATION

The two basic questions that underlie much of the research on the economics of investment in education have to do with how much more or how much less should be invested in education in general and how much more or how much less should be invested in specific types of education (Hansen, 1967). Both issues are of concern to vocational education, particularly the second, which has specific and direct implications.

There are limits to the amount of public funds available for education. In contrast, the demand for expenditures for education is virtually unlimited. Consequently, the allocation of resources to education in general and to various types of educational programs become crucial issues. Kraft (1968) maintained that research on the economics of education will be extremely influential as a basis for policy decisions for guiding education in the future. Weisbrod (1966b), citing education as an area of human resource development that is making rapidly climbing demands upon public funds, cautioned that choices concerning the allocation of resources are not likely to be wise choices when they are made without recognition of the benefits and costs of alternative uses of resources.

There appears to be general agreement with the position that education is a vital element in economic growth. However, the relative contributions of general education and occupational education to economic growth and development have not been delineated clearly. The realization that investment in education contributes to economic growth has led to a new look at the interdependence of the educational system and the occupational structure of the labor force (Woodhall, 1967). The result is that educational planners and policy makers are placing increasing emphasis on future manpower requirements in determining the need for expansion in education and for the allocation of funds within education.

One implication is clear. The study of the economics of education has special relevance to vocational education. It is important that the economics of education become, if it is not now, a primary concern of persons involved in planning, conducting, and evaluating programs of vocational education.

Education and Earnings

Research has shown consistently a favorable relationship between an individual's educational attainment, subsequent income, and prospects for employment (Weisbrod, 1966b; Levin et al, 1971). Innes, Jacobson, and Pelligrin (1965) formulated the following conclusions about the relationship between education and earnings: (1) for males at all ages, annual income increases as years of schooling increase; (2) total lifetime income increases as educational attainment increases; (3) the favorable relationship between income and educational attainment has persisted through the years, even though the amount of formal schooling attained by the population has increased; and (4) when lifetime income is discounted or equated to return on current investment, the contribution of additional education to earnings is positive and significant.

Rate of Return on Investment in Education

The rate of return approach for assessing the economic returns to education involves the relationship between investment outlays and benefits. The present value of lifetime income differentials associated with various levels of education is compared with the incremental costs of the different stages of education. Then net returns from different types of education are compared. Benson (1967) concluded that, in general, returns to education as seen from a societal point of view compare favorably with the yield of investment in physical capital. Schultz (1967) cited evidence showing very high private rates of return to elementary schooling, high returns for high school, and private rates of return to college education that are comparable to private rates of return on other private investments.

Schultz (1967) assessed the use of rates of return as a guide for allocating resources to education and for allocating resources within the educational sector. He maintained that the question of efficient allocation of resources to education was important because education absorbs a large share of our resources; thus, misallocations within education and between education and alternative expenditures could be wasteful. Although the responses of students (and parents) and the decision making bodies that organize and operate schools to changes in rates of return have not been analyzed, Schultz contended that historical evidence indicates that such responses are occurring and that, in general, the responses are in the right directions.

Education and Economic Growth

Those who study economic development in the United States have concluded that education is a significant contributor to economic growth. The basic idea relating investment in education to economic growth is that education has positive effects on the development of human talent and the development of talent, in turn, has positive effects on economic growth (Kraft, 1968). Education produces a labor force that is more skilled, more adaptable to change, and more likely to develop imaginative ideas, techniques and products that are critical to the process of expansion, growth, and adaptation to change. So education, by contributing to worker productivity, is a process of investment in human capital (Weisbrod, 1966b).

Schultz (1963, 1967) stated that investment in schooling is a major source of human capital. Schultz (1963) differentiated the consumption component (immediate satisfaction that people obtain from schooling) and the investment component, which includes future consumption and future producer capability. He maintained that contributions to schooling increase future productivity and earnings.

External Benefits of Education

Most of the research pertaining to the economic benefits to education is based on the assumption that all the benefits of education are captured by the recipient and that none of the benefits of the recipient's education improve the well-being of his neighbors, his employer and co-workers, or society in general (Schultz, 1963). Weisbrod's research (1964) revealed, however, that there are benefits from education to people other than the immediate recipients of that education. Benefits to persons other than the immediate recipient and to persons other than those in the school district in which the education is provided are referred to as external benefits of education.

Weisbrod (1964) categorized persons receiving external benefits from a student's education into three groups: (1) residence-related beneficiaries who benefit by virtue of some relationship between their place of residence and the place of residence of the recipient of education—within this category are included the current family of the student, the future family of the student (intergenerational benefits), neighbors, and taxpayers both in the immediate community of the student and in other communities; (2) employment-related beneficiaries who benefit by virtue of some employment relationship with the recipient of education; and (3) society in general.

COST-BENEFIT ANALYSIS

Cost-benefit analysis is an evaluative technique that relates the total value of benefits of a program to the total costs of the program. Cost-benefit analysis, first used to assess costs and benefits of natural resource development projects, has as its main focus the optimum allocation of resources (Kaufman et al, 1967; Hu et al, 1969). This method is designed to help decision makers maximize benefits for a given level of costs or to minimize costs for a given level of benefits (Kotz, 1967a, 1967b).

The application of cost-benefit analysis to vocational education requires that benefits as well as costs be expressed in monetary terms. Benefits that cannot be expressed in monetary terms cannot be included in the analysis. Spiegelman (1967) pointed out that benefit-cost analysis of vocational education programs permits the assessment of a particular program or project (Does the sum of the benefits of the program or project exceed the sum of the costs?) in addition to permitting comparisons of specific programs or projects (How do the costs and benefits of one program or project compare to the costs and benefits of other programs?).

Identification of Costs and Benefits

The first step in the application of cost-benefit analysis to vocational education is the identification of the costs and benefits of a given program. Both individual and social costs must be quantified in monetary terms, an accomplishment that is termed virtually impossible by Kaufman et al (1967). Mangum (1967) contended that many of the benefits and some of the costs of social programs are nonquantifiable, thereby leaving broad areas of assessment to assumption and judgment.

Individual or private benefits have been defined as the welfare gained by an individual as a result of education. Davie (1967, 1968) listed the following as individual benefits: (1) additional earnings attributable to vocational education net of taxes; (2) fringe benefits associated with additional earnings; (3) stipends received, if any, while enrolled in a vocational-technical program; (4) value of the option to enter other educational programs in the future; and (5) increased psychic benefits. Benefits to society or welfare gained by society as a result of education were listed as the gross additional earnings of individuals attributable to vocational education, the effects of reducing transfer payments, and better citizenship and reduced costs to society of bad citizenship.

Hardin (1967) defined social costs as the value of the productive resources consumed by providing an educational program. The resources include instructional resources; administrative resources; additional resources used by trainees because of training, e.g., travel expenditures of trainees; and opportunity costs of foregone earnings, since the productive manpower of trainees is not available to society while the training course is in progress. Stromsdorfer (1967, 1972) argued that within the context of vocational education, the treatment of costs in a cost-benefit model requires a generalized concept of costs. That is, all costs should be viewed as opportunity costs, for part of the costs of training students in a given skill are the foregone opportunities resulting from the fact that resources used in the training effort cannot be used elsewhere. Stromsdorfer (1967) listed the following types of costs that should be considered: (1) current costs, including items such as teachers' salaries, heat, light, and costs from nonschool system support; (2) capital costs for both physical plant and instructional equipment; (3) cost correction factors to adjust for the fact that nontaxed public resources will buy more goods and services in the market place than taxed private resources; and (4) foregone earnings of students. Private or individual costs of participating in a vocational program are usually categorized as foregone earnings of students and additional expenses incurred while attending school, such as tuition, books, and transportation (Davie, 1967, 1968; Kaufman et al, 1967).

Economists who have conducted cost-benefit studies of vocational education report that the cost data available are highly inadequate. Dueker and Altman (1967) studied 16 comprehensive and 16 vocational schools to identify the kinds of costs and related data that could be obtained to aid in planning and evaluating programs of vocational education. They found that the available cost data do not readily lend themselves to coherent analysis and that cost data pertaining to vocational education are not kept in a way that makes them accessible for rigorous analytic and evaluative purposes. They concluded that data are not easily obtained for realistic cost-benefit studies of vocational education.

Conceptual and Methodological Problems

There are important conceptual and practical problems involved in the application of cost-benefit analysis to vocational education. Davie (1965) and Kaufman et al (1967) emphasized that basic to cost-benefit analysis is the concept that comparisons between programs must be on the basis of marginal or additional costs and benefits. Specifically applied to vocational education, this means that comparisons between vocational education and academic education must be based on the extra costs of training youth in the vocational curriculum and the extra benefits accruing to students in the vocational curriculum.

Estimating the effects of training for a particular training program is a difficult problem. Hardin (1967) stated that the effects of training on output variables cannot be estimated quantitatively and with a great deal of accuracy unless a control group design is used in the analysis. He maintained that the best design is to compare the output variables of trainees with those of comparable nontrainees. Stromsdorfer (1967, 1972) and Weisbrod (1966a) pointed out the conceptual problems associated with a control or comparison group. Of particular importance is the fact that the study group and the comparison group will usually have different socio-demographic characteristics, values, motivations, and other characteristics that affect their labor market experience after completion of a training program. Stromsdorfer pointed out that statistical techniques can help control the differences between the study and comparison groups, but that the different patterns of interaction between variables and within the two groups can never be completely controlled. Hardin (1967), Stromsdorfer (1967), and Weisbrod (1966a) discussed the conceptual issues involved in measuring benefits of occupational education programs.

Discounting Costs and Benefits

Following a quantification of both costs and net benefits in monetary terms, the next step in cost-benefit analysis is the discounting of future costs and benefits to a stream of annual benefits and costs of the program. As Davie (1965) and Hardin (1967) pointed out, both costs and benefits of a training program occur over a period of time; hence, each must be converted to apply to a particular point in time. These converted values, referred to as the present value of costs and benefits, are calculated by discounting the future benefits and costs back to a selected point in time with a chosen rate of discount. The discounted benefits and discounted costs are then summed to obtain the present value of benefits and present value of costs, which will be compared by the benefit-cost ratio. The choice of an appropriate rate of discount is an issue that should be studied carefully by those contemplating cost-benefit analysis research.

Benefit-Cost Ratio

The benefit-cost ratio equals the present value of net benefits divided by the present value of costs. Given the methodology and other assumptions and limitations involved in cost-benefit analysis, the decision rule is as follows: When the benefit-cost ratio exceeds unity, the corresponding activity is economically superior to an alternative activity with a lower benefit-cost ratio. If purely economic efficiency criteria are to be used in determining the investment decision, then the projects or programs chosen first should be those having the highest benefit-cost ratios. Similarly, projects or programs having benefit-cost ratios less than one should not be undertaken. Both Davie (1967, 1968) and Hardin (1967) cautioned, however, that the decision maker may elect to consider additional criteria of a noneconomic nature in the decision making process.

Limitations of Cost-Benefit Analysis

As the foregoing indicates, there are several problems and limitations in evaluating programs of vocational-technical education through cost-benefit analysis. Kaufman et al (1967) cautioned that cost-benefit analysis has disadvantages when applied to programs of education. Davie (1965) listed the following limitations of cost-benefit analysis when applied to educational programs: (1) the treatment of benefits which cannot be measured in monetary terms; (2) the comparison of monetary benefits among different individuals; (3) the search for the best possible programs; and (4) the treatment of benefits which accrue outside a particular community. Kaufman (1967) listed the problems and limitations of cost-benefit analysis as including the following questions: What costs and benefits are to be included? How are costs and benefits to be valued? At what interest rate are costs and benefits to be discounted? What are the relevant constraints? Dueker and Altman's study (1967) of the availability of cost and performance data pertaining to vocational education revealed that an organized body of performance data did not exist and that available cost data were not readily adaptable to analysis.

Rothenberg (1975) described cost-benefit analysis as "a broad emphasis on the importance of carefully sifting out the balance of desirable and adverse consequences of an explicitly formulated set of mutually exclusive alternatives." He indicated also, however, that cost-benefit analysis has attractive strengths as a procedure for providing a detailed framework for sifting out the desirable and adverse consequences in certain more narrow and specific choosing situations. Rothenberg concluded that the usefulness of cost-benefit analysis

> will be most decisively at the mercy of the availability of data. Very serious inadequacy of relevant data exists in almost every area for which cost-benefit analyses have been undertaken. To some extent this has been, and can be, bypassed by sheer human ingenuity in reformulating problems and reconstructing data. But ingenuity is not a perfect substitute for data availability. Analyses in most fields suffer from crude measures in some categories and total exclusion in others (Rothenberg, 1975, 88).

COST-EFFECTIVENESS ANALYSIS

Given the conceptual and practical constraints on the application of cost-benefit analysis to educational programs, economists propose that cost-effectiveness analysis is the more appropriate technique for the objective evaluation of vocational education (Hardin, 1967; Kaufman et al, 1967). Cost-effectiveness analysis of education is a methodological framework for making numerical estimates of the effects of particular training activities on selected output variables and the estimates of the costs of obtaining these effects.

Measuring Benefits

In cost-effectiveness analysis, output variables serving as indices of benefits of specific programs are retained in their raw form. The outputs need not be economic in nature and do not have to be expressed in monetary terms (Hardin, 1967; Kaufman et al, 1967). Hardin listed one group of output variables that pertain to the trainee's performance at the end of training. Examples of these types of variables include the trainee's knowledge, skills, motivation, and other behaviors that may be measured by direct observation or by oral or written tests.

A second group of output variables refer to the trainee's labor market performance. Illustrations of these types of benefits include annual earnings (hourly earnings and annual hours worked), employment stability, labor force participation, skill level of regular job held, degree of utilization of training knowledge and skills in employment, receipt of unemployment insurance benefits or welfare assistance, and geographic mobility. The issues and problems of estimating the effects of training on the output variables (e.g., the necessity for a control group design and the selection of appropriate comparison groups) encountered in cost-benefit analysis are equally applicable to cost-effectiveness analysis.

Effectiveness-Cost Ratio

The outcome of cost-effectiveness analysis is a statement concerning the effect that a particular activity has on selected output variables and on the cost of the same activity. The statement may be in the form of a ratio or in a form that specifies certain effects associated with the costs of the program (Hardin, 1967). It should be emphasized that the application of cost-effectiveness analysis does not require that costs of a program be related to its output variables. Kaufman et al (1967) proposed that it may be useful to study costs of vocational programs separately from the outputs of vocational programs. An obvious advantage of cost-effectiveness analysis over cost-benefit analysis, as a technique for evaluating vocational education, is that it avoids the restriction which requires that all benefits be quantified in monetary terms.

Levin (1975) pointed out that cost-effectiveness analysis must be used with wisdom and caution. Although the case for carrying out cost-effectiveness analyses of social alternatives is a strong one, he cautioned that:

> The conceptualization and measurement of both costs and outcomes have not and probably cannot be routinized. Accordingly, the judgments of the evaluator in setting out decision rules and guidelines for estimating costs and effects represent a crucial variable in determining the outcome of the evaluation. The omission of particular cost components or program outcomes, the selection of a particularly high or low discount rate for future costs or results, and the method of estimation of costs of program ingredients all represent areas where different judgments may alter appreciably the cost-effectiveness ratings of alternatives. The preoccupation with means-ends relations at the expense of considering processes also represents a bias of the approach (Levin, 1975, 118).

SUMMARY

The research of economists indicates clearly that education

is a vital element in economic growth and that investment in education yields a relatively high rate of return both to the individual and to society. It is within the theoretical framework of the economics of education that research on the economics of vocational education must be conducted.

Research on the economics of vocational education is essential if adequate data are to be available for making informed decisions concerning the allocation of resources to occupational education. Data pertaining to the economics of vocational education will bear heavily on policy decisions about occupational education, including the question of what agencies, public schools or otherwise, can conduct occupational education programs most efficiently. If vocational educators want to be involved in the important policy decisions, they must become familiar with the research and concepts of cost-benefit analysis and cost-effectiveness analysis.

The usefulness of cost-benefit analysis as an evaluative technique in vocational education is limited by the requirement that benefits as well as costs be quantified in monetary terms. The more appropriate technique for evaluating vocational education is cost-effectiveness analysis, which allows non-economic as well as economic benefits to be related to the costs of educational programs. Serious questions can be raised about whether either adequate benefit or cost data are available for meaningful and valid economic assessments of vocational education. Vocational educators can make a significant contribution to realistic appraisals of vocational education by identifying and developing appropriate techniques for quantifying appropriate cost and performance data for use in cost-effectiveness analysis.

Warmbrod (1968, 1971) and Stromsdorfer (1972) have reviewed and analyzed research on the economics of vocational education. Ghazalah (1972) and Conroy (1976) have conducted and reported studies relative to the costs and benefits of vocational education programs in Ohio and Massachusetts, respectively. Persons interested in the specific outcomes of cost-benefit and cost-effectiveness analyses of vocational education programs should refer to these reviews and reports.

REFERENCES CITED

Benson, Charles S. "Economics and Education." *Review of Educational Research* 37 (February 1967): 96-102.

Conroy, William G., Jr. "Secondary Voc Ed Measures Up as Positive Investment." *American Vocational Journal* 51 (November 1976): 44-48.

Davie, Bruce F. "Using Benefit-Cost in Planning and Evaluating Vocational Education." Paper prepared for David S. Bushnell (ED 016 077). Washington, D.C.: Bureau of Research, U.S. Office of Education, November 1965.

Davie, Bruce F. "Benefit/Cost Analysis of Vocational Education: A Survey." *Occupational Education: Planning and Programming.* Vol. 2. Edited by Arnold Kotz. Menlo Park, Calif.: Stanford Research Institute, September 1967, 309-30.

Davie, Bruce F. "Cost-Benefit Analysis of Vocational Education: A Survey." *Hearings before the General Subcommittee on Education of the Committee on Education and Labor, House of Representatives, Ninetieth Congress, First Session on H.R. 8525 and Related Bills, A Bill to Amend the Vocational Education Act of 1963.* Part 1. Washington, D.C.: U.S. Government Printing Office, 1968, 105-17.

Dueker, Richard L., and Altman, James W. *An Analysis of Cost and Performance Factors in the Operation and Administration of Vocational Programs in Secondary Schools.* Pittsburgh: American Institutes for Research, October 1967.

Ghazalah, Ismail A. *The Role of Vocational Education in Improving Skills and Earning Capacity in the State of Ohio: A Cost-Benefit Study.* Athens, Ohio: Ohio University, 1972.

Hansen, W. Lee, ed. "Symposium on Rates of Return to Investment in Education." *Journal of Human Resources* 2 (Summer 1967): 291-374.

Hardin, Einar. "Summary Guide for Effectiveness/Cost and Benefit/Cost Analyses of Vocational and Technical Education: A Report of the Conference." *Occupational Education: Planning and Programming.* Vol. 2. Edited by Arnold Kotz. Menlo Park, Calif.: Stanford Research Institute, September 1967, 379-86.

Hu, Teh-wei, et al. *A Cost Effectiveness Study of Vocational Education: A Comparison of Vocational and Non-Vocational Education in Secondary Schools, Final Report.* University Park: Institute for Research on Human Resources, Pennsylvania State University, March 1969.

Innes, Jon T.; Jacobson, Paul B.; and Pelligrin, Ronald J. *The Economic Returns to Education: A Survey of Findings.* Eugene, Ore.: Center for the Advanced Study of Educational Administration, University of Oregon, 1965.

Kaufman, Jacob J. "The Role of Cost-Benefit Analysis in the Evaluation of Vocational and Technical Education." Paper presented at the American Vocational Association, Cleveland, Ohio, December 1967.

Kaufman, Jacob J.; Stromsdorfer, Ernest W.; Hu, Teh-wei; and Lee, Maw Lin. *An Analysis of the Comparative Costs and Benefits of Vocational Versus Academic Education in Secondary Schools.* Preliminary Report, Project no. OE 512. University Park, Pa.: Institute for Research on Human Resources, October 1967.

Kotz, Arnold, ed. *Occupational Education: Planning and Programming.* Vol. 1. Menlo Park, Calif.: Stanford Research Institute, September 1967a.

Kotz, Arnold, ed. *Occupational Education: Planning and Programming.* Vol. 2. Menlo Park, Calif.: Stanford Research Institute, September 1967b.

Kraft, Richard H. P., ed. *Education and Economic Growth.* Proceedings of the First Annual Conference on the Economics of Education. Tallahassee, Fla.: Educational Systems Development Center, Florida State University, 1968.

Levin, Henry M. "Cost-Effectiveness Analysis in Evaluation Research." *Handbook of Evaluation Research.* Vol. 2. Edited by Marcia Guttentag and Elmer L. Struening. Beverly Hills, Calif.: SAGE Publications, 1975.

Levin, Henry M.; Guthrie, James W.; Kleindorfer, George B.; and Stout, Robert T. "School Achievement and Post-School Success: A Review." *Review of Educational Research* 41 (February 1971): 1-15.

Mangum, Garth L. "Evaluating Vocational Education: Problems and Priorities." *Occupational Education: Planning and Programming.* Vol. 1. Edited by Arnold Kotz. Menlo Park, Calif.: Stanford Research Institute, September 1967, 65-90.

Rothenberg, Jerome. "Cost-Benefit Analysis: A Methodological Exposition." *Handbook of Evaluation Research.* Vol. 2. Edited by Marcia Guttenberg and Elmer L. Struening. Beverly Hills, Calif.: SAGE Publications, 1975.

Schultz, Theodore W. *The Economic Value of Education.* New York: Columbia University Press, 1963.

Schultz, Theodore W. "The Rate of Return in Allocating Investment Resources to Education." *Journal of Human Resources* 2 (Summer 1967): 293-309.

Spiegelman, Robert G. "A Benefit/Cost Framework for Education." *Occupational Education: Planning and Programming.* Vol. 2. Edited by Arnold Kotz. Menlo Park, Calif.: Stanford Research Institute, September 1967, 359-77.

Stromsdorfer, Ernest W. "Economic Concepts and Criteria for Investment in Vocational Education." *Occupational Education: Planning and Programming.* Edited by Arnold Kotz. Menlo Park, Calif.: Stanford Research Institute, September 1967, 331-57.

Stromsdorfer, Ernest W. *Review and Synthesis of Cost-Effectiveness Studies of Vocational and Technical Education.* Columbus, Ohio: Center for Vocational and Technical Education, The Ohio State University, 1972.

Warmbrod, J. Robert. *Review and Synthesis of Research on the Economics of Vocational-Technical Education.* Columbus, Ohio: Center for Vocational and Technical Education, The Ohio State University, November 1968.

Warmbrod, J. Robert. "Economics of Vocational-Technical Education." *Contemporary Concepts in Vocational Education.* Edited by Gordon F. Law. Washington, D.C.: American Vocational Association, 1971, 362-73.

Weisbrod, Burton A. *External Benefits of Public Education, An Economic Analysis.* Princeton, N.J.: Industrial Relations Section, Princeton University, 1964.

Weisbrod, Burton A. "Conceptual Issues in Evaluating Training Programs." *Monthly Labor Review* 89 (October 1966a): 1091-97.

Weisbrod, Burton A. "Investing in Human Capital." *Journal of Human Resources* 1 (Summer 1966b): 1-21.

Woodhall, Maureen. "The Economics of Education." *Review of Educational Research* 37 (October 1967): 387-98.

Decision Making Investments in Vocational Education

Charles O. Hopkins

Vocational education decision makers are almost constantly faced with economic problems and issues which stem from a variety of sources. Some citizens think that vocational education is a poor investment of public funds and assert their opinions during public meetings and at the polls. The consumers of vocational education who invest their time, effort and money to prepare for and retain employment in a satisfying occupation must be served effectively and efficiently; limited resources force economic decisions relating to priority of service among groups to be served. There are special needs clientele, the identification and training of whom calls for careful planning of investments. Instructional and instructional support personnel pose certain economic problems—teacher education, for example. The purpose of this chapter is to discuss decision making investments associated with vocational education as they relate to these factor groups.

MAJOR ECONOMIC ISSUES OF VOCATIONAL EDUCATION

Certain people think that vocational education is a waste of resources. These individuals may not be knowledgeable about vocational education, or they may not realize that the nation requires a well-trained work force if economic health and national safety are to be maintained. Furthermore, they fail to realize that most of us must be employed in order to maintain our desired standard of living, and to obtain and retain a position, we must cultivate the required skills, knowledge and attitudes associated with our employment. With approximately 80 percent of the nation's work force employed in jobs requiring less than a professional degree, it becomes increasingly important for educational institutions to provide opportunities for individuals to receive vocational and technical training.

Economic Value of Vocational Education

The economic benefits to be gained from vocational and technical education are many. Surveys have shown that the percentage of employment among those who have received vocational or technical training is much larger than for the population that has not been trained and is seeking employment. The fifth annual report of Project Baseline (a study mandated by Congress and conducted by Northern Arizona University) shows a continuing high employment record of vocational education completers compared to the total labor force in similar age groups. In February 1976, more than a million students from the preceding year were employed and only 150,000 were known to be unemployed. The total labor force unemployment rate at that time for the 16-19 year age group was 19.9 percent, while for secondary vocational completers it was only 13.5 percent. In the 20-24 year age group the rates were 13.6 percent for the total labor force and 8.2 percent for postsecondary completers (Lee, 1976, 33 & 37).

The report concludes: "Two years in a row of consistently higher employment rates for vocational education students than for those without vocational training in a tight money market cannot be ignored. It is probably one of the reasons for the accelerating national interest in vocational enrollment" (Lee, 1976, 35).

If business, industry and other types of employment require a trained work force, the investment in vocational education is a sound one. Not only are people employed, but the money that they return to society in the form of taxes is increased significantly. One study showed that the cost of occupational training was returned within two or three years (Oklahoma State Department of Vocational and Technical Education, 1974). The "pay-back" in that study was based on entry-level income of an average, unmarried 18-year-old who had been trained in a vocational program offered in that state. The same procedure might be used to measure the impact of vocational training on the reduction of welfare recipients.

Vocational education has a responsibility to segments of the population such as welfare recipients. In many instances, those who receive vocational training are able to become self-sufficient. Many times the subsidized individual has a skill but it may need updating, or the person may need to be trained for another type of employment. In either case, the training should result in employment and a reduction in the number of payments for welfare. Another subdivision of the population upon which vocational education has a large impact is that of potential dropouts and individuals who have already dropped out of the formal education system. These people usually have the ability to learn a skill and enter the labor force. In many schools programs are designed to teach dropouts and potential dropouts to learn a skill whereby they can obtain employment and make a contribution to society, thus preventing them from becoming welfare clients.

These social benefits relate to recipients of vocational education; the other facet of economic value pertains to employer and community benefits. Naturally, one of the first assets an industry looks for in a community is the availability of trained workers or, in the absence of such, the capability of a community to provide the training needed for that work force. Employers often credit the vocational training programs of a state or district as being the real reason they chose that particular location to expand or to establish a new facility. If an industry is of sufficient size, it will require some supporting service businesses. So the community receives the benefit not only of the industry, but also of the related service businesses, which provide more opportunities for employment. An incoming industry usually provides a community with real economic gains; it helps increase the school's tax base, raise the real income of individuals, and provide an increased tax base for the state.

Allocation of Resources

One of the most formidable problems faced by vocational education decision makers is the difficulty in obtaining adequate resources. Once the financial resources have been acquired, the next problem for a decision maker is the allocation of those resources among the many client groups who need training. One of the first decisions to be made is whether to allocate the resources to meet the needs of people or the needs of employers. A vocational education decision maker must do both, and this is not an easy task. The allocation of resources depends on the philosophy and objectives of the institution in question.

Many people feel strongly that program planning should be based upon the needs of the people to be trained. Others feel that vocational programs should respond to the needs of business and industry within the local community, region, state or nation. The ultimate decision probably should be a combination of the two; consideration should be given to all beneficiaries of the service. The two needs are not incompatible.

Vocational education is characterized historically by a scarcity of resources and an abundance of needs to be served—a typical economic phenomenon. Its resources may be grouped into four categories: authority, money, personnel and time. These resources must be managed in such a way that they will provide the most satisfaction for the amount invested, which is the crux of the problem.

Society has imposed on vocational education responsibilities for helping solve some of its critical social problems, among them training the disadvantaged—a worthy but usually costly service. This imposes additional demands on available resources. It is essential that surveys of the disadvantaged who need vocational training be specific and accurate, since this type of training is costly and entails risk. Estimates based on general population counts may not provide the kind of training that should be offered. It is a waste of resources to start training programs when it is doubtful that those trained will be employed upon completion of their programs. Probably the worst critics of vocational and technical education are individuals who have been trained and are unable to find employment.

Other factors must also be considered when allocating resources: Which sectors of the population should receive resources? At what educational levels should the training be offered? Which geographical locations should be served? Economically speaking, it is better to offer programs in which representative employers have indicated that there are reasonable employment opportunities.

Vocational Education Finance

Vocational and technical education is more costly than most other educational programs offered by our schools, and someone must pay for the additional costs. Vocational education usually requires more space than other types of education, especially if the particular program utilizes a shop or laboratory. The equipment used is more specialized and usually more expensive than that used in general education. These factors become constrictions for many decision makers, particularly when considering the offering of new or expanded programs.

Wide variations in methods of financing local education programs cause real problems. Many local education agencies would like to offer a larger variety of vocational programs to give students more training options, but the financial base of the school district does not permit this to happen. Largely for this reason, the financing of vocational and technical education has become a joint endeavor of local education agencies, the state, and the federal government. Moreover, this joint funding endeavor must continue to provide the needed occupational training. If local school districts are serious about meeting the population and manpower needs of their communities, increased emphasis must be placed on vocational education.

As this increased emphasis becomes reality, state governments must participate in financing vocational and technical education to a larger extent. There seems to be general agreement that the federal government should continue to increase funding for national priority programs and for persons with special needs for vocational and technical education, and that it should assist in offsetting the increased cost of training. Some states are not providing their share of the financial resources necessary to meet the requirements of their populations. State governments will need to give vocational education a higher priority.

Another possible source of increasing vocational training resources is for employers to help finance training programs that are geared to a specific type of work. For example, where training programs are designed to upgrade productivity within a particular business or industry, perhaps those enterprises which benefit from the training should contribute to its cost.

It also seems reasonable that individuals whose skills are being updated or upgraded could take part in financing their training. Once local, state and federal governments have furnished preparatory occupational training, and those who have completed the training are placed in relevant jobs, then those who wished further training in their field might contribute toward the cost of that training. Such individual inputs would be a small part of the total cost of training, but they probably would pay a large share of the operating costs. A major cost of a training program is the initial cost, which includes building and equipment. It would be extremely difficult for individuals and for businesses and industries to participate to a large extent in financing educational programs on a continuous basis.

Vocational Education Planning

Successful coordination of vocational training with manpower training needs is crucial to the development of viable occupational training programs. Vocational education is often criticized for not being able to diversify its offerings to meet manpower needs. Diversification of offerings is difficult because these needs frequently are not communicated to the agencies that are responsible for implementing the programs. It is essential to devise a system which will allow occupational training funds to be spent in the areas where a need for trained workers exists.

Program planning would be an easy task if there were enough resources to offer training programs in all of the areas needed by industry and business. Since resources are inadequate, the task of planning becomes one of determining the best way to allocate available resources to make an impact on the demands in the most critical areas. Where several critical areas exhibit a need, a method has to be devised to fill them.

Macro-Planning. A procedure known as macro-planning is essential for decision makers. This system consists of establishing priorities among the occupational areas from high to low demand and for the population groups to be served. The underlying concept is that training programs should be offered in the demand areas that show the greatest need for trained manpower and that serve the target populations. From the priority areas that evolve, educational agencies should be asked to consider possible offerings when expanding their systems. This information should be used as a guide; there are bound to be exceptions to the established priorities. These exceptions occur when an educational agency has a need for a training program that is not reflected in the macro-level priorities.

Whether a local educational agency has a need for training may not be established until a needs survey has been conducted. If a need exists for training in the particular area surveyed, the program should be approved. This procedure may be contrary to much current thinking about the way needs for programs should be identified by educational agencies, but it has proved to be a necessary step. One of the nationwide criticisms of vocational education is that programs are initiated in areas where there is little likelihood for students to locate employment. If vocational education decision makers are to be accountable for the use of funds, they must be given some input into the direction that training should take in order to meet manpower demands and serve the target population needs at the macro level.

Vocational education philosophy and planning. The philosophy and objectives of those responsible for planning influence the outcomes of instruction. The traditional belief that training to meet the needs of business and industry takes precedence over the career choices of students affects the outcomes of instruction. An example of what happens when that philosophy prevails is as follows: When a director of a school indicates that there is a need for expansion of training, the decision makers (state board, local board, or others) give that institution a list of manpower needs for their area of interest. The school administrator can then use this information to survey the student body for students who would like to enroll. This procedure is widely used by the administrators who participate in program planning at the local level. Decision makers do not dictate to the educational agency which programs should be initiated, but rather show them the priority areas that fit the manpower training needs.

The greatest obstacle facing vocational program planners is the fact that the limited resources available for program expansion or redirection each year are not allocated to the programs that make the greatest contribution to the economy and the training needs of business and industry. Facing this problem has created an awareness that other methods must be developed to ascertain which programs should be offered.

Linear Programming. Linear programming is a procedure that can be used to forecast the training programs needed. This method allows the decision maker to examine rationally the available alternatives which would produce the best return to whatever objectives were stated. A difficult task is the selection of objectives necessary to generate the kind of program that vocational education hopes to achieve. The system provides a method of rational decision making because judgment is removed from the final task—the process would not work if several alternatives were not available to the decision makers. Some of the alternatives that are available to a decision maker are: to maximize the entry-level wages of persons trained, to maximize the total number of jobs filled, to maximize the placement of students, to minimize the cost of training, and to maximize the number of students served. The process allows the decision maker to assemble the data and to examine what the decision would be if one of the objectives mentioned above were maximized In order to do this, a large amount of data must be available.

There are several constrictions under which the system operates: First, more training programs in a particular area than the manpower demand allows cannot be implemented. Second, an unlimited pool of potential trainees from which to draw does not exist—the aptitudes and abilities of many do not meet occupational requirements. Third, there is a limited amount of capital to be invested in operations, new buildings and equipment. The advantage of linear programming is that once the information is available to decision makers, a tool is available for utilizing the data and arriving at the best possible alternative.

Several benefits can be derived from a rational approach: First—as mentioned earlier—it reduces the chances of human error and bias in planning. Second, it facilitates the matching of a particular population group's interests, abilities and aptitudes with requirements of the occupational area, which results in the initiation of training programs that promise the greatest return on investment. Third, it allows educators to work with industries, to show employer groups the profiles of the population groups of a given geographical area that would be suited to the industry. Fourth, the process can be reversed to indicate the types of industries or industrial development that should be sought by the community to maximize the economic potential of the population. Finally, it provides the decision makers at the macro level with the information necessary from the standpoint of capital investment in facilities, equipment and operations to meet the needs of the population and business and industry.

Any constraint or restriction can be inserted into the model, and an alternate plan or objective can be developed and examined in order to induce better decisions pertaining to the kind of training programs that should be offered. Such alterations may result in reducing the cost of training and in achieving the greatest output from available resources.

A planning issue. A recurring question is whether decision makers should try to include programs for new and emerging occupations as a regular planning procedure. This is a critical issue facing vocational educators today. It is extremely difficult and dangerous to establish training programs for new and emerging occupations because there is a possibility that this manpower will not be needed.

There are some ways that this problem can be dealt with: A contingency fund can be budgeted to meet the needs of new and emerging occupations. A special division can be created to keep in contact with the industrial development of business and industry. When a new or emerging occupation is identified by business or industry, the agency responsible for providing a trained work force can provide specialized training until an ongoing program is established to meet the manpower requirements. This process would give vocational education a great deal of flexibility in meeting training needs.

INVESTMENTS AT VARIOUS EDUCATIONAL LEVELS

When vocational education should begin and where it should be offered are issues that are continuously being debated by decision makers throughout the nation. Vocational education has a place at all levels in our educational system, and its contributions at the various levels should be considered as educational systems are designed.

Occupational Awareness and Exploration

Recently much emphasis has been placed on the occupational awareness and exploration stages of vocational development and their bearing on occupational preparation within our school system. With the present composition of the work force, students should be made aware of what career opportunities are available and suitable for them to pursue. Cultivation of this awareness should start in the early grades and continue into the exploration stage at the junior high level in our school system. Too often, the first time that a student is introduced to vocational education or to any type of occupational training is when that individual enrolls in a vocational training program to prepare for a career already chosen. This situation has created many problems in motivation, most of which stem from not knowing enough about career alternatives to make the proper selection of an occupational field.

Our society has used the educational system as a method of upward social mobility. This concept has contributed to pressure on students to continue their schooling at least to the baccalaureate degree to prepare for professional employment. This is worth consideration, but other alternatives may be as appropriate for a given individual. An investment in career awareness and exploration programs would be very beneficial to the educational process. It would allow students the opportunity to realize what a large variety of job opportunities exist throughout society and give them an opportunity to explore careers before entering a specific training program. Skill training programs likely would have a greater retention rate. Students probably would enroll in programs compatible with their interests, aptitudes and abilities. This would permit much more efficient and successful program operation beyond the occupational awareness and exploration stages.

Secondary School Vocational Programs

Some critics have indicated that vocational education should be offered only after students have completed the secondary school requirements. This would create many problems in our educational system. As students progress through secondary school, they begin to prepare themselves for the career that they hope to pursue at the completion of high school. The intent of vocational education offered at the secondary level is to enable students to learn the skills necessary to earn a living after completion of their formal education. This practice does not prohibit students from continuing their education beyond the twelfth grade if they want to acquire a higher degree of skill or knowledge before entering the work force; but it allows those students who do not choose to continue their formal education, or who cannot afford postsecondary education, the opportunity to receive training that will make them economically self-supporting.

Additional reasons supporting secondary school level vocational education may be gleaned from the school and work history of 18-25 year-olds: A large portion of our population enters the labor market at age 18. Data in some states show that at the end of the freshman year in college approximately 40 percent of the students do not register for the second year. Also, a large percentage of the junior and community college students do not complete their second year. National data indicate that approximately 25 to 30 percent of the students who enroll in college as freshmen complete a baccalaureate degree. Placement and follow-up data collected by the state departments of education and reported to the U.S. Office of Education indicate that 18-year-olds usually do obtain employment if they have received skill training while enrolled in the secondary schools.

Another factor to be considered is the public school commitment to prepare all students with a saleable skill by the time that they complete their 12 years of training. Vocational education is just as important at the secondary level as any of the curricula offered and even more important to students who terminate their formal education after high school graduation. A survey of approximately 1,200 manufacturing industry employers in Oklahoma revealed that they would employ high school graduates at 18 years of age if they were properly trained in a skill (Harris, 1971). Information such as this, coupled with the employment record of high school graduates of vocational training programs, makes a strong case for offering vocational education at the secondary level.

When deciding whether or not to offer vocational instruction at the secondary level, a number of factors should be considered: (1) It requires an enormous amount of resources to provide the facilities and equipment necessary to reach the large number of students requiring training in order to enter the labor force. (2) The most opportune time and place for vocational education is while the students are still in their local community and in the local school environment. (3) It is much more economical for students to learn occupational skills in secondary programs than in other ways. (4) Many more postsecondary institutions would be required to reach the number of students who need to be trained.

Postsecondary Vocational Education

A strong need exists for training beyond the high school level for persons who wish to improve their skills. The secondary schools are engaged primarily in training students to enter the labor market at entry levels. Their initial jobs may be at the lower end of the pay scale. To enable students who have completed secondary training to improve their skills (and salaries) upon entering the labor market, it is necessary to offer instruction at a higher skill level. Many times, the job market demands that workers possess a higher level skill, i.e., at the technician or the semi-technician level.

Many students who have completed their secondary schooling have never been exposed to occupational education of any type. Persons who enroll in the four-year college programs frequently discover that it would be more advantageous to obtain training at the skilled and technician levels, rather than pursuing a baccalaureate degree. Postsecondary institutions should provide for this segment of the population.

Persons who become disenchanted with their current employment may wish to enroll in training institutions in order to redirect their careers. This can be accomplished at the postsecondary level. There are many sources where students can learn postsecondary-level skills, such as junior and community colleges which offer an associate degree that can be earned during a two-year period. Junior and community colleges have been criticized because they emphasize transfer credit to baccalaureate degree-granting institutions. This criticism is becoming a thing of the past. Many junior and community colleges have very strong vocational education departments at the associate degree level and have programs designed to teach a complete spectrum of needed skills.

Area vocational-technical institutes. Since 1963, area vocational-technical training institutes have assumed an important postsecondary training role. Area vocational-technical institutes (AVTIs) are not limited to postsecondary instruction. Frequently these institutions also conduct programs for the secondary and part-time adult populations. Area schools make programs feasible in many of the high-cost training occupational groups where small schools cannot afford to have a comprehensive program of vocational and technical education. AVTIs have taken on many designs. Some of the schools are state supported; some are part of a junior college system; and some are tax-base schools in districts that are autonomous school districts within a state. Regardless of the way an area school is formed, the instruction given in these schools usually is of high quality. They are not designed to offer degree credit, but to teach skills which will allow the recipients to earn a certificate upon completion of the requirements. There are exceptions to this description, but basically these are the characteristics of AVTIs.

Some interested parties wonder whether the AVTIs are needed. These institutions entered the vocational education scene at a time when very little postsecondary vocational and technical training was offered by the public schools. Since 1968, emphasis has been on postsecondary instruction, and colleges and other institutions have begun to redesign their programs to meet the changing manpower demands of business and industry. When the area schools were introduced, they were designed to offer a comprehensive program of vocational education for secondary and postsecondary students, as well as for adult workers within a community. These schools are community based, with emphasis on meeting the population needs and manpower needs of business and industry.

AVTIs have contributed immensely to the improvement of the image of vocational education. It was thought in the past that vocational education was for low achievers—that is, for someone else's children. Today's AVTIs provide high-quality instruction and have been the primary means for increasing the scope of vocational education. A primary purpose of area schools is expressed in the 1968 Vocational Education Amendments, Declaration of Purpose, namely that these schools serve "... persons of all ages in all communities of that State. . . . [with instruction that is] realistic in light of actual or anticipated opportunities for gainful employment and which is suited to their needs, interests, and ability to benefit from such training" (U.S. Congress, 1968). They are community-oriented training institutions that are trying to meet the needs of the various populations within that community.

Technical institutes. Technical institutes throughout the United States also offer postsecondary instruction. One of their missions has always been to prepare students at the post-high school level to enter the labor force. Technical institutes have contributed significantly to the promotion of vocational education at the post-high school level. Their graduates enter the labor market well trained and highly skilled at wage levels that enable the training institutions to attract well-qualified applicants for the various training programs.

It is almost impossible to discern whether all of the institutions engaged in postsecondary vocational education are essential to current training needs. There doesn't seem to be an oversupply of vocational instruction. Nationally, postsecondary vocational education is barely scratching the surface of population needs for training. Program duplication is not evident. Each of the occupational area programs is designed for a specific purpose and for a particular population. All types of institutions seem necessary in order to provide the comprehensive postsecondary training required by the present labor force.

Comprehensive versus specialized institutions. While all types of institutions may be needed to fulfill the needs of the various population groups and occupational area manpower demands, research is needed to identify the most effective and efficient delivery systems for the several types of needs. Postsecondary educational institutions may be divided into two broad categories—those whose primary orientation is vocational education and those favoring broader general educational outcomes. Each may be more appropriate for particular areas of occupational preparation. If vocational education goals are secondary to the mission of the institution, then the use of the resources allocated to them will not provide as much return on investment as the use of resources that are placed in institutions that have training as their primary goal.

The primary mission of area vocational-technical schools and technical institutes is to help people prepare for employment. AVTIs have provided a strong incentive for business and industry to establish themselves within local communities where such institutions exist by providing the kind of training required to maintain their labor force.

AVTIs basically have the capability of providing occupational training to individuals at less cost to the student than do the junior and community colleges. The primary reason for this is that the area schools have their own tax base and are able to absorb the bulk of the training cost. Junior and community schools, on the other hand, usually charge tuition for registration in vocational skills courses directed toward employment.

Adult Vocational Education

Adult vocational education, whether it be for occupational preparatory or supplementary purposes, is one of the most rapidly growing educational fields. It also is a level of vocational education that is very confusing to many decision makers because there are so many alternatives to examine. The problem is where to invest capital in order to reap the highest returns in terms of meeting population and manpower needs. Adult vocational education calls for much more flexibility than that of the secondary and postsecondary levels, particularly that of the occupational supplementary type, because most participants are employed and are subject to the time constrictions of earning a livelihood.

Preparatory training. The area which definitely would contribute the highest return to investment—either to the individual or to society—is preparatory training which teaches beginning skills to workers who plan to enter an occupation field. Included among the enrollees in adult preparatory classes are workers from other fields who want to be retrained in a new occupational field. Another type of student in the preparatory program is the unemployed worker who once held a position but for some reason—economic or technological change or personal—finds that he/she is unable to use the skills possessed. Returns on investment in training the unemployed are economically rewarding because these individuals do not contribute significantly to the economy of a community, state, or nation; in addition, they may be drawing unemployment compensation or receiving welfare payments. Thus, adult preparatory training helps the economy and decreases the burden of taxpayers.

Supplementary training. Supplemental instruction consists of training for the purpose of updating or upgrading the workers' competencies. *Updating* means bringing the worker up to date in the area of instruction; *upgrading* means preparing the worker for promotion to higher rank within the occupational field for which the instruction is being given. Both types of supplemental training need to be designed for specific target populations. Some decision makers believe that the cost of this type of training should be primarily the responsibility of the recipients and not a burden of the taxpaying public.

Avocational instruction. Some of the most popular instruction that is taking place today is in the avocational realm. Skills are taught, but individuals are enrolled in these programs in order to learn an avocation—something that they can use during their leisure time. It is commonly agreed that the cost of this investment should be the sole responsibility of the individuals who are cultivating the skills for the avocation of their choice.

Unfortunately, most states stress training at the secondary and postsecondary levels and leave the financing of adult vocational education to the individual. Adult vocational education instruction should receive increased support in the near future. The return on investment in training on this educational level is relatively high.

VOCATIONAL EDUCATION INVESTMENTS IN TRAINING PERSONS WITH SPECIAL NEEDS

Since the Vocational Education act of 1963 and particularly since the 1968 Amendments and the 1976 legislation, individuals with special needs have become a primary target group for vocational education. Resources have been appropriated and special allotments of funds have been designated to meet the training needs of this group. Vocational education has been assigned the task of assisting with the solution of social problems relating to today's youth. Decision makers have been charged with the responsibility of training the educationally disadvantaged, the physically handicapped, the economically deprived, the emotionally disturbed and the mentally retarded. A real need for occupational instruction exists among the members of these groups. Also, if individuals with such needs can be taught the skills that qualify them for gainful and useful employment and help them develop a sense of accomplishment and a feeling of self-confidence, this training is well worth the cost of investment.

The cost of providing this type of instruction is extremely high, largely because of the low student-to-teacher ratio and the additional time and services required. Costly as it may be, the investment is a good social investment. Many of the people who are classified as disadvantaged or handicapped can be prepared for employment. If the handicapped and disabled do not acquire saleable skills, they cannot gain employment, thus becoming a financial burden to society. They may develop a pessimistic outlook on life and lack a feeling of self-esteem.

The investments and returns to society and individuals for groups with special needs are difficult to measure compared to the regular population. Critical questions facing decision makers are: What priorities should be assigned to these groups in the total vocational and technical operation, and at which levels should resources be allocated in order to reach them? Is it economically and socially more beneficial to allocate the available resources to the general population? Is it a good investment to use a large percentage of the resources for high-cost training required by those with special needs? Most decision makers tend to favor the regular population and manpower needs. Current trends seem to be in the direction of satisfying those with special needs, equipping them with saleable skills and directing them into the mainstream of education and employment.

TEACHER EDUCATION AS AN INVESTMENT

One of the most critical limitations in the expansion of vocational education today, and in the future, is the restricted supply of competent teachers. Frequently there are occupational programs that should be started in response to manpower and population needs, but the unavailability of capable teachers prevents them from being implemented. Supply and demand for teachers is one of the most critical problems in vocational education—one that requires a high degree of sophistication on the part of decision makers. Teachers are a prime factor in the quality of instruction. This teacher quality factor is reflected in the productivity and occupational adjustment of those who have completed a training program. If quality instruction is not maintained, recipients of the training will not meet the population and manpower needs and lesser returns to social and private investments will ensue.

Many workers have the skills and knowledge necessary to hold a job, but they lack the competencies necessary to teach others effectively. Too frequently, an error is made by organizing a training program without carefully investigating the availability of well-qualified instructors, then conducting a search to find an instructor who fits the program. This situation must be corrected if quality vocational education instruction is to be offered. Certification requirements frequently have to be relaxed in order to temporarily certify an individual to teach a class. Unfortunately, some of these individuals are not strong teachers of the subjects and the program suffers from complaints of dissatisfied students or disgruntled employers of graduates. The fact that students are not motivated to learn may very well imply that the teacher is not able to provide instruction that is relevant to the needs of students. Certification standards should be scientifically developed and adhered to.

Inservice teacher education is extremely important for both the teachers who have been prepared in an undergraduate vocational teacher education program and for those recruited from business and industry. The type of preparation given at the preservice baccalaureate degree level by established teacher education departments may not produce the type of teacher that is needed to cope with the needs of today's technology in some of the occupational training areas—hence, established teachers need inservice updating. Since many of the instructors are recruited from business and industry, they should be given inservice training to increase their skills and improve their teaching practices. Also, there is a strong possibility that teachers who remain in the teaching profession for a number of years may become stagnant and fail to keep abreast of innovations in the areas that they teach. Inservice teacher education should be offered on a carefully planned continuous basis.

Teacher resources must be considered as a limiting factor in planning and establishing vocational education at present. This limitation is just as important as the capital resources required to establish training programs. Any time that a limited resource exists, there is a problem for vocational education decision makers who are trying to provide high-quality instruction at all educational levels.

REFERENCES CITED

Harris, James. *The Employment Acceptability of Eighteen-Year-Old Vocational-Technical Education Graduates in Oklahoma Manufacturing Industries.* Occupational Training Information System, Supplement II (VT 013 050). Oklahoma State Department of Vocational and Technical Education: 1971.

Lee, Arthur M., project director. *Learning a Living Across the Nation.* Vol. V, Project Baseline, Fifth Annual Report. Prepared for U.S. Office of Education and the National Advisory Council on Vocational Education. Flagstaff, Ariz.: Northern Arizona University, November 1976.

Leverenz, Susan K.; Hopkins, Charles O.; and Stevenson, William O. *Management by Objective Implementation Sequence.* Stillwater, Okla.: State Department of Vocational and Technical Education, January 1963.

Oklahoma State Department of Vocational and Technical Education. *The Development and Testing of a Linear Programming Technique for Optimizing Occupational Training Program Combinations.* (OEG-0-72-0699. ED 118 746.) Washington, D.C.: U.S. Department of Health, Education, and Welfare, Office of Education.

U.S. Congress. House. *An Act to Amend the Vocational Education Act of 1963 and Other Purposes.* H.R. 18366, 90th Cong., 1968.

Programmatic Investments in Vocational Education

Carl J. Schaefer

We educators understand remarkably little about the cost of the product we produce—educated youth. This chapter focuses on the investments (costs) in vocational education programs. It explores the pursuit of efficiency in production by explaining selected economic principles in an educational setting and by comparing education to business and industry. Finally, it describes and raises questions about the economics of advisory committees, some delivery systems, and the career education concept. See Chapters 2, 3, and 8 for underlying economic concepts.

ECONOMIC ANALYSIS

One of the most important tasks of business management is to select the most effective and efficient combination of the factors of production in order to produce economic goods and services at the lowest possible cost per unit of output. Business and industrial management, operating as they do in a competitive profit motivated economy, must be cost conscious—something relatively obscure in the educational enterprise. Business and industry must seek the most efficient combination of production factors in order to maximize profits. Quantitative generalizations based on tested economic analyses are a major concern to business management. Briefly stated, two such theoretical generalizations are as follows:

1. Diminishing marginal returns. Initially, when we add more and more equal amounts of a variable input—such as students—to a fixed input—such as teachers and a school facility—we reap increasing returns, but

eventually the amount of extra returns—such as graduates, measured by some index of proficiency—will begin to decline.

2. Economies of scale. By increasing *all* of the factors of operation at the same time and in the same degree—such as doubling *all* inputs—you may find that output such as graduates, measured by some index of proficiency—will more than double. This phenomenon is called *increasing returns to scale.*

Diminishing Marginal Returns

Whatever school business managers may think of the achievements of the theoretical economists in their refinement of production analysis, they normally recognize certain quantitative generalizations as being basic to the technical task of proportioning the factors of production.

For example, given a teacher and fixed shop or laboratory facilities, we may want to experiment to see how large a marginal increase—additional input of students—we can add before diminishing returns are reached. Note in Table 1 that with no increase in the number of students (marginal increase) there is no extra output (marginal return). Now we increase the class size by adding five students to the same amount of teacher input and shop or laboratory equipment and facilities, and if all goes well we should graduate five more students who meet our standards—indexes of proficiency—which happens. When we add another five students, making a total of 25, we realize a marginal return of six graduates rather than five, and our marginal rate of return ratio (marginal return divided by marginal increase) has increased from 1.0 to 1.2. Again we increase the size of the class by five to a total of 30. This time the marginal increase over a 25-student class has returned to five, or a ratio of 1.0. Another increase of five results in a marginal return of three, or a ratio of .60. Soon we reach a point where our marginal return no longer exists and adding more students reduces the number of graduates.

When the class reached a total of 30 students, it became subject to the principle of eventual diminishing returns; the marginal increase—extra output—was reduced by one graduate. Finally, a point was reached where there was no marginal return at all, and when more students were added the number of graduates was less than that of the 15 students

Table 1

EVENTUAL DIMINISHING RETURNS: STUDENT/TEACHER RATIO

Marginal Increase (extra input)	Total No. of Class Members	Total No. of Graduates	Marginal Return (extra output)	Marginal Rate of Return (ratio)
0	15	13	0	
5	20	18	5	+1.0
5	25	24	6	+1.2
5	30	29	5	+1.0
5	35	32	3	+ .60
5	40	32	0	0
5	45	27	-5	-1.0

of the original class. Why did this happen? The falling off of returns results from the fact that the new amounts of marginal input (students) provide less and less of the fixed resources to work with. That is, less of the teacher and less of the shop or laboratory facilities are available to each student, to the point where the students do not receive adequate instruction to meet the index of proficiency.

Economies of Scale

An economic phenomenon that is different from our controlled variation of one factor at a time, such as demonstrated by the law of diminishing returns, deals with the scale of operations. That is, by increasing *all* of the factors at the same time to the same degree—say doubling all inputs—you may find that your output is more than doubled, which is called *increasing returns to scale.*

In our example of adding students while holding teachers and shop or laboratory facilities constant, we eventually reach a point where the return changes to less and less. But if we had increased inputs of teachers and shop or laboratory facilities, we might have been able to more than double the extra output of students. See Figure 1. By increas-

Figure 1

INCREASING RETURNS TO SCALE

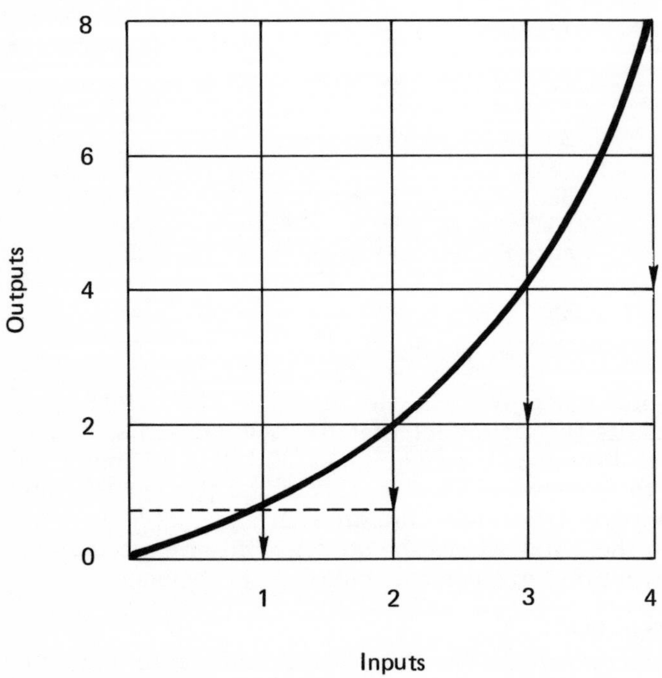

NOTE: When moving from 1 to 2 inputs, we have achieved but constant (equal) output (returns). But at input 3 the returns are double that of point 2, and at point 4 they are doubled again—the benefit of mass or increasing returns to scale. This idealistic situation rests on the assumption that all inputs are variable.

ing *everything,* certain so-called *economies of mass* become operative, involving such factors as reduced cost of supervision and overhead,[1] which make it worthwhile to organize a fairly large operation. If only a few students are to be taught, it isn't rational to establish elaborate training facilities; but if a large number of students are to be prepared continuously, then a greater investment in all of the cost factors may be warranted.

When trying to reach the point of increasing returns to scale, it is important to keep in mind that economies or savings may require changes in production methods. Merely adding another teacher and building another identical shop or laboratory facility will achieve very little economy. However, by teaming an additional teacher with the first teacher, and by adding facilities and equipment which can be used by both, it may be possible to offer a far better program at less cost and with superior results, as verified by our index of proficiency. Unfortunately, very little such thinking has been applied to the expansion of education, with the result that when new facilities have been built and a new staff hired, they usually have perpetuated a one-teacher, one-classroom concept. Thus, any saving only reflected economies of scale through economies of overhead such as administration. Perhaps it is time to think of the fuller use of the economies of scale principle?

Cost of Quality Products

A complex index of proficiency or quality performance by those who have completed their training is required for the operation of an effective and efficient vocational-technical education program. If standards of performance could be agreed upon (e.g., standards dealing with related technical knowledge and manipulative proficiency), it would then be incumbent on program evaluators to quantify the cost factors needed to produce the desired quality of workmanship. Decision makers would then be able to determine what it costs to produce one graduate in terms of capital outlay and operating expenses to meet such a standard. The formula used would be:

$$\text{Cost per Student} = \frac{\text{Cost of Inputs Used to Meet an Index of Proficiency}}{\text{Number of Students Enrolled}}$$

Moreover, if an index of proficiency can be agreed upon and maintained, the cost per student can be changed by varying either the inputs used or the number of students enrolled. Efficiency in arriving at the index of proficiency would then be ascertained by comparing one combination of program inputs with other combinations until the one which produces a product at the least cost without reducing the quality of graduate is obtained. A common example of program comparison, which will be discussed later, is to juxtapose in-school and cooperative education approaches to training certain kinds of workers. Moss and Stromsdorfer point out that it is the complexity of measurement (index of proficiency) of the product of vocational education that continues to plague us.

> . . . the problem of evaluating vocational education is confounded by the fact that its objectives and its outputs are multi-dimensional. The proper specification of its objectives with their relative weights has never been performed. Second, a successful development, weighing and estimation of performance indexes to represent these multiple objectives has never been achieved (Moss and Stromsdorfer, 1971).

When dealing with all of the behavioral objectives of our program, of course, we fall into this multidimensional trap. What appears to be needed is to focus on one of the dimensions (objectives) at a time, and it is the contention of this writer that the place to start is with related technical and manipulative proficiency. This would at least answer the question of what it costs to prepare a graduate who possesses the accepted entry-level skills required of an employee in a given field.

Cost-Benefit Analysis

Moss and Stromsdorfer (1971), as well as others (Corazzini, 1966; Kaufman, 1968; Swanson, 1969; Tomlinson & Rzonca, 1971; Soong et al, 1971; Lee, 1974; Lecht, 1974) have focused on the problem of the costs and benefits of vocational education. *Benefits,* we know, are both of a monetary and a nonmonetary type and have been defined as any outcome of the vocational education process that increases an individual's or society's well-being. Cost-benefit analysis is presently being carried on despite certain methodological and data control handicaps. Such handicaps are also reflected in the determination of "least cost" and exploring the economies of scale with which this chapter deals.

Whether educators realize it or not, they make economic decisions continually. When vocational decision makers decide to start a new program, they have made an assumption that benefits will exceed costs. Otherwise, why invest in a new program at all? The point is, educators should "think economics" explicitly with data, and not just off the tops of their heads.

THE ECONOMIC ORGANIZATION OF VOCATIONAL EDUCATION

Absurd as it may seem in the minds of many educators that there is any parallelism between mass production and education, some analogies do exist.[2] Not unlike the investments that make up vocational education, the tools, machines and equipment used in modern mass production represent a tremendous cost—as do land, buildings, materials used, and other features of modern manufacturing. Although mass production is known best for the manufacture of great quantities of goods, it is distinguished from all previous types of production by its scientific planning and expert management. This expertise, when coordinated with the best-known operating techniques, produces a product of uniform quality at the lowest feasible unit cost.

To carry the analogy between mass production and vocational education one step further, it needs to be pointed out that the essential elements which are considered in mass production have some relevance to those found in the mass vocational-technical programs of today. For example, Table 2 summarizes the parallelism between mass production investment and investments in vocational education.

1. *Graduated learning:* In comparison with the element of mass production—simplification of product production—our objective in vocational education always has been to simplify learning and to move from the simple to the complex. Probably the best example of this is in the teaching of manipulative skills. Here it is a fact that the more complicated skills cannot be mastered before those that are more basic. Thus, by virtue of our "graduating" the learning process we have simplified it.
2. *Commonality in teaching:* As one travels from state to state, or even to other nations, and observes the teaching of vocational subjects, the pedagogy is surprisingly similar. Thus, in a sense we have standardization of parts, much the same as in mass production. For example, the exchange of teachers and processes for the same subject field would be quite similar from one state to another, if not identical.
3. *Use of teaching aids and hardware:* Whereas industry

Table 2

MASS PROTECTION AND INVESTMENTS IN VOCATIONAL EDUCATION

Elements of Mass Production	Elements of Mass Vocational-Technical Education
1. Simplification of product production	1. Graduated learning—basic courses—moving from simple to more complex.
2. Standardization of parts	2. Commonality of teaching as from one teacher to another
3. Use of production and machine tools	3. Use of teaching aids and production of skill and knowledge—the principle of learning by doing and "hands on"
4. Careful arrangement of machines and materials in sequence, combined with continuous motion	4. Physical facilities arrangement, organization and sequence of the curriculum leading to continuous upward movement in the process
5. High volume in quantity and quality	5. Expansion of programs and enrollments, quality control built in by proficiency examinations and testing
6. Planning and coordination of all activities relative to production and distribution (considered the most important of all mass production elements)	6. Planning through the use of advisory committees, community surveys, follow-up studies, assessments and modification of programs

uses production and machine tools, teachers use teaching software and hardware. The intent is to establish a learning environment based on the principle of learning by doing. To accomplish this, the "tools" of teachers reflect those most likely to produce anticipated learnings.

4. *Physical facilities arrangement:* The arrangement of our facilities (shops and laboratories) reflects the best thinking for carrying out the learning process. Like industry, which must have a continuous flow, the flow of education is provided through sequencing of curriculum and through the upward movement of students into more complex courses during the learning process.

5. *Program expansion and quality control:* Vocational education expansion during the last decade is a known fact. But expansion—increasing the volume, as it is called in business and industry—carries with it the need for product quality maintenance. The quality control of all education, including vocational education, is being questioned more and more. Perhaps it is here in the realm of product control that the gap in the parallelism between industry and education is widest. Obviously, some type of quality control needs to be incorporated into the educational system, and vocational education should move toward proficiency or competency based measures.

6. *Planning and coordination:* Planning and coordination through the use of advisory committees, community surveys, follow-up studies, and the like are strongly advocated in vocational education. Just as in industrial production, where the planning and coordination is considered the most important of all managerial functions, so should it be in vocational education.

Therefore, it is not totally unreasonable to suggest that we as vocational educators not only have the obligation and responsibility to those who supply the dollars (taxpayers) for our operation, but we should also be concerned about the cost and quality of education for those we educate. The entire notion of planning, so amply emphasized in the Education Amendments of 1976, becomes imperative when program costs are considered.

THE ECONOMICS OF ADVISORY COMMITTEES

If the planning and coordination functions are considered to be the most important in keeping down the cost in manufacturing, it stands to reason that they are also important in the vocational education enterprise. The use of advisory committees to help plan vocational-technical offerings has been one of the fundamental practices followed by vocational education since its inception. The rest of education is only now discovering the use of advisory committees, as evidenced by the "Eighth Annual Gallup Poll of the Public's Attitudes toward the Public Schools" (Gallup, 1976) when 90 percent of the respondents (parents and others) indicated they would like to serve on educational citizens' advisory committees.[3]

Admittedly, up to this time vocational education advisory committees have been preoccupied with such problems as occupational surveys, verification of course content, equipment and supplies, facilities planning, providing accurate occupational information, and financing and support of proposed legislation (American Vocational Association, 1969). All of these considerations are an important contribution to the functions of vocational education. One might ask, however, have our advisory committees been used effectively enough in coping with the economic aspects of these problems? In fact, if we are concerned about efficiency, it would be interesting to study the difference in operating costs between vocational schools using advisory committees and those that do not.

The "in-kind" dollar and cents contribution of advisory committee membership, if priced out, represents literally thousands of dollars to vocational education at the local level.[4] These highly successful business, industry and labor leaders are chosen for the skills they possess—one of which is in the area of finance. School boards, needless to say, have the final responsibility for budgets and costs; however, they cannot possibly be attuned to all the planning (including costs) involved in providing for and operating the multitude of vocational and technical programs normally offered.

With this in mind, as well as the recognition of the dollar and cents "in-kind" contribution of the advisory committee, vocational education stands to capitalize on such a resource to even a greater extent than in the past.

Just as in the production of a product, good planning saves money, so should good planning in vocational education save dollars. Program planners in this sense need the help of cost-minded individuals such as advisory committee members to help assess the cost factors involved in the educational process. How much did it cost to produce our graduates this year? How effective are they—in a quality control sense? How many were employed? How can the program be improved? These are not only legitimate questions, but ones for which advisory committees are needed when finding the answers. And it should be obvious that the finding of such answers through the use of advisory committees represents dollar and cents savings.

THE ECONOMICS OF DELIVERY SYSTEMS

Vocational education programs have been delivered in a variety of ways, such as in-school programs, cooperative programs, work-study programs and combinations of all three. When a school administrator says, "My school provides vocational education curricula for its students," it is difficult to know just what delivery system(s) he is talking about. And it would make little difference if we assumed that each of the approaches produce the same results. It does, however, make a difference if resources are limited and the variance in cost is large.

In-School Programs

The customary practice is to provide vocational programs as part of a regular in-school offering. It is generally agreed, administratively, that there are fewer problems with this approach regardless of its cost.

Obviously the cost of (or investment in) a vocational program varies within the in-school setting. Theoretically, operating costs by program can be determined by analyzing *direct* expenditures (operating expenditures) such as: teachers' salaries, supplies, instructional materials, heat and light, maintenance of equipment and the like. *Indirect* costs include, among other things, a calculated percentage of administration, custodial services, general maintenance, counseling, and so forth. *Capital* costs consist of investments in such items as the physical facility, land, equipment.

Although operating cost accounting (direct and indirect) for the expenditures made in educational systems would appear to be important, this is not in evidence. All of the studies that have been made, including the more recent "cost-benefit analysis" undertakings, have reported great disparity in the bookkeeping process. Thus, at this time it is next to impossible to determine accurately, by vocational program, what the investments are. Evidence indicates that, in aggregate, the greatest amount is spent by school districts on business and office education programs and the least on distributive programs, with the other fields in descending order being: trade and industrial, home economics, technical, agriculture, and health occupations. This, of course, still does not tell us the comparative costs of each program. In fact, it is impossible to determine amounts of federal dollars spent by program even though enrollments by program are reported (U.S. Department of Health, Education and Welfare, 1973).[5]

Doty (1976), in a study presently under way, has attempted to determine the average cost per pupil for providing vocational education in a comprehensive high school, a full-time AVTS (area vocational-technical school), and a shared-time AVTS. Although this study is but a pilot in nature, the initial data comparisons are worth reporting.

It is obvious from Table 3 that the shared-time AVTS approach (where several school districts cooperate in providing a vocational facility) results in the least cost both for operating and capital expenditures. In contrast to this, the comprehensive school accounts for the highest and the full-time area vocational schools fall in between. Moreover, in each case, the vocational programs are the most costly when comparing them with the college preparatory and general curricula. Although no reason for this difference is given in the Doty (1977) report, it is evident that the shared-time AVTS approach does not include a number of the *indirect* costs, such as physical education program costs, that are found in the other two full-time institutions. The fact that vocational programs cost more in the full-time comprehensive high school than in the full-time area vocational schools is somewhat surprising.

Somers (1971), by averaging several per-pupil vocational cost studies based on pre-1970 data, arrived at what he considered to be a very conservative figure of $1,253 per pupil.[6] Kaufman (1971) found the marginal costs of vocational versus nonvocational senior high school curricula to be from $100 to $220 higher for the vocational student. Thus it would appear, at least for the operating costs of vocational education, that the per-pupil cost runs somewhere around $1,500 regardless of program type, and the vocational "added" costs over the nonvocational costs are in the neighborhood of $200 per pupil. It is submitted that such a differential is not an unreasonable added investment to make in the vocationally oriented student—an investment which may be the last investment of public funds if the student does not continue with postsecondary public schooling.

Table 3

AVERAGE COST PER PUPIL PER TYPE OF EDUCATIONAL GOAL (OPERATING AND CAPITAL EXPENSES) 1973-75

Type of Program	Comprehensive High School	Full-Time AVTS	Shared-Time AVTS
	Operating plus Capital Expenses		
College Preparatory	$3,942	---	$2,519
General Curriculum	$4,035	---	$2,309
Vocational Education	$4,799	$4,060	$3,813*
	Operating Expenses Only		
College Preparatory	$1,427	---	$1,238
General Curriculum	$1,521	---	$1,027
Vocational Education	$1,931	$1,540	$1,315

*This figure is reported at $4,227 when equipment depreciation is included.

SOURCE: Charles R. Doty, 1976.

Some individuals will quickly point out that the initial investment (capital costs) for vocational education is much greater than for the college preparatory and general curricula. This is obviously the case, and those responsible for vocational education programs would be the first to admit that in-school shops and laboratories cost more than general classrooms.

Probably the biggest error by those responsible for in-school vocational education programs has been to ignore the need for depreciating capital investments. Without taking depreciation into account, during any one year when costly equipment needs to be replaced, the per pupil cost of a program can soar. Chow (1976) studied this problem and developed a simple yet comprehensive model for this purpose including: original cost, salvage value, removal cost, life span, and inflation. The major advantage of its use lies in the fact that the revenues of successive years will be charged with equal amounts of depreciation, thus giving more accurate per-pupil cost accounting.

Obviously, when computing per-pupil cost, the "optimum" number of students is an important factor. Following the concept of "economies of scale" it becomes important that vocational education programs enroll an optimum or up-to-capacity number of students.[7] When this is not the case the per-pupil cost will of course rise proportionately, as can be seen by our cost-per-pupil formula.

In sum, it is obvious that vocational education programs cost more than nonvocational programs, both in terms of capital outlay and operating investments. When operating costs are taken alone, the difference is not as great as many people have imagined. Moreover, when capital outlay (including equipment costs) is depreciated on a yearly basis, the total cost reflects a more rational picture. And optimum student enrollment in each and every program is important in order to achieve the economies of program.

Out-of-School Programs

When we speak of out-of-school programs we generally think of cooperative vocational education and work-study type offerings—both of which are partially supported in the federal vocational legislation. The economics of each will be discussed separately.

Cooperative vocational education programs. The accepted definition of this type of program is:

> A program of vocational education for persons who, through a cooperative arrangement between the school and employers, re-

ceive instruction—including required academic courses and related vocational instruction—by the alternation of study in school with a job in any occupational field. These two experiences must be planned and supervised by the school and employers so that each contributes to the student's education and to his employability. Work periods and school attendance may be on alternate half-days, full days, weeks, or other periods of time (American Vocational Association, 1971).

From this definition it can be readily seen that the investment in capital outlay and operating costs on the part of the school is substantially decreased. Little more by way of physical facilities than classroom space is needed to carry out related or theoretical instructional activities. Very little or no equipment and hardware is required, since these are almost entirely supplied by the cooperating employer. A further financial inducement of this program is that students themselves are in school only half the regular school day.

Moreover, business and industry want to participate in cooperative education. According to Burt (1971), industrial executives want to be involved in public education because it:

1. Provides an opportunity for fulfilling a civic and community service.
2. Provides an opportunity for enhancing personal prestige within the companies, among their friends, within their family circle, and among customers and the general public.
3. Contributes to a desire to be known as philanthropic and altruistic.
4. Facilitates a desire to help youth.
5. Offers a springboard for wider public service through either elective or appointive positions.

Cost data on cooperative vocational education programs appears difficult to obtain. For 1972 the total *direct* cost—local, state and federal—based on a national enrollment of 118,024, was $32.8 million or $277 per student. These data pertain to direct costs of teachers and coordinators (U.S. Department of Health, Education and Welfare, 1973).[8] If these data are correct, one can readily perceive the vast saving incurred. This, of course, does not take into account the costs of cooperating employers who provide the instruction, supplies, equipment, and hardware so used. But if Burt (1971) is correct in saying that employers want to cooperate with the schools in providing "on-the-job training," cooperative vocational education programs have been vastly underused, and taxpayers might have saved vast amounts of money.

It cannot be said that cooperative vocational education programs are ineffective. For example, in New Jersey the approximately 16,000 cooperative industrial education students, including disadvantaged and handicapped co-op students, earned more than $11.2 million in some 291 different jobs during the 1975-76 school year. Their average hourly rate was $2.53, some 25 cents more than the federal minimum standard (New Jersey State Department of Education, 1976). In addition, and on a consistent basis, cooperative vocational program students obtain job placement upon graduation at a higher rate than do in-school vocational graduates; the rate has been reported at 80 percent or better for a number of years.

Given the success of cooperative vocational education programs, as well as the low investment needed for their operation, it is surprising that they are not used more abundantly (Lee, 1974). Indeed the question could be asked, if we are at all interested in the "economies of scale," why not try doubling or tripling our investment in cooperative education and making more use of the business and industrial training facilities of our communities to further reduce costs? Cooperative vocational programs account for 5.73 percent of the total number of persons enrolled in secondary and postsecondary vocational education. Why are we so prone to build new and bigger schools when the cooperative education method could be used? Could it be that as educators we are afraid to expose our product (students) to the public before we wash our hands of them at graduation time? Certainly, if education for work is what vocational education is all about, this should not be the case.

Work-study programs. Work-study programs differ greatly from those of cooperative vocational education in that they are defined as:

> A program designed to provide financial assistance, through part-time employment, to students who have been accepted for full-time employment in vocational education programs and require such aid in order to continue in vocational training. The part-time employment is based on the financial need of the student and is not necessarily related to his career objective (American Vocational Association, 1971).

Once the difference in definition is understood, it becomes clear that this federally funded program merely attempts to keep students in school by paying them for productive work. That is to say, the local, state, and federal funds invested in this program go into student wages and do not constitute operating expenses. Indeed, there is but slight operating expense, since students usually are supervised by cooperating public officials and school employees.

If, however, such work-study programs ever took on the aspects of cooperative education and students were paid by other than public funds, investment in them would need to be calculated just as for other educational costs. Until that time arrives, work-study programs will be looked upon as being only supplemental.

Combinations of in-school and out-of-school programs. There are some vocational programs that have combined in-school and out-of-school instruction. Frequently the out-of-school aspect is left to the last semester or last year of the program. Others, such as the practical nursing program, require a certain amount of clinical-type training. Investment in such combinations may well reduce costs substantially, as well as serve as a "quality control" check on the product being trained. Possibly more such arrangements, with the in-school portion being used as a preclinical or preparatory phase, are worth consideration—both from an investment point of view and as a quality control measure.

THE ECONOMICS OF THE CAREER EDUCATION CONCEPT

It should be made clear from the start that vocational education is but one component of the career education concept and not career education in itself. The pedants who scoff at vocational education have accused career education advocates of being one and the same. They are not, and anyone taking the time to study the differences will recognize that vocational education is but one of the contributions to career education.[9]

The career education concept—based on career development—is probably too new to attach any *economic* value to it. However, its very origin stems from the fact that a career is an important part of one's life and the more satisfying that career is, the more satisfying one's life will be. Phrases such as "personal fulfillment," "appreciation for the dignity of work," and "economic independence" have been used in defining this concept.

Whether or not educators as a whole accept the career education concept is hard to discern at this time. It is just too new and it is taking too many diverse forms to assess any collective thrust. However, the fact remains that educators themselves are not happy with their ability to cope with the problems they face. Among these problems are those associated with helping youth make career choices and those pertaining to career preparation. The "Eighth Annual Gallup Poll of the Public's Attitudes Toward Public Schools" (Gallup, 1976) shows that 80 percent of parents deem it desirable to have more emphasis placed on career education and career preparation in the high school, and 52 percent think the elementary school curriculum should include information about jobs and careers.

Such concern is undoubtedly underscored when parents see the unemployment rate of youth rise to an unprecedented level and read U.S. census bureau reports indicating the number of poor (defined as poverty) increased by 2.5 million or 10.7 percent in 1975. Almost anything that education can do, including career education, to change this situation would represent an economy.

More specifically, the economics of career education lies not in its added cost, but in its redirection and reallocation of existing educational resources. As Draper in his study *Educating for Work* expressed it:

> *Special efforts are necessary on behalf of a sizable marginal group of students.* There are considerable numbers of young people who have done poorly so far in school and whose apparent prospects outside school may be poor, too. The causes of their problem are complex and varied. Some have simply never generated much interest in what the school has to offer, perhaps seeing it (not altogether incorrectly) as irrelevant to their style of life. They represent the type who, in previous generations, quit school early, got a job, and did reasonably well—only now that exit is being narrowed. Quite a few of these pupils are alienated to the point of sullen or aggressive hostility; characteristically they have withdrawn from the social and extra-curricular life of the school. Both their school work and their employment prospects are hurt more by their attitudes and personality than by ability lacks. In many cases these factors are compounded by slum backgrounds and the special problems facing minority groups. Common sense dictates that we recognize the futility and waste—and actual damage—in this situation and do what we can about it . . . (Draper, 1967, 112).

What Draper was saying as far back as 1967 was that a redirection of educational resources is necessary if we want to eliminate the waste of our system. He also indicated the need for some type of career preparation at the secondary school level which would involve at least 40 percent and maybe even 55 percent of all students. To test his prognosis, one need but look at secondary school enrollments and compare them with the allocations for staffing and physical facilities. For example, if 40-50 percent of secondary youth need career preparatory training, thus leaving 60-45 percent who do not because they are going on to postsecondary education, then 40-55 percent of the staff and physical facilities should be directed toward career preparation.

Indeed, 40-55 percent of the total school budget should reflect teachers who are devoted and qualified to work with career preparation programs and 40-55 percent of the educational facility should, in addition, reflect this kind of educational program. By mere observation, one can conclude that no such relationship exists within most school systems throughout the United States. Career programs do not take on anywhere near these proportions in most local school situations. In other words, there is a disproportionate amount budgeted for those who do not need career preparation at the expense of those who do.

The concept of career education, then, requires the shifting of allocations in most cases. Such shifts can be made within the bounds of existing faculties and facilities. Moreover, those in elementary and secondary educational leadership roles, if willing to change their emphasis of subject matter, can make a greater contribution to the economies of scale in the education process.

The economy of career education, of course, goes well beyond mere short-run reallocation of educational resources. In the long run, career awareness, exploration, and preparation result in benefits far in excess of any immediate investments. Career education as a total concept should have far-reaching payoffs as measured by more satisfying and rewarding lives. There appears to be ample evidence that the failure of education at all levels has contributed to our present socioeconomic situation and the career education concept may help to remedy some of the imbalance in our school investments.

IN RETROSPECT

If by programmatic investments in vocational education, we mean those costs which are involved in producing our product, we cannot ignore two basic economic principles: (1) the principle of diminishing marginal returns, and (2) economies of scale. Although the direct application of these two theories is not completely applicable to the public sector, educators—and vocational educators in particular—must be aware of their application in relation to the economics of our program operation.

As pointed out by Moss and Stromsdorfer (1971), we lack clear-cut objectives for our programs. The lack of such objectives or indexes of proficiency makes it impossible to arrive at "least cost" economies so as to maximize our investments. Until such indexes of proficiency are agreed upon, little confidence can be attested relative to costs. It is the opinion of the writer of this chapter that the place to begin the study of programmatic investments in vocational education is in the area of performance as measured by the acquisition of cognitive and psychomotor skills.

The economic aspects of the use of advisory committees, various types of delivery systems, and the career education concept have been explored. Advisory committees provide vocational education with an "in-kind" contribution which appears to go unnoticed in our accounting procedures. Our delivery system by the "in-school" method is very expensive when compared with the cooperative education approach. What appears to be needed, if economy of investment is being considered, is to explore further a program combining in-school and cooperative education. Not only would the economy of such an approach be worthwhile, but this combination could well assist decision makers as a quality control index of proficiency of the production process.

The career education concept appears too new to be assessed on an investment basis. What is suggested is the reallocation of existing resources, such as teachers and facilities, to those students who can benefit most from this type of approach. Educational leadership will be necessary for many years to come, if we are to "reverse" the disproportionate investment budgeted for those who do not need career preparation at the expense of those who do.

NOTES

1. Others might be the purchase of instructional materials in larger quantities, combining the use of facilities and hardware, maintaining records, and so on.

2. This is in spite of the scorn and ridicule to which vocational educators are subjected by their liberal arts colleagues who undoubtedly will not see any relationship between the cost of education and the product produced.

3. Twenty-nine percent indicated a desire to serve on committees dealing with career education and 22 percent on committees concerned with educational costs and finance.

4. Even at the modest sum of $100 per person daily consulting fee, the "in-kind" contribution of an eight-member advisory committee would be between $2,000 and $3,000 per year.

5. State Statistical Reports are based on discrete program enrollments, but expenditures are made on the basis of program category; i.e., disadvantaged, handicapped, construction, guidance, research, exemplary programs, etcetera. This reporting discrepancy negates any program-by-program accountability.

6. To show the difference in costs by program is more difficult. A study by Chow (1976) indicates the cost for graphic arts at the Vocational Center, Union County (New Jersey) Vocational Technical Schools was $1,683.13 per pupil compared to a cost of $1,399.26 for the overall pupil cost in some 14 different programs.

7. Optimum does not necessarily mean maximum capacity. It means capacity only in terms of quality product; thus, programs will vary in the number of students accommodated.

8. The figure of $277 per pupil probably does not include all operating costs such as found in total overhead. A more realistic figure appears to be in the neighborhood of $500 per pupil.

9. Reference is made to the misunderstanding of the career education concept as reflected in an article by Grubb and Laverson (1975).

REFERENCES CITED

American Vocational Association. *The Advisory Committee and Vocational Education.* Washington, D.C.: 1969.

———. *Vocational-Technical Terminology.* Washington, D.C.: 1971.

Burt, Samuel M. "Involving Industry and Business in Education." *Contemporary Concepts in Vocational Education.* Washington, D.C.: American Vocational Association, 1971.

Chow, Joshua S. "The Development of an Accounting Model for Capital Expenditures for Vocational Education." Ph.D. dissertation. New Brunswick, New Jersey: Graduate School of Education, Rutgers, The State University, 1976.

Corazzini, A. J. *Vocational Education, A Study of Benefits and Costs: A Case Study of Worcester, Massachusetts.* Princeton, N.J.: 1966.

Doty, Charles R. *Model for Calculating Cost per Pupil for Secondary Vocational, General and Transfer Curricula in Comprehensive High Schools, Shared Time Vocational Schools and Full Time Vocational Schools.* New Brunswick, New Jersey: Department of Vocational-Technical Education, Graduate School of Education, Rutgers, The State University, 1976.

Draper, Dale C. *Educating for Work.* Washington, D.C.: The National Association of Secondary School Principals, 1967.

Gallup, George H. "Eighth Annual Gallup Poll of the Public's Attitudes toward the Public Schools." *Phi Delta Kappan* 58 (October 1976).

Grubb, W. Norton, and Laverson, Marvin. "Rally Round the Workplace: and Fallacies in Career Education." *Harvard Educational Review* (November 1975).

Kaufman, Jacob J. *Cost Effectiveness Analysis as a Method for the Evaluation of Vocational and Technical Education.* Washington, D.C.: Bureau of Research, Office of Education, 1968. (ERIC No. ED 029 983)

———. "Cost-Effectiveness Analysis and Evaluation." *Contemporary Concepts in Vocational Education.* Washington, D.C.: American Vocational Association, 1971.

Lecht, Leonard. *Evaluating Vocational Education—Policies and Plans for the 1970s.* New York: Praeger, 1974.

Lee, Arthur M. *Learning a Living Across the Nation.* Vol. 3. Project Baseline, Second National Report. Flagstaff, Ariz.: Northern Arizona University, 1974.

Moss, Jerome, Jr., and Stromsdorfer, Ernst W. "Evaluating Vocational and Technical Education Programs." *Vocational Education Today and Tomorrow.* Madison, Wisconsin: Center for Studies in Vocational and Technical Education, The University of Wisconsin, 1971.

New Jersey Department of Education. "CIE Kids Earn $11.2 Million." *N.J. Interact* 3 (Summer 1976).

Somers, Gerald G. *The Effectiveness of Vocational and Technical Programs.* Madison, Wisconsin: Center for Studies in Vocational and Technical Education, University of Wisconsin, 1971.

Soong, R.K.; Wetzel, J.; Warren, B.; Hall, J.B.; and Kish, G.A. *Cost-Benefit Considerations of New Careers Program.* Chicago, Illinois: Career Options Research and Development, 1971. (ERIC No. ED 058 440)

Swanson, J.C. *Leadership Role, Functions, Procedures and Administration of Vocational-Technical Education Agencies at the State Level.* Vol. 3. Berkeley, California: School of Education, University of California, 1969. (ERIC No. ED 030 752)

Tomlinson, R.M., and Rzonca, C.S. *An Exploratory Analysis of Differential Program Costs of Selected Occupational Curricula in Selected Illinois Junior Colleges.* Springfield, Illinois: State Board of Vocational Education and Rehabilitation, 1971. (ERIC No. ED 047 679)

U.S. Department of Health, Education, and Welfare. *Vocational and Technical Education: Selected Statistical Tables FY 1972.* Washington, D.C.: Office of Education, Bureau of Occupational and Adult Education, 1973.

Section III: Developing Economic Literacy through Vocational Education

What Vocational Educators Should Know about Economics

William E. Becker, Jr. and Robert W. Reinke

The analytical base of economics has expanded at an exponential rate since the turn of the century (Lovell, 1973). The areas of specialization within this discipline have multiplied to the point where no individual—lay person or Ph.D.—can claim expertise in more than a narrow range of the discipline. These areas vary from economist to economist, in keeping with the individual's personal interests, as exemplified by the tables of contents of the May issues of the *American Economic Review* ("Papers and Proceedings").

Not only has the discipline of economics expanded in scope and sophistication, it has increased in prestige among the sciences. The work of economists, unlike that of other social scientists, for example, is now recognized for Nobel Prize honors. Economists have become developers of analytical skills and concepts rather than simply using knowledge emanating from the other sciences.

It is unrealistic, therefore, to expect elementary and secondary school teaching personnel to be knowledgeable about all economic concepts and analytical skills currently in use. However, many of the analytical skills employed by economic specialists are based largely on a limited number of basic economic concepts. This makes it realistic to expect teachers and students to possess a working knowledge of selected economic concepts and the mastery of certain associated skills.[1] These concepts and skills can be applied to their personal and social problems. Most of them can be incorporated into the content currently being taught by vocational educators.

If Hansen's assertion in Chapter 12 is correct—i.e., that increased economic literacy of our school-age population can most effectively be accomplished by placing emphasis on "personal economic decision making, where it is apparent to students that what they learn will benefit them directly" —then what better place is there to teach economics than in vocational education? Vocational educators take pride in holding to knowledge and skills that are real and of direct benefit to students in their careers. It is precisely through the students' applications of basic economic concepts and skills to problems which are of real consequence to them that they, as well as their teachers, will see the power of an economic perspective, as Becker and Swan (1976) have argued.

The purpose of this chapter is to identify, define, sequence, and clarify a limited number of key economic concepts which may be helpful when analyzing problems and issues of real personal consequence. No attempt is made to specify expected outcomes or desired levels of teacher competency. The identified economic concepts are offered as a foundation upon which vocational educators can build their respective competencies.

RESOURCES

The first economic term to define is *resources*. It serves as our starting point because resource constraints—together with human desires—form the basis of and need for economic analysis.[2] Anything which is or could be used, either singly or in combination, to acquire or produce other things is a resource. There are four broad categories of resources: natural, human, capital, and time resources.

Types of Resources

Natural or land resources are items of nature which can be used in production; therefore, they are called factors of production. Natural resources are measured by surface area, mass and volume. Since natural resources exist in finite amounts, their use in current production implies a depletion of natural resources available for future production.

Human resources—also referred to as labor and human capital—consist of the physical and mental productive abilities of people. Historically, the labor force has been measured by population size and hours of work. More recently, measures reflecting the training of the labor force have been developed. Typically, these measures include years of schooling completed or the amount of accumulated literature in a given occupation or profession. At any given time, there is a finite population available for labor force participation. Over time, however, the quality and quantity of human resources can and do change.

Capital resources—also referred to as physical capital—are items which are or can be used in production, such items having been produced previously. Capital resources include such things as tractors, shovels, and buildings. Unlike natural resources, the items referred to as capital resources require the input of human effort for their existence. The human modification or improvement of natural resources and existing capital is known as *capital creation.* Simply producing more of the same capital is referred to as *capital deepening.* The act of capital creation leads to more specialized resources which tend to be better suited for a given use. For instance, the fastening of a sharp stone to a stick makes a crude axe which transforms natural resources (wood and stone) into a capital resource (an axe). The axe is a specialized piece of capital. This piece of capital, in turn, can be used to make other specialized capital resources such as cabins and tables. Capital deepening, on the other hand, means that more axes, cabins or tables are produced.

Time resources are the most limited resources we possess. Everything we do requires time; no production process is without a gestation period. Even if human, natural and physical resources were available in infinite amounts, a finite life span would necessitate choosing or ordering what to produce. Finite time forces people to choose between leisure activity, sleep, or work activity.[3] It is the existence of finite resources such as time which leads to scarcity.

Scarcity and Opportunity Costs

It is possible to think of an individual who can obtain desired material things without deliberate personal effort. For example, Aladdin possessed a magic lamp and ring with which he commanded two genies which gratified his material desires. He had to forego nothing as long as he held the magic lamp and ring.

Similarly, it is possible to conceive of a world with infinite time and nondepletable resources. In such a world individuals would be able to produce and consume all that they wanted. Effort might be involved in the production process, but individuals would have an infinite amount of time to develop all that they desired. There would be no need for a decision as to what to consume later; nothing would have to be foregone. In such a world nothing would be scarce.

Scarcity refers to the fact that in the real world the acquisition of desired things requires both choices and effort. Scarcity implies that individuals must give up something in making a choice and therefore face *opportunity costs* in decision making. An opportunity cost is the benefit, or value of the benefit, that is foregone by choosing one alternative over another. The scarcity of time and the related opportunity costs resulting from time-use decisions can be seen in the following conditional statements: If I choose to play golf on Saturday afternoon, I must be willing to forego the enjoyment of playing tennis, at least temporarily. If I choose to become a professional musician, I must forego being a professional economist.[4] Similarly, in the case of a scarce land resource, a conditional statement reflecting an opportunity cost might be: If we choose to have a school garden, we must forego having a baseball diamond. Economics provides "rules" by which such decisions can be made in light of the associated opportunity costs.

BEHAVIORAL CHANGE

To the economist, the reasons individuals or groups behave, or are inclined to behave, in a particular way are integrally tied to differing sources of opportunity costs and beneficial incentives.

Incentives

There are many forces which compete for superiority when we make decisions. These forces become stronger or weaker for each of us depending upon the situation, its scope and its short- and long-term impacts. One force, e.g., feeling good because you are well dressed, may become dominant when a personal consumer decision is made relating to the purchase of a new outfit. Another force may put overwhelming pressure on us when a time-use decision is pending (go to work or stay in bed). It is important to realize that human decision makers are not equipped with identical behavior stimulators. To the contrary, each person has his/her method of organizing and acting upon these forces which direct behavior.

Those forces which tend to stimulate behavior or determination will be referred to as *incentives*. Incentives represent a broad category of forces which can be broken down into three sub-categories: pecuniary incentives, material incentives, and psychic incentives.

Certainly *pecuniary incentives* provide the motivation for a large segment of the population to get up early in the morning, forego sleep, fight early traffic, and spend eight hours in the production of goods or services from which someone else will gain the benefit. Pecuniary or money incentives in the form of wages, interest, rents, and dividends from profits provide the motivation for individuals to make services and capital available to others. These money incentives, however, are only effective because of the things for which money can be exchanged. Money or nominal prices indicate the rate at which money can be exchanged for goods. For example, a nominal price of $8.00 per bushel of apples means one bushel of apples can be exchanged for eight dollars or one-eighth of a bushel of apples can be exchanged for one dollar.

Material incentives are closely aligned with pecuniary incentives. The human desire for material devices which allow a person to live more comfortably in the environment will many times stimulate structured activity. Man's need for an extra outer body covering has caused the American Indian, the frontiersman, the Eskimo, the cotton planter, and the sheep herder to organize and execute a daily ritual for the express purpose of acquiring for themselves or others material rewards.

An understanding of pecuniary and material incentives is essential for the proper analysis of choice. People make choices which are directly dependent upon these types of actual or expected rewards. Behavior, i.e., particular choices made by individuals, cannot be explained, however, just by using these two incentive categories.

Psychic incentives are just as important as pecuniary and material incentives in explaining human behavior. Psychic incentives are not easily identified, for they represent feelings found within an individual. A man may choose to use his time lying on the beach watching the sun shimmer on the water, because "it makes me feel good inside," i.e., the incremental psychic reward of lying on the beach is greater than or equal to the pecuniary wage or psychic reward he could obtain from doing something else. A woman may turn down a large money or material reward for returning a lost wallet because the feeling of pride in doing the right thing is reward enough—accepting the pecuniary reward would be an over-payment in accordance with this person's value structure. An individual who can barely afford a Cadillac may buy a Cadillac anyway because the psychic benefit compensates him for the other goods he will have to forego.

Economics is a behavioral science and it becomes more real and fascinating when behavior is discussed. An analysis of incentives and opportunity costs provide us with the background to understand the decisions of others and make decisions for ourselves which are more in keeping with our values.

ECONOMIC EFFICIENCY AND MARGINALISM

Historically economists have defined individual decisions as *economically efficient* (or rational) when no other choice can lead to a greater attainable level of satisfaction or benefits (as defined in terms of psychic, pecuniary, or material rewards). This understanding of efficiency is based upon a method of decision making which associates prices or incremental costs with incremental benefits resulting from a given action.

To understand this *marginal method* of making choices better—i.e., decisions based on comparing incremental benefits and costs—refer back to the individual on the beach.[5] Remember he has decided to lie on the beach and watch the sun shimmer on the water because of psychic rewards associated with that behavior. Note that the individual is not deciding to be a "bum" but is making a rational choice based upon the respective costs and benefits of that decision. At this point, the questions that must be asked are, why or how long will he pursue this activity. To analyze these questions, assume that the individual is economically efficient, i.e., no other choice can lead to a greater attainable level of benefit or satisfaction. Assume also that the opportunity to pursue athletic activity is always available at a fixed rate of one set of tennis per hour (the opportunity cost in this example may represent any alternative pecuniary, material or psychic incentive). Given these assumptions, and knowing that the person is currently lying on the beach, the conclusion can be drawn that the psychic benefit of beach reclining for the first hour is greater than, or at least equal to, the benefits associated with one set of tennis.

The psychic benefit for the second hour of lying on the beach will probably be less than the benefit derived from the first hour—*diminishing marginal satisfaction.* If, however, the psychic benefit of lying on the beach for this second hour is still greater than, or equal to, the reward associated with the alternative benefits of time spent playing tennis, a decision to remain on the beach for a second hour will be made. An individual will continue to stay on the beach until the psychic rewards from being there one more hour are less than the benefits derived from playing a set of tennis. (Note that a change in tennis-playing conditions or climate could drastically alter the final time use decision.)

Similarly, a social system is economically efficient when no change is possible which can make an individual or group of individuals better off without making someone else worse off. Here, too, a method of decision making which associates costs with incremental benefits of individual and collective actions is used.

Economic efficiency, although sought by many, cannot be accomplished without an operational understanding of its key elements. Ideally, individuals and groups will put marginalistic decision making techniques into practice with each choice leading to the greatest level of personal and social well-being.

THE MARKET

Individual decisions can be analyzed in terms of the interaction among pecuniary, material, and psychic benefits, and opportunity costs. On the other hand, group behavior, that is, buying and selling particular goods or services, is typically analyzed in a market setting. A *market* is the total number of buyers and sellers of a particular good or service during a specific period of time. The buyers and sellers establish the price and quantity of the good or service exchanged through their negotiations.

Demand and Supply

Two key forces determine the price at which goods and services will be exchanged, namely, the forces of demand and supply. *Demand* is a relationship expressing the various amounts of goods and services which prospective buyers would be willing to purchase at different prices during a given period of time, with all other prices, income, and tastes remaining the same. *Supply,* on the other hand, is a relationship expressing the various amounts of a good or service which prospective sellers would be willing to sell at different prices during a given period of time, with all other prices and production techniques remaining the same.

The price and quantity relationship of both demand and supply rests on the respective decision makers' attempts to equalize their own marginal (or incremental) benefits and related costs. In the case of buyers, the market price is at least equal to the cost of producing the last unit of output. The competition between possible buyers and sellers that results from their attempts to equate marginal benefits and costs, i.e., maximize obtainable levels of satisfaction, establishes the market equilibrium price. The *market equilibrium price* will be the price for which the quantity demanded of any particular good or service is the same as the quantity which is being supplied.

In an analysis of forces determining market prices it is essential to remember that variables other than price will tend to cause the demand and supply schedules to shift over a period of time. This in turn will affect the quantity supplied and demanded. For instance, if we construct a demand curve for "previously owned" Cadillacs, given a certain price of gasoline, then the price and quantity relationship of the used Cadillac demand curve will remain fixed if all relevant variables, including the price of gasoline, remain constant. If there is a significant increase in the cost of gasoline, however, the demand curve for previously owned Cadillacs should fall. That is, at each price fewer used Cadillacs will be demanded. Even if we assume that the supply curve of used Cadillacs is unaffected by high gas prices, a lower Cadillac demand should lead to fewer used Cadillacs being sold, a lower used Cadillac market equilibrium price, and in time, possibly, fewer Cadillacs being produced. The standard variables which must be considered in the analysis of demand and supply include: values, tastes, incomes, and the price of other goods and services.

Market Imperfections

There are situations in which events, laws, or restrictions do not allow the market forces of supply and demand to freely establish an equilibrium market price. Such market imperfections take the form of price ceilings or price floors.

A *price ceiling* prevents the market price from rising to an equilibrium level where the quantity demanded and supplied would be equal. An example of a ceiling rate is the Minnesota usury law which fixes the maximum interest rate chargeable on some types of loans at 8 percent. Such a ceiling results in a greater quantity of loanable funds being demanded than financial institutions are willing and able to supply. A *price floor,* on the other hand, refers to a restriction which does not allow the price of a good or service to fall to the point where quantity demanded and supplied are equal. Examples of price floors are the prices established for fair trade items, such as

Winchester firearms, and the limits set in farm subsidy programs.

Externalities

Conceptually, the market pricing component of a particular economic system should reflect all aspects of economic decisions. It does fail to quantify satisfaction derived or lost, to individuals or groups, when some production and consumption activities are not reflected in or amenable to price determination. An example of this situation occurs when your neighbor allows the leaves he raked for fall disposal to blow into your yard. You have incurred lower satisfaction—unsightly leaves in your yard—which is not reflected in prices unless you hire a laborer to clean up the leaves and demand, through small claims court, that your neighbor pay the bill. Note: If the bill is not given to the neighbor, he has no way of knowing the degree of absolute hardship he is creating by letting his leaves blow. Until the bill is enforceably presented, he need not make an economically efficient decision about the matter.

In a similar way, externalities occur on a larger scale. *Externalities* can be defined as the incremental increase or decrease in the individual or collective level of satisfaction not reflected in market prices, but initiated through individual or collective decisions. Industries, for example, make production decisions based upon observable prices. When prices are not available, social and economic inefficiencies can develop. The Japanese chemical industry, by using the Minimata Bay region for its waste disposal, lowered the general well-being of the village fishermen and their families. The chemical waste in the bay caused the fishing industry to become depressed, and the toxic mercury ingested by the villagers caused deformation and death. Although villagers protested the waste discharge, the true cost (negative externality) of the industry was not apparent until expressed in dollar terms through court litigation. This revealed that the total cost of the externality was $3.5 million. With this information the company could calculate the true cost of production and, in turn, modify its supply condition to reflect such costs. As a result, the price for supplying a given quantity of a particular product was raised.

The analysis of externalities presented here is a key to the pollution problem. It directs individuals and groups to use an already existing institution (the market) to foster more efficient and knowledgeable choices. It must be noted that this procedure may not stop the pollution, but it will allow choices which rest upon the marginal benefits and costs resulting from a given action.

Real versus Nominal Measures of Value

In any market decision on a good's money value, it is essential to differentiate between the level of the good's money price (or money value) and the price of the good in terms of other goods. One should not be so interested in whether a given money price is high but whether that price is too high in relation to the price of another good, past prices, or expected future prices. *Real measures of value* indicate the quantity of one nonmonetary good, or amount of one's services, which exchange for one unit of another nonmonetary good or service.

Changes in value over a period of time are easiest to interpret by converting the observed money or *nominal value* into an index number. With these index numbers, real values can be computed and compared; for example, real wages, real expenditures, real interest rates. Most index numbers are calculated by dividing observed money value expenditures by the monetary value of the observed expenditures during the period arbitrarily selected as a base. For example, if in 1968 you spent \$9,500 on goods and services, while in 1976 you spent \$13,500 for roughly the same goods and services, then selecting 1968 as the base year yields an index for 1976 prices of

$$\left(\frac{\$13{,}500}{\$9{,}500} \text{ X } 100\right) = 140$$

The calculation of real values from index numbers is as follows. Assume you received wages of \$6.00 per hour in 1968, while in 1976 your wages were \$8.00 per hour. In terms of 1968 prices or purchasing power your real wage in 1976 is

$$\left(\frac{\$8.00}{140} \text{ X } 100\right) = \$5.71$$

This is, prices have risen by 40 percent while your wages only rose by 33.3 percent, so your 1976 wage of \$8.00 per hour is equivalent to only \$5.71 per hour in 1968. An alternative way of saying this is that price inflation was greater than wage inflation by 6.7 percent. Similarly, if the price of apples in 1968 was \$5.00 a bushel, while in 1976 it was \$6.50 a bushel, then the real price of apples in 1976 is

$$\left(\frac{\$6.50 \text{ per bushel}}{140} \text{ X } 100\right) = \$4.74 \text{ per bushel}$$

The real price of apples has fallen. In 1976 apples are cheap (compared to other goods) since their price in terms of 1968 dollars fell from $5.00 to $4.74 a bushel.

The standard price indexes used in the United States are: consumer price index, wholesale price index, gross national product deflator, and commodity price index. The indexes are calculated for particular segments of the population and slightly different methods of computation are used. The national consumer price index is frequently used as a general cost of living index. It is based upon prices for some 400 different goods and services typically purchased by urban wage earners and salaried clerical workers with families.

MACROECONOMICS

Macroeconomics is the study of how an entire economy behaves as a unit. Three basic areas of macroeconomic study are worthy of special attention: the flow of economic activity, economic growth, and income distribution.

Aggregate Flow of Economic Activity

In any economy we can think of two types of transactions—those involving the purchase and sale of complete or final goods and services and those involving the purchase of resources or factors of production which are used to make other goods. Two flows are associated with each transaction in the economy—the flow of money to the seller and the flow of service or product to the purchaser.

Money will flow from firms producing final products to decision makers who control the required factors of production (resources). This money will flow back to the firms as their products and services are purchased. The first money flow is referred to as *money expenditure flow.* Offsetting these money flows are the respective *flows of services* rendered by factors of production and final *product service flows.*

A measure of the *aggregate flow of economic activity* is the real *gross national product.* The gross national product (GNP) is the estimated total output of goods and services—or, alternatively, the total income—produced in a nation during a one-year period. The level of any country's GNP depends upon such things as the resources the country possesses, the sophistication of the corporate and financial structure, tastes and preferences of consumers, and government policy.[6]

Economic Growth

Many economic concepts and theories which developed from the work of Smith, Ricardo, Marx, Keynes, and others gained their impetus from the desire of individuals and groups for more pecuniary, material, and psychic rewards. This insatiable desire for goods and services has continued from early man to present-day society. Material reward seeking has increased in certain parts of the world to the extent that some followers of Thorstein Veblen have classified such conspicuous consumption as sinful, or at least unnecessary. Nevertheless, underdeveloped nations are eager to have a chance at such consumption themselves.

The process of *economic growth* attempts to increase the amount of goods and services through a new or different mix of resources. Aggregate economic growth is usually measured by changes in real GNP divided by changes in population, that is, a rising real GNP population ratio.

Individuals and societies throughout time have realized that their resources were limited because of a lack of resource knowledge, inability to gather resources, or distance limitations. This situation posed the problem of how to obtain material satisfaction, given this relative shortage of resource factors (land, human, capital, time). To achieve economic growth, various changes had to occur. These changes moved individuals and groups away from a short-run survival production process to a long-run growth attitude and procedure. Resources had to be withdrawn from immediate consumption for the purposes of: 1) devising new means of acquiring resources, 2) devising new means of production, 3) devising methods of upgrading existing resources, 4) building capital equipment, and 5) compensating for increased consumption caused by population increases.

Income Distribution

The process of economic growth and its relationship to income distribution can be exemplified by observing the productive procedures followed by a fishing village. In the beginning, all able members of the fishing community except the king and his aide, who set rules and allocated resources, spent most of their waking hours fishing. Fishing entailed walking waist deep into the water with a pointed wooden stick, waiting until a fish swam by, then impaling the fish. This procedure usually led to an income distribution in which each family received one fish per day; the larger families received a larger fish.

This method of catching fish occasionally led to famine. The king directed one of his more intelligent villagers to think of a new way to catch fish. After deep deliberation a new method of fishing was proposed by the thinker. He suggested that many men be freed from the daily fishing routine, which might mean bringing the villagers to near-starvation rations. These men would be directed to build rafts from logs and nets from seaweed. This procedure, assuming that the same distribution techniques would be followed, should guarantee each family more fish each day.

After much thought the king agreed and the experiment began. It took much time and many other resources to accomplish the task—the daily ration of fish per family dropped to one-half fish per day—but finally it was done. More villagers were skeptical, as no one had ever seen this procedure for catching fish. The results, however, confirmed the king's hopes that a new mix of resources could lead to more goods for everyone. When the fishing rafts paddled to shore late that evening, they were piled high with fish, larger and better-tasting than anything ever caught offshore. The catch was so large that every person in the village received two fish. Economic growth had certainly taken place. But even as the village was feasting, the king and the thinker were asking one another: "Is there yet a better way?"

Economic growth in the United States occurs today in much the same way as it did in the fishing village. New resource combinations are attempted in order to improve productivity. Many times a change in one area of production will influence changes in another. The net result is an increase of goods and services made available through the price mechanism—as opposed to the king's equal division scheme—to newcomers in the population, as well as those who desire more material satisfaction.

Population increase represents an important aspect of economic growth. If the population grows, economic growth must occur to maintain the same level of material satisfaction of society's members. For example, if a society of 100 grows by 10 percent, then the material goods of the community must also grow by 10 percent in order to provide the opportunity for each person to receive the same percentage of material goods as before. In this example, if an increase of material satisfaction is desired, which usually is the situation, a new mix of resources must be devised that will add more than 10 percent to the growth of goods and services.

To date many of the world's communities, including the United States, have experienced an economic growth rate exceeding that of their population increase. Some say this occurs because of diplomatic planning, while others say it is a by-product of a market system which advances technology via profits. Whatever the reason(s), it has continued for many years.

Whether economic growth continues, zero growth occurs, or actual negative growth takes place depends on variables that are probably too diverse to analyze using traditional economic understandings. Technological growth in economic analysis must keep pace with socioeconomic change. It is likely, given the history of economic thought, that the basic concepts and skills provided in this chapter will continue to form the building blocks for any future changes in economic analysis.

ECONOMICS IN THE VOCATIONAL CURRICULUM

There is nothing sacred about the list of economic concepts given here. As was pointed out, numerous other economic educators recently have attempted to identify key economic concepts which are at the core of economics. Interestingly, these lists tend to overlap even though they were done independently. It is the job of vocational educators to specify the use of these concepts within their own curricula—curricula that vary from school to school and teacher to teacher.

The potential impact of incorporating economic concepts and skills into vocational curricula seems great and well worth an instructor's effort. This is feasible because vocational education—unlike history, civics, or general social studies education—is founded on the premise that the instruction provided will benefit the student directly. Much of the current thinking in economic education is that a significant increase in basic economic understandings on the part of our student-age population can only be brought about by emphasizing personal economic decision making via problems that are real to students and therefore of immediate concern to them.

NOTES

1. Many economics educators recently have attempted to identify key economic concepts—Fels (1974), Becker and Reinke (1975), Bach (1976), Hansen (1976), and Leftwich (1976). Becker and Reinke identified and reviewed selected elementary and secondary textbooks in accordance with their coverage of economic concepts.

2. Definitions and reasons for studying economics are numerous. At one end of a continuum we have the simple descriptions, e.g., Calderwood and Fersh (1974, 4). At the other end we have the dogmatic prin-

ciples and textbook definitions such as found in Samuelson (1973, 3) who analyzes the costs and benefits of improving patterns of resource allocation.

3. Although the resource of time is often overlooked in the analysis of consumer behavior, economists such as Gary Becker (1965), Linder (1970), and many others have successfully incorporated it into their formal analysis.

4. Recently economist Richard Gill, author of *Economics and the Public Interest,* (1968), decided to join the New York Symphony Orchestra and bore the opportunity cost of not being on the faculty of Harvard University.

5. While the idea of marginal decision making may be a helpful tool of analysis, it is not universally accepted by all economists as a dogmatic descriptor for all human behavior; see Mishan (1961, 1-11).

6. The determinants of aggregate economic activity are hotly debated by economists. Historically, Keynesian economists have argued that government intervention of "incomes policies" could affect real GNP while Monetarists have held that such efforts were of little consequence in the long run; only changes in real money balance affect real GNP; see, for example, Cox (1974). Most recently the Rationalists have argued that the public's expectations can totally defeat any economic policy. For a popular press review of this new theory see *Business Week,* November 8, 1976 (74, 76).

REFERENCES CITED

American Economic Review. "Papers and Proceedings," May issues.

Bach, G. L. "What Should a Principles Course in Economics Be?" *Goals and Objectives of the Introductory College-Level Course in Economics.* A Ninth District Economic Information Series. Minneapolis: Federal Reserve Bank of Minneapolis, 1976, 15-18.

Becker, Gary. "A Theory of Allocation of Time." *Economic Journal* (September 1965): 493-517.

Becker, William E., Jr., and Reinke, Robert W. "What Economics Should the Educator Know?" *Social Studies* (September/October 1975): 195-204.

Becker, William E., and Swan, Craig. "A Student-Oriented, Real Problem Solving Approach in Economics." *Goals and Objectives of the Introductory College-Level Course in Economics.* A Ninth District Economic Information Series. Minneapolis: Federal Reserve Bank of Minneapolis, 1976, 19-25.

Calderwood, James, and Fersh, George. *Economics for Decision Making.* New York: Macmillan Publishing Co., Inc., 1974, 4.

Cox, William N., III. "The Money Supply Controversy." *Some Institutional Aspects of Monetary Policy.* Reprint from the *Monthly Review.* Atlanta: Federal Reserve Bank of Atlanta, 1974, 5-10.

Fels, Rendigs. "The Vanderbilt-JCEE Experimental Course in Elementary Economics." *Journal of Economic Education* (Special issue, Winter 1974): 5-95.

Gill, Richard T. *Economics and the Public Interest.* Pacific Palisades, California: Goodyear Publishing Company, 1968.

Hansen, W. Lee. "The State of Economic Literacy." Mimeographed paper presented at a meeting of the Joint Council on Economic Education, New Orleans, February 1976.

"How Expectations Defeat Economic Policy." *Business Week* (November 8, 1976), 74 and 76.

Leftwich, Richard H. "Objectives of the College-Level Principles of Economics Course." *Goals and Objectives of the Introductory College-Level Course in Economics.* A Ninth District Economic Information Series. Minneapolis: Federal Reserve Bank of Minneapolis, 1976, 26-29.

Linder, Staffan G. *The Harried Leisure Class.* New York: Columbia University Press, 1970.

Lovell, Michael C. "The Production of Economic Literature: An Interpretation." *Journal of Economic Literature* (March 1973): 27-55.

Mishan, Edward J. "Theories of Consumers' Behavior: A Cynical View." *Economica* (February 1961): 1-11.

Samuelson, Paul. *Economics.* 9th ed. New York: McGraw-Hill Book Company, 1973, 3.

What All Workers Should Know about Economics

Robert L. Darcy and Phillip E. Powell

One might think that it would be easy for any articulate economist or experienced economics educator to outline what all workers should know about economics—or what all citizens, consumers, or other functional category of persons should know about the subject.[1] Yet fundamental questions arise that are prerequisite to any useful statement: Which concepts and approaches to economics should be presented? What specific content should be included and emphasized in an abbreviated treatment of the subject? What levels of understanding are appropriate for particular topics? And why should workers know about economics anyway?

Raising such questions may complicate matters unduly. After all, economists surely agree on the basic principles of their discipline.[2] Well . . . more or less; but as orthodox neoclassical economists are fond of pointing out, "a little more or a little less" (marginal analysis) is what it's all about. The subject matter of economics is highly complex, and many of the analytical tools developed and applied by economics scholars are both sophisticated and controversial. So one of the first things that workers, and everybody else, should know about economics is that it is not a simple subject nor a cut-and-dried, purely objective scientific discipline. Yet as long as food, housing, health care, education, jobs, money, taxes, oil, environmental quality, sociopolitical power, and dozens of similar topics continue to be matters of deep concern to so many of us, economics definitely will be a very important subject. Economists and economics educators will try, at least, to understand the economic world and perhaps share their limited knowledge with other people.[3]

Reflecting the view that economics is both complex and important, the section that follows addresses the literal meaning of this chapter's title, dealing with some things that workers should know about the discipline of economics and those who practice it. Some perspective on economics and economics education is also offered. In the second section, we elaborate on suggested economic content—facts, concepts, issues, methods, and principles—which workers might find it useful to know.

SOMETHING ABOUT ECONOMICS

These are the values on which I base my facts.

—Anonymous

Social Science and Values

Answering the four questions posed in the introduction should give the reader information about intellectual orientation, world view, educational philosophy, and even ethical preferences. In our discussion, as in other treatments of economics and economics education, such disclosures can prepare the way for better communication in which value components are less likely to ride unseen as silent partners on the backs of facts and principles.

We view *economics* as the social science that includes the way society organizes and behaves regarding the development, conservation, and employment of productive resources—labor, land, and capital goods.[4] Economic science, therefore, focuses on the three sets of data elements: (1) patterns of social organization and behavior, or *institutions,* (2) the factors of production—labor, land, capital, or *resources,* and (3) practical knowledge and skills, or *technology.*

When analyzing the interactions of resources, technology, and institutions, economists have directed attention to a trio of processes and outcomes: (1) the overall level of economic activity—employment, production, and income generation, (2) the structure and composition of such activity—including the allocation of employed resources and determination of the product mix, and (3) the distribution or sharing of income and wealth. All economic systems are concerned with these same basic questions about employment, production, and income: *How much in total? What? For whom?*

In the United States, the particular values—views of good and bad that serve as criteria of choice—which are used to establish goals and identify priorities for economic performance have changed over time, but few would deny that economic activity is strongly value-oriented. If the American people today are less committed to efficiency and rapid economic growth than they were a generation ago, they have not abandoned these traditional objectives entirely. Nor have they adopted an attitude of indifference toward other criteria for judging the performance of our economy; e.g., conservation of natural resources, job opportunities for all who desire employment, economic security, a noninflationary price level, equalitarian justice, a balanced international position, and basic freedom of choice for consumers, workers, and enterprisers.

People in their capacities as workers, consumers, owners of natural resources and capital, managers, citizens, lawmakers—being human—are value-oriented and constantly making economic decisions reflecting their ideas of good, bad, should, ought, better, worse. Similarly so with the policy decisions and actions of business firms, labor unions, and special-interest groups. This, then, is another important actuality to know about economics: Individuals and organizations are seldom neutral with respect to economic approaches, perspectives, values, goals, processes, and outcomes. (Whether economic communicators openly acknowledge their predilections is another matter.) The doctrinal approach used in this discussion can be characterized as a blend of neoclassical, neo-institutional, and post-Keynesian economics in the traditions of Adam Smith, Alfred Marshall, Thorstein Veblen, and John Maynard Keynes. Our perspective here is societal rather than purely personal, emphasizing the creative role of workers rather than the absorptive function of consumers.

Content and Methodology

Having identified an economic data framework for analysis, three basic economic problems, and some criteria for evaluating economic performance, we now turn to a methodological facet of economics. What do students of the economy do with these central ideas—pegs, on which to hang hundreds of particular and transitory bits of economic information? Employing microscope or "macroscope" as the situation requires, economists isolate, dissect, examine, classify, manipulate, agitate, and in various other ways scrutinize and experiment with the subject matter of economics, employing a set of tools and skills broadly classified under three headings: history, statistics, and theory. By *history* is meant an understanding of technology and institutions, both in terms of empirical information about the past and present and about processes of change. *Statistics* are numbers that—adequately, or in some unhappy cases, inadequately—represent empirical data: facts about the economic world. *Theory* includes abstractions and simplifications—concepts, analytical structures, models, principles, methodologies—designed to identify and show relationships among significant elements in the economic system.[5]

Examples: Tracing the evolution of governmental policy toward labor unions and existing legislation (why, when, where, what, how, and involving whom) illustrates the use of history in analyzing a proposal, say, to prohibit closed shop agreements. Data on labor force participation, employment, and unemployment show how statistics (mostly based on sample surveys) can be used to inject observable facts into economic analysis. The marginal productivity principle of wages and employment illustrates the use of theory in examining an economic issue such as minimum wage standards.

Levels of Economic Understanding

The two preliminary questions remaining—what level of economic knowledge should workers be expected to attain, and why should they acquire economic understanding anyway—are as closely interrelated as the questions of basic approach and specific content. In fact, as economists like to say, everything depends on everything else. The answers to all four preliminary questions are intertwined. Explaining the rationale for a program of worker education can help provide guidelines both for specific content and for determining appropriate levels of understanding with regard to particular bits of institutional, statistical, theoretical, and methodological information. For example, granted that workers should know about the factors of production—labor (human resources), land (natural resources), and capital (goods that have been produced and are available for use in further production)—how much should they be expected to know about the nature, development, conservation, employment, allocation, and payments accruing to particular kinds of the various categories of resources, nationally, regionally, and in local markets?

The answer would seem to depend on the particular learning objectives that have been established. To score well on a multiple-choice test, it may be enough to have heard of an economic datum, to have a vague sort of awareness that, yes, that term "AFL-CIO" fits in a list of economic institutions rather than respresenting an entry in the Periodic Table of Chemical Elements. And it may be adequate for some purposes to recognize the statement, "The laborer is worthy of his hire," as an economic dictum of Biblical origin. But for working people, or young men and women soon to seek their livelihood as labor force participants, a deeper understanding of the worth of one's labor may be desired.

For pedagogical purposes, it is useful to distinguish five levels of knowing, ranging from merely knowing *about* something to knowing *what* it is, *how* it functions, *why* it works the way it does, and finally knowing enough about the subject to formulate a responsible value judgment—*knowing the good.*[6] Limitations of time, interest, current knowledge and learning readiness on the part of students will all influence the setting of educational objectives with regard to particular economic understandings, as will the purpose of the educational program itself. Just how much all workers need to know about the AFL-CIO or the marginal productivity theory of wages cannot really be determined out of context. But curriculum developers and teachers may find it useful to consider the five levels of knowing as they make decisions about the treatment they want to provide for particular facts, concepts, principles, and issues.

Why Economics?

The fourth and last of the preliminary questions posed in the introduction concerns the rationale underlying an economics education program for workers. The answer to that question begins by observing that men and women are far too complex to be treated as abstractions which can be adequately understood in terms of a single economic function they perform, such as participation in the labor force. All but the most ignorant of economists know that workers are people—not commodities, robots, "human capital," or merely another category of "the means of production to be allocated among competing ends." Workers are men and women who live many roles simultaneously: citizen, consumer, job-seeker, job-holder, spouse, parent, friend, religious believer, political partisan, and others.

The immediate question then is: "Why do *people,* especially in their capacity as human resources, want to know something about economics?" Perhaps because they believe that such knowledge will increase their earnings, contribute to self-understanding, or—dare we say it?—show them an escape route from lifelong dependence on wage employment.[7]

Recognizing, however, that most of the demand for economics education comes not from the ultimate consumer, but is synthesized or contrived by others, we are inclined to rephrase the question.[8] Why do *other* people want workers to know about economics, and what do they want them to know? For designers and teachers of educational programs, these are questions of strategic importance.

Viewpoints of Interested Groups

Without attempting a definitive or documented answer to this dual question, insights can perhaps be gleaned from a review of some concerns often identified with various groups interested in economics education.

Educators—including economics educators. Committed to a fundamental human value that more knowledge is better than less, educators see economics education for future workers as making a contribution to social understanding, responsible citizenship, enlightened career planning, and productive participation in economic life. Educators think that knowledge of such matters as supply and demand factors (which influence employment and earnings), returns to educational investments, and occupational opportunities can contribute to practical learning objectives.

Government officials. Convinced that economic literacy is essential for wise choices on candidates and issues—especially those related to taxes, spending, and the regulation of business and labor—many holders of public office from local school board members to state legislators, governors, members of Congress, civil servants, and Presidents of the United States have argued strong cases for programs of economics education.

Public-interest organizations. Proceeding from the assumption that in order to *do* something—e.g., argue persuasively in support of beneficial legislation—you have to *know* something (such as the costs, benefits, and possible side effects of relevant programs), organizations have encouraged and conducted educational campaigns to highlight key facts and pertinent economic concepts and principles.

Business. At times equating the business system with the entire American economy, spokesmen for business have advocated economics education programs in order to encourage a more cooperative, conscientious work effort based on an appeal to the workers' own enlightened self-interest. This application of the economic harmony doctrine, cornerstone of capitalist ideology, often identifies the study of incentives, profits, savings and investment, taxes, unions, and government regulation of industry as priority topics on the checklist of what workers should know about economics. The values of efficiency, growth, and politico-economic freedom are prominent in this world view, along with consumer well-being, worker morale, and social stability.

Organized labor. Reacting against the concentrations of economic power in the hands of business and government, representatives of organized labor support economics education on grounds that a well-informed countervailing power is needed to bargain collectively with employers and exert a more egalitarian influence on government policies. According to organized labor, priority attention in the economics education of workers should be given to studies of collective bargaining, income and wealth distribution, unemployment, poverty, monopolistic power and profits in business, governmental subsidies and tax loopholes, and the role of labor unions in promoting the rights of working people.

The sketches above tend to reinforce a point made earlier, that economics is strongly value-oriented—not just the application of economics to policy problems, but the content and teaching of economics as well. The content students actually devote their time and energy to studying will necessarily reflect other people's values. Again, this observation is not meant to denigrate the values of various interest groups, but only to remind us of their inevitable presence.

ECONOMICS THAT WORKERS SHOULD KNOW

It has been suggested that economics is a study of resources, technology, and institutions interacting to determine: (1) the overall level of employment, production, and income or purchasing power, (2) the structure and composition of productive activity, and (3) the distribution of income. Widespread public concern about the nature of economic outcomes demonstrates the fundamental value orientation of economic analysis. Witness such national goals as the full and efficient utilization of resources; growth of productive capacity and real income; conservation of natural resources; economic security for all members of society; distributive justice; noninflationary prices; reasonably equal and expanding employment opportunities; international harmony; and basic freedom of choice for consumers, resource owners, and business enterprisers. To analyze these processes and issues effectively, historical, statistical, and theoretical information and techniques are used.

Complexity of subject matter and differences in world view, methodology, perceptions, and priorities lead dissimilar economists along a variety of paths in pursuit of economic knowledge and ways of disseminating such knowledge. Thus, there is no such thing as "the" principles of economics or any uniquely correct set of economic facts, concepts, theories, and methods that can be prescribed for teaching.

How to Begin

Once a particular conception of economics is adopted, however, the selection of specific content for a worker-oriented economics education program can be made in a fairly straightforward way, though inevitably involving professional and other kinds of value judgments. Modifications would be necessary to reflect local circumstances, student audience, and any special learning objectives. The resources-technology-institutions analytical framework implies that something should be learned about the nature and types of resources (with special emphasis here on human resources and labor force statistics); the meaning and role of technology (including the principle that resources are a dynamic function of technology); and such key economic institutions as labor markets, unions, labor laws, federal-state programs of occupational information, training, and employment security. Similarly, understanding of the basic questions—How much? What? For whom to produce?—implies the inclusion of a set of specific economic concepts, facts, issues, methods, and principles; and the same is true for elaborations on the economic goals and techniques of analysis previously mentioned.

What follows, then, is an outline of suggested topics for a worker-oriented program of economics education building on the four-idea cluster—data, problems, goals, techniques—discussed earlier, plus a fifth "big idea" prescribing a sequence of steps utilizing the techniques and substance of economics to help solve policy problems. This outline is suggestive, not comprehensive—a globe rather than a detailed highway map. The topics are judged to be appropriate for secondary school students or people already in the work force.[9]

Outline of Economic Content

1. Definition and subject matter of economics: the ana-

lytical framework of resources, technology, institutions, economic roles of the individual as consumer, worker, citizen

2. Basic problems facing the economic system: how much, what, for whom to produce
3. Goals and values: in economics, economic policy, and economics education
4. Techniques of analyzing economic problems: history, statistics, theory
5. Steps in economic reasoning: the rational-empirical-comprehensive method of policy analysis for personal or societal decision making
   a. Define the problem
   b. Identify goals
   c. Consider alternative policies
   d. Analyze likely consequences (benefits, costs, other effects)
6. Resources (emphasizing appropriate historical, statistical, and theoretical facets of the respective topics)
   a. Limited quantities of all resources, dependence on technology, joint use in production, productivity, opportunity costs
   b. Labor (human resources): labor force, employment, unemployment, industrial and occupational distribution of workers, wages and salaries, human capital (including education and training)
   c. Land (natural resources): ownership, types, conservation, rent
   d. Capital: plant and equipment, ownership, investment, interest/dividends/royalties
   e. Quasi-resources: entrepreneurship, time, money, government
7. Technology (meaning, impact on economy and society)
   a. Principles of technological progress
   b. Automation and cybernation
   c. Obsolescence of human resources
   d. Insidious effects on human values
8. Institutions (evolution and present status of selected economic institutions)
   a. The market mechanism, market system, circular flow model, overall level of employment and income (Darcy & Powell, 1974—a circular flow is included)

b. Supply and demand for particular products and resources: elasticity, changes, price and quantity outcomes, product mix, functional and personal income distribution
c. Business enterprise: entrepreneurship, profits, giant corporations and multinationals
d. Labor unions: legislation, collective bargaining, research and education activities, political action, AFL-CIO
e. Money and banking system
f. Governmental (federal, state, and local) economic functions: taxing, spending, regulating, producing, transferring income, stabilizing the economy—monetary and fiscal policies, wage and price restraints, manpower policy
g. Labor markets: structure, geographic differences, "external" vs. "internal" job markets
h. Special work-related governmental programs: occupational information, training, employment security system—job service, unemployment insurance, occupational safety and health, minimum wages, public service employment, equal opportunity standards, and others

9. Some socioeconomic facts, principles, and issues of special significance to workers
   a. Predominance of the "wage-and-salary employee" class of workers
   b. Productivity principle of employment and wages
   c. Aggregate employment: jobs for everyone vs. "musical chairs"
   d. Perceiving the four functions of work: production, income, socio-psychological satisfactions, human development
   e. Income and costs: two sides of the wage coin
   f. Human capital and worker productivity
   g. Economic change and national job trends: occupational, industrial, geographical

Solving Economic Problems

As suggested above, economic knowledge and skills can be used to help solve problems in both the personal and social spheres. Five steps are prescribed for a rational-empirical methodology of policy analysis, or process of economic reasoning:

1. Define the problem: use history, statistics, and theory

to clarify issues and review pertinent facts.

2. Identify the goals: express the policy objectives and underlying values clearly, in operational terms, so that attainment of stated goals will in fact solve the problem as defined.
3. Consider alternative solutions: list the various possible ways (policy options) to pursue stated goals, again relying heavily on history, statistics, and theory.
4. Analyze the probable consequences: indicate the estimated benefits, costs and side effects of each alternative solution.
5. Choose the best available course of action: reflecting what has been learned in steps 1 through 4—having studied the what, how, and why of the problem and possible solutions—now make a value judgment, choosing what you consider to be the course of action that seems best when compared with alternatives.

Although it would be desirable to illustrate this method of decision making with both a societal and a personal economic problem, space limitations allow only brief treatment of one type: our society's unemployment problem (Darcy and Powell, 1973, 297-301).

Step 1: define the problem. During 1975, the number of unemployed workers in the U.S. economy averaged 7.8 million, representing 8.5 percent of the civilian labor force. This was the highest annual unemployment rate since 1941, though far below the 24.9 percent figure in the Great Depression year of 1933 (*Economic Report of the President*, 1976, 196).[10] Data on the composition of unemployment disclose wide variations in the burden of unemployment; e.g., while unemployment lasted less than five weeks for many workers, 1.2 million men and women were jobless longer than 26 weeks; the unemployment rate for nonwhite workers averaged 13.9 percent during the year, compared with 7.8 percent for white workers; the rate for teenage workers was 19.9 percent; blue-collar workers suffered more than double the jobless rate of white-collar workers; and nearly one-tenth of the nation's work potential was lost during the year because of involuntary unemployment.[11] Compared with unemployment rates of 3.5 percent to 5.9 percent in the past two decades, the 1975 statistics indicate an abnormally high incidence of unemployment. What makes it a national problem is that millions of workers and their families suffer the loss of needed income; the economic system loses productive effort worth billions of dollars; and both individual well-being and social stability are jeopardized by the injustice and inefficiency of the economy's performance.

Step 2: identify the goals. What is a realistic objective for reducing unemployment, and what time framework is appropriate for pursuing that goal? This calls for a forthright, though certainly not capriciously arbitrary, value judgment. One set of goals might be to: (1) cut the national rate of unemployment to no more than 5 percent within an 18-month period; (2) ensure that none of a specified list of labor force subgroups shall have an unemployment rate above 10 percent; and (3) maintain such rates for a minimum period of three years. Establishing this policy objective should not imply a rigid, single-minded commitment that ignores other facets of the economy. Goal setting must always be tentative and subject to constant review in light of changing conditions. (Specifying economic goals in measurable, operational terms, while desirable, is both difficult and controversial, again because it is so often the case in economic affairs that everything depends on everything else.)

Step 3: consider alternative solutions. Having selected a goal, the question is how to pursue it. What are the alternative possible ways to achieve the objective, without at this stage prejudging their relative merits? A representative list of some alternative policies for reducing unemployment might include: (1) increasing aggregate demand by cutting taxes, raising the level of government spending, expanding the supply of money and credit; (2) restricting the size of the labor force through a system of work permits—excluding certain men and women on the basis of age, skill, previous employment history, or other factors;[12] (3) providing tax credits or direct subsidies to private-sector employers for job creation; (4) increasing public service employment—state, local, and federal jobs; (5) others. The analytical techniques of history and economic theory, along with creative imagination, can prove highly useful in formulating a wide-ranging set of policy alternatives.

Step 4: analyze the probable consequences. It has been observed that science, including economic science, has two functions: (1) to point out various means for achieving a given outcome; and (2) to indicate the likely consequences of given measures. Insights leading to the development of policy alternatives—formulating hypotheses—can come from a variety of sources; indeed, minds that are unfettered by economic orthodoxy may well conceive solutions that are superior to proposals offered by old hands in the discipline.

On the other hand, the analysis of probable consequences of the alternative measures—testing hypotheses—in most cases can best be carried out by professionals with demonstrated competence in using statistical, theoretical, and historical skills. Whether they succeed or fail on a particular task is a test of maturity of the discipline and skill of its practitioners. (Thinking up innovative solutions hurts nobody; actual implementation of a crackpot scheme could inflict a great deal of harm on members of society.)

Without examining in depth each of the alternatives listed under Step 3 above, we would emphasize the importance of using history, statistics and theory to describe and predict as carefully as possible the benefits (including the extent to which goals are achieved), costs, and other effects that would result from adopting each alternative policy. Benefits and costs should be analyzed not in financial terms, but also with respect to real magnitudes such as physical output, income flows, human welfare, social values, and other considerations.

Step 5: choose the best course of action. After following the steps outlined above, the stage is set for choosing the best course of action: making a value judgment in a manner that is the antithesis of prejudiced and arbitrary decision making. Ideally this judgment reflects a conscientious process of confronting reality, asking fruitful questions, acknowledging the value content of the issue, assuring that innovative proposals receive a fair hearing, and demonstrating the role of logic and empirical data—linked through theory—in searching for knowledge on which to base responsible decisions. The rational-empirical-comprehensive method of policy analysis, or five-step process of economic reasoning, puts into practice the intellectual prescription, too often honored in the breach, that a value judgment is as good as the reasons and evidence that support it and as weak as the reasons and evidence supporting alternative views.

Once a policy choice is made, whether in the realm of societal or personal behavior, thought must be translated into action. Energy, resources, commitment, and vigilance in monitoring are necessary so that appropriate adjustments will be made in timely fashion with respect to both the means and ends of policy, in the light of experience and insights gained.

Workers as Means and Ends: Issues to Consider

We have noted that working people are more than a means of production, not just "human resources." People are also the end-purpose of production, whether viewed quite narrowly in terms of consumer sovereignty, or more comprehensively as participating members of a society dedicated to enhancing human welfare. Out of this dual capacity, as labor economist Sumner Slichter observed a generation ago, certain conflicts of interest arise "between life and work." In this concluding section, we identify seven important ideas that illustrate various types of conflict and challenge in the world of work which could be included in an economics education program for workers.[13]

1. A nation of wage workers. The vast majority of workers in the United States today belong to the class designated "wage and salary employees" rather than being "self-employed." Only 7 percent of all workers enjoy self-employed status, and the figure is even lower for strictly nonagricultural workers (*Employment and Training Report of the President,* 1976, 238). This means that the first fact of economic life for 13 out of every 14 workers—nearly 100 million Americans—is that they are wholly dependent on the labor market for their livelihood and economic status. This is a remarkable change from the situation a century ago, when four out of five American workers were self-employed, and even a generation ago, when the figure was one in every five. Clearly we have become a nation of wage workers, with far-reaching implications for both the individual and society. Among them are a need for better occupational information, more relevant schooling, career counseling and planning, employability training, improved methods of job placement, career ladders, employment security, job enrichment, and progress toward humanizing the work place.

2. The productivity principle. In a private-enterprise market economy, the basic rule determining employment and wages is that the worker must be worthy of his hire, i.e., he must contribute enough to the value of production to make it financially worthwhile for an employer to hire and keep him on the job. Economists explain this entrepreneurial practice in terms of the marginal productivity theory (Samuelson, 1976, Chaps. 27-29). If labor costs exceed the value of the worker's contribution to total output and revenue, what incentive is there for management to carry him on the payroll? If he is not worth his wages, out he goes!

The productivity principle may seem terribly harsh. Does it have any practical significance in the modern U.S. economy? Is it an iron-clad rule governing all jobs? Could it be "repealed" on humanitarian or socially expedient grounds? Without probing deeply into the issue at this time, we do believe there are large numbers of workers, both teenagers and adults, whose productive capacities day in and day out would not qualify them for regular employment under the productivity principle, especially in the face of legal and socially acceptable minimum wage standards. (Whether all these workers can be "rehabilitated" is a moot question. We also are aware that imperfections exist in the labor market that prevent optimal matching of jobs and workers, some of which—discrimination, for instance—can be reduced.) Had the productivity principle of employment not already been relaxed to a considerable degree in the U.S. economy (as in Japan) both in the private and government sectors, the measured unemployment rate would be even higher than it is currently. Thus, the productivity rule has already been partially repealed and the jobs and wages of some workers are being subsidized—by taxpayers, consumers, businesses, or other workers. Proposals to make government the employer of last resort—literally guaranteeing everyone a right to work—are based on a willingness to abandon the productivity principle on a national scale.

It is an indicator of American attachment to the productivity rule not only as an "economic law," but also as an ethical principle, that many people would insist on "word-fact" rhetoric to retain the illusion that public service employment under a last-resort program would indeed be in productive jobs. In actual fact, some of the jobs would meet productivity standards; many others would not. Here again is an example of value-laden economics and the importance of understanding economics at levels beyond the "about" and "what" levels.

3. Aggregate employment. Workers should know that their chances of finding and holding a job depend in part on economic forces far beyond the limits of their work place, and on considerations having little to do with the quality of their own work performance, the efficiency with which a particular plant or office may be operated, or the state of labor-management harmony. The most important factor determining job opportunities is the aggregate demand for labor, which in turn depends primarily on the overall level of spending by consumers, business, and government.

With a total labor force of 100 million workers, when the national economy is depressed and the unemployment rate is 8 percent, some eight million workers at any given time find themselves playing a desperate game of musical chairs. No matter who wins the competition for available jobs—based on age, sex, race, education, work experience, connections, or other factors—there will be an equal number of losers. In times of high national unemployment, say above 3 percent, or 4 or 5 percent, by definition it is just not possible for everybody to find a job. The remedy is not simply for the jobless men and women to try harder, but to restore the economy to high levels of activity by pursuing expansionary fiscal and monetary policies, backed up if necessary by wage and price restraints along with other measures to improve labor markets and economic performance. The fact is that the solution to mass unemployment lies not so much in the economic efforts of individual workers and employers as in appropriate policies implemented by the legislative and executive branches of the federal government. In other words, "politics" may have a lot more to do with a worker's employment and income than "economics."

4. *Perceptions of work.* Few human activities are subject to such wide diversity of experience and perception as work. As indicated before in the quotation from *Working* (Terkel, 1972), work can be perceived as violence to the spirit and body. The Bible calls it a curse. Social philosophers have termed it a necessary evil. However, the poet Kahlil Gibran wrote:

> But I say to you that when you work you fulfill a part of the earth's furthest dream, assigned to you when that dream was born, And in keeping yourself with labour you are in truth living life, And to love life through labour is to be intimate with life's inmost secret (Gibran, 1923, 25-26).

We believe it is just as wrong-headed to treat work essentially in negative terms as it is to perpetuate the myth of the happy worker. What seems appropriate is to stimulate some reflection about the nature and functions of work as observed in the real-life experiences of men and women. What is revealed is a perception of work as an activity that sometimes at least is capable of performing four functions: (1) contributing to production; (2) obtaining income; (3) providing opportunities for satisfying social and psychological needs; and (4) fostering human growth and fulfillment.

5. Two perspectives on wages. While it is no doubt perfectly clear to workers that the wages and salaries they receive represent their incomes—purchasing power to maintain a standard of living and at the same time provide markets that keep the economy humming—it is less often understood that these same wage dollars are viewed by their employers quite correctly as costs of production. The wage coin has two sides, and this is an important basis for conflict of interest between management and labor. Workers would like to maximize the very same magnitude that managers want to minimize. Not that business wants to limit workers' incomes; they merely want to maintain a spread between their total sales revenues and total costs, which by definition is their total profit. The higher the costs (including wages), other things equal, the lower the profits; and that undermines a traditional incentive for owners, managers, and stockholders to engage in business enterprise.[14] Indeed, without holding the line on wage and other costs, a firm's total costs might very well rise above total revenues, resulting in losses, which could force the enterprise to raise prices—if it had sufficient market power—thus feeding inflation, or even suspend operations and cease to exist as a business firm and employer of labor.

The purpose of making workers aware of this double aspect of wages is not to foster an acquiescent attitude concerning wage levels, but to alert them of multiple consequences that might follow their wage demands.

6. Human capital and worker productivity.[15] The quantity (and quality) of output a worker can produce per unit of effort depends on a host of factors, not just how smart he/she is or how hard he/she works. Among these determinants of labor productivity are: technology, tools, other capital goods, materials, skills of workers (including managerial supervision), and the nature of the product being turned out. Which single factor of production is "most important" and deserves the biggest rewards may be interesting as conjecture, but the fact remains that it takes a combination of various resources all working together to produce most of the goods and services that we value. Efforts to measure productivity have yielded useful, though imperfect, results; and this is an area of continuing research among economists specializing in national income analysis, industrial relations, income distribution, economic growth, and human resources.

Since the 1960s, economists in some of these fields have been studying the process by which people enhance their productive abilities through education, training, mobility, health care, counseling, and other investments in "human capital." Research has indicated that workers with more formal schooling, as a group, enjoy higher lifetime earnings than those having less. Efforts have been made to calculate rates of return on investments in education (see Sections I and II of this volume). Increasing attention is being devoted to different forms of human capital such as functional work attitudes, "system awareness," and various personality traits such as leadership ability.

7. *Economic change and national job trends.* In light of the extraordinary achievements in space exploration, growth of our trillion dollar economy, impact of the mass media on national events and lifestyles, and consequences of the energy crisis, it hardly seems necessary to urge that workers need to be more aware of our changing economy and society. Yet it may not be off the mark to suggest that millions of Americans are still impervious to any real comprehension of these forces of change that surround them. Are students aware that technological progress and productivity growth destroy 60,000 jobs a week? Are young people making adequate preparations for jobs and careers in growth occupations, expanding industries, and geographic regions where the most rapid development is occurring? Are schools and colleges well informed about employment trends and the kinds of skills required to perform new and changing responsibilities? The career education movement in elementary and secondary schools throughout the country, along with improvements in occupational information and related developments, will help prepare a number of future workers for the world they soon will enter, but surveys still indicate that most students are woefully deficient in knowledge of the world of work, a fact that challenges educators in general and vocational educators in particular.

Two final observations. Economic understanding and personal development can help individuals achieve success and satisfaction in the world of work, no mean outcome in itself. But equally important, these investments in human capital can qualify young men and women to become agents of change to help bring about not just a healthier economy but a better society.

NOTES

1. An individual typically plays three distinctive roles in economic life: consumer, worker, and citizen—along with numerous more important noneconomic roles.

2. Recall the old saw, "Whenever three economists get together to discuss a problem, one can count on their producing four different solutions." Readers who doubt the wide diversity in economists' outlooks, perceptions, values, methodology, and conclusions—even among mainstream Western economists (Marxists aside)—should compare the works of such Nobel laureates as Paul Samuelson, Milton Friedman, Friedrich Von Hayek, and Gunnar Myrdal.

3. The manic pride that so many economists took in their profession during the sixties has given way to a more humble posture in the seventies. Out of the 1975 annual convention of the American Economic Association came the story of a physician, an engineer, and an economist who argued about which was the oldest profession. The physician pointed out that the healing profession was as old as man himself. The engineer argued that long before the advent of man, God used engineering principles to create order out of chaos. "Touché," said the economist, "and who do you think created the chaos?"

4. Traditional definitions sometimes add the notion that economic activity is directed toward the satisfaction of human wants. There is a broad range of interpretations regarding this statement about purposiveness. Is it merely a reminder that economics deals with human beings, an innocent truism, a crucially significant criterion of bona fide economic activity? Or is it an apologia for whatever private-sector economic activity happens to take place—so long as it is legal—on grounds that it obviously meets the market test of worth or value, since somebody is willing to bear production costs? At this point, without delving into issues of social cost and shortcoming of the market as a valuing mechanism, we shall only observe that most mainstream economists have shied away from conscious involvement in evaluating the *ends* of economic activity, preferring to accept as given, the "preference functions" of consumers, firms, governments, and then concentrating on the *means* by which these ends can "best" be achieved—mainly through the functioning of an institutional arrangement known as the market. This appears strange to American Institutionalists and some other socioeconomists who find proof of the psychological foundations and value orientation of economics in such standard terms and concepts as consumer satisfaction, production of "goods," best-profit level of output, productive versus nonproductive activity, and supply and demand theory of value.

5. Our approach differs from the economics of Dick and Jane or Robinson Crusoe. We feel that teaching economics by simple analogy can have dangerous shortcomings that more than offset the pedagogical advantages of reassuring teachers that there is nothing difficult about economics and motivating students with strong human-interest appeal. Simplistic economics can do more harm than no economics at all: "It's not what you don't know about economics that hurts, it's what you know that isn't so."

6. A favorite classroom illustration of the five levels of knowing is the automobile carburetor. Nearly all high school students and adults have some knowledge of carburetors: (1) virtually all are aware

that a carburetor, being under the hood, has something to do with the engine; (2) many can point to it and tell you it is a device for mixing vaporized gasoline with air for engine combustion; (3) the mechanically inclined are able to describe how a carburetor actually operates; (4) a few students of chemistry and physics can explain why internal-combustion engines are able to function as they do in propelling heavy machinery mounted on wheels at high speed; and (5) a very select number have begun to understand the facts of hydrocarbon fuel production, use, and environmental consequences sufficiently well to begin formulating responsible value judgments concerning the overall subject.

7. Studs Terkel (1972) introduces his best-selling book *Working* as follows:

> This book, being about work, is, by its very nature, about violence—to the spirit as well as to the body. It is about ulcers as well as accidents, about shouting matches as well as fisticuffs, about nervous breakdowns as well as kicking the dog around. It is above all (or beneath all) about daily humiliations. To survive the day is triumph enough for the walking wounded among the great many of us.

Subtitled "People Talk About What They Do All Day and How They Feel About What They Do," the book contains more than 100 case studies of contemporary American workers.

8. See Chapter 12 in this volume for Professor Hansen's observation that student demand for economics education "appears to be weak."

9. For a more comprehensive treatment of the worker role in American economic life, including socio-psychological as well as economic content, see references cited (Darcy & Powell, 1973).

10. Current data are available, month by month, from other published sources.

11. For up-to-date details on unemployment, see statistical appendices of government documents: *Economic Report of the President*, issued annually in January; and *Employment and Training Report of the President* (formerly the *Manpower Report of the President*) issued in the spring of each year, and such current periodicals as *Monthly Labor Review* and *Economic Indicators*.

12. The employment rate is calculated as the number of unemployed workers divided by the civilian labor force. The only workers officially counted as unemployed are bona fide members of the labor force. People who drop out of the labor force, never enter, or who would be eliminated by inability to qualify for a work permit, in this hypothetical example, would not be included among the unemployed.

13. If this sampler of human resource economics fails to stimulate some lively thought and discussion among students and workers, we are obliged to concede that economics still retains its reputation as the dismal science.

14. As usual, outside textbooks, the famous ceteris paribus (other things equal) assumption of neoclassical economics probably would not be appropriate in the case of an actual wage hike. Sales receipts might increase, management might find ways to reduce non-labor costs, or worker productivity could rise sufficiently to cover the increased wages—especially if some marginal workers were let go. Since everything depends on everything else, there is no sure way to predict the outcomes of a wage rise; one must examine all relevant data in specific cases before reaching conclusions.

15. *Productivity* differs from *production* in that the former is a ratio of output to resource inputs, e.g., tightening 400 bolts per hour of work, whereas production is measured simply in terms of output itself, e.g., the 400 tightened bolts.

REFERENCES CITED

Darcy, Robert L., and Powell, Phillip E. *Manpower and Economic Education: A Personal and Social Approach to Career Education.* Denver: Love Publishing Company, 1973.

———. "The Nature of Economic Enterprise." *Vocational Guidance and Human Development.* Edited by Edwin Herr. Boston: Houghton-Mifflin, 1974.

Economic Indicators (monthly). Washington, D.C.: Council of Economic Advisors.

Economic Report of the President. Washington, D.C.: U.S. Government Printing Office, 1976.

Employment and Training Report of the President: 1976. Washington, D.C.: U.S. Government Printing Office.

Gibran, Kahlil. *The Prophet.* New York: Alfred A. Knopf, 1923.

Monthly Labor Review. Washington, D.C.: U.S. Department of Labor, Labor Statistics Bureau.

Samuelson, Paul A. *Economics.* 10th ed. New York: McGraw-Hill Book Company, 1976.

Terkel, Studs. *Working.* New York: Random House, Inc., Pantheon Press, 1972.

ADDITIONAL REFERENCES

Coleman, John R. *Blue-Collar Journal: A College President's Sabbatical.* Philadelphia: Lippincott, 1975.

Heilbroner, Robert L. *The Worldly Philosophers (The Lives, Times, and Ideas of the Great Economic Thinkers).* 4th ed. New York: Simon and Schuster (Touchstone), 1972.

McConnell, Campbell R. *Economics: Principles, Problems, and Policies.* 6th ed. New York: McGraw-Hill, 1975.

Rosow, Jerome M., ed. *The Worker and the Job (Coping with Change).* Englewood Cliffs, N.J.: Prentice-Hall (Spectrum) for the American Assembly, 1974.

Silk, Leonard S. *The Economists.* New York: Basic Books, 1976.

U.S. Department of Health, Education, and Welfare. *Work in America* (Report of a Special Task Force to the Secretary). Cambridge: The MIT Press, 1973 (published under the auspices of the W. E. Upjohn Institute for Employment Research).

U.S. Department of Labor, Bureau of Labor Statistics. *Occupational Outlook Handbook.* 1976-77 ed. Washington, D.C.: U.S. Government Printing Office, 1976.

U.S. Department of Labor, Bureau of Labor Statistics. *Occupational Outlook Quarterly*. Washington, D.C.: U.S. Government Printing Office.

Wirtz, Willard, and the National Manpower Institute. *The Boundless Resource (A Prospectus for an Education/Work Policy)*. Washington, D.C.: New Republic Book Co., 1975.

The State of Economic Literacy

W. Lee Hansen

No one, to my knowledge, has ever asserted that the economic literacy of the American people is particularly high. Nor has anyone concluded that the task of raising the level of economic literacy is an easy one. This does not mean that we must be content with the status quo. What we need to know is whether economic literacy can be increased and if so, how this task can be accomplished. Thus, this chapter attempts to describe the state of economic literacy in the United States today and to recommend ways of raising the level of that literacy.

Never before have we known as much, and yet so little, about the knowledge of economics possessed by our people. Assorted polling and survey organizations now provide a wealth of data monitoring people's knowledge and attitudes about economic issues. But whether the results indicate that the citizenry is reasonably knowledgeable remains unclear—largely, it appears, because little effort has been made to interpret the available data.

Rarely have we witnessed such concern over how much the populace knows about economics and our economic system. At least three major new efforts to raise economic literacy have emerged in recent years. The Advertising Council conducted a huge campaign to educate the general public about economics through comprehensive advertising, mass distribution of a booklet on the American economy, and the dissemination of films and other educational materials. The Business Roundtable sponsored a series of advertisements in *Reader's Digest* to inform its readers about our economic system. And the National Association of Manufacturers staged a campaign to tell the public about the role of government in the American economy.

Amidst this flood of information, it is especially appropriate to ask where we are and where we should be going. The first part of this chapter surveys what we know about the meaning of economic literacy. The second describes the state of economic literacy as it can best be measured. The third suggests why the level of economic literacy is likely to be low. A fourth section describes some of the work now under way to sharpen our concept of economic literacy. And the final section offers recommendations on how to raise the level of economic literacy.

THE MEANING OF ECONOMIC LITERACY

There is need for an operational definition of economic literacy that would make it possible, at reasonably low cost, to determine the extent to which individuals are literate in economics. We would not want the term defined so as to depend upon substantial amounts of formal instruction in economics. However, we would like a definition, the measure of which indicates the level of economic behavior and beliefs people hold about an economic system.

The term *economic literacy* probably crept into our vocabulary sometime during the last two decades, most likely in connection with publication of the report of the National Task Force on Economic Education (Committee on Economic Development, 1961). The report itself did not use this term; rather, it employed the words "economic understanding" to refer to the knowledge of economics thought to be attainable by the average young person upon graduation from high school and necessary for effective citizenship. The report stressed the need for obtaining an overall perspective of an economic system and for applying a rational approach to economic issues. Above all, it emphasized the substantive knowledge of economics—the tools and concepts—that had to be mastered to achieve economic understanding. Some unspecified blending of these elements would lead to economic understanding or economic literacy.

Beyond the task force report, one finds little help. Textbooks frequently set forth goals and objectives, but far too often these are couched in nonmeasurable terms. This makes it difficult, if not impossible, to know what the authors mean by economic literacy. Some texts have been more specific, stating as their objective, for example, the development of students' abilities to become more effective and critical readers of newspaper articles about economics. Again, the terms *critical* and *effective* are not defined, so laymen and perhaps even student readers experience difficulty in knowing what the stated goals mean.

The lack of definition is difficult to explain. Perhaps economists have already attempted and given up what appears to be a difficult task; traces of such efforts are reflected by imprecise statements found in most textbook introductions. It is also possible that any search for a precise measure is illogical because of the improbability of developing a useful metric. Whatever the cause, it seems clear that we, as educators, must decide whether it is worthwhile to define the concept of economic literacy and, if we agree, to develop an operational measure of it.

WHAT DO WE KNOW ABOUT THE ECONOMIC LITERACY OF THE AMERICAN POPULATION?

If we could agree on a definition of economic literacy, could we measure it? And in the absence of a definition, can we judge the extent of economic literacy in the United States today? Is it possible to determine the areas of knowledge in which people display the greatest strengths and weaknesses? What can we infer from existing data?

One approach is to examine the scores on standardized tests in economics for information on the literacy of students. At least three such tests exist. One is the Test of Economic Understanding (TEU) devised for use at the pre-college level. Another is the Test of Understanding College Economics (TUCE). Both instruments were designed to assist in evaluating the effectiveness of economics instruction. They reflect an operational concept of economic literacy. Another instrument, the College-Level Examination Program (CLEP), a test in economics, is designed to find out whether students have acquired sufficient knowledge of economics through their own efforts, rather than through college courses, to warrant receiving college level credit.

All three examinations reflect the mastery of economics obtained through rather conventional courses in economics. Although these tests have been normed, a decision must be made as to the interpretation of the scores. Does literacy imply a score of a certain percentage of correct responses? Or does it mean achieving at least, say, 50 or 75 percent correct responses on each part of the examination, regardless of the overall score? Or should we discount the test results, knowing that five years later the average student will have retained no more than half of what he learned? Regardless of how this question is answered, we still do not know whether mastery of a conventional course, as reflected by these tests, provides a useful measure of economic literacy.

A related approach to measuring economic literacy may be found in the model of the National Assessment of Educational Progress (NAEP), which attempts to monitor student knowledge in a variety of subjects. Several problems arise. Because the social sciences test includes little or no economics, no conclusions can be drawn until the number of economics questions is expanded greatly. Even then, the NAEP stresses the value of the results for showing what testees know, not in trying to pass judgment about the levels of knowledge demonstrated. Thus, efforts to use the NAEP results to measure economic literacy would almost certainly be resisted by NAEP representatives.

We must seek another approach. The most obvious one is to review the results of public opinion surveys in hope of finding a variety of questions and answers indicative of some level of economic literacy. This approach has both advantages and disadvantages. One noteworthy advantage is that the questions asked in opinion polls reflect changing issues and problems in the world rather than what people have learned from a course in economics.

A review of the public opinion surveys shows that they provide seven categories of potentially useful information:

1. *Facts.* The importance of these facts and the degree to which they reflect the knowledge required for economic literacy must be determined.
2. *Assessment of the most important problems currently facing the economy.* The answers reflect what is uppermost in people's minds, including such concerns as inflation and unemployment. Whatever way people reach their conclusions, the answers provide a measure of the impact of economic forces on them.
3. *Assessments of the future of the economy over the coming months or year.* Because the accuracy of these judgments can be determined later, it is possible to evaluate how well those polled understand the workings of our economic system. Of course, we must remember that professional economists often hold

substantially different judgments about the future course of the economy.

4. *Evaluations of actions necessary to deal with specific economic problems.* In some cases no clear consensus on appropriate action exists among economists. In cases where a consensus exists, we can determine whether the respondents' views agree with the conventional wisdom.
5. *The behavior of people under certain specified conditions.* On the one hand, such answers provide an indication of people's self-interest. On the other hand, such answers often indicate how individuals may be swayed by considerations of public interest, for example, after a presidential speech calling for individual sacrifices justified for the common good.
6. *People's priorities based on "what ought to be" questions which reflect their value judgments.*
7. *People's attitudes toward the economic system and its effectiveness.* This also is based on evaluative types of questions.

From these seven types of information, what can we learn about economic literacy? It is clear that categories six and seven are less informative because they reflect normative positions. Category two is somewhat ambiguous because the responses may reflect positive or normative positions, or both. This leaves us with categories one, three, four, and five as having potential value in assessing economic literacy. Whether these will be useful in fact will depend heavily on the way the questions are worded and the alternative responses provided. A brief summary of evidence for categories one, three, four, and five follows:

Category One—Factual Knowledge

That many Americans remain grossly ignorant of the most basic facts about the economy is revealed by several recent polls. When asked to estimate the average rate of profit after taxes on sales in American business, the medial response was 33 percent in early 1975, up from 28 percent about a year earlier; for oil companies the estimate was 61 percent, and for automobile firms, 39 percent (*Opinion Research Corp. Public Opinion Index,* April 1975). In 1974, actual profit rates averaged 5.2 percent for the economy, for oil companies 7.2 percent, and for automobile firms 1.9 percent. The general public was far off the mark! The belief that profit rates were so high undoubtedly led 55 percent of the public to state that government should impose a limit on profit levels.

If the ignorance of the general public seems appalling, college students do not perform much better. In a 1975 poll, college students estimated the rate of profit on sales for large national corporations was 45 percent (*Gallup Opinion Index,* no. 123, Sept. 1975). When asked about the income tax rate on corporate earnings, they reported a 15 percent figure, well below the actual rate.

A 1973 poll revealed the widespread belief that the gains from increased productivity go primarily to stockholders and management rather than to consumers and employers (*The Harris Survey,* 1973). This is contrary to the empirical evidence that productivity gains are widely dispersed across the economy through increased wages and profits, and lower prices.

These are only a few examples of many that could be cited showing how little our populace knows about the fundamental facts of the economy. Interestingly, pollsters ask about profit per dollar of sales rather than profit per dollar of capital invested; this reveals their own lack of sophistication in economics.

Table 1

ECONOMIC EXPECTATIONS (IN PERCENTAGES)

	Better	Worse	Stay Same	No Opinion
Latest	42	36	16	6
March 1975	35	50	12	3
Feb 1975	30	56	10	4
Nov 1974	16	71	10	3
Sept 1974	15	69	11	4
Aug 1974	13	68	15	4

SOURCE: *Gallup Opinion Index* (July 1975), 10.

Category Three—Assessment of the Future of the Economy

A regularly scheduled question is, "Do you think the economic situation in the United States during the next six months will get better or worse?" Similar questions about future unemployment levels and price changes are also asked. Exactly what "better" or "worse" means is not made clear. But presumably these terms reflect the areas of principal economic concern—prices and employment. The way in which people's assessments change is shown in Table 1. In general, these percentages seem to move slightly ahead of changing business conditions. Even more striking is the fact that as conditions change, either from better to worse or from worse to better, the college-educated group is always in the vanguard (though the data are not presented here). Moreover, the "no opinion" report is always largest for the least educated.

Although perceptions of major economic problems show little difference according to levels of schooling, expectations about future conditions do. The cause of this difference is not readily apparent. It may stem simply from differences in the kind and amount of exposure to economic news through the media and perhaps the types of jobs these people hold. That economics education influences these results seems unlikely, since most people receive no exposure to economics instruction at any level of formal education; thus, their knowledge must have originated from other sources.

Category Four—Analysis of Economic Problems and Issues

The ability of people to pinpoint the causes of economic problems and ways to remedy them cannot be assessed easily through questionnaires; on the other hand, no obvious alternative method exists for doing this. What can polls tell us?

In late September 1974, people were asked to indicate the "chief cause of inflation." Given that economists could not agree on this question, it is interesting to learn what the public thought just after the President's inflation summit meeting. The results, first for the entire population, and then by level of education, are shown in Table 2.

Several comments are in order. First, there is the obvious problem of coding people's responses. If a range of possible answers is listed, the respondents have to live with a forced set of choices. Second, given the choices, how unreasonable are those responses? Twenty percent of the people gave more than one response, even though they were asked for a single response. Nonetheless, the range of answers does seem unreasonable. Third, we do observe some dramatic differences

Table 2

PUBLIC OPINION ON THE CHIEF CAUSE OF INFLATION SEPTEMBER 27-30, 1974 (IN PERCENTAGES)

	National	College Education	High School Education	Grade School Education
Price/Wage Spiral	26	22	28	23
Poor Government Planning	12	7	12	20
Government Overspending	11	17	9	9
Consumer Overspending	8	13	6	7
Good of the People	8	8	9	5
Labor/Wage Demands	6	8	6	3
Excess Business Profits	6	8	6	5
Fuel Prices	5	10	4	1
Others	22	20	24	17
Don't Know	18	10	18	25

SOURCE: *Gallup Opinion Index* (November 1974), 27.

by level of education. The percentage responding "don't know" was inversely related to level of education. Whether this indicates that college graduates or grade school graduates are more knowledgeable is a matter of choice. The college-educated group responded somewhat more specifically, a larger percentage of their answers being "government overspending," "consumer overspending," and "fuel prices." Right or wrong, these answers are more informative than the blanket response, "poor government planning."

At the same time, people were asked, "How, in your opinion, should inflation be dealt with?" The responses are shown in Table 3. The responses were distributed equally among the various methods, fewer multiple responses occurred, and "don't know" responses came from more than one-third of all respondents. Twenty-eight percent of the respondents indicated price and/or wage controls, which, combined with "government control of business," yields a total of 32 percent, dominating fiscal policy.

The "don't know" responses declined with increases in education, and alternatives to wage/price controls were much more likely to be considered by the college level group. Only a month later (October 1974), when people were asked in a forced choice question to indicate whether wage/price controls should be reimposed, 64 percent favored this measure and 36 percent were opposed (*Gallup Opinion Index*, 1974). Opposition rose with educational level once again. Obviously, no firm judgment can be made about these results without introducing one's own value judgments unless a consensus among economists about the advisability of reimposing controls exists. It did not.

Category Five—Self-Interest

This type of question asks people how they would respond to a particular situation which may or may not be favorable to them. The results indicate the importance of self-interest in guiding economic behavior. Whether this self-interest evolves out of one's participation in the economy or through formal or informal study is not clear.

The situation in which people are asked how their use of automobiles will be affected by possible increases in gasoline price is a case in point. The data in Table 4 indicate that people in general are sensitive to price changes. We cannot determine how different subgroups of the population respond because the results are not presented by educational level. Apparently, people do see themselves responding in ways that

Table 3

PUBLIC OPINION ON HOW TO DEAL WITH INFLATION
SEPTEMBER 27-30, 1974
(IN PERCENTAGES)

	National	College Education	High School Education	Grade School Education
Price Controls	13	11	15	12
Wage/Price Controls	12	14	12	7
Cut Government Spending	8	14	7	5
Consumers Spend Less	8	12	7	5
Cut Foreign Aid & Exports	5	4	7	4
Government Control Business	4	5	4	2
Wage Controls	3	3	3	1
Others	23	27	23	17
Don't Know	36	24	36	50

SOURCE: *Gallup Opinion Index* (November 1974), 28.

appear to be reasonable. Table 4 is only one of a number of examples that illustrate this point.

Although we focus on cognitive learning in our teaching, attitudes (category 7) receive less attention. Attitudes reflect some ultimate judgment or evaluation: they go beyond the simple matter of value judgments. The nature of attitudes is reflected by questions asked recently on confidence in the "American economic system, free enterprise." Over 40 percent of the respondents, as shown in Table 5, indicated some, very little, or no confidence in the system. Grade school graduates were least able or willing to offer an opinion. Those expressing the most confidence were people with a college background, and those with the least confidence—about half as many—had the lowest educational background. One might argue, however, that the college-trained group gains the most from the system and naturally tends to favor it. Hence self-interest clouds the determination of attitudes.

Status of Our Knowledge of Economic Literacy

The available data reflecting economic literacy offers both reassurance and discomfort. People do seem to be aware of many economic issues and their conclusions about them often make sense. On the other hand, inadequate knowledge of the facts can affect seriously many of the judgments people make

Table 4

PUBLIC OPINION ON IMPACT OF INCREASED GASOLINE PRICES ON AUTOMOBILE USE

Use of Car (in percentages)	Price Rise per Gallon (in cents)				
	10	20	30	40	50
As much as now	54	35	24	22	22
A little less often	34	32	25	15	11
A lot less often	10	28	41	48	46
Not at all	1	3	8	13	17
Not sure	1	2	2	2	4

SOURCE: *The Harris Survey* (August 4, 1975), 2.

Table 5

CONFIDENCE IN THE AMERICAN ECONOMIC SYSTEM (IN PERCENTAGES)

	Great Deal, Quite A Lot	Some, Very Little, None	No Opinion
National	54	42	4
College background	70	29	1
High school education	53	44	3
Grade school education	38	47	15

SOURCE: *The Gallup Poll* (July 10, 1975), 7.

on economic issues. Perhaps we are left in much the same position we were in at the beginning of this report—overall, most people have a muddled understanding of economic issues, an understanding that must be largely intuitive because of the limited exposure of people to economic instruction. We cannot say that most people are literate economically, but neither can we conclude that they are grossly illiterate.

Another source of survey information requires brief mention: the *National Survey on the American Economic System* (Compton Advertising, Inc., 1975). Compared to public opinion surveys, this survey goes into greater depth and employs open-ended questions to a much greater degree. The scope of the questions is wide, covering matters such as the nature of economic systems, the role of specific groups in the economy, and the view of regulation, profits, and dividends. Finally, the results are presented not only for the general population but for special groups (e.g., businessmen, educators, clergy); in addition, the results are tabulated by sex, age, race, education and so on. The authors of the report conclude:

> Economic understanding of the American Public is incomplete and fragmentary. Few adults are highly knowledgeable and few are totally informed. Most of the population discuss economic concepts in general, even vague terms. Even in the best educated groups and among those who are directly involved in the business world there are deficiencies in information, albeit to a smaller degree than in others.

The only caution to be added is that the Advertising Council survey may focus more on formal knowledge of the system than on what might be done in particular situations. The polls may be more informative on the latter. In any case, the conclusions about the level of economic literacy do not differ greatly.

CAUSES OF SHORTCOMINGS IN ECONOMIC LITERACY

We are already in trouble because of uncertainty about the meaning of economic literacy. At the same time we harbor the belief, backed by fragmentary evidence, that people's knowledge of economics is severely limited. Given the nature of our political, social and economic system, with its heavy dependence on individual decision making, we must ask why better progress has not been made in developing the economic literacy of our people so that more of them can grapple with questions of economic importance above the elemental, intuitive level.

The answer, it seems, is that far greater attention has been given to the supply side than to the demand side of the market for economic knowledge and understanding. A review of the literature on economics education reveals that considerable effort has been devoted to increasing the number and quality of the producers of economics education (teachers), improving the means of transmitting economic knowledge to learners (curriculum materials), and giving the subject more appeal (innovative teaching strategies). The underlying assumption is that once we discover the right mix of factors and the right approaches, students and the public will be eager to acquire economic literacy. But there is little evidence to back this assumption. For example, though economics enrollments have risen recently at the college level, most college students never take an economics course; and those who enroll frequently do so only to fulfill a curriculum requirement. Although an abundance and wide array of adult evening courses are offered, economics courses are relatively few in number. Furthermore, there seems to be no great demand for economic news and reporting. How many newspapers have reporters who claim any knowledge of economics and write regularly on the subject? In how much depth is economic news reported in the media? In short, it is conceivable that even with well-trained teachers, first-rate materials, exciting approaches, and increased exposure, economics education might still be stymied for lack of effective demand. We may be at a standstill right now.

One source of the problem may be the very success of the economics profession during the past few decades. With the emergence of the Council of Economic Advisors and the spread of professional economists into key policy making positions throughout the public and private sectors, there is no doubt that more people have come to believe the state of the economy is in reasonably good hands. With more than enough economists available to offer advice to government officials and other decision makers, people are likely to wonder why they should spend time trying to learn what is reportedly a difficult and dull subject.

Also, it is uncertain that communities place a high value on economic understanding as it might be taught in economics courses or social studies classes in elementary and secondary schools. A recent Gallup poll (Gallup, "Seventh Annual Gallup Poll," 1975) asked the public to rank nine high school graduation requirements for students not planning to attend college. Ranked as "very important" by over 85 percent of the respondents were reading, writing, arithmetic, and having a saleable skill. Knowledge about the U.S. government and our history were ranked "very important" by 68 and 75 percent of the respondents. Knowing something about other nations and about the humanities were checked as "very important" by 49 and 33 percent. Where economics fits into this picture is difficult to determine—it probably would fall somewhere between "government-history" and "other nations-humanities" requirements. If this placement of economics is correct, parental and community demand surely must be judged as weak. This information indicates that the public believes the magnitude of the external benefits of economics instruction is limited.

Student demand also appears to be weak. In part, this may reflect parental influence and lack of demand. But other forces also appear to be at work. Most students think they will gain few direct, private benefits from the study of economics. Most of the benefits from understanding economics and economic policies by government, for example, accrue only indirectly to them. The economics that might provide them with more value for their personal economic decision making is generally not viewed as economics by most economists. Perhaps this draws too fine a distinction between economics education for improved citizenship and for individual economic decision making. Yet examination of the textbooks at both high school and college levels shows that they take the "citizenship approach" by preparing students to understand the larger economic issues. Almost no attention is given to individual decision making. An example of a book at the other extreme is *Sylvia Porter's Money Book* (1975) written specifically to help individuals make more informed decisions about how to allocate their resources and adapt to changing economic circumstances. Voluntary purchases kept this book on the best-seller list for eight months. It seems clear that the value of the book to individuals has been judged by the market to far exceed that of typical economics textbooks. Does this have a message for us?

The distinction—admittedly a polarization—between what can be called "citizenship economics" and "personal economics" bears further exploration. Assume for the moment that economics, as currently taught, focuses on effective citizenship. This means that the analyses apply to the large questions of efficiency and equity, stability and growth, and the like. Students learn quickly that much time and effort is required to master knowledge that will yield few future benefits to them. Thus, even though school resources are provided by society, the motivation for students to supply the necessary effort to acquire this knowledge of economics is low. We subsidize economics instruction, but by no means do we have control over the student's input of intellectual effort (though we may have control of his time!). For this reason we cannot be assured that the desired output is forthcoming.

Contrast this situation with one where the emphasis is on personal economic decision making, where it is apparent to students that what they learn will benefit them directly: e.g., career choices, alternative saving and investment opportunities, and budgeting of personal funds. The motivation to acquire this knowledge should be much greater. In the language of economists, students may see large private benefits relative to the resource costs they would incur anyway (given that school attendance is compulsory).

The dominant approach to the teaching of economics, as exemplified by curriculum materials and the formal economics training of teachers, indicates the root of the problem. The effort and resources devoted to producing economic literacy for effective citizenship are wasted to a large extent because the students perceive the benefits as being minimal. Although students are likely to be more receptive to personal economics, the interest and ability on the part of suppliers (teachers) is limited.

What can be done about the situation? Should we try to emphasize the benefits from effective citizenship literacy so that students will be motivated to learn economics? Or should we move the other way, by providing in economics a much higher component of content relating to personal decision making, recognizing that we can help individuals prepare for making decisions of personal importance? A middle ground would approach that elusive but optimal mix in which the learning of personal decision making economics would be linked inextricably with citizenship economics; as a consequence, both types of economic literacy would increase.

How to strike the balance between these two types of literacy is an important but frequently ignored issue. The introduction of case problems and of current newspaper reports in the classroom reflects a move away from the formalism of a decade or two ago. More important is the recent emergence of courses in personal economics and career economics at the secondary level, marking a sharp break with the past. Whether such courses actually meet the personal decision making needs of students is difficult to assess. We do not know the extent to which the content of such courses is linked to citizenship economics. Clearly, a major task for us is to investigate ways in which the two kinds of economic literacy affect the demand for economic understanding and for related competencies that may not always be viewed as economics by economists.

Another important but overlooked force preventing student demand for economics education, whether personal or citizenship, from becoming effective is the low level of general literacy which prevails. General literacy, as used here, refers to the entire range of basic skills, not just the ability to read and write. Unless students possess the necessary basic skills, they will experience considerable difficulty in learning economics. Apparently there has been no systematic study of the kinds of knowledge and skills necessary for economic understanding. Nevertheless, various skills seem essential: the ability to read, reason, perform simple mathematical operations, interpret graphs and tables, and comprehend some basic knowledge about the social-political-economic system.

Until recently we have been largely ignorant of student abilities in these and other areas of learning. Recent data from the National Assessment of Educational Progress, an ongoing effort to appraise the extent of learning among young people, ages 9, 13, 17, and 26-35, shed light on the knowledge and skills students can demonstrate at these ages. (See various reports of the National Assessment of Education Programs published by the Education Commission of the States, Denver, Colorado.) The results deserve study by economists and educators alike. Here are a few highlights from these studies. On the average, young people read as well as the experts had anticipated. Their writing skills—by which they customarily demonstrate what they learn—suffer from serious deficiencies. The mathematical skills of students also leave much to be desired, particularly in consumer mathematics, where young people had difficulty with operations such as figuring taxes and balancing a checkbook. Students' knowledge in social studies and citizenship was weak, as was their ability to read and interpret graphs, tables, and maps.

This brief summary of a wealth of data suggests that the teaching of economics cannot be effective until the general level of competency in a variety of learning areas is upgraded. How to do this is receiving increasing attention by the general public and educators alike. Because of recent declines in student ability and achievement reflected by national Scholastic Aptitude Tests and the American College Test scores, we may have to wait some time for the right conditions. Alternatively, we might want to think about the possibility of placing economics more centrally in the curriculum and using it as a base to develop general literacy along with economic literacy.

A NEW TASK FORCE REPORT

Important new work is under way that may help us get a better grasp on this elusive thing called economic literacy. Several years ago the Joint Council on Economic Education decided the time had come to reappraise and refocus its efforts to improve the teaching of economics in the nation's elementary and secondary schools. Not only had it already completed a major project through its Developmental Economic Education Program (DEEP), but it recognized that in the years since the 1961 task force report, changes had occurred in the discipline of economics, in the economic problems receiving general attention, and in approaches to teaching economics. This led to the development of the Master Curriculum Project, the purpose of which is to give new impetus to the teaching of pre-college economics.

The first and perhaps key element is the preparation of what amounts to a new task force report. While building on the original report, the new report (Hansen, 1977) takes account of what has been learned in the past 15 years and sets the course for economics education through the rest of the 1970s and into the 1980s.

A central concern in the report is the formation of a definition of economic understanding or literacy. The committee drafting this report takes as its starting point the belief that people should be equipped to understand several broad classes of economic issues, and to reach judgments about the effects and/or advisability of economic actions and policies. The committee also recognizes that these issues will be encountered by people largely through their exposure to the media, and in a more limited way through their roles as consumers, workers, savers, members of organized groups, and citizen members of various governmental jurisdictions. The question is how to best equip people to achieve economic understanding or literacy.

We have made a special effort to identify the major elements of the concept of economic understanding. This step is essential because we know that usually it is easier to learn and apply a broad concept if the various steps in the reasoning process can be isolated. As individuals gain experience, the separate steps will merge gradually into a single, almost instinctive process. With such an approach, we think that some of the mystery about what constitutes economic understanding will disappear.

We have identified six major elements of economic understanding. (The earlier task force report emphasized only three elements: numbers 2, 3, and 4.) They are as follows:

1. *Identifying the issues.* This calls for an ability to recognize that many current issues have important economic dimensions and consequences, and that it is important to distinguish between the positive and normative aspects of these situations.
2. *Practicing a reasoned approach.* This represents a reworking of the approach outlined in the task force report: it calls for applying a systematic method in thinking about economic issues, one that examines the relationship between means and ends, the effects of alternative choices, the process of reaching one's own judgment on issues, and so on.
3. *Possessing an overview of the economic system.* This provides a broad framework which helps people sort economic issues into several broad classes—the basic economic problem of scarcity and choice, resource

allocation and the distribution of income, and economic growth and stability.

Taken together, these three elements help move individuals to the point where they can bring more detailed information and knowledge to bear on economic issues.

4. *Understanding the basic concepts, including economic concepts and various statistical concepts.* This element is central to the framework because we emphasize the need to concentrate on teaching a limited number of important concepts and to work hard to ensure that students have a firm grasp of these concepts. We have selected twenty-four basic economic concepts and six statistical concepts. Some readers of the report will be disappointed to find familiar concepts either omitted or given a less than first-rank priority. Others will note that the absence of some concepts reduces the range of economic issues that can be addressed. Offsetting these criticisms is the belief that we can identify the concepts that are most powerful and have the most universal applicability. By concentrating on these concepts we can achieve the greatest return on the resources invested in economics education.
5. *Utilizing criteria for evaluating economic actions and policies.* This element, although overlapping somewhat with the reasoned approach, provides a variety of measuring devices against which different economic actions and policies can be evaluated—efficiency versus equity, growth versus stability, freedom of choice versus security, and so on. We recognize that any judgments people make ultimately will reflect their values in part, but we hope that attention to these criteria will sharpen students' abilities to analyze economic issues and highlight the role of their own values in the process.
6. *Applying the elements of economic understanding.* The real test of economic understanding lies in the ability to combine all of the elements above so that actual economic issues can be explored intelligently by individuals in their various activities and roles. We develop a categorization of news reports on economic issues and illustrate the concepts that are most appropriate for specific news reports within each category. We also indicate by way of illustration how all

of the elements can be applied to several specific economic issues. We believe that considerable experience of this kind must be provided so that students can acquire facility in the most difficult of all tasks: that of putting all of one's knowledge to effective and practical use.

The Joint Council's master curriculum guide will not attempt to recast the elements of economic understanding into an operational measure or set of measures for assessing economic literacy. But the elements can be transformed without great effort. This requires translating each element into a statement of the competencies expected of students. This is how they might appear:

1. Students must be able to distinguish economic issues from other kinds of issues.
2. Students must be able to indicate the various steps in practicing a reasoned approach.
3. Students must be able to identify the broad outlines of the economic system and recognize the interdependencies in the system.
4. Students must be able to articulate correctly the basic economic concepts.
5. Students must know the criteria for evaluating economic actions and policies and recognize the tradeoffs which they entail.
6. Students must be able to take everyday economic issues and apply the various elements listed above to reach an understanding of the issues and then make a personal judgment about them.

Obviously, much work is needed to fill out the details of the testing procedures and the level of competency required to demonstrate different degrees of economic literacy. This work must also recognize that the elements reflect various levels and kinds of cognitive learning ranging through most of the levels in Bloom's taxonomy. Once the levels of economic literacy and the testing procedures have been established, the most effective ways of teaching the elements of economic understanding and appropriate grade placement of the material must be worked out. Only in this way can we hope to build gradually the elements of economic understanding so that by the time young people move into the world of work and advanced schooling, they will be reasonably well-equipped to bring all of the elements together. This will be demonstrated by their ability to apply the sixth element to a variety of issues they will face in the future.

WHERE DO WE GO FROM HERE?

Because there is so much we do not know, it seems wise to forego any long list of recommendations and to indicate instead the major areas of ignorance and concern. Five major problem areas are cited:

First, what is an appropriate definition of economic literacy? What does economic literacy or economic understanding mean? Exactly what knowledge and skills help people develop ways of thinking about and acting intelligently on economic issues? The forthcoming Joint Council on Economic Education report goes further than any prior effort in identifying the components of the concept of economic understanding and in suggesting how these elements can be brought together for the achievement of greater economic literacy. The work of curriculum development groups should highlight any deficiencies and give us an opportunity to make appropriate revisions. In the meantime, there is no reason why others should not devote time and effort to the task of defining what we are trying to produce through economics instruction.

Second, how useful are existing measures? In fact, we have no instruments which purport to measure economic literacy. The standardized tests measure certain types of achievement, but it is not clear how closely these achievements reflect what economic literacy really is. The data from public opinion polls have never been analyzed with enough care to determine what kinds of knowledge and attitudes they reflect. Only recently have surveys been undertaken that probe people's knowledge of economics more deeply; these have yet to be evaluated. Much work must be done to find out how to make effective use of data which already exist and are collected regularly.

Third, can we devise an effective measure of economic literacy? What is the likelihood that we can translate whatever definition we produce into operational terms so that we can measure the behaviors exhibited by people and thereby reach some judgment about their levels of economic literacy? In the Joint Council on Economic Education report, we have not developed such measures, but this does not mean that the task is impossible. On the other hand, it will not be easy to develop instruments to measure what is ultimately a rather subtle mental process—the demonstration of economic literacy or understanding.

Fourth, what explains the low level of economic literacy? For those people who have had some exposure to instruction in economics, what accounts for their low level of literacy? Is it poor teaching, inadequate materials, the inherent difficulty of the subject, or a belief that economic literacy is not of great importance and value? The last explanation is particularly intriguing. If there really is low demand for the subject, then all efforts to improve instruction will miss the mark. This suggests that the links between "citizenship economics" and "personal economics" deserve much more attention. And for those with no exposure to economics, what causes their low level of literacy? Is it because their general education literacy is low, their informal education received via the media is weak, or they too have made a quick benefit-cost calculation which indicates that there are better ways to spend their time? Again, we know almost nothing about the nonformal methods of economic instruction and the way in which these methods might help to overcome the resistance of potential consumers.

Finally, what are the links between general and economic literacy? Our effort to set forth the elements of economic understanding, combined with the review of the National Assessment studies, suggests that general literacy and economic literacy go hand in hand. The usual practice in schools has been to develop the general literacy of students and then to introduce economics. Instead, perhaps both kinds of knowledge and skills should be developed simultaneously. It might even be possible to test this hypothesis by comparing schools in which economics is introduced into the curriculum in the early grades with schools where it is taught much later.

Finding answers to these difficult questions poses a stern challenge for economists, economics educators, and teachers of economics in the nation's schools. We must begin seeking the answers immediately, because a clearer vision of our task is essential if we hope to increase the effectiveness of our efforts to raise the economic literacy of our youth and eventually all Americans.

REFERENCES CITED

Bach, George Leland. *Economic Education in the Schools: Report of the National Task Force on Economic Education.* New York: Committee on Economic Development, 1961.

Compton Advertising, Inc. *National Survey on the American Economic System.* New York: Advertising Council, Inc., 1975.

Gallup, George H. "Seventh Annual Gallup Poll of Public Attitudes Toward Education." *Phi Delta Kappan* 57 (Dec. 1975).

Gallup Opinion Index, no. 113 (Nov. 1974). Princeton: American Institute of Public Opinion, 6, 27, 28.

Gallup Opinion Index, no. 123 (Sept. 1975). Princeton: American Institute of Public Opinion, 15-16.

Gallup Opinion Index, no. 121 (July 1975). Princeton: American Institute of Public Opinion, 10.

The Gallup Poll (July 10, 1975). Princeton: American Institute of Public Opinion, 7.

Hansen, W. Lee. *Basic Economic Concepts: A Framework for Teaching Economics in the Nation's Schools.* New York: Joint Council on Economic Education, 1977.

The Harris Survey. Chicago: Chicago Tribune (Feb. 19, 1973): 1.

The Harris Survey. Chicago: Chicago Tribune (Aug. 4, 1975): 2.

Opinion Research Corporation Public Opinion Index 33 (April 1975). Princeton: American Institute of Public Opinion, 1-3.

Porter, Sylvia. *Sylvia Porter's Money Book.* New York: Doubleday and Company, Inc., 1975.

Section IV: Economic Roles, Goals, and Curricula for the Major Vocational Education Service Areas

Economic Roles, Goals, and Curricula in Agricultural Education

Jasper S. Lee and John R. Crunkilton

Agricultural education is intended to provide for the basic needs of human beings; food, clothing, and shelter are among these needs. The kind and amount of education required for individuals to function efficiently as workers in the agricultural industry have undergone considerable change since colonial times. Agricultural education has come to focus more directly on the economic aspects of the agricultural industry. Full knowledge of the technology of this industry is of little practical use unless such knowledge is tempered with economic understanding. In short, the application of modern technology must be based on economic reality and answer the question, "Will the particular technology in question result in more efficient and profitable means of meeting the basic needs of humans?"

The purpose of this chapter is to interpret vocational agricultural education in terms of the basic economic understandings pertaining to the agricultural industry. This will be achieved by briefly tracing the rise of the agricultural industry, making an analysis of selected basic economic characteristics of the agricultural industry as related to the national economy, reviewing the contributions of curricula to the development of general economic understandings, and looking at future directions for curriculum and instruction in improving economic literacy in agricultural education.

RISE OF THE AGRICULTURAL INDUSTRY

The importance of economic literacy has increased with the emergence of the modern agricultural industry. Self-sufficient farmers in the late 1700s needed relatively little knowledge of economics. They produced at home almost everything they needed and, by and large, were not concerned with commerce. With the advent of certain major items of farm machinery, such as the reaper by Cyrus McCormick and the steel plow by John Deere in the early and mid-1800s, the emergence of the industrial revolution, and the development of improved systems of communication and transportation, farmers became more concerned about commerce. And as they became involved in commerce, the need for an understanding of the rudiments of economics developed. With changes in the characteristics of agriculture, modern agricultural industry emerged to give new meaning to the careers and life-style of people employed in agricultural occupations.

Economic insight into the agricultural industry cannot be achieved without knowledge of the scope of the industry itself. The agricultural industry is broad and includes all activities involved in producing plants and animals and delivering their products to the consumer in desirable form. Further, the agricultural industry includes establishing and maintaining plants and animals for aesthetic purposes; two such areas of activity are called ornamental horticulture and wildlife. The terms *agriculture* and *agribusiness* are commonly used when discussing the agricultural industry. Agriculture is defined by many authorities as being virtually synonymous with farming. The agricultural industry is a result of specialization and decentralization in farming. Many of the functions traditionally performed on the farm, such as growing seed and processing the crops, are now done off the farm. Collectively, all the businesses and industries concerned with providing inputs (feed, fertilizer, and so on) for farming and getting the crops to consumers (processing, packaging, and so on) comprise *agribusiness.* Agribusiness supports farm production in much the same manner that a ground crew supports the transportation performed by an airliner. Agriculture (farming), agribusiness, and closely related areas, when bound together, form the agricultural industry.

Economic understanding is fundamental in all agricultural education efforts. Education in agriculture is provided in several settings. Youth and adults are served through vocational education in agriculture provided by the public schools. In common usage, the term *agricultural education* does not refer only to vocational education programs, but includes different programs carried on by various government agencies and by private industry. Two examples of efforts receiving federal support, in addition to public school vocational education in agriculture, are (1) land grant colleges and universities, which were originally established under the Morrill Act of 1862, and (2) the Cooperative Extension Service, established through the Smith-Lever Act of 1914. Nearly all of the major business corporations in the agricultural industry conduct some type of educational program. These range from the highly specialized training offered by agricultural machinery manufacturers for employees of local dealers to the instruction that field supervisors give farmers and ranchers who are producing crops or animals under contract, as in the production of broilers.

The casual observer may feel that there is considerable overlap in agricultural education programs. This, however, is not the case if both the purpose and the clientele are considered. Vocational education in agriculture is provided under the direction of the public schools to train youth and adults for job entry or advancement in agricultural occupations below the professional level. No other agency is responsible for formal instruction in agricultural education for occupations at this employment level.

THE ECONOMICS OF THE AGRICULTURAL INDUSTRY

The economics of the agricultural industry is rooted in the efforts of people to satisfy their wants for food, clothing, shelter, and non-essential conveniences and luxuries. A very complex economic relationship exists in the agricultural industry. The part of economics which deals with these relationships is known as *agricultural economics,* the study of the economics of production and distribution of agricultural products. Research is used to provide information for improving technology and education; it is also the vehicle for disseminating research findings. Research, education, and consumer preference are the purposes that form the bases for allocating available resources to the various functions in agricultural industry.

Economic Resources

From the standpoint of economics, the resources available in agricultural industry are much the same as in other industries. These are natural resources, human resources, and capital resources; economists often refer to them as the *factors of production.* For agriculture, the factors of production are land, labor, capital, and management. Labor and management are both human resources, but they assume separate roles in the operation of the agricultural industry.

Natural resources include land, water, air, minerals, sunlight, and temperature. Man-made improvements which are attached to the earth and not easily removed are a part of the land, an example being a man-made lake. An applied branch of economics dealing directly with one area of natural resources is *land economics,* which is concerned with economic relationships between humans and land. From the standpoint of the land economist, land is ". . . the sum total of the natural and man-made resources over which possession of the earth's surface gives control" (Barlowe, 1958). As a factor of production, land is thought of as a natural source of food, fiber, minerals, energy resources, building materials, and other kinds of raw materials.

Human resources or *labor* includes both physical and mental efforts. The use of human resources runs the full range of employment levels in the agricultural industry. Some of the occupations are farm tractor operator, dairy farm worker, feed mill worker, livestock auctioneer, logger, veterinarian, research agronomist, wildlife preserve worker, and floral designer. The efficiency of labor is a concern in all areas of the agricultural industry; and educational and training programs are used to help improve efficiency. Vocational education in agriculture provides formal in-school and adult education programs aimed at improving the capability and productivity of workers.

Capital includes economic goods used by labor in conjunction with land in production. Examples of capital are man-made tools, machines, and facilities, known as *property capital.* In addition, capital is sometimes thought of as money, or *money capital.*

Management is concerned with the organization and coordination of land, labor, and capital for efficient production. In the agricultural industry—except for the large farms and businesses—the managers usually are also the entrepreneurs. The success or failure of a farm, ranch, or agribusiness is related to management. People who own farms, ranches, or agribusinesses run the risk of losing what they have invested. Thus, the need for using successful management practices is paramount, for if a business fails the owners lose.

Economic activities in the agricultural industry contribute to meeting the economic goals of the United States. These activities may be classified into four main functions: (1) production, (2) exchange, (3) distribution, and (4) consumption. Each of these will be analyzed as related to the agricultural industry.

The Production Function

Production is concerned with creating goods and services which satisfy wants, known to the economist as *utility*. With the agricultural industry, this includes growing crops and livestock; manufacturing chemicals, feed, and other materials needed in farming and ranching; and supplying food and fiber to the consumer in the desired form. In examining the production function, the reader is reminded that the agricultural industry is much more than growing crops and raising livestock. All of the supportive production efforts to make possible the culture of crops and livestock in abundance are included. Further, all of the activities in processing, packaging, and transporting crops and livestock so that they reach the consumer in an acceptable form must be included.

All output in the agricultural industry revolves around the four factors of production mentioned above. The first three —land, labor, and capital—are combined in various ways to achieve the overall purposes of the agricultural industry. Management has the responsibility of bringing about a mix of the other factors that will maximize returns to the entrepreneur.

The production function in the agricultural industry includes a large number of areas. A few examples are:

Supplies used by farmers and ranchers. These are supplies such as chemicals, feeds, fertilizer, seed, fuel, and animal medicines. A number of agribusinesses, ranging in size from small to large, are involved in the production of these supplies.

Machinery used by farmers and ranchers. This includes the manufacture and maintenance of farm tractors and equipment such as planters, harrows, and harvesters. Several large and a considerable number of small-to-medium-size manufacturers are involved in producing this machinery. Numerous local dealers and servicing centers distribute this machinery to the farmer and rancher.

Processing what farmers and ranchers produce. This includes the activities involved in converting plants and animals into forms desired by consumers. For example, the meat packer converts animals into meat products; the dairy processor prepares milk and manufactures ice cream and other dairy products; the cannery preserves many kinds of food until needed. What a processor does to crops and livestock is an essential step in the production function, if production is defined as increasing the capacity to satisfy human desires.

Population trends in the agricultural industry have moved toward fewer workers on farms and ranches and more workers in agribusiness. Production units have become larger, and individual operators handle larger units. Farms and ranches have increased in size, and many of the smaller farms and ranches have disappeared. Other small farms and ranches have been absorbed into larger units; some have become industrial or residential areas; and some remain idle. In 1976 there were approximately 2.8 million farms, compared to 6.5 million in 1920 (U.S. Department of Commerce, 1975). Less than a third (about 800,000 farms) produce 88 percent of all the food and fiber (Hueg, 1976). In the next few years, more small farms will disappear, with many being absorbed into larger, more efficient units. This continuous trend would not be possible without modern technology and specialization in the agricultural industry.

The Exchange Function

Agriculture in the early history of the United States was a way of life. Nearly everyone lived on farms and produced almost everything needed at home; they were self-sufficient. In fact, there was very little to be bought. As technology and specialization emerged, the exchange function became important. Specialists in blacksmithing and harness making, to name a few, exchanged their goods for the crops that farmers grew. This was known as *barter*.

Exchange is very important in the modern agricultural industry. Farmers and ranchers could not live very well if they could not exchange what they produce for what other workers produce. Of course, bartering has been replaced with our monetary system. The tractor mechanic exchanges labor for money, which is used to obtain food, clothing, and other goods and services. The florist designs arrangements of ornamental plants which are exchanged for money. These are but a few examples of how the modern agricultural industry depends on the exchange function.

The exchange function is very complex and involves two basic activities in the agricultural industry. These are (1) placing a money value on goods and services and (2) performing essential marketing activities. Placing a money value on goods and services results in a price. Farmers and ranchers are vitally concerned about the prices they receive for the commodities they produce because there often is a considerable spread between what consumers must pay and what farmers and ranchers receive. A good example is the common loaf of bread. The wheat farmer usually receives no more than three to five cents for the wheat in a loaf of bread costing ten to fifteen times that amount. The difference in cost can be attributed to a number of marketing and processing activities. Of course, most of these marketing activities are a part of the agricultural industry.

Marketing is more than buying and selling, although these are essential to the marketing function. In the agricultural industry, *marketing* is broadly defined to include all of the steps taken in bringing a commodity from the producer to the consumer. This includes primary and secondary activities. Primary activities involve preparing and delivering products, while secondary activities facilitate the primary activities.

The *primary activities* in marketing relate to the physical handling and processing of commodities. This includes assembling, or getting commodities from a number of farms or ranches together; standardizing and grading, often using U.S. Department of Agriculture standards; storing, transporting, and dividing and packaging. Processing is usually included as a primary marketing activity, although economists do not fully agree on this interpretation. In nearly all cases, processing is a vital step in bringing commodities to consumers, and therefore, is rightly included as a marketing activity. The primary activities represent a large area of the agricultural industry.

The *secondary activities* in marketing facilitate the primary activities. These include financing, pricing, risk bearing, and providing information about marketing. *Financing* is necessary to provide the capital needed for marketing to occur, such as that needed by a grain-elevator operator in order to purchase soybeans. *Pricing* involves placing a money value on something; it occurs in a free market during buying and selling. *Risk bearing* occurs when an investment is made with the idea of realizing a return on the investment. Price fluctuations cause the greatest problems in risk bearing. *Hedging,* to guard against loss, involves buying and selling futures contracts through a commodity exchange, such as the Chicago Board of Trade. *Market information* is the basis for most buying and selling in agricultural industry. Such information includes all areas having an impact on marketing (e.g., price quotations, weather conditions, and government decisions).

The exchange function tends to regulate the production function in the agricultural industry. This is due to pricing, which may stimulate increased production if the price is favorable or reduce production if the price is unfavorable, i.e., below the level at which the risk bearer receives a return on investment.

The Distributive Function

The distributive function enables each person who takes part in the production of goods and services to receive a share of purchasing power for his input. This occurs when people receive payments for what they contribute to the agricultural industry and to other segments of the nation's economy. Such payments may be derived from wages paid for the work of an individual; rent paid to the owner of land, buildings, machinery, and other capital goods; interest paid on capital; and profits to entrepreneurs after interest, rent, and wages have been paid.

The equitable distribution of purchasing power is a problem in the agricultural industry. All persons who participate in production are entitled to compensation for their contributions; and the assumption is made that each shares in proportion to the value of that contribution, whether it be in the form of services or property. The value of the contribution is generally dictated by the law of supply and demand. Considerable disagreement exists over the equity of distribution. Farmers and ranchers have long felt that they do not receive a fair share of the purchasing power, especially in light of the fact that many are entrepreneurs, and therefore have large investments in land and capital and bear heavy risks. Furthermore, workers in other areas of the agricultural industry often feel that they do not receive their fair share. A few examples follow.

Workers in food processing occupations often receive wages far below those received by workers in jobs at similar levels in other industries. A good example is the food cannery worker. It is paradoxical that persons employed in work so vital to the well-being of our country have been among the lowest paid.

Workers on farms and ranches have often been paid low wages. Exceptions to minimum wage requirements for these people have been legislated, making it possible for them to be paid at rates below the federal minimum wage.

Workers in a number of areas of the agricultural industry must often work long hours. Some of them, such as the dairy farmer, must work seven days a week throughout the year with little time off. This is far different from employees in many jobs, such as manufacturing, that have numerous fringe benefits, including paid vacations and sick leave.

Workers in some areas of the agricultural industry must operate hazardous equipment and use dangerous chemicals. They may do this for many successive days without changing to other tasks. These workers usually receive no extra wages because of the hazardous conditions of their work.

Even though concern over equity of distribution in the agricultural industry exists, considerable improvement has been made during the past two decades. Through mechanization, the drudgery of many agricultural tasks has been reduced and the standard of living of workers has improved. Agricultural industry workers in rural areas now enjoy many of the same benefits received by people who live in the city. This was not true before electric power and other conveniences were taken into rural areas. The quality of life in many rural areas may actually be superior to that in the decaying parts of large cities. This, however, does not completely alleviate concern for inequities in the distribution of purchasing power in the United States.

The Consumption Function

The consumption function relates to the use of goods and services. The aim of the production function is to provide for the direct satisfaction of human wants through consumption. In order for this to take place, the exchange and distribution functions must take place. Today's agricultural industry is consumption oriented. If more broilers are consumed, more will be produced. Production in the agricultural industry is responsive to the wants of the people, even though the industry may be unable to make such adjustments instantly. Time is required to grow a new crop or use up an existing oversupply.

Economists sometimes limit the definition of consumption to those goods and services which directly satisfy consumer wants. This narrow definition fails to recognize the materials needed for the production of these goods and services. In popular usage, consumption also includes the use of goods and services while producing finished products. A considerable volume of raw material is used in this manner in the agricultural industry.

Goods is the term applied to anything, material or nonmaterial, which satisfies human wants. Food and clothing are goods, and so are many other things used in the agricultural industry. There are two kinds of goods: producers' goods and consumers' goods. Raw materials such as fertilizers, chemicals, and machines which are used in the process of producing plants and animals are *producers' goods.* So are the raw materials used to make chemicals, iron ore to make steel for machinery, flowers used by the florist to make floral arrangements, and the logs used by a saw mill to make lumber. *Consumers' goods* are finished and can be used directly to satisfy human wants. These include canned food bought at the supermarket, ready-made clothing bought from the haberdashery or boutique, recreational sport fishing at a fee lake, and shrubbery bought at the garden center.

The agricultural industry is a consumer of many kinds of raw materials. Examples of these materials include supplies and services used by farmers and ranchers, equipment and fuel used in forest production, and unprocessed farm commodities used by food processors. Those goods and services that are finished products to some individuals are raw materials to others. The pesticides farmers and ranchers use are raw materials in the production of crops and livestock, but are the finished goods to the pesticide manufacturer. The wheat which farmers and ranchers grow is a finished product to them, but it is a raw material to the flour mill. In other words, whether or not something is a raw material or finished product depends on its consumption.

THE ECONOMICS OF AGRICULTURAL EDUCATION

As pointed out earlier, many individuals associate the economics of agricultural education with the economics of farming and ranching. However, the spectrum of economics in the agricultural industry includes the entire agribusiness sector as well as the business of farming and ranching. Thus, the importance of identifying economic goals for the total agricultural industry is paramount; agricultural education must give special consideration to its role in achieving these goals. These economic goals are reflected by agricultural policy in the United States.

Economic Goals Served by Agricultural Education

Goals for U.S. agricultural policy, as observed in the past and anticipated for the future, have been enumerated by Roy, Corty, and Sullivan (1975) as follows:

1. To maintain a profitable and viable and efficient agricultural production sector capable of meeting all food and fiber demands while providing satisfactory incomes to farmers for use of land, labor, capital and management.
2. To provide for an efficient, profitable and dynamic agribusiness sector consisting of both suppliers of inputs and handlers of agricultural outputs.
3. To provide consumers with an abundance and variety of food and fiber at the lowest possible cost consistent with the preceding goals.
4. To conduct a food and fiber economy within the framework of a democratic society, relying on the free market system as much as possible, consistent with all preceding goals.
5. To coordinate agricultural policy with all other public policies, including foreign policies, for the best interests of the nation and the world.

These five economic goals represent those that agricultural education programs should address as educators develop course content and design instructional strategies in the area of economics education.

Composition of the Agricultural Industry

The agricultural industry has often been described as a multibillion-dollar assembly line. Various facts are available to fully illustrate the reasoning for such a statement, and some of these facts are identified below.

1. There are 2.8 million farms which contain 924 million acres in crops and grassland, 213 million head of livestock, and 285 million head of poultry.
2. Farmers and ranchers annually spend $13 billion for feed, $5 billion for livestock, $7 billion for fertilizer and lime, $2 billion for seed, $3 billion for taxes on farm property, $12 billion for depreciation of capital items, and $25 billion for various other operating costs.
3. Value of products sold annually includes $18 billion worth of cattle and calves, $8 billion worth of hogs, $380 million of sheep and lambs, $10 billion worth of dairy products, $3 billion worth of eggs, $4 billion worth of poultry, $486 million worth of wool and other livestock products, $8 billion worth of food grains, $13 billion worth of feed crops, $2 billion worth of cotton, $8 billion worth of oil crops, $2 billion worth of tobacco, $3.5 billion worth of fruits and tree nuts, $5 billion worth of vegetables, and $4 billion worth of other crops.
4. To produce this amount of output and to operate farms and ranches annually uses $6.5 billion worth of labor.
5. To market the agricultural products, including labor, transportation, corporate profits, and other costs, amounted to $92 billion in a recent year.
6. In addition, the value of farms, ranches, and buildings is over $420.8 billion and the value of equipment shipped to farmers and ranchers is over $6 billion.

7. The annual export value of agricultural products comes to over $21 billion.

When one considers the total inputs and outputs included above, the dollar value of the agricultural industry is well over $150 billion. In addition to these facts, many people are employed to process and market agricultural products and many businesses are involved in the transportation of agricultural products from the producer to the consumer.

Status of Economic Literacy in Agricultural Education

The importance of teaching economics in vocational agricultural education has been stressed for years. In fact, emphasis on economics can be found throughout the curriculum in nearly all local programs. Most local curricula begin with one or two years of instruction in the basics of the agricultural industry at the ninth and tenth grade levels. The purpose of instruction at this level is to develop certain basic or core competencies which are prerequisite to enrollment in specialized occupational preparatory courses. The specialized courses usually are offered during the eleventh and twelfth grades and in postsecondary vocational education programs. These courses frequently are in line with the seven taxonomical areas listed by the U.S. Office of Education. The seven areas are as follows: agricultural production (farming and ranching), agricultural mechanics, agricultural supplies and services, ornamental horticulture, agricultural resources, forestry, and agricultural products.

Evidence of economics instruction can be assessed by reviewing curriculum guides used in various states. For example, in Virginia the ornamental horticulture curriculum guide includes the following topics: financing a business, records and accounts, determining cost of production, and marketing regulations. In Ohio, the agricultural equipment and mechanics curriculum guide (U.S. Department of HEW, 1974), developed under a contract with the U.S. Office of Education, includes such economics-related topics as: identifying organizational patterns of the agricultural equipment business, computing price and selling margin, and determining the market.

In addition to the inclusion of economic topics in each of the specialized subject areas, agricultural educators use two special approaches in teaching students the importance of economic concepts. Supervised occupational experience programs have been a vital part of the total agricultural education program since 1917. As one part of this educational experience, record keeping and concepts related to management and management decisions have always been stressed. Students maintain record books, decide what the variable costs will be, prepare budgets, calculate inventories, and make decisions affecting the success of the project. The entire educational experience associated with supervised occupational experience programs has a positive effect upon economic literacy in agricultural education.

Another major experience that agricultural education students are exposed to concerns the operation of local Future Farmers of America (FFA) chapters. These youth organizations provide hands-on experience with planning budgets, working with group decisions, directing moneymaking activities, and maintaining accurate records.

While the examples just discussed focus upon secondary school programs, economics-related instructional topics can also be found in postsecondary programs in two-year institutions, adult education programs, and young farmer education programs. Adult education programs have, over the years, stressed management and economics-related topics as a part of the instruction. The handling or mishandling of land, labor, capital, and management directly affects the success of the farm operation. Thus, members enrolled in young farmer and adult education programs have consistently demanded a heavy emphasis upon economics-related topics as a part of their educational programs. Furthermore, as the agricultural industry becomes more complex, topics such as contract farming or ranching and the futures market will become increasingly popular.

The status of economic literacy in agricultural education today would be difficult to assess in terms of scores, percentages, or other objective data. Provision has been made to include economics education at the secondary, postsecondary, and college level. Furthermore, many teacher preparation institutions require prospective agricultural education teachers to take courses in economics, agricultural economics, and business. Since little effort has been made to assess objectively the level of economic literacy of agricultural education students, agricultural educators may want to establish this as a priority area. Peterson, Harvill, and Horner (1973) have developed and standardized the Agribusiness Achievement Test. One of the four subsections of this test deals with the assessment of an individual's level of understanding of management principles. This test might prove to be an effective aid in assessing economic literacy in agricultural education.

Research in the Economics of Agricultural Education

Widespread efforts to assess the returns on investments of agricultural education have been hampered by many of the problems raised in Chapter 12 of this yearbook. Nevertheless, efforts have been made by a number of agricultural educators over the years. Many of these studies were designed to determine the number of graduates placed in jobs or to measure the increase in net farm income of adults attending farm business planning and analysis classes. Two studies will be cited here as examples.

In Ohio, Starling (1968) found that farm operators who enrolled in the Ohio Vocational Agriculture Farm Business Planning and Analysis course for two or more years increased their net farm income an average of $2,608. In Minnesota, Persons et al (1968) reported that over a 10-year period, the business records of 3,518 farmers who attended adult classes were analyzed to determine the relationship between educational inputs and economic outcomes. The findings of his study indicated that: (1) By investing $1.00 in an educational program, a farmer realized a $4.00 return in labor earnings; (2) An investment of $1.00 by a community in an educational program returned $2.00 in benefits to the community through the rise in farm labor earnings; and (3) A gain in farm income resulted during each of the 10 years of the study. In addition, the dollar benefits do not reflect the nonmonetary benefits to the farmer or other monetary benefits to the community through expanded business activity in that community.

Another approach to the study of the economics of agricultural education utilizes a follow-up of former graduates. Again, many studies have been conducted in this area and findings have reported as high as 90 percent of the graduates placed in agriculture-related jobs. Less numerous efforts have been made to assess the job use and value of agricultural skills learned by former graduates during high school. Evidence tends to support the contention that many of these agricultural skills are used, either on the job or in personal life.

As pointed out earlier in this chapter, there are many jobs in the agricultural industry which require the worker to possess certain types of knowledge about agriculture. Therefore, the economics of vocational education in agriculture becomes a very complex process. Furthermore, the economic importance of vocational education in agriculture must also take into account consumer benefits derived from lower costs for food, higher quality products, and higher standards of living.

IMPROVING ECONOMIC LITERACY IN AGRICULTURAL EDUCATION

The need for a better understanding of economic principles and concepts and the ability to apply them will become even greater as technology advances. Furthermore, economic literacy becomes even more critical in agricultural education curricula as farms and ranches become larger, the profit margin per unit becomes smaller, and the need for food and fiber increases.

When planning instruction to improve economic literacy through agricultural education, curriculum designers must take into account the clientele to be served. An examination of the goals of agricultural education and types of programs offered would point to the following groups: secondary and postsecondary school youth, practicing farmers and ranchers, adults associated with agribusiness, and consumers of agricultural products. Members of all of these groups have a strong need for developing economic literacy, and for the most part, these needs must be satisfied by those persons who are responsible for agricultural education in the public schools.

Once these groups have been identified, plans must be developed to improve economic literacy. Again, certain approaches can be identified and implemented for each of the clientele groups. One approach was used by the American Institute of Cooperation (AIC). A major objective of the AIC is to develop an awareness of ways to organize people and other resources to do business in America. An annual conference is held by the AIC to which youth leaders from throughout the nation are invited. The program of the conference usually includes five general areas: choosing a business, planning and organizing businesses, budgeting, types of businesses, and an examination to assess the knowledge of conference participants in these areas.

An approach to developing economic understanding which could be used regardless of the type of clientele is the educational tour. This teaching approach could be directed toward either the private or public sector. Tours of the private sector could include visits to local, state, or regional industry. For example, a tour of a grain marketing industry would provide individuals with exposure to country, terminal, and export elevator operations; the transportation of grain by rail, truck, and ship; and regulations that determine grades and standards of grain.

Educational tours to institutions in the public sector would offer individuals insight into economic policy formulation and evaluation, with the major thrust focusing on the function of government in the role of policy making and evaluation. Examples might include visits with U.S. Congress representatives, lobbyists of special interest groups such as the Farm Bureau and National Farmers Organization, Department of Agriculture personnel, and staff in private foundations.

Another approach to the development of economic literacy is through programs that combine work and study. Educational experiences of this type could be conducted on a small scale in local communities. For example, high school students could arrange for supervised occupational experience with local cooperatives, or adult class members could observe business and management activities of the local florist. Combination work and study programs in which students learn management practices have been initiated by large agribusiness firms such as Gold Kist.

Another approach to improving economic literacy, which has not been pursued a great deal, is the use of business management computer games. Several games have been developed at Pennsylvania State University and Purdue University which focus on decision making in management situations. With the expanded use of computers in education, this approach to improving economic literacy appears to hold great promise.

Other methods of improving economic literacy could be through the use of persons who hold management positions as guest speakers in secondary and adult classes, and the development of simulated role playing activities such as negotiating a sales contract. Also, continuous application of knowledge learned in the classroom to business and management situations will aid secondary students and adults in comprehending economic principles.

Agricultural educators have many sources of instructional material in the area of plant and animal science, FFA, and agricultural mechanics. Some of these include the application of economic principles. However, specific content in the area of economics is usually lacking. Many materials outside of agricultural education could be used in teaching economic literacy in agricultural education. Textbooks on economic principles as related to the agricultural industry should be in high school and postsecondary institution libraries where vocational education programs in agriculture are offered. Teachers and students should have access to newspapers such as the *Wall Street Journal*. Magazines for general audiences, such as *Business Week*, and those which are specific to agriculture, such as *The Farm Journal*, can be important sources of economic information. Other resources, such as case studies developed by the Harvard Business School, materials provided through the American Management and Marketing Association, *Doanes Agricultural Reports*, and reports issued by the extension service or departments of agricultural economics in land grant colleges should be available to the agricultural teacher.

SUMMARY

Agricultural education provides instruction for entry occupations in the agricultural industry. Since the agricultural industry provides for the fundamental needs of people and is basic to the welfare and prosperity of the United States, many economic principles and relationships are involved. These bonds are rooted in the economic functions of production, exchange, distribution, and consumption.

Programs of instruction in agricultural education have included certain areas of economic understanding, often related to farming and ranching. Agricultural education has been and continues to be in a position to be a viable force in the development of economic literacy among a large segment of the population and work force in the United States. Past efforts in teaching economic literacy are being expanded. New instructional approaches need to be used, especially in the broad aspects of the agricultural industry. Instructional programs for youth and adults at the secondary and postsecondary vocational education levels can be enriched and expanded to teach greater economic literacy.

REFERENCES CITED

Barlowe, Raleigh. *Land Resource Economics*. Englewood Cliffs, New Jersey: Prentice-Hall, Inc., 1958.

Hueg, William F., Jr. "Production Agriculture Must Face Issues." *AIC Newsletter* 28 (Oct. 1976): 5.

Persons, Edgar A., et al. *Investments in Education for Farmers.* St. Paul: University of Minnesota, Division of Agricultural Education, 1968.

Peterson, Roland L.; Harvill, Leo M.; and Horner, James T. *Agribusiness Achievement Test.* Boston: Houghton-Mifflin Company, 1973.

Roy, Ewell P.; Corty, Floyd L.; and Sullivan, Gene D. *Economics: Applications to Agriculture and Agribusiness.* Danville, Illinois: The Interstate Printers and Publishers, Inc., 1975.

Starling, John. *Mr. Farmer, Do You Want to Increase Your Income?* Columbus: The Ohio State University, Department of Agricultural Education, 1968.

U.S. Department of Commerce, Bureau of the Census. *Statistical Abstract of the United States, 1975.* 96th annual edition. Washington, D.C.: Superintendent of Documents, 1975.

U.S. Department of Health, Education, and Welfare, Office of Education. *Agricultural Equipment and Mechanics, A Curriculum Guide for High School Vocational Agriculture.* Test edition. Washington, D.C.: 1974.

ADDITIONAL REFERENCES

Coale, Charles W., Jr. "Agricultural Education Focuses on Economic Problems." *Proceedings of the 1975 Southern Agricultural Education Conference.* Williamsburg, Virginia: March 1975.

Dodd, James Harvey, and Hasek, Carl W. *Economics: Principles and Applications.* Cincinnati: South-Western Publishing Company, 1957.

Dorries, W. L., and Hamilton, J. Roland. *Economics for Modern Agriculture.* New York: Exposition Press, 1965.

Hoover, Norman K. *Handbook of Agricultural Occupations.* Danville, Illinois: The Interstate Printers and Publishers, Inc., 1969.

Krebs, A. H. *Agriculture in Our Lives.* Danville, Illinois: The Interstate Printers and Publishers, Inc., 1973.

U.S. Department of Agriculture. *Agricultural Statistics.* Washington, D.C.: U.S. Government Printing Office, 1975.

U.S. Department of Agriculture. *State Farm Income Statistics.* Washington, D.C.: U.S. Government Printing Office, Aug. 1976.

U.S. Department of Agriculture. *Agricultural Outlook.* Washington, D.C.: U.S. Government Printing Office, Nov. 1976.

Wilcox, Walter W., and Cochrane, Willard W. *Economics of American Agriculture.* Englewood Cliffs, New Jersey: Prentice-Hall, Inc., 1960.

Economic Roles, Goals, and Curricula in Business and Office Education

Lloyd L. Garrison

Business and office education makes a significant impact on the nation's economy through the preparation of clerical workers for entry into the labor force. In addition, it offers instruction in economic understandings and personal economic competencies for other vocational and nonvocational students. Labor force entrants are primarily in the office occupations or clerical areas, where more than 15 million are employed. The responsibility for providing appropriate training for a myriad of jobs in the office careers cluster in a dynamic economy is a formidable one. The task of upgrading the level of economic literacy is continuous—never fully achieved—but one of the recognized major goals of business education.

This chapter is divided into three major sections. In the first, an overview of the role of business and office education in the American economy is presented via an analysis of the job market—the demand side of the picture. In the second, the supply side is viewed: preparatory and inservice education for the office occupations. The third section deals with two aspects of economics education: (1) the role and philosophy of business and office education as it relates to economic literacy, and (2) a conceptual framework of the business curriculum, along with a discussion of a number of ways in which contributions to the achievement of economics education objectives can be made.

THE JOB MARKET

Many types of businesses operate within our economic system. The nerve center of a business enterprise usually is found in "the office," where various kinds of information are assembled and analyzed. Business and office education is concerned with the education and training of personnel employed in collecting, recording, and processing information. The appropriateness and effectiveness of management decisions, and therefore the ultimate success or failure of a business, may well depend on how effectively and efficiently the "office people" do their jobs.

Office workers are employed in all types of business organizations and government agencies. Such employees are found in agricultural operations, manufacturing concerns, retail firms, hospitals, schools, and so on. Thus, business and office education tends to impact upon the economic system in many different ways and to varying degrees.

An indication of the significance of the business and office education area can be gleaned from the number of workers involved—that is, the number in the labor force. The *Occupational Outlook Handbook* (U.S. Department of Labor, 1976) identifies office occupations as one of the 13 "career clusters" and refers to participants as clerical workers. In 1974, as shown in Figure 1, these workers numbered 15 million and constituted the largest occupational group listed (U.S. Department of Labor, 1976, 16). This figure also reveals the sex distribution of workers, showing the predominance of females in the clerical occupations.

Types of Office Work

Various types of workers are included in the clerical category. Many keep records and do other office paperwork; others handle communications, operate computers and office machines, take dictation, type, ship and receive merchandise, and ring sales on cash registers. Still others may be skilled title-searchers in real estate firms and executive secretaries in business offices, or relatively unskilled messengers and file clerks. Despite the diversity of occupations, much clerical work is concentrated in a few well-known jobs. For example, approximately one of every five clerical workers is a secretary or stenographer, and one in 10 is a bookkeeper.

Although some of the less skilled jobs may require relatively little formal education, secretaries, stenographers, typists, console operators, and others need special skills which must be learned in schools or in other formal training programs. Many clerical jobs require a working knowledge of grammar, spelling, arithmetical skills, and reading compre-

Figure 1

EMPLOYMENT IN MAJOR OCCUPATIONAL GROUPS (BY SEX)

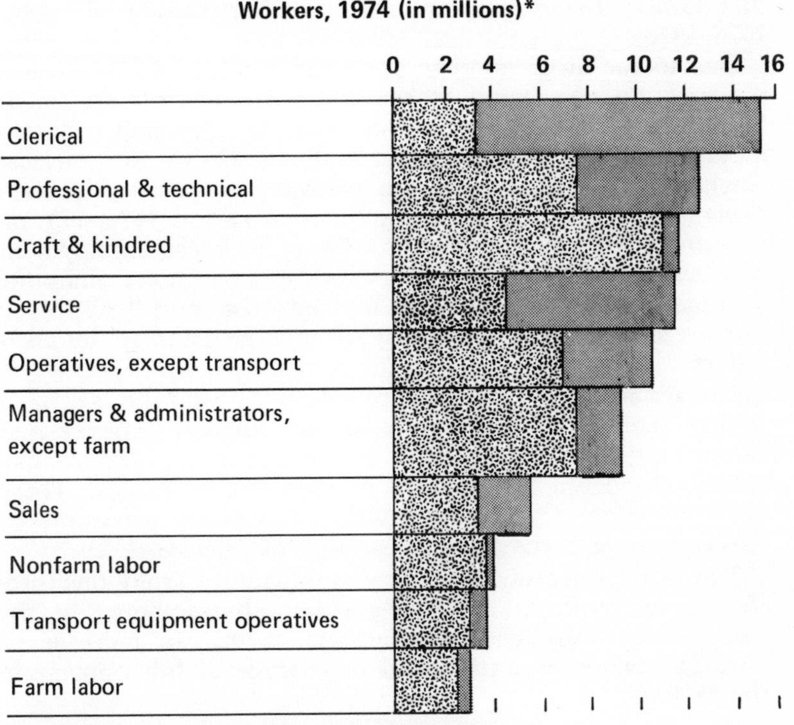

* Includes self-employed and unpaid family workers.
SOURCE: Bureau of Labor Statistics

 Male  Female

hension ability. Employers prefer that applicants for nearly all jobs have basic typing skills.

Employment Opportunities

Employment opportunities, of course, depend upon replacements as well as growth. In general, more jobs will be created between 1974 and 1985 from death, retirement, and other labor force separations than from employment growth. Figure 2 reveals that more than 16 million clerical workers will be needed between 1974 and 1985, with nearly three-fourths of this number being replacements (U.S. Department of Labor, 1976, 18).

Due to the large number of workers employed in clerical occupations, one would expect that a greater number might be needed in the future than in other occupational clusters; in addition, the percentage growth prediction for clerical workers is the highest of the various occupational groups shown in Figure 3 (U.S. Department of Labor, 1976, 17), increasing about one-third from 1974 to 1985. The employment of clerical workers is expected to increase faster than the average for all occupations through the mid-1980s, even though a great deal of paperwork will be handled by computers.

Certain common occupational subclusters can be identified within the office occupations career cluster. Conover and Daggett (1976) have analyzed labor trends for four occupational areas from 1972 to 1985, as indicated in Table 1. These areas correlate quite closely with educational programs or curriculum patterns in business and office education.

The percentage changes vary significantly from one subcluster to another, with the greatest change being in the stenography/secretarial occupations, where an increase of over 60 percent is anticipated in entry-level job opportunities by 1985.

Effect of Automation

The impact of automation on office equipment and procedures is considerable; and obviously it is more important in some occupations than in others. In general, long-term employment prospects are the best in office positions that are not affected by automation, in those which are compatible with computer applications, and in jobs which have developed as a result of new technologies. Automation tends to affect routine jobs the most, and many of these, such as payroll, bank, and file clerks, may be reduced or eliminated. Of course,

Figure 2

OCCUPATIONAL GROUP TRAINING NEEDS AS DETERMINED BY REPLACEMENT PLUS GROWTH

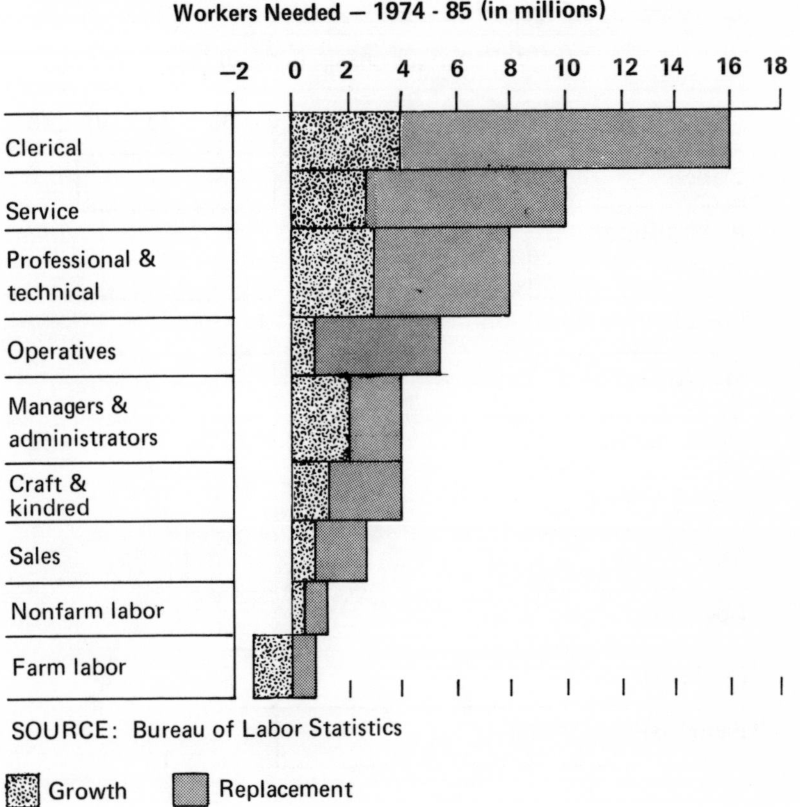

SOURCE: Bureau of Labor Statistics

Figure 3

VARIATIONS IN EMPLOYMENT GROWTH
AMONG OCCUPATIONAL GROUPS

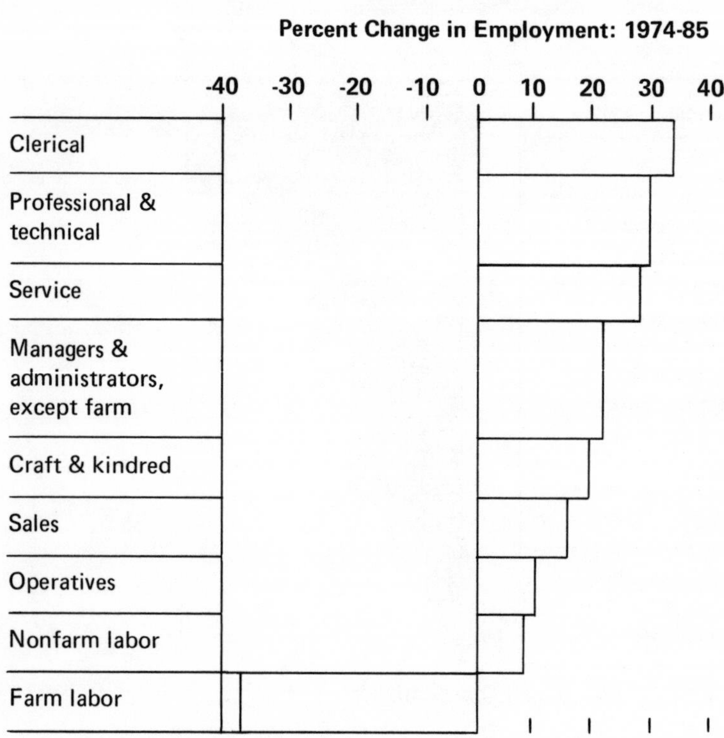

SOURCE: Bureau of Labor Statistics

Table 1

BUSINESS OCCUPATIONS EMPLOYMENT OPPORTUNITIES
1972-85

	Employment (Thousands)			Openings (Thousands)		
	1972	1985	Increase (Percent)	Annual	Growth	Replace
Bookkeeping	1,548	1,900	19.5	118	24	94
Office Practice*	2,210	2,910	31.4	217.8	55.3	162.5
Steno/ Secretary	3,024	4,950	60.8	411	144	286
Data Processing**	480	531	10.6	27	4	23

*Includes file clerks, office machines operators, postal clerks, receptionists and typists.
**Includes console, auxiliary equipment, and keypunch operators.

SOURCE: Conover and Daggett, 1976.

some new jobs will be created for clerical workers as tasks are shifted from clerks to machines. Job opportunities are especially favorable for receptionists, secretaries, typists, and computer operators (U.S. Department of Labor, 1976, 81-82).

Employers are seeking people who have higher levels of education because many jobs are more complex and require greater skill, which may result in part from the effects of automation in the office. A high school education has become standard for American workers, with some occupational areas requiring more than a high school diploma. As new automated equipment is introduced on a wider scale in offices, banks, insurance companies, and government operations, skill requirements for clerical and related jobs are rising. Although automation in the office is still far behind automation in industry, significant developments have occurred recently.

Readers who have not visited a modern office or word processing center in recent years probably would be amazed at the efficiency and scope of operations. The nature of many office jobs has changed drastically, making it imperative that curriculum specialists and vocational program developers be aware of such developments.

EDUCATION FOR THE OFFICE OCCUPATIONS

Program Enrollments

Vocational education, including that for the office occupations, has experienced rapid growth, especially since the Vocational Education Amendments of 1968. Total enrollment in vocational education during fiscal year 1975 was 15,340,426, of which 2,951,065 (19.2 percent) were enrolled in office occupations programs. Enrollment in office occupations by U.S. Office of Education (USOE) instructional program code for the years 1970 through 1975, with projections for 1979, is shown in Table 2. Data used were taken from publications of the U.S. Department of Health, Education, and Welfare (1972, 9-10; 1974, 10; 1975, 1).

During fiscal year 1975, approximately 60 percent of those individuals enrolled in office occupations programs were at the secondary school level; 18 percent, postsecondary; and 22 percent, adult (U.S. Department of Health, Education, and Welfare, 1975, 1). About three-fourths of the enrollees were females and one-fourth were males (U.S. Department of Health, Education, and Welfare, 1972, 7).

The significance of the office occupations programs is further manifested when a comparison is made between the

Table 2

ENROLLMENT IN OFFICE OCCUPATIONS (BY USOE INSTRUCTIONAL PROGRAM CODE) FISCAL YEARS 1970-79

	1970	1971	1972	1973	1974	1975	1979 (Projected)
Office Occupations*	2,111,160	2,226,854	2,351,878	2,499,095	2,757,464	2,951,065	3,601,000
Accounting and computing	301,353	328,281	351,861	385,622	429,708	473,184	525,000
Business data processing systems	165,977	181,313	156,748	155,804	160,000	182,418**	175,000
Filing, office machines, clerical	381,875	364,274	398,226	429,664	508,915	539,562	700,000
Information communication	23,572	26,788	23,826	29,640	31,636	40,705	40,000
Materials support, transporting, etc.	12,441	11,860	10,288	8,636	17,219	9,699	20,000
Personnel, training, & related	9,268	11,924	13,693	20,631	27,492	50,099	50,000
Stenographic, secretarial, & related	470,030	533,221	550,686	606,065	656,522	667,239	800,000
Supervisory & administrative	50,895	70,050	77,730	84,368	109,864	129,971	200,000
Typing & related	555,357	612,770	628,414	628,758	661,730	667,250	850,000
Other	140,392	88,212	141,300	149,927	159,685	190,961	241,000

*Unduplicated total.

**Includes computer and console operators, 25,227; programmers, 26,434; and other business data processing, 130,757.

growth and rank of office occupations OE instructional programs and those of other programs with large enrollments. The top twelve ranking programs are shown in Table 3 (U.S. Department of Health, Education, and Welfare, 2). It may be noted that five of the twelve—the second, third, fifth, sixth, and eleventh—were office occupations programs.

Educational Preparation and Employment Opportunities

The steady growth in enrollment in the office occupational programs is consistent with the growth in employment opportunities. In the first part of this chapter, it was noted that some 16 million clerical or office workers would be needed between 1974 and 1985, based on growth and replacement—the percentage of increase in employment during that period being over 30 percent. Occupational areas in which demand will be great, e.g., secretaries and typists, are also the instructional program areas with large enrollments.

Enrollments in business and office education presented in this section do not include all of the instruction for office workers. Not included are enrollments in proprietary schools, courses other than those classified as "vocational" in secondary school, on-the-job training programs, continuing education, and certain federal programs. The only consistently available national data are those presented earlier which relate exclusively to office occupational programs in the public schools.

Program Costs

Although much enrollment and cost data on various vocational education programs is provided by the U.S. Office of Education's Division of Vocational and Technical Education, cost data for occupational programs per se are not available. Consequently, it is not possible to identify and analyze the costs of the office occupational programs. However, an analysis of expenditures and returns for vocational educational as an "industry" and benefit-cost analysis in vocational education have been presented elsewhere in this yearbook.

Although reliable cost information, either direct or indirect, is not available concerning education for the office occupations—thus making it impossible to quantify the contribution to personal earnings or national income—a reasonable assumption would be that the investment in business and office education is having a significant effect. A worthwhile contribution is being made to the human resources of the nation.

With limited economic resources, society must choose be-

Table 3

INSTRUCTIONAL PROGRAMS WITH THE LARGEST ENROLLMENTS 1969 AND 1974

USOE Instructional Programs	1974 Number	1974 Rank	1969* Number	1969* Rank
Prevocational	1,081,257	1	---	--
Typing & related	661,730	2	458,714	3
Stenographic & secretarial	656,522	3	482,324	2
Agricultural production	552,441	4	645,377	1
Filing & office machines	508,915	5	86,826	4
Accounting & computing	429,708	6	249,209	6
Metalworking	374,628	7	249,248	5
Industrial arts	356,403	8	---	--
Auto mechanics	308,154	9	126,372	9
General merchandise	254,859	10	120,586	10
Business data processing	160,020	11	134,723	7
Fireman training	124,314	12	131,580	8

*Prior to Vocational Education Amendments of 1968.

SOURCE: U.S. Department of Health, Education, and Welfare, *Trends in Vocational Education: Fiscal Year 1972.*

tween the two major modes of investment: investment in humans or in machines. Continuing with this line of reasoning means that we must also make choices among educational programs; for example, whether to fund a business and office education program or one in agriculture, a program in the comprehensive high school or one in an area vocational-technical school. Very likely, a benefit-cost analysis study would be needed in reaching a decision.

The Oklahoma State Department of Vocational and Technical Education has done some pilot work in the area of standardized program costs. The data shown in Table 4 identifies such costs for a business and office education program in a comprehensive high school (Collins, Smith & Hopkins, 1974b, 13) and an area vocational-technical school (Collins, Smith & Hopkins, 1974a, 9). Costs used are primarily those of the 1972-73 period, which can easily be adjusted to current levels by applying price indices. Some adjustment also might need to be made for cost variations in different sections of the country, such as those for instructors' salaries.

BUSINESS AND OFFICE EDUCATION AND ECONOMIC LITERACY

Business education, by its very nature, is an economic undertaking. Every subject in the curriculum addresses itself to an economic problem—whether it be preparing for a particular vocation, understanding the economic environment, or making enlightened voter and consumer decisions (Daughtrey, 1970, 97).

The total goal of economics education, which is to achieve a high level of economic literacy, cannot be achieved in any one course or curriculum area. Economics education is similar to character education in that it must be handled and taught by many different teachers in many different ways throughout the school curriculum. As Hansen points out in Chapter 12 of this yearbook, of course, we lack a precise definition of what is meant by economic literacy, which makes our job more difficult. However, many would agree that a definition of *economic literacy* should include a blending of some substantive knowledge of economics that would enable individuals to obtain an overview of our economic system and to develop the ability to apply a rational approach to economic issues in order to function effectively as citizens in our society.

Table 4

STANDARDIZED PROGRAM COSTS: BUSINESS AND OFFICE DIVISION

Cost Areas	Annual Operating Cost	
	Comprehensive High School	Area Vocational-Technical School
Salary of Instructor	$ 9,550	$ 8,967
Travel of Instructor	88	152
Salary of Supportive Personnel	1,725	6,317
Depreciation of Facilities	465	905
Depreciation of Equipment	1,187	2,264
Operation & Maintenance of Plant (Includes Heating, Air Conditioning, Electricity, Water, & Consumable Supplies)	445	1,188
Annual Insurance of Facilities	70	136
Annual Insurance of Equipment	89	170
TOTAL	$13,619	$20,099
CAPITAL OUTLAY FOR A NEW PROGRAM		
Facilities	$13,950	$27,150
Equipment	14,838	28,300
TOTAL	$28,788	$55,450

SOURCE: Collins, Smith and Hopkins (1974a, 9; 1974b, 13).

Philosophy of Business and Office Education

A philosophy of business and office education that has evolved over the years includes both general and specialized education. The specialized, or vocational phase, prepares students to enter office occupations as capable and intelligent members of the labor force. The general education phase assists individuals in developing an understanding of the American economic system so that they can cast their dollar vote for goods and services and their ballot for issues and candidates from an enlightened position.

A conceptual framework for the business curriculum which is generally accepted today is shown in Figure 4.

The *about* phase includes both personal economic decision making and aggregate economic analysis. The *for* business phase includes instruction designed to prepare persons for gainful employment. Personal use skills are developed in both categories. The instructional goals are to prepare informed citizens and informed workers. The ultimate curricular goal is to improve our economic society. This goal is accomplished when persons understand the system and can participate in it intelligently, which means they are also economically literate.

Business courses in the *about* phase are designed for all students. This area is often labeled "basic business" and includes such courses as general business, advanced general business, consumer economics, business principles and management, and economics. When these courses are treated as a composite, the objective is the same as for economics education: to aid the student in developing an understanding of economics and the American economic system and in acquiring the skills and abilities necessary to perform citizenship and consumer functions effectively in that system (Daughtrey, 1970, 98).

Basic Business Education

The *general business course* has evolved through experiences with several types of objectives, but now is widely recognized as the offering through which business education makes a unique contribution to the achievement of economic literacy, or the objective of economics education. It introduces the deeper concepts of business and economics at a point in the development of students when they begin to encounter adult problems of the world of business—ninth and tenth grades.

In recent years, emphasis in general business has shifted from personal economic skills to an understanding of broader

Figure 4

A CONCEPTUAL FRAMEWORK FOR THE BUSINESS CURRICULUM

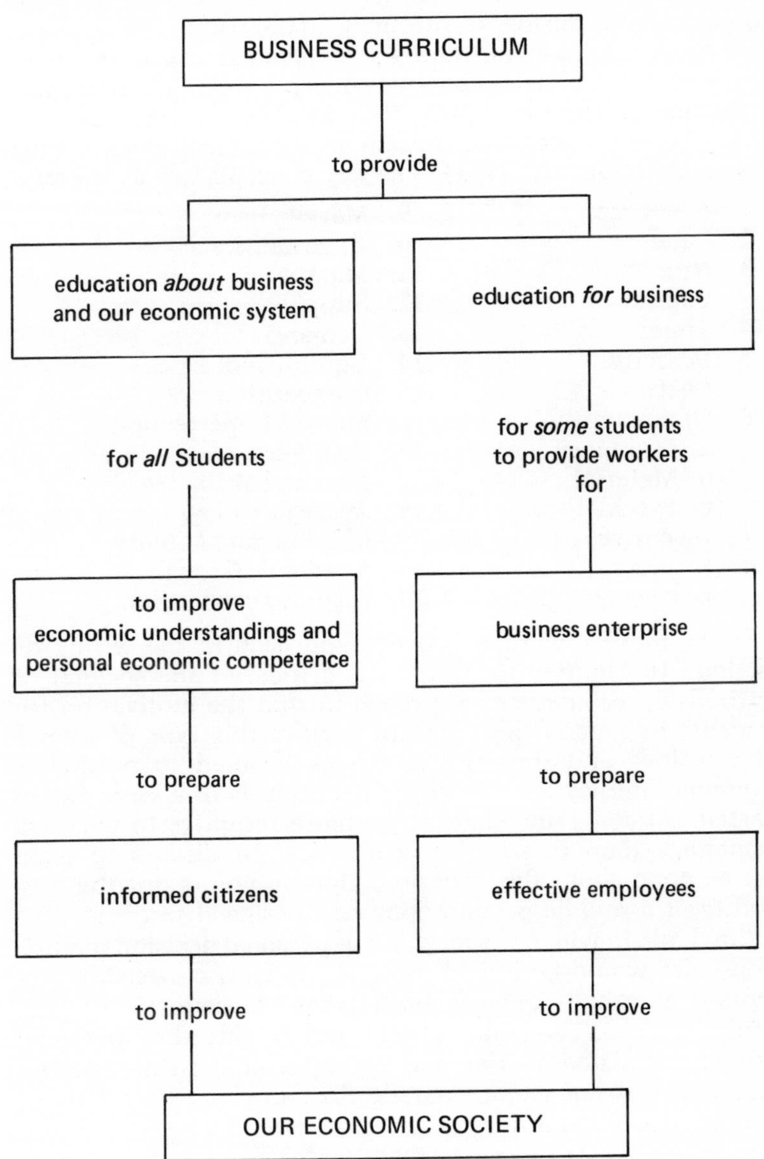

economic concepts. Several years ago this writer, in cooperation with a group of high school general business teachers, developed a syllabus "solely for the purpose of assisting teachers who want to enrich the typical textbook course with materials that provide a better understanding of the nature and functioning of the American economy and of the economic role of business enterprise" (Garrison, 1964). Since that time textbook authors have included much more information about basic economic concepts and understandings.

Becker and Reinke (1975, 203) identify the page location of key economic concepts in one of the current general business texts (Nanassy, 1973). The key concepts are as follows:

1. Resources
2. Land
3. Human Capital
4. Time
5. Scarcity Costs
6. Opportunity
   a. Pecuniary
   b. Material
   c. Psychic
7. Incentives
8. Economic Efficiency
9. Marginalism
10. Externalities
11. Market
12. Supply
13. Demand
14. Equilibrium Price
15. Competition
16. Market Imperfections
17. Real Versus Nominal Measures
18. Aggregate Flow of Economic Activity
19. Economic Growth
20. Income Distribution

Is the move toward a broader approach in the wrong direction? In Chapter 12, Hansen is critical of the societal or "citizenship economics" approach in that the motivation for students to expend the effort to acquire this type of knowledge is low, and thus the resources devoted to producing economic literacy for effective citizenship is to a large extent wasted. Students are likely to be more receptive to personal economics than to societal economics. In discussing what can be done about the situation, Hansen points out the possibility of a middle ground approach designed to achieve an optimal mix in which the learning of personal decision making economics would be linked inextricably with citizenship economics; as a consequence, both types of economic literacy would increase. Warmke (1971) points out that personal economic decision making and aggregate analysis are interrelated and that one cannot pursue the study of either without a knowledge of the other.

According to Daughtrey (1970, 98-99), personal economic

skills in the past were sought as end results in the general business course; while these skills and abilities still form the bulk of the content today, they also serve as launching pads to an understanding of broader economic concepts. An attempt is made to aid students in understanding the relationships between their personal decisions and the total economy. Perhaps this approach accomplishes the earlier objective more effectively and provides an introduction to societal economics as well. An appreciation of the personal-societal relationships may also serve as an excellent foundation on which to build an understanding of broader, more abstract economic concepts later.

An illustration of how the study of a topic can develop from the individual or personal viewpoint to a societal one is given below, using savings investment as the subject (Swearingen & Garrison, 1972, 49-50).

> The savings-investment section of the general business course has traditionally dealt with the decision of the individual whether to save or to spend certain portions of his current income. The opportunities for the individual to invest his money in United States Savings Bonds, in corporate bonds, and in common stocks are discussed. However, the discussion is usually limited to the decision of the individual on making an "investment." For example, the textbook may contain a section dealing with the decision of the individual to "invest" in a home and pointing out some of the important questions relating to home ownership.
>
> The weakness of this section of the ordinary text from the standpoint of economic education is again that the subject is almost never moved beyond the individual point of view; and again it is a relatively easy task to lead the student further. He will readily grasp the idea that business firms may annually be faced with the quetsion of whether their net earning should be paid out as income (dividends) to the owners or be re-invested in the firm. The decisions of many business firms to re-invest a portion of their profits make these firms collectively a major investment factor in the economy. Also beyond the textbook, the student should be led to see the relationship between the decisions of individuals to save part of their income by making deposits in savings accounts at banks and the decision of a local business firm to build a more modern plant and equip the plant with more efficient machinery. The very close relationship between the savings of individuals and the investments of businessmen should be stressed.
>
> There are additional ways of achieving depth in economic education about savings and investments. The economic effects of the decision of an individual to invest in a home (a consumer good) can be compared with the economic effects of the decision of a business firm to expand its plant (a capital good). A distinction can be drawn between the so-called investment of an individual through the stock or bond market (merely a transfer

operation) and the investment of a businessman when he builds a new factory (a creative operation). A distinction can be drawn also between the economic effect of a decision by a person to build a home and the economic effect of a decision instead to purchase a home that was built in some previous period. The fact that business firms may "invest" in other firms, as is typically the case with banks and savings and loan associations, can be pointed out.

The student's viewpoint may well be broadened to include a study of the relationship between the level of investment in our economy and such important factors as the level of our national income, the level of employment, and the rate of economic growth. The investment process is particularly important in explaining why the level of economic activity in our capital goods industries fluctuates more widely than our general level of economic activity. Experience has shown that students are always interested in such problems as depressions and booms, and it is easy to show the mutual interrelationships between changes in the level of capital investment and the fluctuations in the level of business activity.

In our society decisions to save and to invest are made largely by individuals and business organizations operating within the framework of a high degree of freedom. In many other countries these decisions are more directly and more greatly influenced by government policy. There the freedom of the individual and the freedom of the business organization to make decisions regarding savings and investments have been almost entirely sacrificed for other goals which the leaders of the society consider more important.

Considerable attention has been given to the general business course due to the nature of the offering and the contribution it makes to the achievement of economic literacy, and further, due to the fact that it has a larger enrollment than any of the other so-called basic business courses.

The *advanced general business course* is a companion course to general business either at grade 11 or 12. Using macroeconomic content, this course stresses societal economic concepts, providing an opportunity to learn such concepts in a business-oriented framework. The advanced general business courses may serve as a capstone to the economics education program in the business department of the high school, especially if no separate course in economics is offered. It is not a padded general business course nor a watered-down economics class.

The *consumer economics* or *consumer economic problems* business course may serve as a capstone to the economics *course* also has a close relationship to the general business course. It is typically taught in the eleventh or twelfth year. Although the title indicates this would be a personal economics type of course, it is much more than that. It further refines the deeper concepts that may have been introduced in general business, and analyzes the more complex relationships between the consumer and the total economy, e.g., income distribution, economic stability, price determination, real versus money income, savings, investment, credit and monetary policies. An indication of the breadth of the course is revealed by Becker and Reinke (1975, 203) which shows the page location of key economic concepts contained in one of the leading consumer economics texts (Warmke, et al, 1971).

The *business principles and management course* usually is found only in large high schools. The course may be considered partly vocational and partly basic business in nature. It should acquaint the student with types of business organizations, problems of production and management, causes and effects of business failures on the economy, and evolution of the field of management.

The *senior high school course in economics* is making a slight comeback. Several states have added economics as a separate course or as units in other courses. It may be offered through either the social studies or business education department. The course is much improved over earlier high school courses in economics. Much effort is now being exerted to make it realistic and functional, partly through personal economic illustrations and an understanding of relationships of the personal to societal economic activities. Improvements in teacher qualifications, materials, and enrollments are also evident. Nevertheless, much remains to be done.

There may be other basic business courses such as business law and economic geography in which economic concepts are included, but obviously no one school or program will include all of those discussed here. A curriculum which includes a general business course, well organized and taught, in the ninth or tenth grade and a similarly effective advanced general business or economics course in the eleventh and twelfth grades will go far toward enabling students to achieve some modest level of economic literacy. Even though economic concepts and understandings are integrated in many different courses, both within or outside the business curriculum, a carefully developed capstone course is necessary to bring together and extend such learnings in a rational way.

Specialized or Vocational Business Education

We might interpret the training for a person's vocation as

the most important type of economics education; however, vocational business education is normally not considered by definition to be part of economics education. Such a statement does not mean, however, that the vocational courses or those concerned primarily with education *for* business do not contribute substantially to a person's economic literacy. There are opportunities in most of these courses to integrate economic topics into the subject matter, especially in showing relationships and reinforcing the learning from other courses.

Persons employed in business-office occupations are concerned primarily with "cost and supply" considerations. They must combine available resources in the most efficient manner to cut costs and increase the productive supply potential. Office workers facilitate business operations by recording, retrieving, analyzing, organizing, and reporting data for business decisions. Courses designed for career entry into office occupations include the "big three" of typewriting, bookkeeping, and shorthand, plus such courses as office procedures, systems analysis, and data processing.

In *typewriting and shorthand* the teacher can help students increase their business and economic vocabularies through selected copy materials. Naturally, the primary emphasis is and should be on developing the specific business skills for which the courses are designed.

In *data processing* there is ample opportunity to help the student develop an understanding of the role of automation in the economy. Information technology will have increasing implications for the economy and a place in the curriculum for developing an understanding of it must be found.

Bookkeeping, or accounting, as the high school level course is now called, cannot be taught effectively without the inclusion of certain economic concepts and ideas. To make bookkeeping practices and accounting principles meaningful, the student needs to understand how systematic records form the basis for making business and economic decisions.

To illustrate some of the economic concepts and understandings that can be used to enrich the accounting course, several examples are provided for various units or modules in the course. The area of study is given, followed by a listing of some appropriate concepts (Guyton, 1963, 68-88). An explanation is also given of how these concepts can be developed in the learning situation.

Starting an accounting system. The beginning unit provides an excellent opportunity for developing certain economic concepts and understandings, such as the following:

1. Prices are simply expressions of value in terms of money.
2. Private ownership of property has great economic implications.
3. Exercise of the right to organize or form a business organization, such as an individual proprietorship, in a free enterprise economy serves certain economic functions.
4. Business operates within, and as a part of, a system of economic organization, which in this country is known as American capitalism or the American enterprise system.

Profit and loss or income statement. To supplement the basic profit and loss information and to relate it to the American economy, the teacher could present the following economic concepts:

1. Profit is a reward for initiative and risk bearing.
2. Profit may be the result of luck or monopoly.
3. Profit is the motivator of our economic system.

Bank deposits, checks, reconciliation. The following general concepts may be presented:

1. The use of money serves several important economic functions.
2. The volume of money in circulation and the level of spending in our economy greatly affect the total performance of the economy, as may be illustrated by the major flows of "money payments" and "goods and services."
3. The Federal Reserve System operates in such a way as to contribute to economic stability and to promote economic growth.
4. The budgetary or fiscal policy of the government has major effects upon the performance of our total economy.

Handling purchases and sales of merchandise on account. The study of credit should involve an analysis of the following subjects:

1. Credit in its relationship to purchasing power.
2. The effect of credit transactions on the price level.
3. Credit as a factor in economic stability and growth.

Taxes and payroll records. The material in this unit provides an excellent springboard for launching a brief study of the federal budget and the role of government in our economy.

Study of these additional subjects should enable most of the students to gain further insight into a variety of economic concepts, including the following:

1. Businesses as well as individuals pay large sums of money each year in taxes.
2. Government budget policy, if appropriately developed, can play an important stabilizing role in the economy.
3. The role of government in the economy of the United States is an ever-changing one.
4. It is a fundamental responsibility of every citizen to participate constructively in economic decision making by governments.

Partnerships, corporations, and cooperatives. Under the guidance of an interested and capable teacher, the students participating in this total process should bring out certain economic understandings and concepts, such as the following:

1. Specialized needs of our society call for different forms of business organization.
2. Businessmen adopt that form of organization which seems best for helping them organize and carry on their particular activities.
3. Separation of ownership and control in large corporations has resulted in a new type of decision making based upon the idea of stewardship on the part of expert managers.
4. With the development of the large corporation, management must consider not only the best interests of the corporation but also those of society.

Depreciation of fixed assets. Through the use of classroom discussion and related activities, the following economic concepts may be developed:

1. Many kinds of capital, or man-made aids to production, are essential for the production of goods and services required for meeting the needs and the demands of the American people.
2. Savings and investments are necessary in our economy to provide those tools of production.
3. Variations in the amount of investment in capital goods have important effects on the total economy.

Such questions as the following may help to launch a study of the topic of capital formation: What are capital goods? Are all fixed assets capital goods? Why is capital necessary to the businessman and to our total economy? How is capital formation accomplished? Are savings necessary to capital formation?

These questions may lead to the cooperative formulation of a brief topical outline involving:

1. The definition of capital.
2. Capital formation—what it is, how it is accomplished, and why it is important to the individual, the business firm, and our whole economy.
3. A further consideration of the role of savings in capital formation.

Financial reports. The subject of national income accounting may be presented with this unit in the following five steps:

1. A definition of gross national product (GNP) and a discussion of its significance as a measure of the performance of the total economy.
2. An analysis of the major components of GNP.
3. An analysis of the costs of producing GNP and their significance as incomes to the basic factors of production.
4. An explanation of how double counting is avoided in computing GNP.
5. An explanation and illustration of the flow of spending and the flow of output, or the flow of money and the flow of goods and services.

SUMMARY

Business education encompasses both general and specialized education; that is, education *about* business and education *for* business. The objective of general or basic business education is essentially that of economics education or the development of the economically literate student. Included would be both personal and societal economics. The specialized phase of business education is concerned with the preparation of workers for careers in the office occupations. This curricular area will include much that may be identified as economics education, but the primary thrust or contribution to economic literacy comes through the basic business education curriculum. The two areas are indeed compatible and interrelated, each enriching and giving meaning to the other. In fact, it might be logically assumed that students preparing for office careers would and should be taking basic business courses.

REFERENCES CITED

Becker, William D., Jr., and Reinke, Robert W. "What Economics Should the Educator Know?" *The Social Studies* 66 (Sept./Oct. 1975): 203.

Collins, Bill D.; Smith, H. Gene; and Hopkins, Charles O. *Capital Outlay and Annual Operating Costs for Area Vocational-Technical School Program Planning*. Report 1. Stillwater: Oklahoma State Department of Vocational and Technical Education, Division of Research, Planning, and Evaluation, Planning Unit, 1974a.

———. *Comprehensive High School Vocational and Technical Education Program Planning*. Report 3. Stillwater: Oklahoma State Department of Vocational and Technical Education, Division of Research, Planning, and Evaluation, Planning Unit, 1974b.

Conover, Hobart H., and Daggett, Willard R. "Business Education—The Changing Tide." *The Balance Sheet* 58 (Sept. 1976): 16-17.

Daughtrey, Ann Scott. "The Responsibility of Business Education for the Development of Economic Understanding." *The Emerging Content and Structure of Business Education*. National Business Education Yearbook, no. 8. Edited by Ray G. Price. Washington, D.C.: National Business Education Association, 1970.

Garrison, Lloyd L. *A Syllabus for Teaching Economics in the High School General Business Course*. New York: Joint Council on Economic Education, 1964.

Guyton, Percy L., ed. *A Teacher's Guide to Economics in the Business Education Curriculum*. New York: Joint Council on Economic Education and National Business Education Association, 1963.

Nanassy, Louis C., and Fancher, Charles M. *General Business and Economic Understandings*. 4th ed. Englewood Cliffs, New Jersey: Prentice-Hall, Inc., 1973.

Swearingen, Eugene L., and Garrison, Lloyd L. "Teaching Economic Concepts in General Business." *Economics in the Business Curriculum*. Edited by George L. Fersh. New York: Joint Council on Economic Education, 1972.

U.S. Department of Health, Education, and Welfare, Office of Education, Bureau of Occupational and Adult Education, Office of Adult, Vocational, Technical, and Manpower Education, Division of Vocational and Technical Education. *Summary Data Vocational Education: 1975*. Vocational Education Information, no. I.

U.S. Department of Health, Education, and Welfare, Office of Education, Center for Adult, Vocational, Technical, and Manpower Education, Division of Vocational and Technical Education. *Trends in Vocational Education: Fiscal Year 1972*. Vocational Education Information, no. II.

———. *Trends in Vocational Education Fiscal Year 1974*. Vocational Education Information, no. II.

U.S. Department of Labor, Bureau of Labor Statistics. *Occupational Outlook Handbook*. 1976-77 ed. Washington, D.C.: Government Printing Office, 1976.

Warmke, Roman F.; Wyllie, Eugene D.; Wilson, W. Harmon; Eyster, Alvin S. *Consumer Economic Problems*. 8th ed. Cincinnati: South-Western Publishing Company, 1971.

Warmke, Roman F., ed. *Teaching Personal Economics in the Business Education Curriculum*. New York: Joint Council on Economic Education, 1971.

Economic Roles, Goals, and Curricula in Distributive Education

Neal E. Vivian

Distributive education is a program of occupational instruction in marketing and distribution. It is designed to serve the needs of youth and adults who have entered, or are preparing to enter, distributive occupations. Since marketing and distribution functions relate to products and services, which are present in all types of business and industrial institutions, distributive occupations are present in all retail, wholesale, and manufacturing enterprises, in personal and business service firms, in finance, real estate, transportation and communication businesses, and in public utilities.

Distribution functions very much like the distributor of an automobile performs in converting gasoline into power; in an economic context, distribution directs the flow of goods and services in our market-centered economic system. Both are essential elements of satisfactory performance in the systems to which they belong. Distribution is the link between production and consumption: it is a broad generic term that encompasses marketing. Marketing relates to the activities that take place wherever goods and services are bought and sold, whether that be in a retail store, a local service establishment, or a large central wholesale market. Marketing functions are described in Chapter 10. The discussion in this chapter also pertains mostly to the realm of marketing.

DISTRIBUTION IN OUR ECONOMY

Education for careers—and positions—in distribution has received increased visibility in recent years because of the growing realization of the influence of marketing and distribution on the economic growth of our nation. Distributive occupations workers and costs of distribution are difficult to identify for two main reasons: (1) distribution tasks frequently are combined with those of other occupational fields; and (2) distribution is a function of many types of institutions, as alluded to in the opening paragraph of this chapter. Nevertheless, ardent efforts have been made to classify occupations and identify distribution costs.

Distributive Occupations

Distributive occupations workers constitute roughly one-fifth of the civilian labor force; half of the labor force perform some distribution tasks. Because of the heterogeneity in the kinds of tasks allocated to the positions held by many workers, a common practice is to arbitrarily assume that those workers whose assignments are 50 percent or more in the realm of marketing are distributive occupations workers. Therefore, most of those employed in retailing and wholesaling are classified as distributive—but not all of them. This means that a large majority of the nearly 12 million retail workers (about 14 percent of the labor force) and the nearly 4 million wholesale workers (about 5 percent of the labor force) are in distributive occupations. (U.S. Department of Commerce, 1975, 235 and 238). In addition, there are nearly 1.75 million buyers, purchasing agents, and sales managers and about 1 million managers of wholesale and retail businesses whose functions are mainly distributive. A large percentage of those employed in the real estate industry are in distributive occupations. Proportionately, there are fewer distributive workers in manufacturing, finance, and transportation.

Personnel classification problems make it difficult to analyze economic problems, particularly at the macro level. Statisticians in the Departments of Commerce and Labor and in the U.S. Office of Education are working on the improvement of employment data.

The one occupation that is unquestionably distributive is that of sales workers. There were more than 5.5 million sales workers in 1970 (slightly less than 7 percent of the labor force). The demand for this type of work is increasing at a rate which corresponds to the growth of the civilian labor force. During the decade from 1960 to 1970, there was a 10 percent increase in the number of male workers and, interestingly, a 30 percent increase in the number of females.

The total increase of sales workers was 17 percent, which was about the same as that of the civilian labor force. For comparative growth rates among occupational groups, see Chapter 14, Figure 3.

Gross Product

Approximately 43 percent of the GNP in 1971 ($1,050 billion) may be attributed to three categories of industries which contributed most to distribution. Contributions of the three groups were as follows:

Wholesale & retail trade	$180.8 billion	17.3 percent
Finance, insurance & real estate	150.7 "	14.3 "
Selected services	122.7 "	11.7 "

By contrast, manufacturing contributed 24.7 percent and agriculture, 3.2 percent. The purpose of these data is to communicate the impact of distribution on our economy rather than to suggest the needs for training.

The Economic Function of Marketing and Distribution

As the intermediary between production and consumption, distribution acts as a catalyst on its counterparts; it stimulates potential consumers to purchase goods and services, and it motivates manufacturers and service establishments to produce them. Assembling goods, negotiating prices, and distributing them are important functions, but the stimulation of demand is the force that changes the speed of the wheels of business and industry. Nothing happens until a sale is made.

The world will not beat a path to the door of a person who builds a better mousetrap. It is the efforts of distributors to motivate potential users to change their habits and raise their standards of living. Contrary to popular belief, purchasing power is highest during depression and recession periods. This catalytic role of distribution was aptly expressed by L. T. White, formerly a Vice President of Cities Services, Inc.:

> Distribution is more than a series of channels between production and consumer. Distribution provides a force, a pump, in addition to the path along which goods flow. The forces of distribution are powerful ones; they are persuasion by the marketer and desire by the user (White, 1974, 20).

DISTRIBUTIVE EDUCATION

Distributive education was not one of the three original

vocational education fields—trade and industrial education, agricultural education, and home economics education—that were federally reimbursed under the Smith-Hughes Act of 1917. It was introduced in the George-Deen Act of 1936 as an adult education program for employed workers to aid small businesses and stimulate the economy, which was still in the Great Depression. The only way for high schools and postsecondary schools to meet the employment requirement and to participate in federal reimbursement was to use the cooperative part-time vocational education plan under which student-trainees were employed at least as many hours as they attended school, thereby meeting the requirements of being employed. The consequences of this restriction affected programmatic investments until 1963, when the recipients of distributive education were redefined to include those undergoing preparatory training.

Enrollments

Enrollments in distributive education during the 1940s and 1950s were dominated by the adult program. For the fiscal year (FY) ending 1938, the first year that enrollments in distributive education programs were reported, 89.8 percent were in adult education. A quarter century later, in FY 1963, the adult enrollment was 84.4 percent of the total. During that year postsecondary enrollments were still less than 1 percent of those enrolled. During the past decade emphasis has switched to preparatory programs at the high school and postsecondary levels, as shown in Table 1.

Goals of Distributive Education

The major purpose of distributive education is to prepare people for employment in distributive occupations. Three goals which have been generally accepted by distributive educators describe the contributions of the field:

1. *The educational contribution*—to offer instruction in distribution and marketing.
2. *The social contribution*—to develop an understanding of the social and economic responsibilities of those engaged in distribution in a free, competitive society.
3. *The economic goal*—to aid in the improvement of the techniques of distribution.

The American standard of living is based on effective and efficient distribution, as well as on effective and efficient production of goods and services. It depends largely on the

Table 1

ENROLLMENTS IN DISTRIBUTIVE EDUCATION 1965-66 TO 1974-75

School Year Ending	Total Enrollment	Levels of Instruction (Percent)			Number of Teachers
		Secondary	Postsecondary	Adult	
1974-75	873,224	40.5	18.7	40.8	18,239
1973-74	832,905	42.4	16.0	41.6	16,505
1972-73	738,547	41.1	14.3	44.6	14,804
1971-72	640,423	41.0	16.1	42.9	13,795
1970-71	578,075	41.7	14.9	43.4	11,974
1969-70	529,365	43.5	15.5	41.0	10,458
1968-69	563,431	32.7	10.8	54.6	9,741
1967-68	574,785	30.6	7.8	60.8	8,610
1966-67	481,034	31.5	4.4	63.1	7,523
1965-66	420,426	24.2	3.8	71.6	---

SOURCE: U.S. Department of Health, Education, and Welfare, *Trends in Vocational Education: Fiscal Year 1975.*

development of human capital, which was discussed in Chapters 2 and 3. Distributive education not only aims to increase the human capital of those enrolled in distributive occupations training, but also serves the need for marketing competencies required in other occupational areas.

Curriculum Content

Distributive education content has been divided into five competency categories as follows: (1) Marketing competencies—knowledge, skills and attitudes common to the marketing functions of all distributive occupations, (2) Technical competencies—the knowledge and skills relating to a product or service that are characteristic of a specific occupation or subcluster, (3) Economic competencies—sufficient economic literacy to make appropriate occupational decisions, (4) Social competencies—the personal-social behaviors necessary for success in distributive occupations, and (5) Basic skills—the applications of communication and mathematical skills. This chapter focuses on the marketing and economic competency areas.

Marketing. A new definition of marketing which expands the scope of former concepts has been proposed by McGarry.

> Marketing is that phase or aspect of an economy that has to do with and results in the changes in custody of, responsibility for, and authority over goods, to the end that goods produced by many agencies are made available for the convenience and satisfaction of different users (McGarry, 1971, 134).

McGarry notes that marketing as defined above is not restricted by production and consumption; instead, it is a pervasive element that penetrates every part of the economy. The definition also includes the main purpose of marketing—the essential reasons for the process.

The components of marketing and its relationship to other disciplines have been plainly and meaningfully described—and graphically portrayed—by Kelley and Lazer (1967). This description will be helpful to investigators who want a quick overview of marketing.

Macro and micro approaches. Both marketing and economics are studies at two levels—macro and micro. The micro approach applies to a specific segment of the economy such as the behavior of individual consumers, and single firms or industries—sometimes called "economics of the firm" or "managerial economics." An understanding of both macro and micro levels is essential for decision makers in distributive occupations.

Since marketing is an integral part of any economic system, some kind of mechanism must be developed to decide what and how much is to be produced and by whom, when and to whom the product will be distributed. Irrespective of the type of economic system, macro-level objectives are basically to make goods and services available to consumers when and where they are needed (McGarry, 1971, 6-11).

Marketing creates three of the four basic economic utilities —time, place and possession. Provision of these utilities is a significant part of any economic system. In addition to the internal organization activities of a marketing institution, there are external forces that act upon and affect the marketing process. The impact of government through its regulatory agencies, activities of the Federal Reserve Bank, levels of employment and income all have powerful effects on the marketing system. However, in a free enterprise economy, the market per se really directs the flow of goods and services —not the government or a central planning agency. Basically, marketing decisions are made by businessmen—the market managers. Micro economics provides the underlying theory for managerial marketing which became quite popular in the late 1950s (Bartels & Jenkins, 1976).

The marketing functions. At both the macro and micro levels of marketing we find the same basic functions, sometimes referred to as economic activities: buying, selling, transporting, storing, grading, financing, risk taking, and market information. All of these functions should be an integral part of the distributive education curriculum. As the marketing functions are learned, the economic aspects of those functions should be assimilated by distributive education students.

While an understanding of economics and marketing is essential on both macro and micro levels, greater emphasis should be placed on the micro level in distributive education. Distributive education is in a unique position to teach those competencies pertaining to specific marketing strategies and activities in the firm as they relate to product distribution that is satisfactory to customers and profitable to marketers.

RELATED LITERATURE AND RESEARCH

The importance of understanding and applying economic principles has been emphasized since the inception of the distributive education program. Economics was included in the training of retail "salesgirls" by Lucinda Prince in 1906.

Since the passage of the George-Deen Act, when distributive education was adopted into the family of federally reimbursed programs, some mention of economics has been made in nearly every U.S. Office of Education bulletin.

Literature on Need for Economic Competencies

One of the earliest and most significant articles on the relationship of economic education to distributive education was submitted by Beaumont (1958). In a chapter of the 1958 yearbook of the National Business Education Association, he emphasized the importance of distributive education students' being able to understand the business-economic environment in order to function effectively as workers. He further stated that combining economic understandings and vocational skills should result in an awareness of the principles of economics.

Warmke, in a summary of a paper presented at the First National Clinic on Distributive Education in 1963, stated that the disciplines of economics and distributive education are intertwined in both intent and content.

> One must understand the role of distribution to know economics, and one must understand economics to know distribution . . . economic educators and distributive educators share similar concerns and content. Interdisciplinary programs involving the two areas would seem more difficult to avoid than to implement (Warmke, 1963).

Other students of distributive education have underscored the relationship of economics and economics education to distributive education. Upon examination of the contributions of distributive education to the general goals of secondary education, Crawford and Meyer (1972) made the point that distributive education graduates become more intelligent consumers—an economic role—through their study of merchandise information. This, they stated, has proved to be a valuable outcome, though not a stated objective, of the program.

Samson (1973) presented a paper at the National Business Education Conference which stressed the need for an understanding of the free enterprise system as a prerequisite for students pursuing distributive occupations careers. As a foundation for an apperceptive base, he recommended a fundamental understanding and appreciation of the profit motive, freedom of choice in all matters, the functioning of supply and demand, and the operation of a market-centered economy.

Research on Economic Understandings

Little research pertaining to the teaching of economic knowledge, skills and attitudes in distributive education was reported prior to the mid-1960s. Until the National Clinic on Distributive Education in 1963, little attention was given to this aspect of content. Without doubt, teachers were including economic competencies in distributive education courses without identifying them as such, but it took the National Clinic of 1963 to arouse the consciousness of 100 distributive education leaders to the need for a systematic study of the relationship between distributive education and economics. A variety of uncoordinated efforts followed.

Economic competency needs of workers. When early investigators turned to the literature for help in identifying the economic competencies required of workers in distributive occupations they located a study by Overman (1954), the purpose of which was to determine the basic economic concepts that selected business leaders believed should be understood by everyone. Through this study, Overman established a list of 49 frequently appearing economic concepts. He also found that most of industry's economics education efforts were directed toward employees and that some business organizations were cooperating with the schools and colleges to this end. More than a decade later Ertel (1966) studied the tasks and related knowledge in the merchandising operations of retail firms without identifying economic understandings per se.

Crawford (1967) completed a classical study which identified the competencies needed by distributive education teacher-coordinators. It entailed the derivation of a list of tasks and competencies needed by the recipients of distributive education. Although a number of concepts having a direct relationship to economics emerged from the study, the competency area of economic understandings needed by workers in distributive occupations was not fully developed.

Samson (1969) studied middle management related knowledge in department stores. He dealt with 30 broad competency areas, only a few of which were in the realm of economic understandings, e.g., "to relate the functions of production, distribution and consumption."

At the collegiate level, Smith (1963) did a study of economic concepts that are basic to an understanding of introductory marketing courses. He found that a pattern of relationships exists between a broad range of basic economic concepts and subject matter of the collegiate introductory marketing course and groups of related topics therein. He indicated that without an understanding of these essential economic concepts, the student is unable to gain the total significance of those portions of marketing subject matter to which economic concepts are related.

Eggland (1976) completed a study to determine and verify the economic competencies required of distributive occupations employees so that a competency based curriculum can be completed and utilized in distributive education. The stated objectives of the study were (1) to determine which of the economic understandings are thought to be most important by economists and economics teachers generally, (2) to refine and translate those economic understandings into competencies, and (3) to learn specifically the value of these economic competencies to persons working in various segments and levels of the distributive occupations. After a thorough review of the literature and related research, the investigator was able to identify a list of 300 economic concepts thought by various authors to be essential to the economic literacy of the general populace. With the advice of a panel of consultants, the 300 concepts were categorized and combined into 56 performance oriented economic competencies. A sample of distributive business personnel was asked to respond to each of the competencies regarding its value to successful job performance in various distributive occupations. A hierarchy of 56 competencies, based on the mean reaction of this jury, was presented in the final report.

Economic understanding needs of teachers. A *Test of Economic Understanding* (TEU) was developed by the Joint Council on Economic Education (1963). This instrument was used extensively on a variety of respondents in the research that followed. (See comments on tests of economic understanding by W. Lee Hansen in Chapter 12.) Meisner (1966) used it to measure the relationship between the amount of teacher preparation in economics by distributive education teachers and the level of economic understanding achieved by their students. Vivian (1966) also used the TEU to measure achievements of high school students who had formal instruction in economics, or had participated in a Junior Achievement project, or were participating in the distributive education program. He found that there was no significant relationship in achievement among the three groups of students. Ganser (1969), Jones (1971), and Kim

(1973) also used the TEU when comparing the economic understandings of business and distributive education students with other students. The results were generally the same: The business and distributive education students did not differ significantly in their understanding of economic concepts from their general education counterparts.

The latest research pertaining to the teaching of economic understandings in distributive education to be reported in this chapter was completed by Renshaw (1976). He identified marketing knowledge needs of secondary school distributive education personnel. "Economic concepts relating to marketing" was one of 69 areas of need under the category "marketing concepts and principles." The 10 concepts included in this category, all of which ranked high in importance, were: (1) business/economic cycles, (2) capitalism, socialism and communism, (3) competition, (4) entrepreneurship, (5) free enterprise, (6) governmental influence and control, (7) laws of supply and demand, (8) monetary theory, (9) price theory, and (10) profit.

Instructional materials. Production of student and teacher material specifically designed for distributive education has been slow, to say the least. Klaurens (1965) evaluated experimental student and teacher materials on economic concepts taught to student-trainees in cooperative vocational education programs in Minnesota. The results, which were measured by the TEU scores of participants, indicated a significantly higher gain score for the experimental group that used these specially developed materials.

A course guide for teachers—including transparency masters—titled "Economics for Young Workers" was developed by Minnesota teacher-coordinators under the direction of Meyer (1966) with U.S. Office of Education support. The proposed instruction attempted to link important economic concepts to persistent life situations of workers and their employment by a business firm. The publication is out of print.

The only commercially published student material exclusively devoted to distributive education use that the writer located is a manual titled "The Economics of Marketing" prepared by Klaurens (1971). It is one of 17 manuals in a series called "Occupational Manuals and Projects in Marketing" designed for use at the secondary and postsecondary levels. On the other hand, economic understandings have been integrated into secondary school marketing textbooks by authors such as Nolan and Warmke (1965) and Mason and Rath (1968) and in later editions of their textbooks.

STATUS OF ECONOMIC LITERACY

A study by the National Management Advisory Council (1974) aroused wide concern. Distributive education students and an equal number of nondistributive education students in 130 high schools located in 38 states participated in the survey. The two objectives of the study were to answer these questions: (1) What are the attitudes of distributive education seniors toward the American business and economic system, and what is the extent of their knowledge concerning the workings of the American economic system? (2) To what extent do the attitudes about American business and the knowledge of the workings of the American economic system, as held by distributive education seniors, differ from those of high school seniors not enrolled in the distributive education program? Although the title and both of the stated objectives dealt with the extent of knowledge of the "workings of the American economic system," the study was primarily a survey of attitudes. The survey revealed many areas of relative strength and relative weaknesses in the business world as viewed by students.

A companion study relating to distributive education teachers was done in 1975. Results were compared to similar data obtained in the 1974 survey of high school seniors; findings were encouraging. Six generalizations merit repeating here:

1. Overall, D.E. teachers express a higher level of positive attitudes towards business than do the D.E. seniors.
2. Teachers appear to be pragmatic about business. They are aware of many of the deficiencies, but apparently see no better system and are willing to exist within the current structure, and perhaps even try to improve it. However, there are indications that the overall structure of the teachers' attitudes is also changing.
3. The students are aware of their world, business, and the economy. Although they may disagree with their teachers on specific issues, they do not differ as much on absolute judgments of what is being done.
4. The attitude data suggest that teachers may not be communicating their knowledge to the students.

Specific questions regarding known facts substantiate this finding.

5. When asked directly, most teachers felt the business system is basically good, while the students exhibited a mixed reaction.
6. The D.E. teachers indicate widespread use of the various materials they are furnished, and in general feel the materials provided by publishers and manufacturers are better than those provided by educational agencies.

In conclusion, it seems that distributive educators are somewhat aware of the need to teach economic concepts, skills and attitudes. By and large, they have at least a fair understanding of economics, but apparently they can benefit from some assistance in transmitting their expertise to their students. Teaching support materials are available, but there is room for further development and extension of their use.

Improving Economic Literacy in Distributive Education

Assuming that the observations above are reasonably accurate, what action should be taken to improve the teaching of economic literacy? If distributive education is to play a significant role in improving economic literacy among its students, the attainment of economic-understanding objectives cannot be left to chance. Economic competencies cannot be treated as incidental outcomes or outcomes that will flow naturally from the instructional program. As in the achievement of other desirable outcomes, economic competencies must be treated as essential goals of distributive education, and those goals should be explicitly stated. This means that the study of economics must be integrated into the distributive education curriculum, that specific outcomes should be sought, and that those objectives and goals should be understood by teachers, students and administrators.

Application of the systems approach is a recent development in distributive education. The specification of precise learning objectives and the selection of appropriate instructional strategies are important tools in achieving desired economic outcomes. An example of this approach is the Interstate Distributive Education Curriculum Consortium (IDECC), which consists of 500 learning activity packages covering 983 competencies. Presently, the system is being enlarged to encompass the economic competencies identified by Eggland (1976).

Much more could be said concerning the systems approach, but the remainder of this chapter will treat the selection and use of instructional strategies in the development of economic competencies.

INSTRUCTIONAL STRATEGIES

The identification and selection of appropriate learning activities is a difficult, yet essential, teaching task. Although no formula to assist the teacher in these tasks exists, three principles may help teachers in their selection of learning activities: (1) No one strategy is the most effective for all learners, (2) A variety of strategies and techniques must be employed, and (3) Students learn best when they are involved in meaningful learning activities.

A creative distributive education teacher today has a wide variety of educational settings from which to choose: classroom, business community, the youth organization, and the actual training station in which the student is employed. The activities that have proved most helpful to teachers and which seem most appropriate when teaching economics in distributive education are: (1) problem solving, (2) projects, (3) role playing, (4) case studies, (5) simulation, (6) games, (7) field trips, (8) DECA activities, and (9) on-the-job learning assignments.

Problem Solving

Problem solving requires the manipulation of data as a part of anticipating and evaluating the likely results of alternate decisions. This approach simulates the kind of situation in which, at some future time, students are most likely to use their economic knowledge. It also improves insight into the nature of decision making that involves both economic and noneconomic considerations.

The value of the problem solving approach is greatest where the problem encountered is based on a real situation, even if a degree of simplification is needed. An examination of suggested solutions to a problem would form the basis of an analysis of its advantages and disadvantages. This approach is one of the most effective classroom techniques for developing the ability to do independent decision making.

Projects

The use of projects is closely related to problem solving. The term *project* recently has acquired a somewhat different meaning in distributive education. Essentially, it involves conducting and reporting an inquiry that is planned and executed largely by the students themselves. The term *project* usually refers to an individual and self-contained activity by the student. A student is expected to select—with teacher guidance—a suitable topic for investigation. Over a long time period, perhaps the entire school year, the student collects and analyzes information relevant to the topic and finally presents the findings in a report. Although projects are done on an individual basis, they also may be performed by small groups (Bayles, 1967).

Several interesting examples of economic projects have been reported, and it is clear that teachers who use this method usually find it to be very effective. Like any other learning procedure, care must be taken that the component activities are directly related—or closely related—to the student's career objective and to the stated objectives of the progam.

A project that generally has been used successfully is "Establishing and Operating Your Own Business." This project has high potential in the development of economic competencies within the marketing framework. Obviously, it relates to micro economics or economics of the firm. Some appropriate activities that have important economic implications are: (1) List all of the ways that time, place and possession utilities are performed by your firm. How do they add value to goods and services? (2) If you were operating this business in another type of economy, what might be some of the differences in operations and goals? (3) What types of capital are used in your business? What effect does the capital used have on the productivity of the workers in your firm? (5) Give examples of how the following factors have affected your business: population changes, family income, increased home ownership, inflation, fuel shortages, increased taxes, and so on.

Role Playing

Economic role playing elicits the students' powers of introspection through an attempt to understand economic implications of their actions (Ryba, 1975, 126). In role playing situations, the assumed roles are developed in a business or economic setting. Different roles are assigned to students so that they may understand not only their own roles, but also the interplay which takes place among the role players. They also learn the economic principles governing the development of the situation being simulated. One such situation might be a board of directors meeting where students assume the roles of chairman of the board, comptroller, treasurer, economic consultant, and vice president in charge of marketing. This technique is closely related to problem solving—a specific problem is presented to the simulated board of directors, and different approaches in attacking and solving the problem are discussed and analyzed.

Case Studies

A case study in economics may be defined as any detailed study of a particular situation by means of which the relevance of economic concepts can be shown. It has been used for many years on the collegiate level to teach law and business management and has found favor in teaching economics. The publication of case study materials by various organizations and commercial publishers has increased notably. Closely related to problem solving, the case study is actually a problem situation that requires a solution. Effectively used, case studies may become media for developing decision making competencies. They stress logical thinking and exploration of all possible alternatives rather than the use of rote memory.

Good teachers have always used examples to illustrate principles. In case studies the process is reversed; the principles themselves are examined as they evolve from a single case or a succession of cases. Principles are learned through the study of actual situations, institutions, industries, firms, and the like. Recent research has strengthened the appeal of case studies in teaching economic concepts. Building economic understanding by induction from real world situations has become popular (Sanford & Bradbury, 1975, 243-53).

Since case studies are specific to a place, a time and a concept, they lend themselves to teaching micro economics or micro marketing rather than to macro economic learnings. Real cases within the knowledge of the students that are associated with their own community are interesting and meaningful to students. One of the greatest merits of case studies is that they require the direct participation of students. When properly chosen they are likely to evoke lively and interesting responses.

Case studies are available for a number of economic principles that are directly related to distribution. Pricing policies and their relation to elasticity of demand and cross elasticity with other products, the selection of channels of distribution, the reevaluation of currencies and their effect on the sale of products manufactured by a local industry, alternative techniques for raising capital are all topics which can be converted to case studies and related directly to specific economic principles.

Simulation and Games

Simulation and games are not new to distributive education. The terms have often been used interchangeably; although there are many similarities between them, however, there are also some distinct differences. A simulation has been described as a reproduction of a real life situation, containing elements which the author identifiies as necessary to the goals (Popham et al, 1975, 139). One definition of *game* is "a contest conducted according to a set of rules and undertaken in pursuit of educational objectives (Blucker, 1973). Although both games and simulations may involve students in decision making and may approximate reality in many ways, there are several basic differences between them (Popham et al): (1) The input for simulation should approximate real life input; the input for the game is often the result of chance, (2) A simulation requires students to perform as they would in real life; a game involves symbolic performance—often the movement of a pawn on a board, (3) The outcome of a simulation is feedback for each individual participant; the outcome of a game is usually some degree of winning or losing (Popham et al, 1975, 140). Similarities are that both use structured role playing to develop understanding of economic principles and both are simplified versions of models of a real life situation.

Daughtrey (1974) reports that recently the number of simulation games for economics has so mushroomed that over four hundred are available. They range from simple, free games to the complicated computerized type. Some of the available games that may be appropriate for use in distributive education secondary or postsecondary classrooms will be described here.

Manual Games

A game that utilizes the paper and pencil approach is titled "Economic Decision Game" (Rausch, 1968). The areas covered are: the market, the firm, collective bargaining, the community, scarcity and allocation, banking, the national economy, and international trade.

Another game titled "Market" (1971) can be used to introduce the concepts of price determination, supply and demand, and allocation of resources. Students play the roles of retailers and consumers. Retailers compete for profit; and consumers, given a limited budget, must decide how much to buy, what to pay, and so on. After the completion of the games, students are expected to discuss the underlying economic principles involved.

In another game called "Economic Systems" (Coleman & Harris, 1969), students take the roles of manufacturers, workers, farmers, and mine owners. The goal is to make a profit and maintain a high standard of living. Decisions must be made on how to make best use of productive potential, how much to buy, sell, produce and consume at what price. The purpose is to illustrate graphically the operation of an economic system—including the interdependence of its parts, the way group demands cause an individual to modify his behavior, and how individuals can influence group demands and collective goals.

Computer Games

Computer games also are available for use in high schools and postsecondary classes. They range from simple to very complex. "Computerized Management" (1959) is designed for high school use. Student teams represent management functions—sales, finance, production, and so on—and analyze options leading to managerial decisions. They must coordinate their efforts with company objectives and compete with other companies that also are student teams. The companies compete in converting raw materials into finished inventories and in distributing their products at a profit to supply a demand established weekly by the computer. Topics covered include: bidding and the market, cash position, capital expansion, and stock dividends. When a certain seller in the game withholds temporarily some of his products from the market, a student may say, "So that's what is meant by the effect of inelastic supply schedule on the determination of equilibrium price."

Although most teachers report favorable results from the use of simulations and games—particularly from the learner motivation standpoint—they also report some caveats. They contend that simulations and games require careful selection and much planning by the teacher. Also, they are time consuming; therefore, some teachers question the amount of time spent in relation to the benefit derived.

Field Trips and Studies

A field trip can be used to develop student skills in the application of economic theory. Field trips can encompass many aspects of economics. Moreover, concomitant skills may be acquired through observation, collection, and analysis of data from primary sources. Again, specific objectives or desired learning outcomes must be identified and communicated to the students. Illustrations of potential outcomes of a field trip to a local business establishment are to acquire a better understanding of: (1) business behavior and the theory of the firm, (2) wage determination, (3) industrial location, (4) price determination, and (5) relationship between national and local economic activity.

Field studies that include observations of a number of firms, agencies or organizations—or of economic activities within a community or region—might focus on macro economic theory. Some possible topics to be addressed are economic planning, the labor market, prices and demand in the local market, and other concepts related to macro marketing. Field studies can augment both the learning of economic theory and the development of skills in its application. Some real problems related to its use are: acquiring the time necessary to use the method properly, ensuring its proper application to distributive occupation competencies, and making the proper initial business contacts. Through their obvious relevance to real life activities, field trips and field studies can stimulate student interest in the economic aspects of marketing and distribution.

Youth Organization Activities

The Distributive Education Clubs of America (DECA), official youth organization for distributive education, is regarded as an integral part of the instructional program because it provides opportunities for students to apply and refine competencies initiated in the classroom or on the job, and to learn new ones. Perhaps DECA's greatest contribution is its motivation of youth to learn for a purpose. Opportunities abound at the local, state and national levels for further development of economic competencies and for the learning of new economic concepts and principles. In the competitive activities of DECA there is a chapter project—"Creative Marketing"—and an individual project called "Individual Studies in Marketing" which lend themselves well to the improvement of economic literacy.

"Creative Marketing Projects," supported by Sales and Marketing Executives International, is designed to encourage DECA chapters to recognize marketing as a medium for the economic and social improvement of a community. One of the criteria used in evaluating these projects is measurable improvement of the marketing performance of a community. Some potential projects might relate to finding new markets for local products, promoting the community's resources, increasing the trade area, increasing employment opportunities, creating better shopping facilities, and exploring problems or challenges affecting the marketing process.

The purpose of the "Individual Studies in Marketing" project is to improve, expand, or evaluate marketing principles and practices in selected industries and to provide opportunities for individuals to study and do research in the area of their career objective. Another competitive activity with excellent potential for the improvement of economic literacy is a project involving the *Area of Distribution Manual*, in which students acquire experience in research and in selecting and organizing information for practical use in one of the areas of marketing or in a phase of marketing and distribution.

Similar competitive events occur in the Junior Collegiate Division of DECA. However, these events are designed to reflect a middle management or managerial level of creativity or decision making in the area of marketing and distribution. Here special attention could be given to the development of economic understandings at a higher level than for high school students. A new thrust has emerged recently in the DECA competitive events—competency based competitive activities. Much more emphasis is being placed on the development of managerial and economic skills.

DECA members may learn economic concepts through local chapter activities. These activities could include such things as guest speakers at chapter meetings or conducting surveys to study economic phenomena such as levels and types of employment in the area, consumer preferences, customer buying habits, and other types of information that help to improve the economy of the community—and at the same time contribute to the growth of economic understanding of the chapter members.

The Cooperative Education Plan

The cooperative vocational education plan combines vocational instruction in the classroom with supervised experiences and training on a distributive occupations job and youth organization experiences. The term *cooperative* reflects the working relationship between the school and employers of the business community in providing student-trainees with learning experiences related to their distributive occupational career objective.

The cooperative plan affords a unique approach to learning economic behavior. It offers student-trainees an opportunity to apply economic theory and policy in a real work environment under actual business conditions over a period of time. Learning experiences can be planned to embrace most of the aspects of micro economics. Economic skills and understandings are learned through observation, collection, and analysis of data from primary sources. In effect, occupational experiences and on-the-job training provide practical real world laboratories for experiments in applied economics. This direct experience in economic situations is the feature that distinguishes cooperative vocational education from other methods of increasing economic understanding; student-trainees may learn firsthand many economic concepts that are not readily grasped in an academic setting.

Under the cooperative plan, students can assess the effect of suggestion selling on the economy of the firm and on profits. The same applies to the elimination of waste, the encouragement of customers to carry small packages rather than having them delivered, and many other similar economies. Student-trainees may consider such questions as: Do labor unions affect wage levels in my firm? If so, how? What are the factors that influence the location of the business for which I work—price of land, availability of customers, etc.? How do fluctuations in economic activity affect the business of my firm? What is the effect of local employment rate and personal earnings on business activity of our firm? How are prices determined and under what circumstances are they altered? and many others. Affiliation with a business firm alters the perspective of students and elicits reflective thinking of students when economic phenomena are made the focus of learning.

CONCLUSION

A relatively high degree of economic literacy is an especially important criterion of the preparation of distributive occupations workers, particularly at the secondary school level and also in postsecondary education. Unlike many occupations, the products of one's labor in distribution are intangible and not easily understood by the population in general. Time, place, and possession utilities seem nebulous and academic to many youths—and their parents—and lack the glamour associated with the material outcomes of the occupations served by the traditional vocational fields. Therefore, during these times when many young people hold high concerns for the common good and seek identity through their work, some rationale is needed to justify socially the careers they pursue.

A better than average understanding of the way our economic system works, especially the role of distribution in the American economy, together with a concern for consumer service can contribute a great deal to the preparation of a productive, well-adjusted work force in distribution. It seems evident that distributive education would benefit a great deal from a reexamination of its economic purpose and the economic component of its curriculum.

REFERENCES CITED

Bayles, Ernest E. "Project Method in Education." Presented at the National Seminar in Distributive Education, Lansing, Mich., May 7-12, 1967.

Beaumont, John A.; Kahn, Gilbert; and Popham, Estelle. "Economic Education through the Vocational Business Courses." *Educating Youth for Economic Competence.* National Business Education Yearbook, Vol. 15. New York: National Business Association, 1958.

Blucker, Gwen. *An Annotated Bibliography of Games and Simulations in Consumer Education.* Urbana: University of Illinois, and Springfield, Illinois: Superintendent of Public Instruction, 1973.

Coleman, James S., and Harris, Robert T. *Economic Systems.* New York: Western Publishing Company, 1969.

"Computerized Management." Chicago Heights, Ill.: Computer Games, Inc., 1959.

Crawford, Lucy C. *A Competency Based Approach to Curriculum Construction in Distributive Teacher Education.* Vols. I-IV. Blacksburg, Va.: Virginia Polytechnic Institute and State University, 1967.

Crawford, Lucy C., and Meyer, Warren G. *Organization and Administration of Distributive Education.* Columbus, Ohio: Charles E. Merrill Publishing Company, 1972.

Daughtrey, Anne Scott. *Methods of Basic Business and Economic Education.* Cincinnati: South-Western Publishing Company, 1974.

Eggland, Steven A. "The Determination and Verification of Economic Competencies Required of Persons Employed in Distributive Occupations." Paper presented at the annual convention of the American Vocational Association, Houston, Texas, December 1976.

Ertel, Kenneth A. *Identification of Major Tasks Performed by Merchandising Employees Working in Three Standard Industrial Classifications of Retail Establishments.* (USOE Project No. 7-0031. ED 010657.) Moscow: University of Idaho, 1966.

Ganser, Carl Joseph. "An Evaluation of the Understanding of Economic Concepts by Business Education and Social Studies Undergraduate Teaching Majors at Wisconsin State University—Whitewater." Ph.D. dissertation, University of Wisconsin, 1969.

Joint Council on Economic Education. *Test of Economic Understanding.* John M. Stalnaker, Committee for Measurement of Economic Understanding. Chicago: Science Research Associates, Inc., 1963.

Jones, Ronald O. "A Study of the Relationship Between Economic Understanding, Business Education Curricula, and Certain Personal Factors of Business Education Seniors in Selected Delaware High Schools." Ed.D. dissertation, Pennsylvania State University, 1971.

Kelley, Eugene J., and Lazer, William. *Managerial Marketing: Perspectives and Viewpoints—a Source Book.* 3d ed. Homewood, Illinois: Richard D. Owen, Inc., 1967, 685-87.

Kim, Paul Y. "An Analysis of Personal Economic Understanding Developed in Selected General College Business and Economics Courses," Ph.D. dissertation, University of Minnesota–Minneapolis, 1973.

Klaurens, Mary K. "An Evaluation of Experimental Materials in Economics for Minnesota Part-time Occupational Training Programs and Recommendations for Revision. M.A. paper, University of Minnesota–Minneapolis, 1965.

———. *The Economics of Marketing.* Occupational Manuals and Projects in Marketing. New York: Gregg Division of McGraw-Hill Book Company, 1971.

"Market." Westchester, Ill.: Business Games, 1971.

Mason, Ralph E., and Rath, Patricia Mink. *Marketing and Distribution.* New York: Gregg Division, McGraw-Hill Book Company, 1968.

McGarry, Edmund D. "Functions of Marketing Reconsidered." *Conceptual Readings in the Market Economy.* Edited by John C. Narver and Ronald Savitt. New York: Holt, Rinehart and Winston, Inc., 1971.

Meisner, Wayne A. "The Effect of Distributive Education Teachers' Preparation on the Learning of Economic Understandings." M.A. paper, University of Minnesota–Minneapolis, 1966.

Meyer, Warren G. "Economics for Young Workers: A Suggested Course Guide for Developing Economic Competencies." Developed pursuant to a contract with the U.S. Office of Education. Washington, D.C.: Department of Health, Education, and Welfare, 1966.

National Management Advisory Council (for AVA Distributive Education Division). "A Survey of Distributive Education and Non-Distributive Education High School Seniors: Their Attitudes toward Business and Their Knowledge about the American Economic System." Washington, D.C.: American Vocational Association, 1974.

———. "A Survey of Distributive Education Teachers: Their Attitudes Toward Business and Their Knowledge about the American Economic System." Washington, D.C.: American Vocational Association, 1975.

Nolan, Carroll A., and Warmke, Roman F. *Marketing and Sales Promotion.* 6d ed. Cincinnati: South-Western Publishing Company, 1965.

Overman, Glenn D. "Basic Economic Concepts about the American Business System which Business Executives Believe Everyone Should Know." Ph.D. dissertation, Indiana University, 1954.

Popham, Estelle L.; Schrag, Adele Frisbie; and Blockhus, Wanda. *A Teaching-Learning System for Business Education.* Gregg Division, McGraw-Hill Book Company, 1975.

Rausch, Erwin. *Economic Decision Games.* Chicago: Science Research Associates, 1968.

Renshaw, Paul Obert, Jr. "Basic Marketing and Marketing Related Knowledge Needs of Secondary School Distributive Education Instructional Personnel." Ph.D. dissertation, University of Minnesota–Minneapolis, 1976.

Ryba, R. H. "Teaching Methods and Aids: a Survey." *Teaching Economics.* Edited by Norman Lee. London: Heinemann Educational Books, 1975.

Samson, Harland E. *The Nature and Characteristics of Middle Management in Retail Department Stores.* Madison: Distributive Education Resource Center, University of Wisconsin, 1969.

———. "Objectives of Career Education for Distributive Occupations." Paper presented at the Annual National Business Education Research Conference, Chicago, 1973.

Sanford, C. T., and Bradbury, M. S. "The Use of Core Studies in Economics." *Teaching Economics.* Edited by Norman Lee. London: Heinemann Educational Books, 1975.

Smith, Lloyd George. "Economic Concepts Basic to an Understanding of Introductory Marketing." Ph.D. dissertation, Indiana University Graduate School of Business, 1963.

U.S. Department of Commerce, Bureau of the Census. *Statistical Abstract of the United States.* 94th ed. Washington, D.C.: Government Printing Office, 1975.

U.S. Department of Health, Education, and Welfare, Office of Education. *Trends in Vocational Education: Fiscal Year 1975.* Vocational Education Information, no. II. Washington, D.C.

Vivian, Neal Edward. "Economic Understanding of Distributive Education Students." Ph.D. dissertation, University of Minnesota–Minneapolis, 1966.

Warmke, Roman F. "The Relationship of Economic Education to Distributive Education." *Implementation of Vocational Education in Distribution.* Paper presented at the National Clinic of Distributive Education in Washington, D.C., October 14-18, 1963. Collated by Harland E. Samson. Madison, Wisconsin: Distributive Education Office, Department of Curriculum and Instruction, School of Education, University of Wisconsin, 1967.

White, L. T. "The Importance of Distribution in our Future." *Strengthening Distributive Education.* Edited by William P. Dannenburg and Carroll B. Coakley. Danville, Illinois: The Interstate Printers and Publishers, Inc., 1974.

ADDITIONAL REFERENCES

Garmon, E. Thomas. "Economic Concepts We Don't Understand . . . What Now?" *Journal of Business Education* 48 (Nov. 1973): 77-78.

Grashof, John F., and Kelman, Alan P. *Introduction to Macro-Marketing*. Columbus, Ohio: Grid Inc., 1973.

Lee, Norman, ed. *Teaching Economics.* London: Heinemann Educational Books, 1975.

Moorman, John H. "A Study of Basic Economic Concepts in the High School Curriculum." Ph.D. dissertation, University of Iowa, 1949.

Narver, John C., and Savitt, Ronald. *Conceptual Readings in the Marketing Economy.* Holt, Rineheart and Winston, Inc., 1971.

Shaw, Milton Eugene. "Economic Concepts Believed by Selected Business Leaders to be Essential to an Understanding of the American Business System." D.B.A. dissertation, Indiana University Graduate School of Business, 1969.

Economic Roles, Goals, and Curricula in Health Occupation Education

David R. Terry

Conceptually the economics of health is the application of economics to the health industry, not just to medicine; thus, to approach the economic roles, goals, and curricula in health occupation education is to examine subsets of the concept. This definition is not very explicit, even to health economists —particularly to health occupation educators. In fact, since health services fall outside the traditional parameters of applied economics, it is only during the past decade that an increasing number of economists have worked actively on the problems of the health industry. Mushkin (1958) believes that economists have paid little attention to the health industry because it provides so many exceptions to the economic principles that explain the behavior of the market. Many economists who have inquired about health services support this view (Boulding, 1958, 255; Buchanan, 1960, 400; Samuelson, 1955, 122; Weisbrod, 1961, viii). It may be helpful, therefore, to examine a definition of health and to review the nature of the health industry prior to considering the distinctive characteristics of the industry which have been of concern to economists.

HEALTH AND THE HEALTH INDUSTRY

Health

Health is a broader concept than that usually held by health occupation educators, whose immediate concerns are most frequently associated with preparing a cadre of health personnel whose primary responsibilities are caring for the pathological conditions of the human, the animal, or the environment. The preamble to the constitution of the World Health Organization supplies a concept of health which certainly adds a broader perspective and encompasses the American dream of opportunity: "Health means more than freedom from disease, freedom from pain, freedom from untimely death. It means optimum physical, mental, and social efficiency and well being."

The definition above probably is too broad to furnish practical guidance regarding a complex society's true aims for health, and too vague for evaluating exactly where society is in approaching the goal. However, the definition does serve to challenge health occupation educators as they consider further development of manpower resources which have been technology based and centered on acute medical care. Certainly society is not looking for a left carotid artery specialist or technician, as avid as medical technology is about the development of one (Kinsinger, 1970). Although the lack of a workable definition of health is at the heart of the problems faced by both health economists and health occupation educators, a review of the present health industry will clarify some issues.

Health Industry

Definition. The health industry is a term used by the U.S. Department of Labor in its Standard Industrial Classification Code to designate both public and private "establishments primarily engaged in furnishing medical, surgical, and other health services to persons" (U.S. DOL, 1967, 87). Establishments that are privately owned (voluntary or proprietary), as well as those federal, state, and local government agencies primarily engaged in giving care or service to patients, are included in the industry. Also, since almost all health occupation educators have themselves been prepared initially in a health delivery occupation and are most likely providing some health service in connection with their educator role, they too are counted in the health industry.

The health industry in the United States, then, consists of a loosely associated network of agencies and facilities such as medical centers, hospitals, extended care centers, health maintenance organizations (HMO), medical and dental clinics and offices, government agencies, educational institutions, and, most importantly, practitioners, all of which function through hundreds of types of activity to maintain, restore and protect the nation's health. However, because of its fragmented, disjointed, and increasingly specialized functioning, the health industry is characterized as a nonsystem and has not totally lost its identification as a cottage industry.

Personnel. As of 1900, it is estimated, the health industry employed 350,000 persons. By 1967, the industry's labor force had grown to 3.36 million (U.S. Dept. of HEW, 1969, 21). The latter figure is indicative of the industry's growth just prior to the actual effects of implemented federally legislated programs designed to stimulate health manpower resource development. (See Appendix F, U.S. Dept. of HEW, 1970, 79, for an inventory of federal programs that supported health occupation training.) As a result of the federal programs, the labor force increased by another 1.33 million persons in only seven years—4.70 million direct employees in 1974 (U.S. Dept. of HEW, 1975, 9). In 1973, the industry was the third largest industry in the United States. Because of both the drop in employment within the construction industry and the continued manpower growth in the health industry, the latter was considered the largest American industry in 1976.

And yet, large as the health industry is, it nevertheless functions with only two principal types of personnel: (1) a cadre of physicians and dentists who are considered the primary providers of health care, and (2) a larger cadre of auxiliary personnel who work directly or indirectly with or through the primary providers of health services. An examination of some of the relationships between the primary providers and the auxiliary providers of health services provides ample indication that significant changes are taking place within the industry regarding who is providing health services.

Physicians and dentists active in medicine, osteopathy, and dentistry numbered about 450,000 in 1973 (U.S. Dept. of HEW, 1976b, 108). Between 1900 and 1973 these practitioners increased almost three-fold (2.9 times). However, as a proportion of the aggregate health manpower work force, they declined from 44 percent to 10 percent of the total. Over the same period, the number of dentists alone increased numerically 3.5 times, while as a proportion of the aggregate of dentists and dental-related auxiliaries, dentists declined from 86 percent in 1900 to 39 percent in 1973. In 1900, there was one person working in an auxiliary health occupation for every physician; by 1940 there were five; in 1950 there were seven; and in 1973 there were twelve (U.S. Dept. of HEW, 1970, 68; 1974a, 9). In 1980, with 400,000 physicians and proposed national health insurance, there may be an increase to 16 or 17 to one.

In 1973 there were 170 primary occupational titles and 465 alternate titles among the health occupations (U.S. Dept. of HEW, 1974a, 515). These 635 occupational titles did not include occupations within the health industry for which no special education or formal training is required (e.g., many business, clerical, and maintenance occupations which are essential to but not unique to the health industry). The number of primary and alternate titles grew from 125 and 250, respectively, in 1967, an increase of 45 primary and 215 alternate titles. Growth was accounted for both in actually new occupations and from enlargement of the scope of occupations included within the health industry.

The health occupations have generally been divided—in part by federal programming—into three groups: (1) the medicine, osteopathy, dentistry, veterinarian, optometry, pharmacy, and podiatry (MODVOPP) group; (2) professional nursing; and (3) the allied health occupations group—broadly defined to include the professional, technical, and supportive workers in patient services, administration, teaching, and research who are engaged to actively support, complement, or supplement the functions of MODVOPP and registered nurses. In addition, personnel engaged in organized environmental health activities are included in the allied pool (U.S. Dept. of HEW, 1974a, 133).

The professional (registered) nursing group includes not only those with initial preparation at the baccalaureate level, but also both those diploma graduates of two- or three-year hospital based programs and those two-year associate degree graduates of community college programs. Other nursing related occupations are included in the allied health pool. As in registered nursing, there is no classification among the allied health occupations free of ambiguities. Some two-year preparatory occupational programs are tied by title to graduate technologists or therapists—as are some four-year program titles—while other two-year preparatory programs are titled to graduate technicians or assistants. Based upon occupational titles, therefore, it is difficult to adequately identify the work roles and relationships among the health manpower workers in both nursing and the allied health group. In addition, these ambiguities have, together with certification requirements, contributed to the lack of career lattices and ladders for occupational mobility.

Facilities. As noted earlier, facilities identified by type and numbers within the health industry are numerous. Health services proffered for health care are usually classified as inpatient or ambulatory with respect to where individuals receive health services. Inpatient services are those provided in facilities listed on the Master Facility Inventory (MFI) of the National Center for Health Statistics. Included on the MFI in 1972 were 7,481 hospitals and 22,000 facilities providing nursing care. In addition, there were an unspecified number of other facilities which provide services such as training and sheltered care rather than medical or nursing care, e.g., homes and other facilities for the mentally retarded, the emotionally disturbed, dependent children, unwed mothers, blind or deaf, and the physically handicapped (U.S. Dept. of HEW, 1974a, 345, 528). Among ambulatory and nonpatient health services are those provided by hospital outpatient departments, emergency rooms, and clinics as well as by emergency medical ambulance services, blood banks, clinical laboratories, comprehensive health service programs (including HMOs), medical and dental group practices, dental laboratories, family planning facilities, home health services, optical-related establishments, pharmacies, poison control centers, crisis prevention centers, auditory establishments, psychiatric outpatient services, and rehabilitation facilities (U.S. Dept. of HEW, 1974a, 530).

Employment within hospitals, nursing homes, and related institutions currently accounts for the majority of the work force in the health occupations. For example, in 1972, 74 percent of all active registered nurses and 56 percent of all active licensed practical nurses were employed within these settings. Aside from those in the MODVOPP group, employment of most other technicians, technologists, therapists, assistants, and aides is at or above the 80 percent level within inpatient facilities.

Expenditures and sources of income. Nationally, expenditures for health care (national health budget) increased 18-fold in the 30 years from 1940 to 1970 (U.S. Dept. of HEW, 1976b, 7). From 1970 to 1975 the health budget grew 36 percent to $114 billion (current dollars) and accounted for over 8 percent of the Gross National Product (GNP). The federal health budget amounted to an estimated $32 billion in 1974, with over 79 percent of it allocated to health services (Center for Health Policy Studies, 1974a, 2; 1974b, 3). In 1974, the federal budget funded nearly 40 percent of all health services provided by the health industry (U.S. Dept. of HEW, 1976a,

15). These latter expenditures were made primarily through Medicare and Medicaid under authorizations of the Social Security Act.

What do the billions of dollars represent? They include expenditures for health services provided by hospitals, physicians, dentists, registered nurses, allied health occupations services, public health programs, medical research, commodities, training of health personnel in hospitals (where training costs are added to expenditures for services) and integrated educational institution-hospital programs, and a large part of the capital expenditures for physical plants. Excluded from the data are expenditures for medical and related education outside of hospitals, except as noted, and the value of contributed services of hospital volunteers, including those of physicians. Also excluded are expenditures for food, water, housing, personal health education, and transportation to and from doctors' offices and pharmacies. Also not included are those indirect costs of disease and injury (loss of output) such as disability assistance.

Sources of funds for included expenditures have shown that while there has been a shift from private to public sources, there has also been an expansion in private insurance coverage. For those covered by some form of third-party prepayment source—90 percent of those under age 65 in 1971 (AMA, 1973, 67), third-party payments in fiscal year 1974 accounted for 90 percent of hospital care, 61 percent of physician's services, but only about 14 percent of dental services (U.S. Dept. of HEW, 1976a, 42). The latter figure indicates that more of the costs associated with dental related education are being met by direct patient expenditures than are those costs of medical related education where educational costs are added to the respective service prices and billed to the third-party payment source.

ECONOMIC CHARACTERISTICS OF THE HEALTH INDUSTRY

Having presented an overview of the health industry, it is appropriate to return to a discussion of some of its distinctive characteristics which have tended to prevent economists from applying their tools to this major segment of the American economy. The distinctions cited by Klarman (1965, 11-17) in his overall review of the economics of health will be described briefly.

Uneven and Unpredictable Incidence of Illness

Apart from preventive medicine procedures, requirements for health services are based upon incidence of disease and injury rather than upon the more stable and predictive units of market. Because of the economic disadvantages incurred when the health services are required and because the provider of health service cannot make repossessions, prepayment plans have been developed to meet the exigencies of the patient and to take the payment risks from the providers. Further, health services are often associated with pain, discomfort, and personal indignity and are sought only because of possible drastic consequences.

External Effects

In economics, external effects are those positive and negative results for others which result from one's own behavior; e.g., immunization against a debilitative disease agent will produce greater rewards to the society than to any single individual. Coupling education and research to the delivery of services is another example of a way to increase positive external effects.

Consumer Ignorance

In very few industries is the customer so dependent upon the producer for information concerning the quality and quantity of the product (services). Most typically, the consumer even accepts without question the provider's recommendation. Indeed, it is stated flatly in an American Medical Association publication that, "The 'quantity' of hospital services consumed in 1962 was determined by physicians" (AMA, 1963-64, vol. 1, 19). Infrequency of specific service purchases by the consumer is said to contribute to the problem, which is further heightened by the provider's positive attempts to keep him or her uninformed. The consumer's ignorance and helplessness places a heavy responsibility on the integrity and competence of the provider. This relationship is supposedly made explicit and formalized through licensure, which in fact, however, contributes further to the problem.

Restrictions on Competition

Whereas in most industries one can anticipate that vigorous competition will provide information and dispel consumer ignorance, just the reverse is true in health services. Three factors contribute to the problem. First, entrance restrictions for labor into the industry are assured through the provider's control of education, certification, and licensing. Second, advertising (consumer education) is forbidden and price competition is lost in schedules of "usual and customary charges." Third, critical comment and evaluation of the output of other providers is regarded as unethical. From the provider's point of view, it is alleged that these established strictures provide a mechanism to maintain control on substitution of services, which may reduce consumer outputs by persons in occupations requiring less formal training than those currently providing "approved" services. Formal education for the health occupations, however, has not been based upon identified service tasks and levels of responsibility; only of late has the work been started to identify service tasks and to relate them to levels of responsibility (Terry, 1973).

Health Care as a Need

The right to good health and to receive health care is the expressed consensus of the American society. The individual's need for health and health services is generally taken as the basis of his right to receive it, regardless of ability to pay. However, when a service, such as health service, is to be provided on the basis of "need," then those paying for it would seem to have some right to inquire into the actual presence of "need" and an obligation to determine whether or how much the service actually satisfies the need (Fuchs, 1972, 8). It would appear that the American consumer of health services either has not recognized this right and obligation or has delegated it to third-party prepayment sources, as evidenced by society's succumbing to this payment system with its built-in priorities of care and payments for expenditures.

Nonprofit Motive

In an industry which has traditionally been viewed as not making a profit on the sick and where health service centers have grown up from voluntary nonprofit organizations, it is difficult for the economist to apply the tools normally applied in studying industries based on maximizing profits. Historically, the health auxiliary's low wages have been based not only on a nonprofit motive structure, but have also served to maintain the monopoly on authority (responsibility) by the primary providers of health service.

Health Services and Education as Joint Products

It is often stated that conducting a good educational program in a hospital, dental or medical office enhances the quality of service rendered. This is based upon the proposition that a teaching atmosphere and the presence of students foster student curiosity and challenge the providers to perform at their best. But there is a dissenting position which states that the interests of the patient and of the provider-teacher may not be mutual. Health service expenditures have tended to be higher in teaching hospitals than in nonteaching hospitals, and over a third of the hospitals in the United States are designated as teaching hospitals.

Rapid Rise of Health Service Costs

In an economy based upon increased productivity rather than upon expansion of the labor force, health service expenditures have risen at a faster rate than the consumer price index for all items, and hospital service expenditures have risen faster than all others (AMA, 1973, 107). In the face of increasing use of health services and even greater expected use under anticipated national health insurance, it is not likely that these labor related costs will be reduced.

The foregoing review of both the health industry and some of its economics related characteristics is intended to be neither all-inclusive nor complete. Rather, it is hoped that the content provided will stimulate the health occupation educator and provide greater insight into the nature of the health industry as a whole, and of places within the current nonsystem where marginal contributions can be made to effect greater efficiencies. Changes in educational programs and curricula can be made which can ultimately affect allocations of the health manpower (labor) resources in a way that will improve the last (marginal) inputs of resources.

HEALTH OCCUPATION EDUCATION

The majority of health occupation educators fall into four categories. First, there are those who are currently teaching in a specific health occupation preparatory program. A second category includes those who are teaching individuals from specific health occupations to be teachers of the occupation (teacher educators). In the third category are the teachers of teachers of teachers—teacher educators who specialize in teaching advanced graduate students. Finally, a fourth category includes those in various leadership positions, among which are persons in state offices of adult and vocational education and those on health education commissions supervising postsecondary educational institutions.

Each of these audiences will have reacted somewhat differently to the economic considerations presented in the foregoing discussion and therein lies a dilemma for the health economist. Some in each category work in the immediate environment where health services are being provided and thereby serve as a part of the final input, while others work in environments far removed from such opportunities. Each has a different perception of his or her role relative to the entire industry, as well as a perception of the role which can be translated immediately into recognizable health service functions. Any evaluation of the services provided by one of the groups, however, must take into account the health of the society. And that brings us back to the door of the economist for help in discussing whether or not our marginal inputs are providing increases or decreases in health service and health.

When the economist refers to the health industry, the focus is on the health services rendered by (1) labor—the personnel engaged in the health occupations who are also making use of (2) the physical capital—the plant and equipment used in the delivery, and who are calling for (3) intermediate goods and services—drugs, purchased laundry services, etc. (Fuchs, 1972, 8). In the presentation which follows, the focus will be upon these issues in which health occupation educators and economists can work together. The coverage given to each issue is not meant to be complete nor are the number of topics covered meant to be all-inclusive. Rather, the intent is to provide stimulus for action.

Management Regarding Clinical Decisions

By definition, resources in general are limited and must, therefore, be most efficiently utilized to effect the highest good for the society. Human capital (labor), as a resource, is perceived as a quantity limited in part by its well-being—health. Hence, the crucial question faced by society is what expenditures society is willing to make in maintaining this resource at some agreed-upon level of health. Differences in expectations among members of the society will tend to diminish as federal health insurance becomes reality. The opportunity cost related to policy of this kind is at the very crux of the whole economic system. On the one hand, without labor, other resources are not manageable, and on the other hand, if too much is expended on health, that which must be foregone may be intolerable.

An example will illustrate. Thyrotoxicosis can be treated medically, surgically, or with radiation therapy. If each is about equally effective, the question then becomes: What is the most cost-effective intervention? To continue developing a labor force capable of offering each treatment as if the whole society were going to have all three would require gigantic expenditures. Research must be permitted to discover alternatives for case management, but after two or more alternatives are available, a policy decision must be made as to which types of health occupations will be needed to deliver the service.

In another example we see the case for making policy regarding the length to which the primary investigator (provider) may go in satisfying himself as to a course of action. A patient with hypertension sees a family practitioner, nurse practitioner, or physician's assistant in rural America, and a blood pressure measurement is taken. If it is high, medication is started. Expenditure to patient (or third-party payer) is $10 to $15. The same patient sees a specialist in a teaching hospital's clinic and after 10 days of diagnostic workup (requiring all kinds of labor inputs) and treatments, the expenditure is $1,800. Allowing for educational effects, the real costs to the society, as well as the expenditure incurred, may have been too large in the latter case.

In the face of a third-party prepayment system, society must create policy which will allocate its limited resources to provide minimal acceptable services. *Minimal* must not be construed to be negative if the standard is satisfactory. As noted in the cases above, the decision of what kind of service, and how much of it, has been left solely to an individual practitioner. The patient, as long as he must pay some portion of the expenditure, must have an opportunity to participate in the decision making process.

Health occupation educators stand at the "cutting edge" of change. The practicing vanguard of practitioners are not as easily motivated to accept change as are those in preparatory classrooms.

Education: Where and at What Costs

As noted earlier, health occupation education and health services have existed as joint products in the health industry —a relationship quite unlike formal preparation for any other industry. However, since the skyrocketing costs in hospital expenditures of the late 1960s and since the development of health occupation education programs based in community colleges and universities, with the concomitant closing of similar hospital based educational programs, more attention has been given to assessing the real need of requiring the "clinical education" to be done in the hospital.

In 1968-69 this writer developed and implemented a campus based respiratory therapy program that incorporated a simulation laboratory in which the students learned and practiced the fundamentals of equipment maintenance and delivery of services. Students were rotated through six hospitals and nursing care centers to learn the basics of providing service, rather than being sent to one hospital to become experts in performing the specified techniques of care used therein. The writer also revamped a radiologic technology program designed to teach the students the fundamentals of x-ray in a simulation x-ray service facility. Using relatively inexpensive commercial x-ray cabinets and models, the students became completely familiar with the nature of x-rays, the equipment, and the uses of x-rays before ever seeing a patient. Considering cost differences in operating these programs on the college campus versus in the hospital, the former proved to be more efficient, despite the fact that the eventual employer of these providers still had some on-the-job training to do, as do employers in most industries. Also, considering the sources of recovering expenditures for operating the different programs, the campus based program drew its resources from tuition referenced funding (student, state and federal tax bases) rather than from a sick patient and a prepayment system based upon some limited portion of the public.

A recent federal study of educational costs associated with the clinical education for the seven MODVOPP health occupations and registered nursing has provided data on their net educational expenditures—total education expenditures less portion of expenditures returned through income from instructor generated research and patient care (U.S. Dept. of HEW, 1974b). Two shortcomings of the method used in the study result from (1) the assumption that medical interns, for example, cannot be taught by regular medical school faculty, as is done in the case of nursing, and (2) the failure to assess the income generated by patient care provided by students—an assumption that the students are not producing outputs. The Hartford Hospital *Study of the Cost of Education Programs* (1972) suggests that when student outputs are considered, the net education expenditures can be reduced to near zero or below (net gain). These latter findings are important in light of federal capitation grants being made to offset alleged positive net educational expenditures in the eight occupational education programs noted above. The point also should be made that in the federal study, differences are not taken into consideration between sources of income to pay salaries of hospital house staff—medical residents serving as instructors—and to pay those of nursing instructors. Again, salaries for the former are derived from the patients and their prepayment plans, whereas in the case of nursing, the salaries are derived from a general tax base. Health occupations educators in nursing and in the allied health programs have the charge to investigate these differences in funding bases with the tools of the economist.

Health Service Supply

Economists follow the supply side of the health industry by assessing three main elements: (1) the supply of factors of services—labor and capital, (2) changes in production, and (3) the degree of monopoly control that influences supply availability to consumers. The last of these elements was discussed earlier. The first two will be discussed after describing the credentialing processes which impact upon them.

Credentialing is the formal recognition of professional or technical competence—inferential measures of ultimate health outputs. The term is currently used in the health industry in referring to the processes of registration or certification of individuals by professional associations; licensure of individuals by government; and accreditation of formal educational programs by voluntary agencies, upon which the government bases qualification for federal manpower training expenditures.

Supply factors. Health manpower economists look not only at manpower by numbers of individuals in the industry, but also at the characteristics of that labor which affect service inputs and ultimately outputs. Those inputs are, in large part, effected by the educational programs preparing the potential members of the labor force. The number and kinds of educational programs, as well as their enrollment capacities, determine the potential inputs to service as well as the potential availability of labor. A crucial question for the health industry regarding labor is whether or not it will have to pay inordinately high wages (1) to attract the labor and (2) for the productivity of the labor force. The latter point is painfully noted by the increasing number of occupational specialties, each with its limited scope of input (including responsibility). This fractionation increases the necessity for larger and larger quantities of labor in an economic system based on reducing labor costs.

The number and kinds of health occupation programs are

limited, in part, by federal policy. High costs of capital resources and instructor salaries for the programs have been made available by federal funding—predominantly through capitation grants currently, and only in the MODVOPP and nursing programs. The health manpower training acts of the 1960s and their amendments are examples. While the MODVOPP and registered nursing education programs have continued to receive considerable federal support, the allied health educational programs have been significantly reduced at the federal level. Health occupation educators have tended to support and maintain differences in federal funding policy among the health occupations, as measured by their demands for funding by occupational title rather than by funding based upon more efficient methods of labor input that are founded on new and expanded functions and relationships among health manpower inputs.

Formal educational requirements for the health occupations are most often determined directly by requirements for credentialing in all of its aspects, as well as indirectly by the informal pressures of certain health occupations to protect their own status—usually expressed as statements to the effect that, "Certainly no one else can do what I do unless they have had to meet all of the requirements I had to meet." The triteness of these formalized and informal pressures is given focus in the example of a student, currently enrolled in a course offered by this writer, who became a Certified Laboratory Assistant and after working for four years in the hospital in which she was trained, found herself permitted to perform almost every function in the medical laboratory and to sign out the reports as the only one responsible before a report was returned to the patient's chart. In order to raise her salary, however, she went back to school to meet the educational requirements to become a Medical Laboratory Technician (MLT). Upon completion of this program, she returned to the same hospital to continue doing the same work but at a higher salary. Registered Medical Technologists in the same laboratory received identical salaries as the MLTs, but one was required to be a Medical Technologist (MT) to have a supervisory position. The individual in question went back to school for the MT, went back to the original hospital, and became a supervisor at a higher salary, but doing many supervisory functions for which none of the education had prepared her. Now, given that patient morbidity rates were not affected by the above use of labor—it must be assumed they have not, for the practice has continued for several years—then the educational requirements and credentialing for this occupation must be reviewed in terms of service costs and health expenditures.

Licensure statutes often contain stipulations relating both to courses, by title, to be taken in formal educational preparation for a health occupation, as well as to functions (tasks, services) which can or cannot be performed by those licensed. Certification requirements, whether for licensed or non-licensed health occupations, are made explicit through examinations, the content of which has also contributed to the respective educational curriculum. In a similar manner, accreditation has tended to establish uniformity within an occupation by stipulations which offer little or no opportunity for crossover of faculty between two programs or for the sharing of curriculum or physical plant between two allegedly different occupations or levels of an occupation.

Health occupation educators have, for the most part, limited their respective curricula by not going beyond the narrowest limits of practice as defined by the most limiting credential. For example, dental hygiene graduates of Illinois schools cannot practice to the full extent of the licensure act of the state of Washington. Health occupation educators should be preparing a potential labor force capable of functioning to at least the greatest level of service recognized for a given occupational title, and it would be expected that they would be pursuing their ultimate responsibility by being in the vanguard in producing new and more effective health service inputs.

Health occupation educators should know that a little-known time-bomb continues to tick away (set to go off December 31, 1977) in Section 1123 of the Social Security Amendments of 1972 (U.S. Congress, 1972, 90). In this section, policy has been set which states that after that date, individuals providing health services shall not be denied federal reimbursement for services based upon the fact that they do not meet the formal educational, professional membership, or other specific criteria currently established for determining qualifications. Rather, proficiency of service will be the standard. This policy, notwithstanding a counter proposal contained in the federally proposed Recommendation III for credentialing health manpower (U.S. Dept. of HEW, 1976a), should encourage greater academic freedom in preparing health service providers through more cost effective means as well as to prepare them to make greater contributions to productivity.

Productivity. In the absence of reliable measures of health output, productivity is difficult to assess (Berman, 1976). It is possible, however, that the practice of having a plethora of health service specialists whose independent activities and expensive procedures are part of today's "best practice" techniques is not worth the costs. Studies by Patterson and Bergman (1969) on the use of auxiliary personnel have shown, for example, that pediatricians use a registered nurse in essentially the same way they do a medical assistant whose training is only six months. Smith, Miller, and Golladay (1972) found similar findings in other medical services which used either medical assistants or licensed practical nurses instead of registered nurses. The point is that one possible reason why greater economies of production have not been observed may be the restrictions on which types of personnel may perform what tasks. This fact may be preventing the technically (and economically) efficient solution to production from being attained. Health occupation educators must work with economists to find, or prepare, delivery systems for economic study.

Health occupation educators must reach beyond the immediacies of educating and training manpower whose productivity is measured by the mechanical acts of a current technology. That kind of productivity will mean in the future, if not now, uselessness (Willers, 1971).

REFERENCES CITED

American Medical Association. *Commission on the Costs of Medical Care Reports.* 3 vols. Chicago: American Medical Association, 1963-64.

———. *Socioeconomic Issues of Health.* Chicago: Center for Health Services, 1973.

Berman, Edgar. *The Solid Gold Stethoscope.* New York: Macmillan Publishing Co., 1976.

Boulding, Kenneth E. *Principles of Economic Policy.* Englewood Cliffs, N.J.: Prentice-Hall, Inc., 1958.

Buchanan, James M. *The Public Finances.* Homewood, Ill.: Richard D. Irwin, Inc., 1960.

Center for Health Policy Studies. *Chartbook of Federal Health Spending, 1969-74.* Washington, D.C.: National Planning Association, 1974a.

———. *Federal Health Spending, 1969-74.* Washington, D.C.: National Planning Association, 1974b.

Fuchs, Victor R. "Contributions of Health Services." *Essays in the Economics of Health and Medical Care.* Edited by Victor R. Fuchs. New York: Columbia University Press, 1972.

Hartford Hospital. *Study of the Cost of Education Programs.* Hartford, Conn.: Hartford Hospital, 1972.

Kinsinger, Robert E. "Personnel Resources Development for Health Occupations Education." *National Conference on Health Occupations.* Edited by Robert M. Tomlinson, et al. Urbana, Ill.: University of Illinois, 1970.

Klarman, Herbert E. *The Economics of Health.* New York: Columbia University Press, 1965.

Mushkin, Selma J. "Toward a Definition of Health Economics." *Public Health Reports* (Sept. 1958): 785-93.

Patterson, Patricia K., and Bergman, A. B. "Time-Motion Study of Six Pediatric Office Assistants." *New England Journal of Medicine* (Oct. 1969): 771-74.

Samuelson, Paul A. *Economics.* 3d ed. New York: McGraw-Hill Book Company, 1955.

Smith, Kenneth R.; Miller, M.; and Golladay, F. L. "An Analysis of Optimal Use of Inputs in Production of Medical Services." *Journal of Human Resources* (Spring 1972): 208-25.

Terry, David R. *Determining Behavioral Content of the Curriculum in Occupational and Professional Education Programs.* Urbana, Ill.: University of Illinois, Bureau of Educational Research, 1973.

U.S. Congress. *Comprehensive Health Manpower Act of 1971.* P.L. 92-157. 92nd Cong. Washington, D.C.: Government Printing Office, 1971.

———. *Social Security Amendments of 1972.* P.L. 92-603. 92nd Cong. Washington, D.C.: Government Printing Office, 1972.

U.S. Department of Health, Education and Welfare, Division of Allied Health Manpower. *The Allied Health Professions Personnel Training Act of 1966, as Amended: Report to the President and the Congress.* Washington, D.C.: Government Printing Office, April 1969.

———, Bureau of Health Professions Education and Manpower Training. *Health Manpower Source Book 21.* Washington, D.C.: Government Printing Office, 1970.

———, Bureau of Health Resources Development. *The Supply of Health Manpower: 1970 Profiles and Projections to 1990.* DHEW Pub. (HRA) 75-38. Washington, D.C.: Government Printing Office, 1974a.

———, Health Resources Administration. *A Proposal for Credentialing Health Manpower.* Washington, D.C.: Government Printing Office, June 1976a.

———, Health Resources Administration, Center for Health Statistics. *Health, United States 1975.* Washington, D.C.: Government Printing Office, 1976b.

———, Institute of Medicine. *Costs of Education in the Health Professions.* DHEW Pub. (HRA) 74-32. Washington, D.C.: Government Printing Office, 1974.

———, National Center for Health Statistics. *Health Resources Statistics 1974.* DHEW Pub. (HRA) 75-1509. Washington, D.C.: Government Printing Office, 1974.

———. *Health Resources Statistics 1975.* DHEW Pub. (HRA) 76-1509. Washington, D.C.: Government Printing Office, 1975.

U.S. Department of Labor, Manpower Administration. *Technology and Manpower in the Health Service Industry 1965-1975.* Manpower Research Bulletin 14. Washington, D.C.: Government Printing Office, May 1967.

Weisbrod, Burton A. *Economics of Public Health.* Philadelphia: University of Pennsylvania Press, 1961.

Willers, Jack C. "The Quality of Life in the Seventies and Implications for Vocational Teacher Education." *Changing the Role of Vocational Teacher Education.* Edited by Rupert N. Evans and David R. Terry. Bloomington, Ill.: McKnight and McKnight Publishers, 1971.

Economic Roles, Goals, and Curricula in Home Economics Education

Alberta D. Hill and Helen J. Westrum

Home economics is a field of study or discipline that synthesizes knowledge drawn from its own research and from other disciplines, including economics, and applies this knowledge to the lives of families and individuals.

Both the terms *ecology,* a study of the interrelationships of organisms with their environment, and *economics,* which is derived in part from the Greek word *oikonomikus,* meaning "skilled in the management of the household," were considered by the founders of home economics as appropriate labels for the field. The *economics* of home economics has not been always apparent to the public, or even vocational educators. The purpose of this chapter is to underline the economics of home economics education.

HOME ECONOMICS: SCOPE AND PURPOSE

The core of home economics was delineated by its founders:

> Home Economics in its most comprehensive sense is the study of the laws, conditions, principles and ideals which are concerned on the one hand with man's immediate physical environment and on the other hand with his nature as a social being, and is the study especially of the relation between these two factors . . .

The American Home Economics Association (AHEA) reconfirmed this statement as essentially the basic mission of home economics for the 1970s. The AHEA says in its 1975 statement of purpose that:

> The core of Home Economics is the family ecosystem: The study of reciprocal relations of the family to its natural and man-made environments, the effect of these singly or in unison as they

shape the internal functioning of families, and the interplays between the family and other social institutions and the physical environment (AHEA, 1975).

Vocational home economics education is an integral part of the total home economics profession. The historic perspective, statement of purpose, and understanding of the content origin of home economics summarized here provide the context within which the economic roles, goals, and curricula in vocational home economics programs are discussed.

CONTRIBUTIONS OF HOMEMAKING TO THE ECONOMY

Problems in Measuring Economic Worth of Homemaking

A major purpose of vocational home economics education is to prepare persons for the occupation of homemaking. The work of the home, as defined by Walker (1976), ". . . comprises a multiplicity of activities performed in individual households that result in goods and services that enable a family to function as a unit." This work has been performed traditionally by females. Preparation for the occupation is often limited to only an informal apprenticeship-type training in the parental home. There have been no regular working hours, salary scale, or tenure. The activities of the individual homes are extremely varied and hard to quantify. For all these reasons, the work of the home is usually excluded from discussions of manpower needs or status of the economy.

Walker (1976) points out that for many years economists interested in the measurement of national income have included in their estimates only an apology for the omission of household production. Documentation of such "apologies" is presented in quotations from 1930 and 1969 publications of the National Bureau of Economic Research. King and Epstein (1930) minimized the omission of an estimate of the value of the services of the "housewife" by indicating that the value of the service of the "head of the household," presumably male, who "manages the family business" was also excluded in the estimates of national income. (Note: The authors of this chapter perceive management of the "business" of the family as an integral part of home economics!)

The solution to the perplexing problem of quantifying the economic worth of homemaking has been further confused by some facets of the women's movement. In the worthy attempt to gain equality for women in employment outside the home, the occupation of maintaining homes has been downgraded. This situation, clouded by lack of empirical data of the economic worth of homemaking and by emotional debates, is not apt to be resolved until sex stereotyping of homemaking has been eliminated.

Progress is being made in the recognition of the economic contribution of homemaking to the family, if not to the national economy. Developments in Social Security plans and benefits are at an embryonic stage, but promising. There have been gradual changes in deductions allowed for some homemaking activities, notably child care, in calculating income tax. The following quote from a recent state cooperative extension service release reflects another trend. (Editor's comment: The salary quoted is more than minimum wage but less than a certified experienced checker at the supermarket!)

> If you're a full-time homemaker with two children—and one of them is less than a year old—you're worth about $7,600 a year to your family.
>
> Your worth in dollars goes *down* as the children get older, presumably because they're more able to take care of themselves. But, if you became sick or died and had to be replaced with paid help, the family's budget would really suffer. Depending on the ages of her children, the homemaker's contribution of cooking, washing, ironing, cleaning, and the few other jobs you do around the house comes to between $3,000 and $9,000 a year.
>
> These figures reflect what most families know—but do nothing about. Few women have bothered looking into disability insurance for themselves. This kind of policy is being pioneered by a few companies. The need is great, but the companies say there is little demand (Washington State University, 1977).

Walker, who has given leadership to the research at Cornell University focused on measuring the value of household work, has completed a monumental study of *time use* as a measure of household production of family goods and services (Walker & Woods, 1976). This study recognized the limitation created by the fact that household work is variable and discontinuous and that it is not possible to record the precise beginning and ending of work. Though the Cornell studies have several limitations, they have provided a wealth of data to assist in placing a dollar value on household work. Walker points out that "additional research is needed to determine appropriate methods for incorporating household production into national indicators for economic analysis."

Homemakers' Contributions to Economic Goals

The total number of persons included in various censuses of the "work force" does not include the 28 million homemakers who are not gainfully employed (i.e., receiving wages or salary) outside the home (Gordon & Lee, 1972). Their contribution to the economy, however, can be considered as important as the contribution made by many who are listed as gainfully occupied.

Homemakers contribute to the economy as: (1) producers of goods and services, (2) consumers of goods and services, (3) decision makers, and (4) producers of knowledge, skills and attitudes. These, of course, are not discrete categories. The "teaching" function—producer of knowledge, skills, and attitudes—is one of the services produced, but it is separated from the other services in this discussion to permit placing greater emphasis on this important function.

The homemaker as producer. The output of goods and services of the home may be difficult to quantify, or price, but they are observable and are, therefore, often the only recognized economic function of the home.

Earlier in the century there was no doubt about the production role of the homemaker, who provided most of the family food through gardening, baking, canning, raising chickens and churning. The worth of the homemaker was established by the observable activities of cleaning and maintaining the household, baking, laundering, mending clothing and household linen—tasks accomplished without the help of modern laborsaving devices. These tasks were carried out in addition to assuming full responsibility for children.

Changes in food production and distribution, technological developments in textiles, and the development of so-called laborsaving devices have obscured the economic significance of the homemaker. The nature of work has changed in a way that may make it less apparent, but there continues to be a multiplicity of activities performed in households that result in goods and services enabling a family to function as a unit. The small size of the household unit—and therefore the apparent economic insignificance when viewed in terms of other businesses and industry—the high percentage of females engaged in this occupation, and the nonmonetary aspect of the work have contributed to the lack of recognition of economic worth. It is extremely difficult to make an accurate estimate of the monetary value of these goods and services. Monetary contributions can be appreciated only when one is trying to hire a household worker to replace the "built-in" homemaker.

One way to estimate the value of the goods and services produced in the home is through a study of time spent in homemaking activities. The extensive study made by Walker and Woods (1976) was referred to earlier. Activities included in that study were: marketing, household management, household record keeping; food preparation and after-meal cleanup; house care, house maintenance, yard care and car care; washing, ironing and special care of clothing; and physical and other care of family members.

The homemaker as consumer. Population increases and frequent changes in family structures make it difficult to provide up-to-date figures on the number of households in the United States. According to Gordon and Lee (1972, 8), there are 63 million households. Individually and collectively, these households are the basic consuming units in the economy. The family income gives family members the purchasing power to buy goods and services to satisfy their needs and wants; the family decides which goods and services they will purchase.

In 1971, the United States produced goods and services worth one trillion dollars. Consumer expenditures accounted for two-thirds of the gross national product, including $103 billion for food, $107 billion for housing and shelter, and $42 billion on recreation (Troelstrup, 1974, 5). Collectively, consumers had $667 billion in disposable personal income in 1970 (Gordon & Lee, 1972). These statistics document the magnitude of the homemaker's economic role.

The power of family units as consumers supports the need for them to be well-informed about the variety, cost, quality and availability of goods and services and the effects of their decisions upon the national economic structure.

The homemaker-home manager is constantly making decisions about using human resources (i.e., abilities, skills, attitudes and knowledge), and nonhuman resources (i.e., time, money, goods, property, and community facilities) to reach family goals and realize family values (Nickell, Rice & Tucker, 1976, 109). These decisions, which have far-reaching effects upon quality and costs of production, help determine the kinds and number of jobs that are available and have great impact upon the environment.

The homemaker as decision maker. The function of the homemaker-manager is partly one of making decisions as a consumer. The decision making function is, however, broader in scope than choosing among the many alternatives in the marketplace. Although most decisions made by homemakers have some relationship to goods and services, the impact upon the social and economic structure and well-being of the society goes farther than the production or use of goods and services. The decision making role of homemakers is an *administrative* function. Family administration may be shared but, in terms of business and industry, involves establishing goals, developing long-range management plans, and setting personnel policies. The administrative role in the family unit may include deciding on numbers and spacing of children, establishing educational goals, deciding when to move to a retirement home, dividing responsibilities among family members, and establishing rules for teenagers' conduct. Collectively, these family decisions affect demand for housing; cost of public education, welfare and protective services; and total population growth. The administrative, decision making role in itself has an economic value. If not performed within the family, such roles would have to be assumed by outsiders who would be reimbursed.

The homemaker as producer of knowledge, skills and attitudes. Society, by law and social mores, has assigned to families the responsibility of care and guidance of children. Although schools, child care centers and nursery schools for the young child may assist in this task, the family is legally responsible for the behavior as well as the care of the young. Despite changes in patterns of family life, one function of a family continues to be that of providing experiences that aid children in personality development, in acceptance of roles, and in learning to do tasks needed for independent living.

There is ample evidence to support the idea that the family unit is more influential than any of the other experiences of children in the development of knowledge, skills and attitudes. There is a direct and measurable relationship of skills and knowledge learned at an early age in the home to the human resources available to each individual. More important than skills and knowledge are the attitudes and the related value system which, by intent or default, are taught in the home. These are the values and attitudes people retain throughout their life. The value of work as a part of life, the desire to strive for quality in workmanship, the feelings about cooperative effort and competition, and the acceptance of persons different from self are generally those taught in the home. Attitudes that are learned as part of the early socialization process in the family will also direct behavior regarding use of land, the disposal of garbage, use of water, the conservation of electrical energy, and recycling.

ECONOMIC GOALS OF VOCATIONAL HOME ECONOMICS

A General View

Vocational home economics programs at all levels have included instruction in "personal and family finance" and "consumer education"—or, at least, "consumer buying"—since the 1920s, but the *economic* goals of home economics have not been, nor are they now, limited to those labeled as family or consumer economics.

Because home economics involves working closely with families, which are the basic economic as well as social units of society, the outcomes of the program have significant impact upon other economic units of society. All of the knowledge and skills needed for management of the home have an economic component: the feeding, clothing, and housing of family members; providing psychological support and security for family members; and caring for the young and elderly and managing resources to achieve individual and family goals. Special emphasis has been given in vocational home economics programs to meeting special situations. Programs during the Great Depression of the 1930s helped families "make do" with limited resources; World War II programs developed the skills needed to extend limited health care services and use substitutes for scarce goods; home economics educators in the 1970s include an analysis of the consequences of consumer decisions upon the environment in their programs.

Home economics is a discipline that focuses on improving the welfare of individuals and families. Therefore, economic goals of home economics programs reflect social developments and changes in family structure as well as changes in the status of the economy and the economic structure. This does not mean that the goals of home economics ignore basic concepts underlying our economic system nor that the goals are to promote self-centered and selfish behaviors. The goals of home economics are to help families apply the knowledge of our economic system to personal choices. The focus on the individual and family does mean, however, that goals are realistic for individuals and families in all segments of society. The focus on people means that consumers are seen as individuals with varying goals and abilities and certainly with freedoms and social responsibilities. In home economics, consumers are seen as individuals who are born with certain resources and accumulate other resources as they move through life, making decisions on how to use these resources which will affect their lives, the lives of their families, and the welfare of the nation and the world.

Goals Established by Legislation

Economic and social developments, or at least the public's perceptions of these developments, are often reflected in legislation of state, national and local governments. The U.S. Congress has, since 1917, periodically revised vocational education legislation to conform to changes in employment patterns, the economy and needs of individuals. Each change in legislation has directly affected the goals of home economics.

Subpart 5 of Title I, Vocational Education Public Law 94-482, enacted in the fall of 1976 (U.S. Congress, 1976), supports educational programs in consumer and homemaking education for all educational levels *for the occupations of homemaking.* The law states that this is to include "consumer education, food and nutrition, family living and parenthood education, child development and guidance, housing and home management (including resource management), and clothing and textiles." Each of these content areas has an economic component.

The law also reflects the economic goals and social concerns of the nation by stating that these programs are to:

1. Encourage participation of both males and females to prepare for combining the roles of homemakers and wage earners.
2. Encourage elimination of sex stereotyping in consumer and homemaking education by promoting the development of curriculum materials which deal with increased numbers of women working outside the home and increased numbers of men assuming homemaking responsibilities and the changing career patterns for women and men.
3. Give greater consideration to economic, social, and cultural conditions.
4. Encourage outreach programs in communities for youth and adults giving considerations to special needs.
5. Prepare males and females who have entered or are preparing to enter the work of the home.
6. Emphasize consumer education, management of resources, promotion of nutritional knowledge and food use, and parenthood education to meet current societal needs.

Economic Goals of Consumer Education

Criticisms of home economics programs—possibly justified—have been that too much emphasis has been placed on "buymanship" and too little on understanding financial facts of the economic system, the process of decision making and the consequences of decision making. A review of curriculum guides developed in the last ten years gives a different view. For example, *Concepts in Personal Finance Education,* developed in Oregon in 1972, lists "Purchase of Goods and Services" as only one of five concepts. The others are: Employment and Income, Money Management, Credit and Rights, and Responsibilities in the Marketplace.

A project carried out by North Dakota State University (1974) gave emphasis to structuring and organizing consumer education. One dimension of the framework developed was a statement of four competencies which are as follows:

The consumer can use at mastery level:

1. The *inquiry* process in relation to consumer behaviors.
2. The *valuing* process in relation to consumer behaviors.
3. The *decision* process in relation to consumer behaviors.
4. The *rational* consumer action process.

These behaviors were presented as a spiral development with levels building upon one another.

LEVEL I—Consumers choose, buy and use according to present needs and wants.

LEVEL II—Consumers are part of current consumer movement—value clarification is at beginning level.

LEVEL III—Consumer behavior shows results of integration of personal values with judgments based on facts.

LEVEL IV—Consumers set priorities and exercise their influence upon the public and private sectors of the economy to improve conditions for present and future generations.

The general categories described above give an indication of the scope of consumer education goals within home economics, but the characteristics which distinguish consumer education in home economics from consumer education or personal finance taught in other disciplines are more apparent in statements of specific objectives. These objectives focus on the family and the interrelationship of consumer decisions with all other personal and family decisions.

Priority Goals for 1970s

A review of the capabilities of the discipline of home economics and the current social and economic situation are used as criteria for selecting a few priority goals. The goals selected by the authors are those which have met the criteria of appropriateness for our times and for home economics.

Assist individuals to assume responsibilities and accept rights of a consumer. Home economics has the responsibility to assist individuals in assuming the responsibilities and accepting the rights of a consumer.

Responsibility is an important qualification for the occupation of "consumer." This quality of responsibility, a part of the individual decision making process, is based on knowledge and directed by positive attitudes about the economic system and the rights of others. Each consumer has a responsibility to the businesses and industries which supply personal needs, a responsibility for helping maintain a workable and equitable economic system, and responsibility to neighbors and fellow citizens. This responsibility extends to setting a pattern that will be followed by future generations of his or her family.

The consumer also has rights; the right to be informed, the right of redress, the right to be protected against dangerous consumer goods are but a few. These rights, stated in law, are important for a consumer to know and use because, if not used, they could be lost.

Ensure efficient use of resources. To ensure the efficient use of human and nonhuman resources is a major economic goal in vocational home economics programs. To be able to utilize resources efficiently, one has to be able to identify, assess, and develop resources. At the present time it is estimated that only 4 to 10 percent of human potentialities are being used (Nickell, Rice & Tucker, 1976, 157). The goal of efficient use of human resources is far from being met, but the fact that this underuse has been recognized is significant.

Diminishing natural resources and continuing world population growth mandate a new look at goals related to the conservation of material resources. Decision makers need new knowledge and changed attitudes regarding the use of nonrenewable resources, one-use disposables and convenience tools and appliances. Limited land resources will require revised plans and attitudes about housing. Food use may become influenced more and more by the total world food supplies and requirements.

Provide for economic stability and security of family units. Economic security is a goal that is important to individuals and families. This fundamental survival need is related to being able to make decisions, handle resources, and hold an adequate job.

Prepare for dual role of homemaker-wage earner. The

preparation of men and women for the dual role of homemaker-wage earner has two economic facets. Achievement of the goal leads to: (1) the well-being and economic stability of the home, and (2) increased satisfaction and productivity of workers, men and women, in their employment outside the home. With most men *and* many women in the labor force, it becomes imperative that time spent at home is well managed. All family members are partners in this challenge. This means that all family members need a variety of skills and knowledge in resource management, child care, and maintaining supportive family relationships.

Studies of time spent on household activities support the general observation that most women who are employed outside the home spend almost as much time carrying out homemaking activities as they did when they were full-time homemakers. Men, on the other hand, increase only slightly the time they spend on homemaking tasks when the wife works. One reason for this situation is that men and women have been taught that certain tasks are rightfully female roles and others male roles. A second reason is that many men have not been prepared to perform those homemaking tasks perceived as "women's work." Preparing males as well as females for the work of the home is an essential part of making all occupations equally available to both men and women.

CONTRIBUTIONS OF HOME ECONOMICS TO DEVELOPMENT OF SALEABLE SKILLS

Home economics has joined other vocational programs in contributing to the economic goal of preparing persons for the labor market. This activity within vocational education supplements but does not replace preparation for the occupation of homemaking. Training that is planned and carried out by home economics educators prepares persons for work in those occupations which use the knowledge and skills of home economics.

Influence of Vocational Education Act of 1963

Records of home economics education conferences in the early 1920s give some accounts of discussion of wage-earning programs. There is some historical evidence of cooperation (and conflict) between home economics and trades and industrial education food service programs; one author of this chapter phased out a food management program in 1942. These are examples of sporadic and isolated programs. Preparation for earning wages did not become one of the major goals of home economics education until the passage of the Vocational Education Act of 1963. This legislation, designed to increase employment opportunities for all persons in all communities, gave home economics both the resources and impetus to expand instruction for using the skills and knowledge of home economics to help persons enter employment outside the home.

Occupational Opportunities

The occupations for which training can best be included in home economics are those closely related to the *content* areas of the discipline. These can be identified as occupations related to: (1) child care, (2) clothing, apparel and textile services, (3) family and community services, (4) food service, (5) housing and interior design, and (6) institutional and household maintenance.

Studies completed in a number of states verify the need for better-trained workers in all of these occupational groups. Labor statistics indicate that jobs available in service occupations will continue to increase, but it is difficult to ascertain the number and kinds of positions available except on a local level. Data regarding some food service occupations are more adequate.

Each of the occupational areas which use home economics content include occupations at several levels, including those of the professional level requiring a bachelor's degree. This condition requires that educators distinguish among levels, analyze the tasks required at each level, and then match training to the competencies needed for each level. A two-year post-high school program for an entry-level food service job which would require only six weeks or 12th grade training is an economic waste—a waste of educational resources and the learner's time. It is equally wasteful, however, to lead persons to believe that they will be able to obtain employment with secondary school training if additional training is required.

Economics-Related Problems in Wage-Earning Programs

Two major problems face home economics educators who are involved in wage-earning occupations. First, many of the occupations which use the knowledge and skills of home economics are occupations with low pay scales. The second problem is the low status of many of these jobs. Both problems stem from the fact that the jobs are seen as an extension of homemaking tasks, which have had low status and non-measurable economic returns. It is also true that many of these jobs have been traditionally assigned to minority groups.

In some occupations employers report interest in better-trained employees, but admit that they will pay those trained no more than those with no training. Some food service occupations, many of which have been traditionally filled by men, are an exception, but even in this field many important tasks of the industry are carried out by low-paid workers. Institutional and household maintenance workers, tasks often filled by minority groups, are notoriously low-paid. Jobs such as care of children and clothing maintenance tasks, once done by maiden aunts, grandparents or a "nice little Irish immigrant" when the homemaker needed extra help, are still among the low-status, low-pay group.

Educators interested in upgrading these occupations need to look beyond task analysis and curriculum development. They need to assume leadership in mobilizing groups concerned with services to people in settings such as homes, nursing homes, day-care centers, or school lunchrooms. A concerted effort is needed to improve the public image and pay scale for many home economics-related occupations if these occupations are to provide viable employment opportunities.

Successful Programs

The problems cited above are real and a serious handicap to the contribution home economics could make to employability. In spite of these handicaps, a number of successful programs are in operation. It is not the purpose of this chapter to describe these programs, but recognition must be given to:

1. Entry-level courses at secondary school level which encourage trainees to continue in a paraprofessional program at postsecondary level.
2. Employment of homemakers who have an opportunity for training to build on their homemaking skills.
3. Competency based child guidance programs in community colleges which will make possible formal certification of trainees.
4. Occupational courses which have made secondary school meaningful and acceptable to disenchanted students.
5. Programs which have made possible a real career, with opportunities for advancement, to those who

did not want, or could not afford, a four-year college program.

ECONOMIC LITERACY IN HOME ECONOMICS

Economic literacy is discussed here within the context of the definition and scope described by Hansen in Chapter 12.

A 1970 survey of the status of consumer education in home and family life programs in the state of Washington included a study of the teachers' perceptions of their preparation for teaching each of 28 major topics. The large majority perceived themselves to be well-prepared in their undergraduate teacher education program to teach topics related to selection of consumer goods, bases for consumer decisions, sources of consumer information, credit and sociocultural influences upon consumer decisions. Topics which were most often perceived as those for which they were *not* well-prepared included economic security plans, taxation, consumer in the larger economy and estate planning. It was possible to generalize from this 1970 study, at least for this one state, that vocational home economics teachers had a good background of knowledge about consumer goods as services. The data can be used also to generalize that home economics teachers were better prepared in the sociological, cultural and psychological supporting disciplines than in economics.

New tests, teaching materials, and curriculum guides can serve as aids to the home economics teacher in improving the economic literacy of youth and adults in their roles as homemakers and wage earners. A greater improvement can be achieved by improving the economic literacy of those who teach. This greater literacy for teachers requires effort of three different types:

1. Include more study in business and economics in preservice and inservice teacher education programs. Home economists focus programs on personal and family needs and home-based decisions, which often seem minor, even mundane, and unrelated to such things as the GNP or international monetary plans. These *little* family decisions, when added together and multiplied by 60 or 70 million, are not micro, but macro concerns. Home economists then need to have the economic background that allows them to see the global picture of how people's decisions interrelate with other sections in the economy.

2. Team approach to teaching. A cooperative team approach can help avoid gaps and repetition in a program and utilize the resource represented by different subject matter specialties. A team approach does not necessarily require team teaching. It does require that each member of the team become aware of expertise of other members of the team. It also requires that each member of the team have the sense of security and feeling of self worth that makes it possible to accept teammates and to share.
3. Continuous self-directed education. Home economics educators will not learn all they need to know in a preservice, four-year teacher education program, nor will they keep updated by an occasional inservice class or conference. They can utilize the expertise of the economics, distributive education, or agriculture teacher to supplement their own knowledge, but this will not substitute for their own economic literacy. Continuous, self-directed education will take different forms for different teachers, but will include: (1) extensive reading—books, editorials in daily newspapers, business sections of weekly magazines, the *Federal Register*, and (2) contacts with economic planners through community organizations, political affiliations, visits to managers of industry.

EPILOGUE

Vocational home economics education programs have *economic* goals; achievement of these goals contributes to the national economy. The economic contributions are directed toward:

1. Preparing people to enter the labor force by developing competencies needed for:
   a. occupations in businesses, industries and service agencies which use the knowledge and skills of home economics.
   b. the dual responsibilities of homemaking and wage earning.
2. Preparing all people for the occupation of homemaking.

The occupation of homemaking is essential for maintaining the basic unit of society. Although individually these are small units, collectively they are the greatest force in the economy. The level of ability of homemakers in production, decision making, consumerism and teaching affects all other units of production, distribution and service.

REFERENCES CITED

American Home Economics Association. *Home Economics—New Directions II*. Washington, D.C.: American Home Economics Association, 1975.

Gordon, Leland J. and Lee, Stewart H. *Economics for Consumers.* New York: D. Van Norstrand, 1972.

King, W. I., and Epstein, L. *The National Income and Its Purchasing Power*. Publication no. 15. New York: National Bureau of Economic Research, 1930.

Nickell, Paulena; Rice, Anna; Tucker, Susanne P. *Management in Family Living*. New York: John Wiley and Sons, 1976.

North Dakota State University, College of Home Economics. *Consumer Education Curriculum Modules, A Spiral Approach: Guide*. Washington, D.C.: Superintendent of Documents, 1974.

Oregon State Department of Education. *Personal Finance Education Guide.* Salem, Oregon: Oregon Board of Education, 1972.

Troelstrup, Arch W. *The Consumer in America.* New York: McGraw-Hill, 1974.

U.S. Congress. *Education Amendments of 1976*. Public Law 94-482. 94th Congress. Washington, D.C.: Government Printing Office, 1976.

Walker, Kathryn E., and Woods, Margaret E. *Time Use: A Measure of Household Production of Family Goods and Services*. Washington, D.C.: The American Home Economics Association, 1976.

Washington State University, Cooperative Extension Service, Tape Service. News release. 1977.

Economic Roles, Goals, and Curricula in Trade and Industrial Education

Max Eddy

Available evidence suggests that the human species has been busily engaged in work from earliest times. At first, labor was concentrated on satisfaction of the most basic needs: food, clothing, and shelter from the elements. Having accomplished this, the next priorities were security, comfort, pleasure, recognition, status, and other personal purposes. Being creative, homo sapiens consistently sought ways to ease the burdens of work by improving the methods of his economic quests. Initially, various discoveries produced crude technologies. As gross as the first applications of those innovations might have been, they precipitated drastic changes in the existent mode of life, and they generated a mind-set of alertness for additional knowledge. The extent, refinement, and cumulative effect of the technologies of antiquity "blow our minds" as we examine artifacts of civilizations that predate the Christian Era by several thousand years.

EMERGENCE OF TRADE EDUCATION

An important social and economic consequence of early technology lies in the fact that it required a division of labor among the people affected. Such divisions were defined eventually and became discrete, gained social recognition, and finally were formalized. The emergent occupations which dealt with the acquisition and conversion of natural resources into consumer products—and related repair, maintenance, and service—came to be known as the skilled trades and crafts.

Following the advent of trade training, one finds a series

of methodologies and techniques which were adopted to meet the needs of the progressing times. A chronological account of the learning practices includes: (1) conscious imitation; (2) deliberate instruction in a natural family setting, where the father taught his son(s) his craft; (3) adoption of a son to maintain a family trade tradition; (4) a systematic contractual apprenticeship arrangement between a youth, his father, and a master craftsman that provided instruction through productive work supervised by a church, a guild, or a unit of local government; (5) private and church-related schools to train orphans and other indigent children and youth; and (6) public supported, institutionalized forms of trade and technical education designed to achieve state and national economic goals.

Evolution of trade training practices did not preclude the earlier methods and techniques; all have survived with modifications (Evans, 1971, 14). In fact, each successive practice provides a backdrop of traditions which furnishes an array of diverse alternatives for economic considerations.

England's primary motive for establishing the American colonies was economic. The raw materials needed by the mother country to feed its expanding industries in order to improve its position in world trade were abundantly available from the newly discovered continent. Also, the colonies were viewed as a built-in market for British manufactured goods. Manufacturing and processing in the colonies—even for colonial consumption—were discouraged and in some cases forbidden. The colonists, for the most part, were intent on their newfound personal, religious, and political freedoms and on the taming of the land which provided opportunities for ownership and independence, the like of which was unknown in Europe. Thus, concern with industry and the development of the trades and crafts was not a matter of economic concern and was deferred.

But this was to change. The seed of independence and freedom grew in the colonists. They resented the restrictions and general exploitive bent of the crown. Finally, the conflict—both political and economic—opened a breach between England and its subject which fomented the Revolution. The colonists were freed from their bonds; the republic was created; and the new nation set about generating political and economic goals of its own making. As might be expected, the new nation chose to enter world competition in the production and distribution of consumer goods. This choice necessitated the accumulation of capital and use of skilled labor, each of which was in short supply in the developing country.

Shortly after the Civil War, the United States began to pursue its industrial potential with vigor and determination. It soon became evident that a prime missing ingredient in our industrial development was a corps of skilled mechanics and tradesmen. Imported skilled manpower from Europe was insufficient, and the workers from American farms, although willing, lacked the skills that were sorely needed in industry. There was no alternative; the nation was confronted with the necessity to prepare its own skilled workers in order to meet the requirements of expanding vital industries and to enhance its economic goals.

Around the turn of the century, a variety of educational movements emerged which purported to improve the competencies of industrial workers. Some were helpful and foresighted, but none measured up to the needs of the times. Also, a variety of directly related private and corporate schools came into existence, many of which were on target, but their output was too meager to impact very much on the larger national needs. Furthermore, industry contended that its function was to produce a product at a profit, while the public school's responsibility was "essential" education—including economics education and trade and industrial education.

The public schools were reluctant to respond to the challenge, but the demands of the supporting economic order and the working classes were adamant. So during the first decade of the twentieth century, trade education classes were organized in some high schools, and a relatively large number of public trade high schools were established. But the time was ripe for much more. Industry, business, labor organizations, certain professional and trade associations, and vocational educators demanded that the responsibility for trade and industrial education be placed squarely upon the shoulders of the secondary schools as a matter of national policy. The movement was expedited by the Society for the Promotion of Industrial Education. Then with support from agriculture, a women's interest group, and concerned political leaders, plus further pressure on industrial production growing out of World War I, Congress passed the Smith-Hughes Act in 1917. Thus, trade and industrial education (T&I), a function of public education focused on the economic needs of industry, became a national policy—and remains so today.

THE PROGRAM: ITS PRINCIPLES AND GOALS

Growing out of an unrelenting, chronic need for increasing the nation's skilled manpower for industrial production and services, trade and industrial education provided training for the most critical, highly skilled trade and craft occupations—among them were carpenter, plumber and steamfitter, tool and die maker, machinist, printer, draftsman, electrician, and blacksmith.

The Program

Preparation for the trades was targeted at a variety of populations: (1) high school youth, (2) adults currently employed in industry, (3) industry apprentices, (4) youth in "dead-end" jobs, (5) youth who dropped out of school without appropriate occupational credentials, and (6) teachers of trade subjects.

Secondary school classes. Two delivery systems were used for trade preparation of high school youth. The most common was a school based arrangement called a "day trade" class—sometimes referred to as a "Smith-Hughes" class. A day trade class addressed one particular craft and was designed to provide selected learners the necessary skills and knowledge for successful job entry. Developing somewhat later was a "cooperative trade" methodology in which school and industry worked together in education and job training of selected youth. Industry provided training in trade skills in its shops, while the school furnished instruction in related subjects.

Evening trade extension classes. These classes were developed to provide adult workers an opportunity to keep up to date and expand their trade competencies for job security and advancement purposes. Classes were offered during nonworking hours in a school or industrial setting. Meeting hours and number of sessions were very flexible in order to deal with actual learner needs.

Part-time trade extension classes. This instruction provided a ready vehicle for public school involvement in apprentice training. While industry provided the skill training for future journeymen, the school furnished the instruction in related trade subjects—mathematics, science, drawing, safety and others. A minimum of 144 hours of instruction per year was required.

Part-time preparatory classes. These offerings were a response to the needs of young, out-of-school youth who were employed in "dead-end" jobs. They enabled such students to prepare for entry into a more promising trade or craft. Classes met during regular working hours. Thus, when current employers chose to be contrary, the training was in effect unavailable to target clientele.

General continuation classes or schools. Their purpose was to provide early school leavers an opportunity to continue their education in order to enhance their social and civic development.

An interesting offshoot of general continuation programs in the early 1930s was a multi-occupational, cooperative part-time program called "Diversified Occupations" (D.O.). It was reasoned that if a general continuation program would bring dropouts and school leavers, who were at work, back to school to improve their social and civic development, why not provide potential school leavers currently in school pursuing a general education an opportunity to learn an occupation through employment? This program worked well for nearly 20 years until a congressional committee spotted an obvious legal discrepancy: (1) the Smith-Hughes Act provided for "segregated" classes in each program area and did not allow "mixed" classes in reimbursed programs, and (2) D.O. classes, in their mix of occupations, included training situations not covered by any of the categories in existing federal legislation, i.e., office, public service, personal services. Thus, federal funds were being used for *non-segregated classes* and to support training in *occupations not covered by the federal acts.*

Trade and industrial teacher training. Teacher training was mandated by the Smith-Hughes Act; in order for a state to receive its trade and industrial allotment, it had to show how it would prepare trade teachers. Teacher training duties usually were delegated to teacher education units in established colleges and universities where curricula in vocational-industrial education were offered. Characteristically, inservice teacher training was given a high priority by such units. This type of teacher education set the general pattern of trade and industrial education for half a century.

Principles of Trade and Industrial Education

It is generally accepted that trade and industrial education was promulgated to enhance economic goals. In order to assure that appropriate results accrue, certain firm principles have been adhered to. Prominent among the basic tenets are these:

1. Instructional substance must be derived by a process of trade analysis.
2. An instructor's basic qualification is trade competency—but he/she must also know how to teach what is known.
3. Vocational instruction requires a substantial time block for practical "hands-on" experience.
4. Educators should heed the wisdom and respond to the real needs of industry by utilizing craft advisory committees.
5. Follow-up studies and product evaluation are essential to maintain program validity.

Trade and industrial education, operating under the original legislative act and its supplements, has focused on and deliberately served state and national economic goals through a variety of critical times: the economic prosperity of the 1920s, the Great Depression, a second world war, the subsequent period of economic realignment, and an era of unparalleled economic and technological expansion which followed. The contributions were significant, affording trade and industrial education a high priority among the vocational education service areas.

Changing Goals of Trade and Industrial Education

By the end of the 1950s it became apparent that the national commitment to vocational education was inadequate, the scope of vocational education was much too narrow, and the target emphasis of vocational education was improperly focused in light of the times and projected future needs. After a critical study of economic, manpower, and people needs, a new national policy was established, which evoked and demanded some significant adjustments in organization, procedures and priorities.

Encouraged and stimulated by the Vocational Education Act of 1963 and its subsequent revisions, state and local agencies have moved to expand, revitalize, and redirect trade and industrial education with the following goals:

1. Primary emphasis on *individuals* and their personal and economic needs.
2. Expansion of the levels of instruction to include prevocational, secondary, postsecondary, and adult instruction.

3. Offering programs for a broader array of industrial pursuits at a variety of entry levels to enhance employment opportunities—somewhat diminishing the "trade craft" emphasis of the past.
4. Continued support of secondary and postsecondary cooperative industrial education programs and other models of practical work experience programming at all educational levels.
5. Promotion of group and personalized instruction and economic education for individuals with special needs.
6. Encouragement of life-long program planning—preparatory, supplemental and retraining—with elimination of upper age limits and restrictions.
7. Cultivation of grass roots level, as well as state and national, political support for industrial education.

The current national policy, which emphasizes individual economic concerns as opposed to national goals, has not diverted trade and industrial educators from the basic operating principles previously cited. In effect, the new stance tends to make local trade and industrial personnel accountable primarily to their local constituency, which is close at hand. Thus, their concern with principles related to quality outcomes is increased.

ECONOMIC EFFECTS OF TRAINING

The economic justification of vocational education has typically been based on faith rather than on proof. The American people and their elected legislative bodies have demonstrated their faith with legal sanctions and financial support for this practical education which "promotes the general welfare, assures economic growth and well-being, and contributes to the national defense." With this justification, trade and industrial educators have felt relatively secure. Indeed, until recently trade and industrial education had little concern for actually proving its merit—its virtue was inherent and its support broad based.

The complacency of the past has been shaken by conditions of late. Our production supremacy is being challenged by rising industrial powers. Critical natural resources, once bountiful, are being depleted. The essence of national security is a matter of question in a nuclear age. An extended period of inflation with recessions has created doubts about our future economic security and job security, and the accelerating costs of education have stimulated people to question the wisdom of the public investment. Thus, trade and industrial education, along with its counterparts, now feels compelled to "prove the pudding." The need for solid evidence of worth has sent educators and researchers on urgent quests to generate supportive data, develop communication systems, and perfect techniques and models that justify their past and assure their future.

Although many approaches have been examined, the effort lacks the maturity and sufficient evidence to face all of the contemporary challenges. But the effort is well under way, and evidence of the economic value and impact of trade and industrial education is mounting.

In the following discussion, selected data and research studies which relate to the economic and social effect of trade and industrial education are reviewed. The available data and information suggest some pertinent questions:

1. Is the magnitude and nature of instruction such that it really supports the productive work force of the nation?
2. Is current effort and output aligned with the more critical needs of industry?
3. Is the public making a sincere effort to provide financial program support?
4. Are the costs of this vocational service area reasonable?
5. Do the recipients and the public receive a fair return for their expenditures?
6. What benefits accrue that are not necessarily measurable in monetary terms?

While the answers to these questions remain a matter of conjecture, certain evidence suggesting answers is presented in the remaining sections of this chapter.

Enrollments in Trade and Industrial Education

As previously noted, trade and industrial education, as an element of public policy, was generated out of the need to increase the number and skills of workers in America's industrial production and service work force. Historically, skilled and competent workers in many basic industrial categories have been in short supply, even in normal economic periods, and the situation has been critical in periods of economic expansion and of armed conflict. Thus, it could be assumed that enrollment can be considered one measure of the economic contribution and impact of trade and industrial education.

In general, the trend in enrollments has been steady increase, except for some regression during the Great Depression and again during and immediately following World War II. Total enrollments from 1918 to the present have exceeded 50 million. This total is of such magnitude, and the areas in which training was provided so basic, that undoubtedly the economic contribution has been significant in terms of numerical measure alone.

As shown in Table 1, since the Vocational Education Act of 1963 was passed, there has been a dramatic increase in total enrollments. In fact, enrollments have made a threefold increase during the past 13 years, growing beyond the 3 million mark in 1975.

Not only has the total increased yearly, enrollments through each of the levels have steadily increased as well. Particularly apparent are increases in secondary and postsecondary programs. Some people are concerned about the apparent high priority accorded preparatory programs; others hold that current economic and demographic conditions justify programming that emphasizes the preparation of young workers for entry into industrial production and service. Adult programs, however, while showing numerical growth, have lagged in the proportional sense. This is viewed with some consternation in an era when "the typical member of the labor force without a college education holds twelve different jobs during a 46-year working life" (Lecht, 1976). Trade and industrial education, however, remains committed to adult education and its proportional downturn may be more related to proliferation of services than to the lack of proper emphasis.

Alignment With Industry's Needs

Data reported by the U.S. Office of Education (U.S. Dept. of HEW, 1976) showed a total enrollment of 3,016,509 during 1975, with 690,030 program completions. Although these figures are impressive, it is difficult to assess the degree to which these enrollments and completions relate to manpower needs and employment opportunities. One problem faced in making such comparisons is the variance in how jobs are classified and categorized by national, state and local agencies generating manpower data (U.S. Dept. of HEW, 1974, 73-76). No attempt is made here to make the systems compatible, but perhaps the findings of the 1976 Report of the Conference Board (Lecht, 1976, 47-48) contributes a new note of enlightenment to the situation. This report utilizes

Table 1

ENROLLMENT IN TRADE AND INDUSTRIAL EDUCATION CLASSES BY LEVEL: 1963-75 (IN THOUSANDS)

Year	T&I Total*	Secondary		Postsecondary		Adult	
		No.	Percent	No.	Percent	No.	Percent
1975	3,017	1,305	43	475	16	1,235	41
1974	2,824	1,218	43	413	15	1,193	42
1973	2,702	1,134	42	345	13	1,123	45
1972	2,397	925	39	357	15	1,089	45
1971	2,076	790	38	310	15	956	46
1970	1,906	692	36	261	14	953	50
1969	1,721	459	27	174	10	1,042	61
1968	1,629	422	26	138	9	1,031	63
1967	1,491	368	25	123	8	966	65
1966	1,269	319	25	116	9	804	63
1965	1,088	252	23	60	6	757	70
1964	1,069	249	23	53	5	766	72
1963	1,002	209	21	46	5	726	73

*The sum of enrollments by level will not produce the T&I total for years prior to 1973, since certain "special" program enrollments were reported under this category during that time.

SOURCE: *Summary Data, Vocational Education* (HEW, 1976).

a term, "penetration rate," to depict the relationship between enrollment in occupational training programs and employment in the target occupation. For trade and industrial education, it was estimated that 10 persons were enrolled in training for each 100 persons employed in trade and industrial pursuits, for a penetration rate of 10—slightly below the median in the array of vocational program areas.

Another way to express alignment is to compare anticipated changes in enrollment with projected changes in employment. Here the Board projects:

> The most striking increase in the projections is the growth of enrollments in the trades and industry programs. . . . Projections of more rapid growth in enrollment in this program area than of employment in related fields suggest a marked increase in the enrollment-employment ratio in the coming decade. (Lecht, 1976, 47-48).

EXPENDITURES AND COSTS

Expenditures for vocational education in general have been increasing consistently. Likewise, expenditures for trade and industrial education have increased. Looking at the past two decades, expenditures amounted to $56 million in 1955, advanced to nearly $155 million in 1965, and approached $1 billion by 1975. It would be no surprise were the public to ask, "What are we getting as a result of increased expenditures?"

Comparative Costs of Trade and Industrial Education

A 1975 report from Virginia (Woolridge, 1975) compared the costs of teaching vocational subjects and nonvocational subjects. Three school systems provided data: a large urban district, a medium-sized district, and a rural system. Only those costs "having a direct bearing" on teaching of the subject were considered.

When the costs per pupil per year by subjects were computed, trade and industrial classes ranked (in increasing cost order) as follows among the vocational education areas: (1) business education, $111.75; (2) trade and industrial education, $126.97; (3) distributive education, $135.40; (4) home economics, $141.40; (5) industrial arts, $141.57; and (6) agricultural education, $154.98. In this study vocational education instructional costs were about 28 percent higher than those of academic subjects. While conceding this fact, the researcher attributed those higher costs to two factors: the comparatively low pupil loads of vocational teachers (21 percent) and the extended contracts which many teachers command (7 percent). One point of interest is that in each district where special education, driver education, and military science were offered, they were more costly than trade and industrial education.

Operational Costs

The state of Ohio has developed a system for analyzing operating costs of vocational education as one of the six elements of PRIDE—Program Review for the Improvement, Development, and Expansion of Vocational Education and Guidance (Ohio Department of Education, 1975). The system utilizes an internal analysis of the costs of operating a vocational education program under the expenditure categories: Administration, Supervisor Vocational Area, Principal/Director, Vocational Counselors, Nonvocational Counselors, Vocational Teachers, Vocational Texts and Supplies, Vocational Shop-Laboratory Equipment, Other Expenditures, and Operation Maintenance. Costs are assigned to each of these categories and are summated to produce a total annual program cost (T). The average cost of a class hour of vocational instruction (X) is computed by dividing the total cost by number of instructional hours for the class during a school year. Also computed is the average cost of one pupil hour of instruction (Y), which is the cost of one class hour of instruction divided by the number of pupils in the class.

The PRIDE analysis shows that the average trade and industrial education costs (T, X, and Y) hold close to the averages of vocational education in general. Vocational agriculture and business/office programs costs were higher in all categories, while health and distributive education costs were lower.

When the T&I programs with the highest student contact hour costs were examined, it was found that the enrollment typically was below average and the instructor costs were above average. It was also common for textbook, supply, and equipment costs to be considerably above the mean. When looking at the programs with the lowest cost, the only striking common factor was higher than average class enrollments.

T&I COST-BENEFIT ANALYSES

It is not cogent to assume that the vastly increased expenditures and the increasing enrollments of trade and industrial education guarantee appropriately greater public and private returns. Therefore, the procedures of cost-benefit analysis have been applied to this vocational area. Selected examples are reported here in order to assess the extent to which costs have produced benefits, both social and private.

Inter-Program Rates of Return

In 1972 a study was conducted in Ohio (Ghazalah, 1972) to evaluate the social and private costs and returns of vocational programs offered at the high school level. The benefit-cost criterion used was the "internal rate of return." The criterion was applied to both social and private considerations, and separately for males and females. Two measures of rates of return were calculated—Rate of Return I included a foregone-wages factor; Rate of Return II did not. The time period for accrued benefits was a lifetime for Return I, but only a five-year period for Return II.

When the social rates of return of the 18 schools in the sample were averaged across 14 occupational areas, trade and industrial programs were standouts, as shown in Table 2.

T&I programs rated at the top in terms of social rate of return, exceeded only by General Merchandising. General Merchandising was enhanced by the fact that it was a one-year program with a high trainee-instructor ratio. It also provided a considerable amount of high-paying, part-time work for trainees during their training period, lessening both social costs and foregone wages. It should also be noted that females had the very highest Return I rating for General Merchandising, but their next highest rating was in Drafting —a T&I program.

In terms of private rates of return, trade and industrial programs maintained the same levels of rank, with some internal shifts. In general, the programs which produced the higher social returns also produced the greater private returns.

Projected Benefits from Program Expansion

In 1975 a study (Ghazalah, 1975) was conducted to assess the net effect of increasing vocational enrollments to include 40 percent of all 11th and 12th graders by 1974, and adjusted to 44.4 percent by 1977. Since program expansion involves costs and benefits to both society and individuals, knowledge of potential net benefits were deemed to be an important adjunct in future planning decisions.

This study included all vocational education program areas and provided an estimate of monetary value and rank for each occupational classification in terms of a "social present

Table 2

MEDIAN SOCIAL RATES OF RETURN BY PROGRAM

Program	Rate of Return I (percent)		Rate of Return II (percent)		Return I Rank	
	Male	Female	Male	Female	Male	Female
Welding	76.8	---	214.5	---	2	---
Auto Mechanics	62.3	---	210.6	---	4	---
Auto Body	59.3	---	139.1	---	6	---
Machine Shop	73.3	---	257.6	---	3	---
Drafting	61.8	45.6	176.8	98.8	5	2
Cosmetology	---	14.7	---	31.5	---	7
Agric Mechanics	40.5	---	47.9	---	8	---
Agric Production	44.7	34.1	49.7	13.1	7	3
Steno & Secretarial	---	27.4	---	61.2	---	4
General Office	34.3	22.6	86.6	39.1	10	5
Accounting	35.6	22.5	93.8	43.3	9	6
Gen Merchandising	103.7	127.2	148.1	79.7	1	1
Food Preparation	24.6	13.7	44.2	9.3	11	8
Child Care	---	-5.1*	---	**	---	9

*A negative percentage means that benefits did not equal costs.
**Rate of return too low to calculate.

SOURCE: *The Role of Vocational Education in Improving Skills and Earnings in the State of Ohio: A Cost-Benefit Study* (Ghazalah, 1972).

value." Separate data and rankings were provided for males and females. Data were derived from four vocational education planning districts in Ohio, involving 38 secondary schools.

Mean Social Present Values were computed for 56 vocational programs, 26 of which were T&I classifications, as shown in Table 3. It is noteworthy that in the case of males, 18 of the 26 T&I programs were among the upper one-half of program ranks for Value I (time consideration: a working lifetime) and 20 of the 26 for Value II (time consideration: five years). Women in T&I occupations accounted for 13 and 15 of the top ranks for Values I and II, respectively, under the same assessment—with females being represented in only 17 T&I programs. When all vocational programs were grouped by vocational education area, trade and industrial education had "the highest social present value" (Ghazalah, 1975, 37). Following in order were agricultural education, distributive education, health occupations, business and office education, and home economics (gainful).

Cost Benefits in an Underdeveloped Area

In 1971 a cost-benefit study (Puerto Rico Department of Education, 1971) was conducted to document the cost and effectiveness of vocational technical education in Puerto Rico. During the 1969-70 school year, 26,500 graduated from vocational-technical programs at a cost to the government of $23.5 million. During one year of work, the graduates created private benefits of $58.4 million and social benefits of $116.9 million. The social benefits brought back to the government $16.4 million—allowing the government to recover its expenditures within a period of 17 months.

From the revenue return standpoint, distributive education, human resources, industrial arts, trades and industry, and office occupations were high contributors. Private benefits per program, arranged from highest to lowest, established T&I in the number two position with $15.3 million—second to distributive education with $22.4 million. The average cost-benefit ratio of trade and industrial programs was 2.5:1. Ranking highest among T&I programs in terms of this measure were: Electrician, 4.3:1; Draftsman, 1.8:1; Cabinet Maker, 1.2:1; and Plumber, 1.1:1.

Statewide Analysis of Four Programs

Harris (1972) reported the results of a study of the cost-effectiveness of four vocational programs in Florida's area vocational centers. The study included graduates and leavers

Table 3

MEAN SOCIAL PRESENT VALUE PER INDIVIDUAL WITH RANKINGS: (TRADE AND INDUSTRIAL PROGRAMS ONLY)

Program	Mean Social Present Value I				Mean Social Present Value II			
	Male	Rank	Female	Rank	Male	Rank	Female	Rank
Appliance Repair	$11,240	24	$5,178	10	$2,693	23	$1,916	15
Body & Fender	11,298	22	4,852	13	2,952	21	2,116	11
Auto Mechanics	16,344	9	7,556	2	4,007	11	2,813	3
Auto Specialist	11,936	20	5,020	11	3,197	20	2,330	10
Aircraft Maintenance	16,533	7	––	––	4,215	9	––	––
Business Machine Maintenance	13,432	17	5,319	9	3,677	12	2,586	5
Commercial Art	10,894	25	4,358	14	3,234	19	2,385	9
Carpentry	14,263	13	––	––	4,434	6	––	––
Electricity	24,973	2	––	––	6,119	2	––	––
Masonry	15,948	10	––	––	3,402	17	––	––
Glazing	17,316	6	––	––	4,357	8	––	––
Drafting	13,649	15	5,656	8	3,587	15	2,515	6
Electronics	15,313	12	6,473	4	4,446	5	3,244	1
Industrial Electronics	15,702	11	7,138	3	3,611	13	2,452	8
Radio/TV	6,305	40	2,219	28	2,412	26	1,937	13
Foreman/ Supervisor	6,486	37	2,516	25	1,438	45	1,063	33
Graphic Arts	12,221	18	4,865	12	3,470	16	2,495	7
Foundry	26,622	1	––	––	6,368	1	––	––
Machine Shop	17,492	5	––	––	4,403	7	––	––
Sheet Metal	20,673	3	––	––	5,197	3	––	––
Welding	18,204	4	8,510	1	4,485	4	3,153	2
Cosmetology	5,229	46	1,187	42	1,713	38	1,234	27
Quantity Foods	4,718	51	1,707	37	1,539	40	1,228	28
Small Engine Repair	11,118	23	––	––	2,888	22	––	––
Tailoring	4,766	50	2,155	29	796	54	628	42
Occupational Work Ex- perience	8,234	32	3,840	18	1,822	37	1,324	23

SOURCE: *Vocational Education Planning District in Ohio: An Economic Evaluation of Foregone Benefits from Limited Participation* (Ghazalah, 1975).

covering a three-year period, 1968-1971. Programs under study were auto mechanics, air conditioning and refrigeration, practical nursing, and cosmetology.

The average rate of return in this case was 76 percent per year on the investment of public funds and 54 percent return per year on student's time and money. On the average, society would recoup its average investment of $1,716 per student in 1.3 years, while the student would have his $2,411 investment returned in 1.9 years.

Greater average public benefits resulted from the nonsecondary portion of the sample than was the case of the secondary portion, $1,224 and $940, respectively. Private benefits also gave the advantage to nonsecondary students. However, nonsecondary programs were more costly than secondary, due mainly to the greater average number of hours of instruction involved.

FOLLOW-UP STUDIES

Despite known shortcomings, information derived directly from vocational program graduates and their employers is useful in assessing benefits, efficiency, and improvements needed. Selected results of several such studies are reviewed here in order to focus more clearly on the public and personal impact of trade and industrial education.

A National Follow-up Study

Eninger (1965) reported the findings of a nationwide survey of trade and industrial education graduates based on a representative sample of high schools offering three or more programs. His report covers the experience of 5,500 T&I graduates (covering the years 1953, 1958 and 1962) in comparison with academic curriculum graduates.

The occupational history section of this report provides the following interesting findings:

1. *Placement.* Time required for graduates to obtain a job was related to the general level of unemployment, but it took academic graduates over one month longer to find full-time employment than was required by T&I graduates. Black graduates required two times as long to find full-time jobs when compared with all other graduates.
2. *Relation of first full-time job to training.* The percentages of 1953, 1958, and 1962 T&I graduates who found jobs in the particular trades for which trained were

roughly 33, 28, and 30, respectively. Only 17.3 percent of black graduates were placed in jobs directly related to their vocational training.

3. *Employment security.* T&I graduates enjoyed a high level of employment security. Expressed as a percent of employable time in months spent in full-time employment, the median was 95. This level was substantially higher than that of academic graduates.
4. *Employment stability.* Vocational graduates had significantly greater employment stability than academic graduates. After 11 years, two-thirds of the 1953 graduates had held only three jobs or less.
5. *Job satisfaction.* The great majority of T&I graduates indicated overall satisfaction with the jobs they had held—combined mean of 3.12 on a 1 to 4 scale.
6. *Job relatedness.* Expressed as the mean of the "relatedness rating" of each job held to vocational training received, the reading would be only "slightly" related, on the average.
7. *Initial earnings.* The hourly wage rate of the T&I graduates and the academic graduates were not significantly different, computed on basis of the first full-time job.
8. *Present earnings.* T&I graduates working in jobs related to their trade training tended to earn more than those employed in unrelated jobs. When graduates without college experience were compared, vocational graduates had higher earnings than academic graduates after two and six years.
9. *Earnings progression.* Two years after graduation T&I graduates had a slightly higher mean earnings progression than academic graduates. The difference was reversed in six years and increased in favor of academic graduates 11 years after graduation. Thus, T&I graduates had an initial advantage but lost it after six years.
10. *Job mobility.* T&I graduates were not prone to move; the majority of those who did tended to stay within 300 miles of home.

State and Local Follow-up Studies

More recently follow-up data from graduates of South Dakota's seven public vocational-technical schools was assembled (Stover, 1976). Data were gathered from groups at time of training program exit, one year after exit, and five years thereafter. Employers of graduates also responded to a follow-up of the questionnaire.

At the time of exit, trade and industrial graduates were evidently pleased with the training received. Ninety-three percent indicated that they would recommend training to others who were interested in the same occupations.

Over 500 individuals who had completed their training the previous year reported their current hourly earnings. Most wage rates were in the $2.00 to $4.00 range. However, 29 individuals reported earnings above this category; of this group, 22 were T&I graduates.

Almost 9 out of 10 of the T&I graduates reported that their first full-time job was in the field of their training or a related one. A large majority indicated that their training was a requirement or was helpful in gaining their first job. After one year at work, virtually all graduates (99.4 percent) rated their previous training as average or excellent.

Individuals who had graduated from vocational-technical schools five years earlier reported current employment in 22 occupational areas, 14 of which were industrial occupations. Hourly wage reports indicated that those employed in industrial pursuits were doing well compared to those employed in other lines. Of 16 occupational areas where one-half or more of the respondents were earning over $4.00 per hour, 12 were trade and industrial classifications. It is also interesting to note that current employment five years after graduation was still related to previous occupational training in most cases. In fact, in 10 of the 14 T&I classifications, 60 to 100 percent of the respondents claimed that their current job was related to their vocational training.

After five years on the job, nearly one-fourth of the graduates regarded their training to be "exceptional," while 70 percent held it to be "adequate." Eighty-seven percent would recommend their training program to others.

When employers rated T&I graduates currently working in their firms, 43 percent were judged to be "excellent," 47 percent "average," and 10 percent "poor." Of those individual graduates who were employed in the occupation for which trained, 87 percent would be rehired by their current employer. Ninety-four percent of the employers would recommend the hiring of T&I graduates to other employers.

Data derived from a study of 11 of Kentucky's vocational-technical school exits for the 1971-72 school year (unpublished) confirm certain of the above points. For instance, out of 671 exits, 105 earned an hourly wage of $3.51 or more. Eighty-seven (83 percent) of the highest-paid individuals had received their training in trade and industrial areas. Eighty-three percent of those employed T&I exits responded positively to their present job and the vast majority found employment near home.

A study of public and parochial schools in Lansing, Michigan (Bournagas, 1963) compared the experience of trade and industrial graduates with samples of nonvocational graduates. Observations of subjects were conducted over a period of about five and one-half years. As in the case of the Eninger study, the T&I graduates had a higher degree of job stability and enjoyed a higher degree of job security. Approximately one-half of the T&I graduates had entered and continued to be employed in jobs related to their occupational training.

ECONOMIC LITERACY

Few would fault the proposition that trade and industrial education graduates would be better prepared for work life if they were fully competent in their occupational skills, knowledge and attitudes, *plus* possessing a general understanding of our economic system and their economic roles in it. However, this situation does not exist, and its prospects are not promising. Evans (1971, 122-23) points up the fact that instruction in economics has not been a part of vocational curricula and that schools do not have the capacity to provide instruction in that area as part of general education at present. He also asserts that "most vocational teachers have had little contact with the study of economics, and except for a few in business education, none are prepared to teach it." How true this rings in trade and industrial education!

Trade and industrial education teachers, as a group, are unique in that the prime requisite for certification and employment is occupational experience and competency. These qualifications are acquired through productive work in a bona fide position in industry rather than in the halls of higher education institutions. Thus the "tradesman-turned-teacher" typically comes from a blue-collar world to teach skills, information, and concepts that relate to a relatively narrow spectrum of knowledge—an occupation. They are likely to conceptualize themselves as workers, wage earners, or craftsmen. Many cling to a worker and craft-oriented outlook in harmony with the labor movement economic perspective rather than with classic economic systems or models.

Many of the teachers, even in the secondary schools, have not earned a college degree, and a large majority of those who teach part-time and adult classes are nondegree instructors. Most of those who do have degrees have had no more than a survey course in economics. Thus, neither their previous experience nor their professional education prepared them for a high level of economic literacy. Therefore, they are inclined to teach what they know best—occupational skills, information and related concerns.

It should not be inferred, however, that trade and industrial education teachers are oblivious to or ignore economics. Indirectly or deliberately, they teach certain general principles and values of economic consequence. It can safely be assumed that the relationship of employment opportunities and wage increases to a robust economy and to industrial expansion are appreciated and transmitted to their students. Students discuss the consequences of governmental regulation and priorities for their work, their jobs, the work environment, earnings, and the like in formal and informal sessions. Most instructors fully appreciate and stress the efficiency and cost implications of absenteeism, tardiness, downtime, and poor workmanship.

Almost all trade teachers deliberately emphasize certain basic principles and attitudes affecting the production of goods and services. They are intent on developing pride in workmanship and a desire to satisfy an employer with high output of superior quality. Similarly, the principle of "a day's work for a day's pay" is emphasized in the instructional setting. The economic and personal implications of safety, materials conservation, and honesty when dealing with others are stressed at all instructional levels. Likewise, the value, proper care, and respect for tools, materials, and equipment are a focal point of instruction.

With reluctance, it must be conceded that trade and industrial education is not a strong force in upgrading economic literacy of secondary and postsecondary vocational students—much less the industrial work force—in terms of societal and personal economic understandings. In fact, it does not appear likely that a breakthrough will occur as long as we retain the current source of teacher recruitment, the typical teacher preparation curricula, and the priorities which this service area has so long embraced.

SUMMARY OF THE ECONOMIC IMPACT OF TRAINING

During the sixties and seventies, we have witnessed a significant beginning of the assessment of economic and social effects of trade and industrial education. Data and information that are highly supportive of the outcomes of this vital educational service are mounting. Evidence seems to support the following assertions pertaining to trade and industrial education:

1. Industrial production and efficiency are enhanced by the substantial number of workers who have received preparatory and/or supplementary training.
2. Programs embrace occupational areas that are vital to the economic well-being of the nation. Although there is less than a perfect mesh between industrial manpower needs and individual choices, as reflected by program enrollment and completions, the match is such that the goals of each are served.
3. The public has confidence in the worth of this educational service, as evidenced by its demands for additional operational units and its financial support of expansion. Program expansion produces a multiplier effect on the benefits of training and grass roots support.
4. The operational costs of this type of vocational edution are rather modest in relation to those of the other services; nevertheless, they do exceed substantially those of public education in general. Low teacher-learner ratios, training laboratory equipment, consumable supplies, and relatively high teacher salaries appear to be major contributors to the higher cost.
5. This vocational service produces both social and private benefits in return for investments. Cost-benefit analyses show that the public usually receives a quick and generous return on its investment and that private monetary benefits are realized quickly and are substantial.
6. Evidence supporting the efficiency of this service is manifest. Program graduates find jobs quickly; they enjoy a high degree of job security; tend to be stable workers; and remain in their local labor market area. Jobs resulting from this training command high earnings compared to other vocational service areas. Employers of graduates are satisfied with their

performance and productivity, and the graduates themselves react positively to their training experiences and the opportunities afforded thereby.

SOME CURRENT CHALLENGES

During the six decades since the Smith-Hughes Act, trade and industrial education has addressed the vocational education needs of the nation. Few would deny that this program area is a stellar performer in the realm of education for work. But what is adequate today, or even superior, may be woefully wanting as new challenges unfold. Therefore, it is incumbent upon the educators of this field to continually make adjustments and improvements. The six challenges that follow require attention—now:

1. Trade and industrial education has not adequately outgrown certain limiting characteristics of Smith-Hughes origin. Current legislation mandates that vocational education serve *people*—as people happen to be, not as vocational educators wish they were. Therefore, practitioners should take fuller advantage of the flexibility afforded by current laws to provide multi-level, broad based learning opportunities in order that all who aspire to employment in industrial pursuits may profit from suitable instruction.
2. Minority groups are not enjoying equal benefits from instruction completed. Industrial education personnel should assume a role of active advocacy in their behalf. Determination and dedication, new thrusts, cooperative planning, organized placement services, and continuing counseling and personal services are among the requirements for progress in this area.
3. Trade and industrial education has been and continues to be the domain of males. Less than 15 percent of current enrollment is female. Women in trade and industrial occupations are clustered, for the most part, in the low-paying, traditionally "female" programs—cosmetology, quantity food preparation, textiles, and public service. This is a great untapped source of growth.
4. Trade and industrial personnel led early efforts to provide practical vocational instruction for persons with special needs. These beginnings failed to reach maturity as the "special needs" program area emerged. Current emphasis on mainstreaming as opposed to

segregated special needs instruction presents a pedagogical challenge and a professional opportunity for trade and industrial education.

5. Decision making in both institutional program planning and student curriculum selection should be based on a clear understanding of the manpower needs and requirements of the labor market. Industrial educators must learn to utilize available national, state and local manpower data more effectively and to take the lead in generating relevant data that are not available from other sources. Accountability pertaining to the alignment of employment opportunities and vocational preparation is badly needed.
6. Historically, vocational educators have chastised school counseling and guidance personnel. From this time forward it is highly desirable that trade and industrial education and counseling personnel form a relationship of mutual respect and cooperation so that the highest order of benefits may result from career education, training and job placement, and continuing vocational education services.

Trade and industrial education's capability to serve the needs of the population and of industry will be significantly enhanced as decision makers and practitioners rise to confront and master the problems cited above. And they will!

REFERENCES CITED

Bournagas, Kimon. *Vocational Education: Its Effect on Career Patterns of High School Graduates.* East Lansing: Bureau of Educational Research Services, Michigan State University, 1963.

Eninger, Max U. *The Process and Product of T&I High School Level Vocational Education in the United States.* Pittsburgh: American Institute of Research, Sept. 1965.

Evans, Rupert N. *Foundations of Vocational Education.* Columbus: Charles E. Merrill Publishing Company, 1971.

Ghazalah, I. A. *The Role of Vocational Education in Improving Skills and Earnings in the State of Ohio: A Cost-Benefit Study.* Athens: Division of Business Research, College of Business Administration, Ohio University, Nov. 1972.

Ghazalah, I. A. *Vocational Education Planning Districts in Ohio: An Economic Evaluation of Foregone Benefits from Limited Participation.* Columbus: Department of Education, State of Ohio, Feb. 1975.

Harris, Marshall A. *Benefit-Cost Comparison of Vocational Education Programs.* Tallahassee: The Florida State University, 1972. (ERIC No. ED 074223)

Lecht, Leonard A. et al. *Changes in Occupational Characteristics: Planning Ahead for the 1980's.* New York: The Conference Board, Inc., 1976.

Ohio Department of Education. *System for Analyzing the Cost of Operating Vocational Education Programs.* Columbus: Ohio State Department of Education, 1975.

Puerto Rico Department of Education. *A Cost-Effectiveness Analysis of the Vocational Education Program in Puerto Rico.* Washington, D.C.: Department of Health, Education, and Welfare, Office of Education, 1971. (ERIC No. ED 073303)

Stover, Keith M. *Follow Through—Management Information System.* Springfield: University of South Dakota, June 1976.

U.S. Department of Health, Education, and Welfare, Office of Education. *What is the Role of Federal Assistance for Vocational Education?* Washington, D.C.: Department of Health, Education, and Welfare, 1974.

U.S. Department of Health, Education, and Welfare, Office of Education. *Summary Data: Vocational Education.* Washington, D.C.: Department of Health, Education, and Welfare, 1963-1975.

Woolridge, R. W. *The Comparative Cost of Teaching Vocational and Non-Vocational Subjects in the Senior High Schools of Three Virginia Localities.* Blacksburg: The Virginia State Advisory Council on Vocational Education, 1975.

ADDITIONAL REFERENCES

Kaufman, Jacob J. *A Cost Effectiveness Study of Vocational Education.* University Park: Institute for Research on Human Resources, Pennsylvania State University, 1969.

Law, Gordon, ed. *Contemporary Concepts in Vocational Education.* Washington, D.C.: American Vocational Association, 1971.

Little, J. Kenneth. *Review and Synthesis of Research on Placement and Follow-up of Vocational Education Students.* Columbus: The Center for Vocational Technical Education, The Ohio State University, Feb. 1970. (VT 010175)

Roberts, Roy W. *Vocational and Practical Arts Education.* New York: Harper and Row, 1971.

YEARBOOK AUTHORS

William E. Becker, Jr. is associate professor and director of the Center for Economic Education, University of Minnesota. He is also executive director of the Minnesota State Council on Economic Education and consulting editor for *The Social Studies*. Dr. Becker has received awards from the Federal Deposit Insurance Corporation, International Paper Company Foundation, and the National Science Foundation. He is the author of numerous articles in professional journals in economics, economics education, human relations and finance.

George H. Copa is associate professor of vocational education in the Division of Agricultural Education and associate director of the Minnesota Research Coordinating Unit for Vocational Education at the University of Minnesota. He was the first editor of the *Journal of Vocational Education Research* and has authored numerous journal articles and research reports. Dr. Copa was a senior scholar with the Ministry of Education in Portugal as a vocational education planning and evaluation consultant. He teaches courses in vocational education planning and evaluation.

John R. Crunkilton is associate professor of agricultural education in the Division of Vocational and Technical Education, College of Education, Virginia Polytechnic Institute and State University. Dr. Crunkilton has been a teacher of vocational agriculture in Ohio. He served as a research assistant at the Center for Vocational and Technical Education, Columbus, and in the Department of Agricultural Education at Cornell University. He was the editor of the *Journal of the American Association of Teacher Educators in Agriculture* from 1970 to 1974.

Robert L. Darcy is a human resource economist whose background includes the directorship of centers for economics education at Ohio University and Colorado State University, where he was professor of economics until 1975. Recently returned from an assignment in Saudi Arabia, Dr. Darcy is now a consultant in Washington, D.C., specializing in the areas of manpower and education. His publications include an innovative world-of-work textbook for secondary schools, which is co-authored with Phillip E. Powell.

Max Eddy is currently professor of industrial education, School of Technology, Purdue University, where he has been a faculty member since 1956. Dr. Eddy has been active in trade and industrial education for 30 years, including 10 years as head of Purdue's Department of Industrial Education.

Lloyd L. Garrison is professor of business education and head of the Department of Administrative Services and Business Education in the College of Business Administration, Oklahoma State University. He has authored numerous journal articles and book chapters, primarily in the areas of economics education and accounting education. Dr. Garrison has held positions of leadership in state, regional, and national professional organizations. He was the recipient of the 1972 Mountain-Plains Business Education Association Leadership Award.

Katy Greenwood is currently a staff member of the National Project for Improving Institutional Capability to Prepare Vocational Education Leaders and Teachers at the University of Minnesota. She is associate director of the national project "Interpreting Vocational Education" at Texas A & M University and serves as special consultant to the Career Education Project for the American Vocational Association. Her major research emphasis has been in the history and philosophy of vocational education.

W. Lee Hansen is professor of economics and of educational policy studies, University of Wisconsin–Madison. In addition to numerous articles and books in economics and economics education, he recently co-directed a National Science Foundation-sponsored conference on economics education, the proceedings of which will be published in 1977. He also chaired a committee of the Joint Council on Economic Education, which will issue a report during 1977 outlining a new framework for teaching economics at the precollege level.

Garth A. Hanson is an AVA associate director. Before joining the AVA staff in 1973, Dr. Hanson was an associate professor of business and office education at Utah State University. He has also worked as a state teacher educator and served as executive director/secretary for the Utah Vocational Association.

Alberta D. Hill is dean of the College of Home Economics at Washington State University, Pullman, where she has been a faculty member since 1969. From 1969 to 1975 she was professor of vocational and technical education in the College of Education and consultant for the state Home and Family Life Education Program. Dr. Hill has also served as chairperson of the Department of Home Economics Education at Iowa State University and program specialist in the U.S. Office of Education.

Charles O. Hopkins is coordinator of planning, Division of Research, Planning and Evaluation, Oklahoma State Department of Vocational and Technical Education and associate professor, Department of Occupational and Adult Education, College of Education, Oklahoma State University, Stillwater. Prior to joining the State Department in 1969 he was a vocational agriculture teacher. He is responsible for the annual and long-range state plans and is co-director of an Educational Professional Development Act training project. Dr. Hopkins has published several bulletins and conducted many workshops on management by objectives.

Charles J. Law, Jr. is state director of the Division of Occupational Education, North Carolina Department of Public Instruction. Dr. Law has had extensive experience as a vocational teacher and has served in leadership positions at the state level for a dozen years. He also served as an assistant professor of the Department of Adult and Community College Education at North Carolina State University. He has written a number of publications and articles.

Jasper S. Lee is an associate professor in the Department of Agricultural and Extension Education at Mississippi State University. Dr. Lee has held various positions in teacher education and curriculum materials development in agricultural and vocational education at Virginia Polytechnic Institute and State University and Mississippi State University. He is author of several books and journal articles and a contributor to the 1976 AVA yearbook. He is editor of *The Journal of the American Association of Teacher Educators in Agriculture* and special editor for *The Agricultural Education Magazine.*

Darrell R. Lewis is an associate dean of the College of Education and professor of economics education at the University of Minnesota, where he teaches courses and conducts research in both economics education and the economics of education. Dr. Lewis has had extensive experience as a teacher educator, curriculum developer and researcher. He has written numerous books, journal articles and monographs.

E. Charles Parker is an associate professor of business education at Utah State University. He is director of projects involving cooperative education and inservice training for vocational administrators and has had extensive experience in developing curricula for cooperative education teacher training. He spent nine years working for the Utah State Board for Vocational Education in data and curriculum development and as a specialist of office occupations.

Phillip E. Powell is coordinator of economic, environmental and conservation education, Arkansas Department of Education. Mr. Powell has had extensive experience as an economics education teacher, curriculum developer and administrator in Ohio, Colorado and Arkansas. His publications include a world-of-work textbook for secondary schools co-authored with Robert L. Darcy. He has served as president of the Arkansas Association of Supervision and Curriculum Development and is a member of AVA and Arkansas Vocational Association.

Robert W. Reinke currently occupies the position of 9th grade social studies teacher in the Robbinsdale (Minnesota) Public Schools and is Assistant Director of the Center for Economic Education, University of Minnesota. Mr. Reinke has won top honors in both the National Kazanjian Economic Education award program and the International Paper Company Economics Award program. He is also author of several articles on economics education and a Ph.D. candidate.

Carl J. Schaefer is professor of education, Department of Vocational-Technical Education, Graduate School of Education, Rutgers–The State University. Dr. Schaefer served as teacher and local director of vocational and adult education, as director of the Ohio State University Instructional Materials Laboratory (T & I) and assistant state supervisor of trade and industrial education in Ohio, and as assistant professor of trade and industrial education in Pennsylvania. He was the founder of the Department of Vocational-Technical Education at Rutgers and served as its chairman for several years. His latest book, co-authored with Merle Strong, is *Introduction to Trade and Industrial Education.*

David R. Terry is associate professor of allied health professions in the School of Allied Health Professions at Northern Illinois University. He has recently published a report determining the behavioral task content of health occupations programs, and has co-edited with Rupert Evans *Changing the Role of Vocational Teacher Education.* Dr. Terry's report "Competencies for Teachers" has had wide acceptance. He has had extensive experience as a medical technologist, radiologic technologist, vocational educator, curriculum developer and researcher.

Neal E. Vivian is professor of distributive education at The Ohio State University in Columbus. He has been a high school and a junior college teacher, an adult instructor, and a state supervisor of distributive education. Prior to his present assignment he was a research specialist at the Center for Vocational-Technical Education, The Ohio State University. Dr. Vivian has edited and authored numerous journal articles and other publications. He has been very active in professional organizations and served as president of the Council of Distributive Teacher Education.

J. Robert Warmbrod is professor of agricultural education at The Ohio State University, where he conducts research and teaches graduate courses in research methods and data analysis. He was president of the American Vocational Education Research Association in 1976. Dr. Warmbrod is currently a vice president of the American Vocational Association representing the Agricultural Education Division. Included in his publications is *Review and Synthesis of Research on the Economics of Vocational Education.*

Helen J. Westrum is associate professor of home economics at Eastern Washington State College, where she teaches vocational home economics, consumer education and personal finance. Dr. Westrum is a consultant to the state staff in home and family life education.